DATE DUE

F

ALEXANDER BRYAN JOHNSON
Philosophical Banker

A NEW YORK STATE STUDY

ALEXANDER BRYAN JOHNSON

Philosophical Banker.

Charles L. Todd • Robert Sonkin

SYRACUSE UNIVERSITY PRESS   1977

Copyright © 1977 by SYRACUSE UNIVERSITY PRESS, SYRACUSE, NEW YORK 13210

ALL RIGHTS RESERVED

First Edition

Library of Congress Cataloging in Publication Data

Todd, Charles L
  Alexander Bryan Johnson: philosophical banker.

  (A New York State study)
  Includes index.
  1. Johnson, Alexander Bryan, 1786–1867. 2. Scholars—
United States—Biography. 3. United States—Intellectual
life—1783–1865. I. Sonkin, Robert, joint author.
CT3990.J6T63   191 [B]   77-15598
ISBN 0-8156-2188-4

ALEXANDER BRYAN JOHNSON

was composed in 10-point Linotype Times Roman and leaded two points,
with display type in Times Roman,
printed letterpress in black ink on 55-lb. P & S Vellum Offset
by Joe Mann Associates, Inc.;
Smythe-sewn and bound over boards in Columbia Tanoflex
by Vail-Ballou Press Inc.;
and published by

SYRACUSE UNIVERSITY PRESS
SYRACUSE, NEW YORK 13210

MANUFACTURED IN THE UNITED STATES OF AMERICA

for Clare *and* Sylvia

CHARLES L. TODD holds degrees from Hamilton College and Columbia University. He is Professor Emeritus and former Chairman of the Department of Speech at Hamilton. In 1969 he co-edited, with Russell T. Blackwood, *Language and Value,* a collection of studies by distinguished American and foreign scholars of Johnson's philosophic and economic works, and is the author of numerous articles in magazines and journals. In 1977 he was co-producer of a Bicentennial television series, "The Heritage of Central New York," seen on public broadcasting stations throughout the state.

ROBERT SONKIN, Professor Emeritus of Speech at City College of SUNY, holds degrees from City College and Columbia University. He is co-author with Levy and Mammen of *Voice and Speech Handbook* and a contributor to *Language and Value,* and he has written numerous articles on language for scholarly journals.

Todd and Sonkin collaborated on a series of field recordings for the Library of Congress documenting the great "Okie" migration to California during the late 1930s, and they wrote several articles in the New York Times *Magazine* based on their experience.

Foreword

THIS IS THE STORY of Alexander Bryan Johnson, who came to America as a boy not long after my ancestor, Kunta Kinte, but under somewhat different circumstances. He settled in the Mohawk Valley of New York State, grew rich, married the granddaughter of President John Adams, and until 1812 owned a black slave named Frank. He also, in 1828, wrote a unique book on language, undiscovered for a century, which showed how words are used as whips, and can distort our view of reality. How differently, he pointed out, in 1828, white Americans view the word *black* when it refers to the color of night on the one hand, and on the other, to the color of a man's skin. The questions he raised about language and reality are still being asked by philosophers today.

Alexander Bryan Johnson had roots, but he kept them hidden from his friends and his Adams relatives—and often from himself. His ancestors were distinguished rabbis in Europe, and his father had changed his name voluntarily, unlike Kunta Kinte. There was a *griot* in his family, however, his Cousin Rachel in London, who wouldn't let him forget, and he censored her letters with ink and scissors, though not quite carefully enough. Charles Todd and Robert Sonkin, after ten years of digging through the voluminous papers of this strange and brilliant man, have told the story, which began in 1787 and ended shortly after the Civil War. It is part and parcel of the American dream—and the American tragedy.

Alex Haley

Contents

Illustrations

following page 170

A. B. Johnson, probably in his mid-thirties.
The Burney's Academy, Gosport, England.
View of Utica, 1807.
Abigail Adams Johnson, in her mid-thirties.
John Adams by Gilbert Stuart.
Residence of A. B. Johnson, now the "Bank with the Gold Dome."
Cover page of pamphlet of Johnson's first lecture on language.
John Quincy Adams, sixth U.S. President.
View of Utica, 1840.
View of Utica, 1844.
View of Utica, *c.* 1850.
Oneida Institute, Whitesboro.
A. B. Johnson, probably in his early fifties.

Acknowledgments

Had it not been for the generosity of four of Alexander Bryan Johnson's many descendents—Alexander Bryan Johnson and Mrs. Leonard Jarvis Wyeth of New York City; Bryan Johnson Lynch, formerly of Barneveld, N.Y., and Mrs. Waldo Cary Johnston of Old Lyme, Connecticut—this biography could not have been written. Our debt to each of them is immeasurable: to Mr. Johnson for the fair copy of his great-grandfather's twelve-hundred-page manuscript autobiography plus many bound volumes of his correspondence with his friends, relatives, and notables here and abroad; to Mrs. Wyeth for the original rough draft of the autobiography; to Mr. Lynch for numerous personal documents and reminiscences passed down through his family; and to Mrs. Johnston for photo copies of Johnson's voluminous correspondence with John and John Quincy Adams, and other members of the families into which Johnson married. All of this material was made available to us and was placed on permanent loan in the Library of Hamilton College in Clinton, N.Y., where it has been useful to a growing number of scholars concerned with Johnson's pioneer forays into the world of American philosophical, economic, and political theory.

Prior to this windfall from the Johnson family which made a biography of the man himself possible, our attention was first drawn to Johnson's published works, largely lost and forgotten for a century, by numerous scholars to whom we are deeply indebted for sharing with us the products of their early research and enthusiasm. Our thanks go first to S. I. Hayakawa, the author of many books which Johnson would have called "kindling appliances" in his lonely search for the meaning of words. It was "Don" Hayakawa, currently a U.S. Senator from California, who introduced us in San Francisco, back in 1966, to some of Johnson's writings, and to Stillman Drake, now Professor of the History of Science at the University of Toronto, whose tireless investigations during the 1940s produced the first nearly complete bibliography of Johnson's published works and the first twentieth-century reprint of Johnson's now well-known *A Treatise on Language.* Drake, in turn, brought us together with David Rynin, Professor of Philosophy at the University of California, Berkeley, whose collated edition of the *Treatise* and the earlier *Philosophy of Human Knowledge,* including a long critical essay, brought the Utica banker-philosopher to the attention of scholars throughout the world. We are deeply obliged to both Drake and Rynin for providing many of the clues that led us eventually to the complete Johnson story, and for sharing with us many of the fruits of their research. Our thanks go likewise to Columbia University's distinguished economic historian, Joseph Dorfman, and to Hamilton College economist, Sidney Wertimer, Jr., for the help they gave us in placing Johnson's writings on banking and economic theory in the context of their time. We are also deeply indebted to David Ellis, Professor of History at Hamilton, and author of several histories of New York State, for sharing with us his vast knowledge of the Central New York region where Johnson lived and worked from 1801 until his death in 1869. We also owe much to another Hamilton historian, David Millar, for his help in dealing with the intricacies of the pre–Civil War political scene, and particularly Andrew Jackson's "war" with the Bank of the United States in which Johnson played so active a role.

Among other individuals who must be included in these acknowledgments are Dr. Walter Pilkington, Hamilton College Librarian; William Murray, president of Utica's Munson-Williams-Proctor Institute, and the Institute's Curator, Edwin Dwight; the late Robert Ward McEwen, former President of Hamilton College, and his successors Richard Couper, John Wesley Chandler, and J. Martin Carovano. We also owe a debt of gratitude to Professor Leonard Richards of the University of Massachusetts, who sent us his notes on Johnson's role in the anti-abolitionist turmoil in Utica; and likewise to John Roberts of the University of Chicago for making available to us his study of Johnson's excommunication by the Utica Presbytery.

In addition to the many people who provided information and encouragement, we are greatly indebted to the Ford Foundation for making substantial funds available to us through Hamilton College, and to the following organizations for the assistance they have given us in providing background information on Johnson's life and times: The Massachusetts Historical Society, the New York Public Library, the New York Historical Society in Cooperstown, The Oneida County Historical Society, the Corning Museum of Glass, the Utica Public Library, and the New York State Library in Albany. Finally, we appreciate the courtesy of S. W. P. Barrell and Sons of Southsea, England, for permission to use certain material, including illustrations, from L. F. W. White's *The Story of Gosport* (1964)—the English coastal city in which Johnson was born.

Finally, we would call attention to recent reprints of Johnson's works which, in view of the rarity of the original editions, have made our task easier.

Deep Sea Soundings and Explorations of the Bottom; or, the Ultimate Analysis of Human Knowledge [1861] (New York: Greenwood Press, 1968).

A Guide to the Right Understanding of our American Union; or, Political, Economical and Literary Miscellanies [1851] (New York: Greenwood Press, 1968).

An Inquiry into the Natural Rights of Man as Regards the Exercise of Expatriation: Dedicated to All the Adopted Citizens of the United States [1813], in C. L. Todd and Russell T. Blackwood, eds., *Language and Value* (New York and London: Greenwood Press, 1969).

An Inquiry into the Nature of Value and of Capital, and into the Operation of Government Loans, Banking Institutions, and Private Credit [1813], with an introductory essay by Joseph Dorfman (New York: Augustus M. Kelley, 1968). Includes as supplements two pamphlets by A. B. Johnson: *The Advanced Value of Gold* [1862] and *Our Monetary Condition* [1864].

The Meaning of Words: Analysed into Words and Unverbal Things, and Unverbal Things Classified into Intellections, Sensations, and Emotions [1854], with an introduction by Stillman Drake (New York: Greenwood Press, 1969).

The Philosophical Emperor: A Political Experiment; or the Progress of a False Position. Dedicated to the Whigs, Conservatives, Democrats, and Loco Focos, Individually and Collectively of the United States [1841], with an introduction by David R. Millar (New York: Greenwood Press, 1968).

The Physiology of the Senses; or, How and What We See, Hear, Taste, Feel and Smell [1856] (New York: Greenwood Press, 1968).

Religion in its Relation to the Present Life [1841] (New York: Greenwood Press, 1968).

Speech before the Auxiliary of the American Colonization Society [1834], in Todd and Blackwood, eds., *Language and Value.*

A Treatise on Banking; the Duties of a Banker and his Personal Requisites Therefor [1850], with an introduction by Sydney Wertimer, Jr. (New York: Greenwood Press, 1968).

A Treatise on Language: or the Relation Which Words Bear to Things [1836], an expanded and revised edition of *The Philosophy of Human Knowledge, or A Treatise on Language* [1826], in a conflated edition of the two versions by David Rynin and with a critical essay (Berkeley: University of California Press, 1947 and 1950), reprinted (New York: Dover, 1968).

Summer 1977

Charles L. Todd
Robert Sonkin

Introduction

BETWEEN 1814 AND 1861, Alexander Bryan Johnson published ten
books, some thirty pamphlets on a multitude of subjects, and
numerous essays and stories in the popular journals of his time. He made
many speeches, and, under a variety of pseudonyms, spoke out on public
issues in the editorial columns of the New York State press. He was connected by marriage with two American presidents, John Adams and
John Quincy Adams, and was on friendly terms with three others:
Martin Van Buren, James Madison, and Millard Fillmore. At one time
or another he also knew or corresponded with General Lafayette, Sam
Houston, De Witt Clinton, Robert Fulton, John Howard Payne, Frances
("Fanny") Wright, and other notables of his time. He was one of the
most influential bankers in the country, served as a director of several
dozen financial institutions in New York State, and played a major role
in Andrew Jackson's "war" with Nicholas Biddle and the Bank of the
United States. He was one of the few nineteenth-century Americans to
be excommunicated by the Presbyterian church, later becoming a pillar
of the westward-moving Episcopalians while carefully concealing his
Jewish antecedents from all but a few prying contemporaries. He never
ran for public office, but politicians constantly sought his counsel. Following in the footsteps of Benjamin Franklin, he produced a volume of
moral precepts which he called *An Encyclopedia of Instruction* (1856),
speculated about stoves and the nature of heat and electricity, and wrote
an autobiography (never published) about certain details of his life
which he felt, as Benjamin Franklin had put it, "my posterity might like
to know."

Among Johnson's books were three dealing with the philosophy of language which, by all the logic of history, should not have been written until the twentieth century. These were *The Philosophy of Human Knowledge* (1828), *A Treatise on Language* (1836), and *The Meaning of Words* (1854). Many modern critics have agreed that they anticipated by nearly a century some of the major speculations of Bertrand Russell, Alfred North Whitehead, Ludwig Wittgenstein, A. J. Ayer, Aldous Huxley, and others. S. I. Hayakawa has termed him "the first American investigator into what we now call semantics." Percy Bridgman, the eminent Physical-Philosopher, suggested that Johnson "at least partially anticipated" his theory of "operational definitions." Albert Einstein once referred to him as "a truly original thinker," and Aldous Huxley saw his *Treatise on Language* as a "minor American classic."* In many of his other writings, Johnson also stole a march on such latter-day "positive thinkers" and "mind cure" advocates as Mary Baker Eddy, Dr. Emile Coué, and Norman Vincent Peale. In 1830 Johnson began work on a "collated dictionary" which, though he never completed it, would have borne a striking resemblance to Roget's *Thesaurus*. Johnson's prescience, however, went beyond the realm of language theories and philosophy, for as early as 1814 he had produced a book called *An Inquiry into the Nature of Value and Capital* that clearly fore-shadowed basic Keynesean "New Deal" premises, along with thoughts on why people spend money that will have a familiar ring to readers of Thorstein Veblen's *Theory of the Leisure Class*. Despite his many forays into the future, however, A. B. Johnson was very much a man of his time—an Englishman transplanted into the wilds of Central New York and obsessed with the American Dream.

As for Johnson's personal eccentricities which might have attracted writers about the oddities of upstate New York—men like Carl Carmer, Samuel Hopkins Adams, Edmund Wilson, and Harold Thompson—the area provided far too rich a lode of Millerites, Oneida Perfectionists, Finneyites, Spiritualists, and other "ultraists" for them to pause over a part-time eccentric who minded his own business and carefully avoided public display. Johnson, in other words, was destined to oblivion by time, place, and his own design. His re-emergence as a personality and a thinker to be reckoned with was almost purely accidental, and it happened in San Francisco.

As pointed out in the Acknowledgments, major credit for John-

---

* The statements by Bridgman, Einstein and Huxley are from letters they sent to Stillman Drake (see Acknowledgments) upon receiving copies of Johnson's *Treatise on Language*, reprinted on a hand press by Drake in 1940. The edition was limited to 42 copies.

son's rediscovery must go to Stillman Drake, now a Professor of History at the Institute for the History and Philosophy of Science at the University of Toronto, and at the time of his lucky finding of *A Treatise on Language* in a secondhand San Francisco bookstore, a statistician for the War Production Board and a former philosophy student at the University of California, Berkeley. Drake's tale of how he became "the first modern Johnsonian in a matter of minutes" is graphically told in his essay, "Back From Limbo: The Rediscovery of Alexander Bryan Johnson," which appears in *Language and Value,* edited by Charles L. Todd and Russell T. Blackwood (New York and London: Greenwood Press, 1969). A portion of the story may also be found in David Rynin's introduction to his collated edition of Johnson's *Philosophy of Human Knowledge* and *A Treatise on Language* (Berkeley: University of California Press, 1959; New York: Dover Publications, 1968). Space limitations preclude a retelling of the long sequence of events which brought Johnson into the world of the twentieth century, for it involves many personalities and a nationwide search that began in 1938 and culminated in 1970 with the emergence of the nearly complete collection of manuscript material now housed in the library of Hamilton College in Clinton, N.Y. What can be told, however, is the story of Johnson's handwritten, twelve-hundred-page autobiography and his carefully preserved correspondence, on which the present work is largely based.

When the authors first came across this manuscript (it existed in both a rough draft and a "fair copy") they were tempted merely to edit it and publish it in its original form. However, Johnson was obviously not writing for public consumption. It was written for his own family and their descendents, and consequently, if we may use a cliché, he "threw in everything but the kitchen sink"—expense accounts, autopsy reports on deaths in the family, inconsequential letters regarding minor business transactions, and other trivia that only a tired old man, writing in his last years and obsessed with his failure to achieve literary recognition, would have put on paper. In Johnson's own words, "I commenced as early as 1812 to keep an account of my expenses and income, and I have a continuous and daily account thereof from the year 1819. I also commenced very early to preserve all the private letters that were written to me whether they were deemed important or unimportant and whether from friends or enemies, from relations or strangers, and I have a collection of them and united them in letter books from about the same period as I have of my expenses." He began the autobiography (first called "The Autobiography of Me, Alexander Bryan Johnson") in 1864 at the age of seventy-eight, and finished it in 1867, seven months before his death. The work starts off in a lively narrative style with Johnson relying on his memory ("mostly visual," he said) of his early days in England. By the time he was about one-third the way through, however, he began to draw more and more on his letter files; and the narrative, with occasional exceptions, gives way to a chronological catalogue of what he considered the major events of his life, each brought to mind by a letter sent or a letter received. As he grew more and more impatient with storytelling his transitions became terse and mechanical, consisting of such devices as: on such-and-such a date "I received the following letter from . . . to which I replied as follows." As a result, attempts to reproduce the raw autobiography were frustrated by Johnson's impatience with his own work and his increasing lack of selectivity. Expense and income statements were tossed into the text indiscriminately together with letters that speak eloquently of America's past. Johnson's excessive concern with the image he wanted to create for his descendents also caused him to omit many letters critical of his performance, or which dealt too intimately with his private life (even some of John Adams' letters were edited at times); and, of course, all of the revealing correspondence with his Jewish relatives abroad was carefully censored. Johnson also ignored, either out of forgetfulness or by design, a number of truly major events in his life, and frequently failed to supply a setting for the events he did record. In short, the "true reflection" of himself which he promised in the introduction to the autobiography did not wholly materialize. The portrait is blurred, and there was an excessive amount of retouching, particularly in those portions dealing with his public career—his posture, for example, *vis-à-vis* the anti-slavery movement, his excommunication from his church, and his unpopular attitudes throughout the Civil War. Fortunately, however, Johnson kept up his letter files and his scrap books meticulously and saw to it that they were entrusted to his sons. Without these, no "true reflection" of him would have been possible.

The reader of this book who may have been intimidated by Johnson's preoccupation with the philosophy of language and other esoteric matters need have no qualms about getting lost in a maze of philosophical speculation as he approaches the Johnson story, for the man revealed here had resigned himself to oblivion in that respect. As early as 1832 he wrote of his first work on language, "The book received no praise, nor censure, nor perusal. I seek not to animate the dead." In the autobiography and his personal letters he made only a few halfhearted attempts to elucidate his theories, and then mostly in a rather petulant, schoolmasterish fashion. What really prompted him to leave these records behind was far more likely a sense of having lived through, and played a part in, a crucially formative period in the building of the

American dream; of having "made it" in a new world blatantly hostile to his finer sensitivities, and finally, of having contrived for himself a life style that he must have known was compounded of oddities and contradictions, and those comic and tragic interludes that make a man's life something more than a simple passage from birth to death.

The late Edmund Wilson, in his final book, *Upstate,* made the entertaining suggestion that we "invented" Alexander Bryan Johnson—a theory shared by several other friends of ours, who have heard parts of the Johnson story and share our enthusiasm for this part of the world. We find Wilson's theory flattering indeed, for no one could have "invented" Alexander Bryan Johnson except the man himself. Readers who are familiar with the annals of "the psychic highway," as Carl Carmer has called the area which lies roughly between Albany and Rochester, or, by others, "The Burned-Over District," will share with us, we trust, the notion that anything could have happened here in the first half of the nineteenth century—including Alexander Bryan Johnson. Did Edmund Wilson, for instance, "invent" those loveable and unloveable people who first populated his "Mohawk and Black River countries"? Did Samuel Hopkins Adams "invent" those improbable Erie "Canawlers" of his, or Carl Carmer "invent" Cooperstown's "Cardiff Giant," Cohocton's Fowler brothers ("the practical phrenologists"), or Palmyra's farm boy, Joseph Smith and his angel, Moroni? No, we assume that, like Alexander Bryan Johnson, they were all self-invented, but we will admit that there must have been something in the air in central New York State that produced, to quote Carl Carmer again, these "creatures of a high-wrought fancy."

ALEXANDER BRYAN JOHNSON
Philosophical Banker

CHAPTER 1

1786–1801

Childhood in England • American Beginnings

I N NOVEMBER 1863, when he was seventy-seven years old, Alexander Bryan Johnson sent a melancholy letter to his old friend in Albany, Simon DeWitt Bloodgood, a writer of sorts who had for years been a faithful reader of Johnson's books and magazine articles. Johnson complained that his friends in Utica were dying off, and that his literary talents were being spent in writing their obituaries. He wondered whether anyone would bother to write his own, or if, like his literary works, his passing would go unnoticed. Bloodgood tried to cheer him up. "I think," he replied, "you do yourself an injustice," and, recalling Johnson's many other exploits, he added, "I believe if you had decided upon an exclusively literary career you would have impressed your opinion upon the age." Bloodgood made a suggestion: "As you are in good health and full enjoyment of your faculties, why do you not prepare an autobiography?"

Johnson let the idea germinate for a while, and then, "after several months of leisure, concluded to essay the project, and every step naturally begat a desire to preserve from destruction the labor already expended till at length the work acquired its present proportions"— nearly twelve hundred pages of manuscript. "Should it fall from my hands wholly unregarded," he said in his preface, "it at least beguiled many hours which might otherwise have been burthensome by inaction." He regretted that he had "nothing more important to say," claiming that his life had been made up of "mere simple transactions"; and he warned the reader not to expect any "sensational confessions"—a warning which must have amused those who knew Utica's venerable pillar of rectitude. "Unlike J. J. Rousseau's," he wrote, "my biography will contain no confessions of drunken revelry or libidinous adventures, and

1

therefore it will lack the spice which has preserved his confessions to this late day: but it will be more acceptable to my descendents for whom it was chiefly written, and to whom alone it may probably be interesting." The autobiography, he vowed, however, would be "as true a reflection of me intellectually and morally as a daguerreotype would be of me physically."

Johnson was born, he said, in the English channel town of Gosport, opposite the Isle of Wight, in Hampshire. His father, Bryan, and his mother, Leah, had lived there during the American Revolution prior to moving to London. His father's business consisted of "obtaining the wages and prize money of sailors and officers of the Navy," and Gosport remained a regular port of call after the family had moved to London. Johnson was apparently born during one of his family's stays in Gosport, a supply station for the Channel fleet, but the city's archives bear no record of the event. He knew little, he said, of his family's antecedents, save that his father was born in Fulham, near London, the son of an impoverished owner of a small windmill. Johnson also recalled that his father had been engaged at an early age "by an opulent friend of the family as a humble companion" on frequent business trips to the continent where he acquired "a great fund of practical information . . . along with some fluency in the German language and many associations with people of high respectability and considerable distinction." Johnson's main regret, which he expressed often in his memoirs, was his father's "deficiency of literary education" which made him indifferent to "all but the simplest forms of English Literature," leaving his son's education "much dependent upon my own volition." However, overshadowing this "deficiency" (which Johnson would overcome in later years through omniverous reading) was his father's "entire abstinence from all intoxicating drinks and from tobacco in any form"—a virtue which Johnson would frequently pontificate upon throughout his long abstemious life.

Of his mother, Leah, whom Bryan Johnson had met in her native Holland and later married in London, Johnson wrote that "her literature was still less than my father's, and having left her native country at an early period of womanhood, had never learned to write or read English, and eventually forgot all she may have learnt of Dutch," although, he added, "she ultimately spoke English with scarcely any foreign accent, but mixing less with society than my father, her choice of words was far less simple than his, and her general information more restricted."

There is a hint in this early portion of Johnson's memoir that Bryan Johnson may have cut more of a figure in London than one would expect, for his son stated that he "long saw in his possession a full-length portrait of himself painted by Benjamin West, when West was first attaining celebrity, and I have never ceased to regret that this picture, owing to its size, was left in England on our removal to America, and its ultimate fate I could never ascertain, but its lineaments, dress of the hair, with curling pins and general appearance, remain very distinct in my memory." Contemporary chroniclers of Benjamin West's works have been equally unsuccessful in determining the fate of this portrait.

That Johnson knew more about his family's antecedents than he claimed is revealed in his carefully preserved collections of "Kith and Kin" letters. Here one learns that his father's family came from Germany where one of his ancestors was a prominent Rabbi. Leah's family was likewise of the Jewish faith, and a descendant of a rabbi in Holland. Two of his father's brothers can be identified by name: William, who settled in Copenhagen, and Jonathan. Both used the surname Jones. Jonathan was, for a while, Bryan's partner, and like him spent his time between London and the Channel ports (Bryan's later decision to emigrate to America may have been precipitated by business disagreements with Jonathan, for Jonathan at one time declared himself bankrupt, and Bryan remained convinced that Jonathan had cheated him out of some money). Some of the persons who appear without identification in Johnson's early chapters can safely be identified as Jonathan, his wife Katherine, his son Solomon, and his married daughter Rachel Robinson— all of whom, except for a temporary lapse on Rachel's part, had remained in the Jewish faith.

In the matter of his own brothers and sisters, Johnson's memories were also vague. His mother, he believed, had two sets of twins who died in infancy, and a daughter Elizabeth, two years Johnson's senior, who died at the age of ten. Elizabeth's death seems to have left an impression. The last food she took was an orange, and Johnson related that his mother had never been able to touch the fruit since. His father had fainted when he heard of his daughter's death, but Johnson remembered that he, himself, had been reluctant to give up his play at the time, and did so finally "rather by a consciousness of its impropriety than by grief."

Johnson could not recall his arrival date in London, but he felt he must have been very young, for it was associated in his mind with his first suit of clothes. He tried to refresh his memory of London in later years by poring through Dodsley's *Annual Register,* but he could find little there that evoked personal recollections. He did, however, manage to bring back some early memories on his own:

The beheading of the King of France is one of the few public events that I recollect to have heard spoken of. I must have been tinctured by the then prevailing republicanism, for while the information was being communicated to my father, and all seemed much interested, I exclaimed, "Damn the King!" My father reproved me and said I was speaking treason, but I told him I meant the King of France.

I remember being taken to Drury Lane Theatre when the King and Queen were to be present. We sat in a box nearly opposite to the royal party, George III and Queen Charlotte, and had a distinct view of their persons, and my recollection thereof is very distinct. The King and Queen entered separately and were greeted with great applause, the King bowing several times and the Queen courtesying, and at each time both to a different part of the house. "God Save the King" was sung with great enthusiasm by the actors, the audience joining in the chorus, and the Queen beating time with her fan on the edge of her box. Two yeomen of the guards called Beefeaters stood motionless on the stage, one at each end of the royal box. They were tall men with a peculiar military dress, and each holding a long pike or halbert in his hand. Over the box was a royal crown, and behind the King's chair stood a lord-in-waiting, and behind the Queen's a lady dressed with large hoops, though they were not then worn except on such occasions. I saw the lady present the Queen with a pocket handkerchief, which the Queen handed back after having used it in wiping her face. The Queen had what seemed to be a white bearskin muff. The same ceremony of bowing and courtesying occurred on their majesties' leaving the theatre as on their entrance.

The King I saw subsequently at Portsmouth, with several of the Princes, his sons, on the occasion of his visit to some Admiral who had captured from the enemy and brought into port several large ships of war. A new three-decker for the Royal Navy was launched in the presence of His Majesty as a further commemoration of the royal visit, and I was in one of the numerous small boats that hovered around to see the launch. I was near enough to see the King and Princes, who were seated on a high platform erected near the ship to be launched, and the ship at the proper time glided slowly but successfully into the water amid cheers of all the spectators on land and water. Nearly every person wore during the day a sash of broad dark blue ribbon slung over the right shoulder, and bearing on it in large golden letters the name of the successful Admiral with laudatory remarks. I wore one, and I never felt before or since so much exaltation as on that day, with anticipations too absurd to relate.

The admiral who was being thus honored was Richard, Earl Howe (1726–1799), who in June 1794, in an engagement with the French fleet, took seven ships as prizes, and towed them into Spithead. Johnson may be forgiven for not recalling that the party did include the Queen, and three of the royal princesses (not princes).

Johnson also recalled standing on the balcony of his school in Finsbury Square in London and watching the Prince of Wales (later George IV) drill a company of artillery men prior to a general review by the King. Far more vivid than his memories of London, however, were those of the Channel ports to which he so often accompanied his father. One of his favorite trips was to the naval supply base at Sheerness.

> The town of Sheerness was very remarkable to me by reason of a part of it called the "Old Ships" and which consisted literally of large old men–of–war ships that had been brought ashore during high tides, and then beached so as to prevent them from again floating however high the tide might subsequently rise at any future time. The old ships were occupied by families belonging to the dockyard or the public offices, and each ship became a sort of village, divided into separate dwellings, the port holes being glazed as windows, and each deck of the ship becoming a street. The rooms were numbered and in many cases furnished very conveniently, making comfortable apartments with all family accommodations, so that a person who had not seen the exterior would never suspect he was on board a ship. Several old ships were thus inhabited, and each was as full of inhabitants, men, women and children, as a beehive.

Johnson at this age frequently ran errands for his father, and on one of his trips to Sheerness he was sent out in a boat to deliver papers to a Captain Elliot aboard a gunboat in the harbor. The captain, after lowering the "accommodation ladder" for the boy, took him to his cabin and offered him a glass of wine—the first he had ever tasted. Johnson recalled later that he had "felt no inconvenience from it." He noted, however, that Captain Elliot was "inclined to drink too freely," and concluded that "he may have asked me as an apology for opening a bottle himself."

While Johnson was in Sheerness in June 1797 the great mutiny of the Channel Fleet took place. It began at Spithead, off Portsmouth, when the sailors rebelled over low pay, bad food, a cutback in the grog ration, and above all, confinement to their ships while in port. The Admiralty in London, after hearing their grievances, promised them amnesty and a redress of their complaints, but a few days later, after no action had been taken, a delegation rowed out to the HMS *London,* the flagship of Admiral Sir John Colpoy, to press their demands. The admiral directed one of his gun crews to fire on the boat, and drove the sailors off.

His crew resented this procedure, hoisted the rebel flag and deposed the officers, sending the Admiral on shore, and ducking some of the minor officers by hoisting them with a rope atached to one of the ship's yards and suddenly loosening the rope, precipitating the victim into the water with a shot attached to his feet that he might sink, though he was drawn up and not drowned. In some cases the plunge was repeated several times according to the enmity felt towards the particular officer. The mutineers now held complete control of the ships and of Sheerness.

Young Johnson had a close look at the climax of that historic affair, including the execution aboard the gunboat *Sandwich* of one of the ring leaders of the revolt, Richard Parker. He recalled the story in graphic detail, obviously fascinated with the spectacle, just as he would be some years later when he attended the public execution of an American Indian near Utica.

As I was there at the time, I went in a small rowboat alongside of the ship to see the execution. I was about eleven years old, but I remember distinctly getting up early, as the execution was to be in the morning. The ship could be seen from the room in which I slept, and we noticed a yellow flag flying from the masthead as signal of the event to be consummated. Our boat was not permitted to touch the ship, but it, with numerous other boats, circled around and, as the day was the thirtieth of June, the weather was serene and beautiful and the sea entirely calm, and we were near enough to see distinctly all that transpired. After no long time, Parker emerged from below and came on deck. A sort of funeral procession preceded him with a chaplain of the ship at its head, reading the funeral service and moving towards a platform that had been made near the bow of the ship and on what is technically termed the catshead, a projection from which the anchor is sometimes appended. Parker was dressed in a suit of black clothes—coat, waistcoat and breeches with short boots and with a white cap on his head. His arms were pinioned at the elbows, but so that he held a white pocket handkerchief in his right hand. He had a rope round his neck, and as the procession reached the platform, he was stationed thereon, and the rope around his neck was attached to a longer rope that depended from one of the ship's yards where it passed through a block and reached down on the other side to the hold of the ship. The rope was sufficiently long to enable all the sailors below to hold on to it, that all might take an active part in his death. Just above Parker's head a round stick of wood, like a large rolling pin, was fastened to the rope to prevent his head from striking the yard when he was drawn up. Entire silence pervaded the immense concourse of spectators and he stood for some moments on the platform with the understanding that he was to be pulled up when he should let drop the handkerchief that he held in his hand. He seemed calm and made no demonstrations of any kind that could be seen from our boat. His clothes seemed new, and his appearance not the least like a common sailor. Finally he let fall the handkerchief, and immediately a cannon that was in a port hole under the platform was fired as a signal to the sailors below, who held the rope, and as the smoke of the cannon ascended, Parker was very slowly drawn up till the stick above his head, reeved into the rope, struck the block at the yard's arm and stopped the further ascent. He struggled convulsively for a few seconds and I noticed that a white shirt protruded somewhat from between his waistcoat and the waistband of his trousers by, I suppose, the inflation of his abdomen which seemed to become tumid. All was speedily the quiet of death.

Another Channel port that fascinated the boy was Deal, whose beaches he later compared to those at Rockaway, outside of New York. He was particularly impressed by the "hovelers," the men of the rescue teams who went out in large open boats to help ships in distress along the coast. Johnson recalled standing at his window with his father's spyglass and marveling at their daring. He also learned the ways of the smugglers who conducted most of the trade in Deal, benefiting from its proximity to the French coast. In Deal Johnson also saw his first semaphoric telegraph, erected in 1776 and modeled after a French device:

It was erected on the highest part of the vicinity, and looked like a one-story house, and was adapted to the occupation of the attendants. I was once inside the building, and I often watched its telegraphic motions from the outside. In the building, but at opposite sides, were fixed two large telescopes, one directed so as to see a telegraph stationed several miles in a direction from London, and the other to see a telegraph equally distant in a direction towards London, to and from which city all communications went and came by means of a high erection on top of the house, and in which were fixed six moveable shutters—two abreast of each other. Each shutter had a large white ball painted in its center to make the shutter more conspicuous, and the mode of communication consisted in raising these shutters from a horizontal to a perpendicular position according to some prescribed meaning. This mode of communication enabled all parts of the coast to communicate with London in a few moments, and was a great improvement over any previous mode.

It was his birthplace, Gosport, however, that provided the greatest excitement for the observant boy, especially at a time when Britain was warring with the forces of revolutionary France. The American Revolution and the Napoleonic Wars had transformed the little coastal village, bounded on the east by Portsmouth Harbor, on the west by Southampton Water, and on the south by Spithead and the Solent, into a bustling naval supply station—the terminus of the Fareham Road running north into the rural areas of Hampshire, and thence to London. Each morning the stages and caravans set off from the Red Lion, The India Arms, and The Bell Savage, carrying mail from the ships, naval personnel and their families, ships' suppliers, and minor functionaries like Bryan Johnson bent on brokerage business for the ships' paymasters. On some of his earliest trips, Johnson must also have encountered many French aristocrats and priests, refugees from the Terror, who had been befriended by the people of Gosport before moving on to Winchester and London.

During his family's earlier residence there, many Americans saw it for the first time as prisoners of war, or "Englishmen guilty of high treason." While Johnson was growing up, however, the Americans had been replaced by French prisoners herded together in Forton Prison. Excursions to the prison contributed to the delights of a Gosport childhood, and Johnson went frequently:

> I often went to look through the rails at the prisoners. They manufactured and sold toy ships, dominoes, dice and various playthings which they would traffic off through the railing. I have been there at rather an early hour of the evening when they were driven into adjoining buildings for the night and the yard cleared till next evening—the guards prodding them with fixed bayonets and exclaiming, "Couchez! Couchez!"

There were other entertainments in Gosport, among them an outdoor boxing ring, and Johnson described some of the sights he saw there:

> I once saw in it a regular fight between two women. They were naked to the waist, and exhibited a shocking sight, while sailors stood around to witness the combats. Women who thus associate with sailors seem almost everywhere a peculiar species of women, being generally large and bloated, the effect probably of intemperance. I saw a sailor and one such woman in the public market at Gosport, where the sailor purchased a string of flounders. The man and woman seemed affectionate, but they got into a quarrel after the purchase, and the sailor struck the woman in the face with the fish till the string broke and scattered the fish on to the ground.

Gosport was well known for its "press gangs," with their bizarre methods of recruiting for the beleaguered British navy. The gangs operated up through the war with America in 1812, but their activities were at a peak during Johnson's boyhood, and he recalled them vividly:

The gang consisted usually of five or six men with clubs in their hands, and commanded by some petty naval officer. Their approach created usually much terror to men liable to their power, and I saw a gang force a man into a boat to carry him on board some ship in the harbour. He struggled against getting into the boat till he was severely beaten with clubs and literally tumbled into the boat. The men liable to be impressed were sailors belonging to merchant vessels, and a difficulty probably existed in discriminating such men from those that belonged to ships of war. On the return home of a merchant vessel and the discharge of the crew, some of them would endeavor to escape the press gang by dressing themselves in long clothes with powdered wigs and various disguises to look like landsmen, and thus endeavor to reach London by a stage coach that plied three times a week between Gosport and London, but they usually encountered a press-gang that was stationed at a turnpike gate a short distance out, and when the appearance of any passenger excited suspicion, one of the press gang would shake hands with him and from the feeling determine whether he was a sailor or a landsman.

Johnson and his family maintained a residence in Gosport until he was nine or ten years old, and for a time, at least, Johnson attended Burney's Academy in a residential section of the town called Cold Harbor. He recalled a couplet about the district that went, "Some say the Devil is dead and buried in Cold Harbor/Some say he rose again and is prentice to a barber"—but what the couplet meant he never knew. The school, he said, was "highly respectable, but I learned little in it." From Burney's, Johnson's father sent him on to a boarding school in Milton in Kent. Here Johnson was instructed in dancing, drawing, and "the ordinary rudiments of English." The board, he said, was "unexceptionable . . . and we had hot rolls nicely buttered at two breakfasts every week." Johnson described some of his other not-very-rewarding experiences at Milton:

On Saturday nights the schoolmaster's wife attempted to plow with a finetooth comb the heads of the small boys, receiving the products in a washbasin partly filled with water. Our dancing school was kept in an assembly room of the town and I was assiduously drilled in a "minuet de la cour" to be danced at the end of the current quarter of the school, and I had for the occasion a pair of light-colored short breeches with knee buckles, and a new pair of dancing pumps. My attainments in drawing were not very extensive. . . . I believe this is the best school I ever attended, but I remained in it not long enough to be of much use to me. My weekly allowance of spending money was sixpence, which the schoolmaster gave me half weekly while no other boy had more than half the sum. The master usually commented on this extra allowance as invidious and not pleasant to him, and he had been especially instructed by my father that I must not be subjected to any corporal punishment, of which the master was not entirely sparing to other boys. I believe my conduct was not intractable or perverse, but I learnt slowly and with great difficulty, and one morning while I was in a reading class and standing with the rest I either read badly or some other way unintentionally aroused the ire of the schoolmaster, and he struck me on my back with a short horsewhip that he held in his hand for such purposes generally. I know not how much he hurt me but I cried pretty loudly, and in the midst of it a servant entered the school room and informed the master that my father had arrived and wanted to see me. The arrival was very inopportune and the master soothed me as well as he could and I eventually went to see my father. The result was his taking me home with him; and thus ended my residence of Milton, much, I have no doubt, to my disadvantage.

Shortly thereafter the family moved to London and Johnson was placed in the Finsbury Square day school. Again, the boy showed little aptitude for formal learning, especially in his French classes, and he attended school only briefly. As he tells us, however, he had other resources:

My want of schooling was somewhat compensated for by an insatiable inclination for reading. The books I read were obtained from circulating libraries, and though they consisted almost wholly of supernatural romances that seem to have vanished from existing libraries, they much assisted in improving my character by infusing into it aspirations to occupy a good social position, and especially to dread that I should pass from life without leaving some worthy memorial of my having existed. . . . I was unfortunate in possessing no one who knew books sufficiently to direct me to more useful reading, but an attorney in London, a Mr. Gillman, whose son I knew, observing my taste for reading, loaned me an English translation of Buffon's *Natural History,* and Buffon's *History of Botany,* and I read them with great pleasure and some profit. Possessing neither brother nor sister, I became more solitary than I should have otherwise been, and being but little at school or with other boys, my talent was very small at ordinary social boyish amusements, and my early life was far more sedentary than the life of boys generally.

There were many temptations in London for a boy just going into his teens and obviously subjected to little parental restriction, but Johnson somehow survived—though many of the places he went to, he confessed later, were "not quite suitable for so young a boy as I was." One of his delights was The White Conduit House, a public tea garden "not more than a pleasant walk from Chiswell Street where we lived." Here Johnson confined himself mostly to tea and hot rolls, "though punch, syllabubs, wine, ham, and other like articles could be obtained." Bands played constantly, "and much company of both sexes were constantly in the gardens though the company was far from select, especially on Sundays." Johnson was usually in the company of older boys, and thus "saw more of London and its various phases than boys of my age usually see," but he ascribed his escape from "injurious consequences" to his "invincible shyness" and to the fact that his companions refrained entirely from drink and tobacco.

Another favorite tour of Johnson's took him to the debtors' prison on Fleet Street, "usually called 'The Fleet.' " One of his cousins (probably Solomon Jones) had a friend confined in the prison "occupying a handsome and well-furnished room with no appearance of a prison." Johnson described "The Fleet" in detail:

> The entrance to "The Fleet" was through a gateway or hall and which brought you into a large open ground filled with prisoners, whose principle amusement was playing at "rackets"—a game in which a small hard ball was struck with a sort of stringed battledore against a very high brick wall which surrounded the prison and whose summit was imbedded with broken glass. At each side of the enclosure was a range of brick buildings which constituted the rooms of the prisoners, and no restraint prevented any of them from entering the yard. Each prisoner could purchase what food he thought proper and cook it himself, or have it brought to his room ready-cooked from adjoining cookshops, and at such time as he desired. The only restraint on the inmates was an inability to pass out of the prison into the streets, but an almost constant flow of visitors in and out of the prison was but little delayed by any personal examination of the passers, though doubtless the men at the gate knew who were prisoners and who not, though the personal scrutiny seemed slight. At a given hour of the night all visitors had to retire or else be locked up and remain in the prison. Connected with the prison was a place separated from the rest and which contained

the poor who were unable to support themselves. This place had a grated opening fronting on Fleet Street, and stationed thereat was constantly to be seen some prisoner exclaiming to the passersby, "Please remember the poor debtors."

Bryan Johnson was undoubtedly a restless man, ambitious for himself, and for his only son. There are indications in the later family correspondence that he was frequently at odds with his brother Jonathan, and there may also have been differences with other members of the family over religious matters, for at some point both he and his son joined the Episcopal church. At any rate, some time in the year 1797, Bryan decided to try his fortune in America. Johnson himself ascribed the decision to the influence of one of his father's older brothers who had gone to America prior to the Revolutionary War, settled in Philadelphia, and returned to England some time after the war, "a perfect enthusiast about the United States." Bryan had no notion as to where he might try to settle in America, but once the decision was made he lost no time in putting his plan into action.

Leah Johnson does not seem to have been party to the arrangements, but Alexander, then no more than twelve years old, was. Bryan, who made his momentous decision while on business in Sheerness, ordered his son to meet him at the Saracen's Head Inn in Snow Hill, just outside of London. The two went to bed for the night. In the morning Johnson awoke and found his father gone,

but presently he came into the room and told me that as the stage approached London and night was coming on, the passengers became alarmed for fear of highwaymen, who were then common in England, and that he had slipped all of his money into his boots. On his retiring he had pulled off his boots, and putting on a pair of slippers left his boots to be cleaned. During the night he awoke and remembered his money. It constituted nearly all of his property, and was in large Bank of England notes. . . . He enquired of some servants who were up and was told that the bootblack lived in a neighboring alley, and that he always took the boots home with him to clean. My father hired one of the servants to go with him to the house of the bootblack, and they went with a lighted lantern, the night being quite dark. They found the house and knocked several times at the door, when a window was opened in one of the upper rooms and the bootblack put out his head and said, "Oh, I know what you want. You are the gentleman who left money in your boot. It is all safe and mistress has it at the bar, and will return it to you in the morning." My father accordingly received the money as soon as the mistress of the house had risen but she told him he was not under much obligation to the honesty of the bootblack, the money having fallen out of the boot as it was lifted up and, she seeing it, made the bootblack hand it to her, at which he was a good deal loth. Thus safely ended this misadventure, which if it had resulted in a loss of the money would probably have detained my father in England, and my whole future life would have been vastly different from what it became.

A few days after this episode, Bryan Johnson departed for Dublin, having sold the house on Chiswell Street and instructed his family to find a small apartment elsewhere in London. Leah and her son were also told "to await further directions"—which they did until February 1801.

Johnson, who adored his father, must have listened many times in Utica to the story of Bryan's arrival in New York, and his trip into the Mohawk Valley:

> At this time the yellow fever was raging badly in the city and my father hastened from it to Albany. He was sitting there one night and looking into the street when sparks of fire seemed to dance before his eyes; and he thought it was a symptom of the commencement of yellow fever. He was much alarmed and sent for a physician and explained to him the symptoms, and when the doctor thought that what my father saw was nothing but fire flies—or lightning bugs as they are ordinarily called—my father became pacified; no such insects existing in England and the present being the first he had seen.
>
> From Albany my father journeyed on to Utica, then called Old Fort Schuyler, from an old fort that had been used against the Indians by General Schuyler and which was then standing. He thought of going on to Canada, but being much pleased with the appearance of Old Fort Schuyler he concluded to remain there, and never afterwards removed therefrom. I, after a time, received letters from him instructing me to direct my letters to him at Old Fort Schuyler, State of New York, and informing me that he was much pleased with the locality, and that I might accomplish much for myself in the new country, if I could acquire a good handwriting, which he advised me to attempt.

Bryan Johnson chose an auspicious day to arrive in Old Fort Schuyler, for it was July 4th, 1797, and the little settlement on the Mohawk was celebrating the nation's twenty-first birthday. The orator for the occasion was Frances Bloodgood, a rising young lawyer who had just moved from Albany, and whose son, Simon DeWitt, sixty-six years later would persuade Bryan's son to write his autobiography. If Bryan was uncomfortable in a crowd which included Nathan Williams, whose family property in New England had been razed by British troops, Erastus Clark, a friend and associate of Alexander Hamilton's, and Colonel Benjamin Walker, aide-de-camp to Baron von Steuben at Valley Forge, it didn't trouble him for long, for in little more than a year he would become one of the town's leading merchants and sit with all three of these patriots on a committee chosen to change the name of Old Fort Schuyler—a process finally accomplished when the name Utica was picked out of a hat.

Old Fort Schuyler, which Bryan had found so agreeable that he never pushed on into Canada, was hardly a setting one would expect to attract a Londoner who had spent his youth in the capitals of Europe. The fort itself, built as one of a chain along the Mohawk to protect the bateaux and wagon trains bringing supplies to Fort Stanwix (where Rome, New York, now stands) was a palisaded mudbank enclosure guarded by a blockhouse at each of the four corners. With the British capture of Canada, Stanwix was temporarily abandoned, but was hastily rebuilt during the Revolution and renamed Fort Schuyler—causing the village downriver to add the word "Old" to its name. The land on which the fort stood was part of a tract of 22,000 acres given by George II in 1730 to Governor William Cosby. After Cosby's death the tract was sold by his widow to three American army generals and Rutgers Bleecker of Albany. By 1773, as white settlers began pushing westward, the four investors parceled off their property at great profit, and by the time Bryan arrived, Old Fort Schuyler was a boisterous, thriving community of some one hundred families, and soon to become, by virtue of its proximity to Trenton Falls and its advantages as a halfway point from New York to Niagara Falls, the stamping ground of such intrepid British travelers as Frances and Anthony Trollope, Harriet Martineau, Captain Frederick Marryat, and a host of others, all of whom would turn up their noses at the hard-drinking, tobacco-spitting yokels who had had the impudence to name their outposts Utica, Troy, Rome, Ilion, Attica, Syracuse, Copenhagen, and Paris. Bryan Johnson, perhaps alone among his many new friends, imbibed no alcohol and chewed no tobacco, but he sold plenty of both products, along with the wheat and potash in which he very quickly cornered the central New York State market.

In London, meanwhile, Leah and her son, Alexander, settled down to a long, tedious wait for the summons from Bryan. They took an apartment on Bunhill Row, overlooking an artillery parade ground, where the boy watched "an intensely painful sight" of a soldier being flogged. Bryan, having scraped together most of his resources for the trip to America, had left his family little cash, promising to send money from America, but it was often slow in coming:

> My father, when he went to America, would have gladly taken me with him, but I refused to go and leave my mother alone. The remittances which we received from him she employed on me without any limit but my own volition, and I never encroached on them unduly except once, in procuring a rather expensive suit of regimentals, gun and all other equipment, to join a boys voluntary military association established in our neighborhood, under the gratuitous tuition of an army officer who once a week drilled us, and though I was probably poorer than any other of the company, I was the first accoutred and always the best.

Many years later, on 4 March 1831, Johnson's cousin Solomon Jones wrote from Brussels that he was sending: "Your Military Boys Jacket having had it in my possession ever since you left England. It may be a pleasing sight for your sons. It is in a very decayed state from age, and may be interesting."

At one point when a remittance failed to arrive, Johnson—then thirteen or fourteen years old—applied for a job as "reader" in a publishing house known as The Minerva Circulating Library, but was told by the manager that the job of reading aloud copy to the proofreader "would kill me in a short time." Johnson took consolation from the fact that the manager deemed him "too genteel for the office," since it required "rougher material." Bryan's remittance finally arrived, however, and his son gave up job hunting in favor of providing himself with some skills which might be useful in America. Living upstairs in the house on Bunhill Row was a lawyer whose son had a basement workshop where he turned out handsome leather pocketbooks. Johnson was invited to learn the craft, and made a few feeble attempts at working leather—"my notion thereof being, like those of most English people at that period, that everything had still to be taught in America." The lawyer upstairs often discussed America with him, arguing that the new country's relationship with England depended entirely on who would succeed Washington as President. Both agreed that Adams and Jefferson were logical successors, but, wrote Johnson later, "he and I both hoped that John Adams would be the successor—though I little suspected at that day he would ultimately become my grandfather-in-law."

Bryan's letters to his son were delivered to The New York Coffee House in London, a tavern popular with American sea captains, and Johnson went there regularly whenever mail was distributed.

To prevent the appearance of using the house gratuitously, I occasionally called for a cup of coffee, but whether the lady of the house who was in the bar saw I did not drink the coffee, or suspected otherwise my motive for ordering it, she told me that I need not call for coffee, but that she was pleased to have me use the room whenever I had occasion. I thought this very kind, and always thereafter availed myself of her offer without any expense, and she came to recognize me when I went into the house, and seemed pleased when she could tell me she had a letter for me.

As he had earlier, Johnson often amused himself during the long waiting period by wandering alone around London, and one of his favorite haunts was the Smithfield cattle market, not far from Bunhill Row. Once a year the area was cleared and became the scene of the famous Bartholomew Fair—"a great day for children and idlers."

I remember one show in the form of a huge tea kettle with musicians stationed around the lid, and another exhibited the German princess "who had as many children as the days of the year." Several stages had mountebanks on them selling patent medicines for the cure of every disorder. Menageries of many ferocious animals were to be seen, and theatricals were exhibited in others, while booths were plenty for the sale of eatables and playthings. Among the eatables were fried pork sausages which as they were frying filled the surrounding atmosphere with no fragrant odor. The whole scene was animated, and adapted, of course, to the people who resorted to it.

There were other "great days" in London to beguile a youth, and Johnson, knowing that his own children and grandchildren would never see such sights, described them in detail:

Also, among the past shows of London that were in full vogue in my day, were the "Milkmaids' Festival" on the first day of May, when they paraded the streets in large companies with their bright milk pails and cans formed into a pyramid, and borne from house to house on a sort of platform, receiving presents from the persons they visited. The chimney sweeps, also, had a day of festival every year, and went around in numerous companies making music by beating together their shovels and brushes. On the twenty-ninth of May was another festival commemorative of the restoration of Charles the Second and of his escape while hid in an oak tree. Oak apples, as they were called, were gilded with leaf gold and were carried around and worn. The fifth of November, called "Guy Fawkes" day, was another festival, commemorative of the attempt to blow up the Houses of Parliament by the papists, as alleged. A large image of the would-be incendiary was carried around seated on a chair with a lantern in one hand and matches in another and at night the image was burnt at a rude gallows improvised for the occasion. In standing to see one of these operations the leg of the image fell off, and some of the party threw it among the crowd of which I was one, and it came near striking me while all on fire.

At some point Johnson also went off to Sheerness to visit his Uncle Jonathan, Bryan's former partner in the ships brokerage business. There he caught his first glimpse of Russian sailors who, he was told, were "entirely unlike English sailors . . . and deemed very gross in their food, and I was told of their stopping a lamplighter and dipping into his oil a red herring which they afterwards ate." Johnson also told of seeing a Negro officer in the crew who "walked arm in arm with the white officers, and public report affirmed that he was a particular favorite of the Empress Catherine." Even more fascinating than the Russians, however, were some Dutch ships and their crews. Because of his mother's ancestry, the boy took a particular interest in the women who lived aboard the ships and came ashore occasionally to sell cheese sprinkled with caraway seeds. Since the women were a "superior race to the English women who associated with sailors," he assumed they were "the wives of the sailors and not their casual companions."

Among his uncle's friends in Sheerness was a comic actor named William Twaits, and Johnson went often to see him perform in the Sheerness theater. The final performance of the season, Johnson recalled, was a comedy about "a gallant eloping with a young female, and it was acted with great spirit, and we all laughed and enjoyed the denouement." However, Jonathan's family had an attractive young lady staying with them at the time who was also an admirer of Twaits, and who ran off with him shortly after the play closed. Johnson, with obvious relish, told what happened next:

I volunteered to go after her, and ascertaining where the company was to make its next station, I started on foot to learn her fate and if possible reclaim her. . . . The place I was to visit was some forty miles or more from Sheerness on the road to London. I started very early and walked till my feet became painful, and I put up for the night at some inn. In the morning I felt refreshed and proceeded on my journey and at dark found myself near Greenwich Hospital—a large government asylum for decayed seamen. Its approach was over a very lonely heath, and I felt fearful of highwaymen, as the place seemed well adapted to their operations. I heard a man behind me and when he came up I ascertained that he was one of the Greenwich pensioners, and I accompanied him as far as the hospital, when he left me. . . . The next day I reached the place . . . where the actors were to exhibit, and I saw in a shop window a playbill announcing, among others, the name of Twaits, so that I knew that I was on the right track. I forget how I found the young woman, but I got an interview with her at the house in which she was boarding, and persuaded her to return with me, after representing to her the anguish she had occasioned to all her friends. She finally returned with me. . . . What eventually became of the young woman I know not, but when I saw Twaits in New York, he seemed not to recognize me, and I cared not to refresh his memory with this crazy adventure of my boyhood and of his misdeeds.

Twaits, according to George C. Odell's *Annals of the New York Stage* (New York, 1927), made his New York debut in 1805 as Caleb Quotem in *The Wags of Windsor,* and appeared in some thirty other productions before his death in 1814. One of his popular roles was that of the First Gravedigger in Hamlet. Shortly after arriving in New York he married one of the famous Westray sisters, better known to New York theatergoers as Mrs. Villiers.

Back in London with his mother as the year 1801 began, Johnson, approaching his fifteenth birthday, began to worry seriously about his father and the long-delayed summons to America. His mother tried to keep him amused by providing him with chickens, rabbits, pigeons, silkworms, and even a monkey to tend, but he was obsessed with fear of what might happen to his mother and himself if his father should die in America. Finally he wrote, begging his father to send for them, and the summons came shortly—accompanied, however, by a money order which Johnson discovered would not be nearly sufficient to cover the passage. Fortunately, among his mother's many indulgences in her son's behalf was a course of lessons on the flute. Johnson became acquainted with his teacher's family, and learned by accident one day that their landlord, a brickmason, had a son who was a cabin boy on a merchant ship just arrived in Liverpool from New York. Johnson obtained the name of the ship and its captain and wrote at once to Liverpool, asking when the ship was to sail again for New York, and proposing himself and his mother as passengers, with payment for the trip to be deferred until their arrival in New York. The captain agreed and informed Johnson that the next sailing would be in three weeks. Johnson wrote his father in Utica telling him what had happened, asking him to meet them in

New York with enough money to pay the obliging captain. Meanwhile, in addition to furnishing him with a way of getting to America, his flute lessons had had an additional side effect on the precocious boy. His teacher, he discovered, was not only a "delightful flutist," but also a "rank atheist" who, among other things, lectured the young Johnson on the antirevelation doctrines of Tom Paine. Johnson wrote later: "I undertook to convert him from his atheism, and in this way became familiar with his doctrines. He is the only person I met who entertained entire atheism, and in its defense he was practiced and fluent, but as I stood on the defensive my arguments fortified my own orthodoxy and prevented me from becoming contaminated with his logic." Years later this musical atheist would appear in Johnson's *Treatise on Language* along with Spinoza, John Locke, and other erring philosophers who failed to realize "that language is impertinent to the whole discussion," and that "verbal incompatibilities afford no cause to disbelieve in the being and attributes of deity."

As the day of departure drew near, the young Englishman, "tinctured" though he may have been by "republicanism," paid some last visits to the landmarks of London:

> I walked around London now with renewed interest, as taking a lasting farewell, as I supposed, of the scenes I had heretofore passed without any particular attention. I went into St. Paul's Cathedral which was situated along my almost daily walks. I had never entered it before, but I now took a close survey of it and stood under its immense dome, where I found suspended numerous tattered flags that had at different times been captured from the enemies of Great Britain. I went also to the Monument which is situated not far from St. Paul's, and gazed particularly at its fluted stone column and read all the inscriptions on its base, and I felt disposed to greet with a goodbye even the pavement on which I trod. Not that I felt depressed at leaving England, but I realized the importance of our pending movement, and wished to impress on my memory all that I could.

Leah and her son packed their bedding, clothes, and what household objects they could, and sent them on to Liverpool in a covered van drawn by eight horses. They moved in with Jonathan's family, and the women busied themselves making pickles "and other things useful for the sea." Leah outfitted her son in a complete sailor's suit with cap, though Johnson refused to don them until he was on board the ship. On the eighth of February 1801, Johnson and his mother, amid much family weeping, climbed into an "accommodation coach" and began the long journey to Liverpool.

The morning after their arrival Johnson set out to find his captain, and brought him back to the tavern to call on Leah. The captain, "a very kind and obliging man," suggested another boardinghouse "as much less expensive, and more congenial to my mother's feelings," and by nightfall, they found themselves ensconced with a widow, her father, and "two handsome full-grown daughters." Johnson remembered the two girls singing a popular Scotch ballad that went, in part, "With his philabeg above his knee and he's the lad that I'll go wi', " but what chiefly delighted the boy, apparently, was the way the "old man mimicked the girls and travestied the words in a way far from delicate." The old man also talked to him "very freely, and said some things worth repeating but not quite proper."

Mother and son passed two pleasant weeks in their boardinghouse before the ship was ready to sail, and Johnson busied himself exploring Liverpool. They went through the usual anxiety of waiting for their baggage to arrive from London, and Leah, acting on the suggestion of the captain, "prepared several large phials of syrup made of milk and sugar" which they were told would be quite a luxury once they were at sea. Finally, when the eventful day came, they went on board where they found four passengers besides themselves. One was an American lady from Poughkeepsie, New York, and the others were three young men—"mercantile adventurers who intended seeking their fortunes in New York." One of the young men had many "instructive books with him," some of which he lent to Johnson, who read them with "much interest and improvement—my orthography having been but little cultivated, and I felt my defects therein quite painfully." Johnson added, "I was ambitious to appear rather learned, and I usually received credit for knowledge above my deserts."

The rest of the trip was by no means as eventful as his father's earlier voyage, but the enthusiasm of a small boy with a flair for the dramatic made up for the absence of French privateers and threatened hangings:

> Our ship finally moved from the dock and we were under way. I had put on my sailor clothes and prepared to be quite a seaman and even wanted to ascend the rope ladder which led up the mast, but the great alarm of my mother ultimately prevented me. Soon the motion of the ship took from me all thoughts but of sea-sickness, and I took to my berth and remained therein many days unable to partake of any food. The drinking water particularly disgusted me, as it tasted of the casks in which it was kept and was also turbid and warm. I longed for nothing so much as a tumbler of good cold water. After a period I

was able to sit up when the sea was not very rough, and the passengers amused themselves in the evenings by playing at cards, and of which I was quite fond and took a part. During the passage we, however, encountered a very severe storm. The cabin windows had to be closed by wooden shutters to keep the waves from breaking the glass and rushing into the cabin. I was lying in my berth very sick, and suddenly I heard an unusual noise in the cabin and ascertained that the fire in our Franklin stove had been thrown out onto the cabin floor by the pitching of the ship, and that the oakum between the seams of the planks was burning and setting the floor on fire. I was so prostrated by seasickness that I heard the danger without alarm, and lay still in bed, indifferent to the result whatever it might prove to be. The fire was soon extinguished by a few pails of water, but the storm continued for nearly twenty-four hours, and then subsided into a calm which restored me, and I commemorated the occasion by a first attempt at literary composition. It was in rhyme, and I remember only the first two lines:

> Hail Aurora, beauteous Goddess of the morn,
> Ne'er more did I expect thy light to see.

I exhibited my poetry to our fellow voyagers and my mother, and they all, of course, expressed much delight, and my personal conse-quence was augmented—in my own opinion at least. . . .

We were at sea on the first of April and were made the subject of some practical jokes by being called on deck at night to see a shoal of porpoises playing around the ship. We hurried up and saw what we supposed we were called to look at, but the whole was a delusion produced by the beating of the waves against the ship. Another joke was heaving the lead to see if we were on soundings. The bottom of the lead was covered with tallow so that it might bring up some gravel from the bottom and thus enable the captain to ascertain our where-abouts. The lead was duly thrown overboard, and on its being hauled up, an English shilling was found imbedded in the tallow, and we were led to wonder at the curiosity, but we were eventually told the shilling had been placed in the tallow before the lead was thrown into the sea—though most of us had invented theories to account for the shilling's being at the bottom of the ocean, and each inventor was as well satisfied with the truth of his theory as most theorists always are.

Only one other adventure occurred on our voyage. It was the ap-pearance of a vessel which was evidently making towards us. Our ship was American and therefore free from capture by any privateer, but we were purposely alarmed by suggestions that the vessel might be a pirate, and consultations were held by the passengers as to the conduct to be observed by resistance or otherwise, but as our ship was unarmed, resistance was out of the question, and therefore each passenger hid his money and other valuables where the pirates would be unlikely to find them. How much of these alarms were feigned to frighten the inexperienced, I know not, but soon the strange vessel approached us near enough to hail, and she proved to be a Spanish brig from Cuba and desiring some provisions, if we had any to spare. Our captain fortunately could spare some and they were sent on board, and we received in return a quantity of sweetmeats, and among them some guava jelly, the first I had ever seen, and we feasted on it abundantly, and I had never eaten anything that seemed so delicious. After these reciprocations, the two vessels parted company, and it occasioned a feeling of loneliness in me that I had not felt previously.

We now rapidly approached New York and could at length see land. We were met outside the Hook by the owner of our ship, who knowing of our proximity had come out in a sloop with several of his friends. They came on board our ship and were regaled by our captain with English cheese and bottled London porter, and which were well relished and praised. They also received our newspapers, and as our passage had been accomplished in thirty days it was deemed quite a quick trip. All the conversation was redolent of politics and of recent triumphs of anti-federalism, and which the speaker seemed to deplore. . . .

The New York of that day was a very small city, containing I believe about sixty thousand inhabitants. As I occasionally walked on Broadway, which was even then the great thoroughfare, I was known to be a stranger and was several times asked if I had not come in the late arrival. My walks extended up Broadway to the Hospital, which still exists, but it was far out of town. I saw no private carriages and very few hacks, and they had to be ordered at the livery stables. The city had a very rural appearance. I looked at every thing with rather a depreciatory feeling, and noted as defect every divergence from English customs. On my landing in New York I was about two months short of fifteen years old.

CHAPTER 2

1801–1805

Boyhood by the Mohawk

PEOPLE AND NEWS TRAVELED SLOWLY in America at the beginning of the nineteenth century, and Johnson and his mother suffered anxious moments as two weeks went by without word from Bryan. New Yorkers then, as now, were not very knowledgeable about Upstate New York, and when Johnson asked several of them about Utica—or "Nootka," as some thought he was saying—they denied any knowledge of such a place. The boy finally remembered that it had once been known as Old Fort Schuyler, and got a more encouraging response. (Johnson, in telling of this incident, recalled that his father, when asked for his suggestions on renaming Old Fort Schuyler, had favored *Kent,* but a member of the committee had "ridiculed it with an indelicate euphemism," and the suggestion was dropped.)

Finally, as the third week of waiting began, the suspense was broken when two gentlemen arrived at the Johnsons' boardinghouse one morning, announcing that Bryan had been detained in Utica by illness, and that they had come to escort the pair to their new home. Johnson was even more relieved when one of the men produced the money to reimburse the patient ship's captain. The man with the money, "of fine appearance and gentlemanly address," was named Jacob Brown, and thus began the rather remarkable series of acquaintanceships with American notables that would mark Johnson's early years in this country. Brown, a storekeeper in Brownsville, New York, and a supplier of potash to Bryan Johnson, had been private secretary to Alexander Hamilton while the latter was Inspector General of the Army, and he was shortly to become one of the heroes of the War of 1812, serving as Commander of the New York Frontier forces, and fighting at Ogdensburg, Sackett's Harbor, Fort Erie, and Lundy's Lane. Later, in 1821, he would be made Commanding General of the U.S. Army, and a rival of Andrew Jackson's for the presidency until, disabled by paralysis, he was forced to retire from active life. On several occasions in later life, Brown would turn to Johnson for consultation on political matters in New York State.

The trip to Utica took five days, with a one-day stopover in Albany. Johnson found the journey pleasant, "everything being new that I saw," and his companions "talkative, intelligent and agreeable." Their fifteen-year-old charge also seems to have done some of the talking, being "ambitious to create a good impression." Spring comes to the Mohawk Valley very halfheartedly in April, but as the party followed the Mohawk through Schenectady, Amsterdam, Herkimer, and Little Falls, Johnson saw turtles basking on logs on the banks, and grey squirrels running along the roadside—both new sights to the boy from London. Brown and Carrington told of the river's history, the conquest of its rapids by the new locks at Little Falls, and the man-made ditches which, prior to the building of the Erie Canal, permitted river traffic to continue on to Oneida Lake and into Lake Ontario. It was late at night when they finally arrived at Bryan's house, a low one-and-a-half-story wooden building on Utica's single street leading toward Whitesboro. Bryan had purchased the house and land in 1800 for $1,200, using the front part for his store and the rear part as a residence, and Johnson found it "convenient and handsome." (After the house burned in 1862, Johnson sold the lot alone for $5,000.) He noted no alteration in his father's appearance, though his voice "seemed much changed and hoarser than when I last heard it." Dr. Carrington told the boy later that Bryan had implored him, when he became sick, "Doctor, keep me alive till I see my son and I will ask no more!"

The morning after his arrival, Johnson awoke early to view the sights of Utica. His father proposed he take a brief horseback ride, and he gladly accepted "though my feats of horsemanship had heretofore been confined to a few rides in London livery stables where boys are permitted for a few pence to ride an hour up and down a long yard." Johnson took off alone down "a new road that was being made by the Seneca Road Company" (now Genesse Street, Utica's main thorough-fare), getting as far as New Hartford, larger than Utica at that time, and boasting a church where Utica had none. The view of the spire pleased him "as the recurrence of a familiar sight."

Johnson told nothing of his mother's early experience in Utica, though it is evident from what he said on the occasion of her death years later that she rarely left the house except to attend whatever church her son took her to. Bryan, however, lost no time in introducing his son into local society. Utica was a small workaday world, but it had attracted an adventurous group of men who had left New England and often Europe behind for a frontier outpost where, with luck and good connections, large fortunes could be made. One of the first of Bryan's neighbors to meet the youthful arrival was Peter Smith, "one of those extraordinary men that new countries are apt to produce." He had arrived in Old Fort Schuyler two years before Bryan, and was one of the few men who were able to outdo him "in the quick acquisition of capital." He began, as did Bryan, with a small store, but soon discovered the advantages of learning the tongue of the Oneida Indians and trading with them for furs. In 1794 he negotiated a 999 year lease on a 50,000-acre Oneida tract in what later became Madison County. The federal government concerned over Smith's dealings with the Oneidas, sent Timothy Pickering, who had recently resigned as Secretary of State after a disagreement with John Adams, to try to curtail Smith's activities, but the canny Utican was too much for the suave diplomat. A year later Smith formed a partnership with John Jacob Astor, and the two of them cornered the Indian fur trade in the East. Though the Smith estate never reached Astor proportions, it did well enough. Peter Smith's son, Gerrit, a boy of Johnson's age when they met, was to use his wealth in support of the abolitionist movement (his home in Peterboro became one of the most important stations on the underground railroad). He also became an ardent supporter of Elizabeth Cady Stanton and Susan B. Anthony in the women's rights crusade, which began in nearby Seneca Falls.

Young Johnson was not much impressed by Peter Smith's "literary education," but he was learning, and would learn more painfully later, that young America did not place a high premium on such cultural attributes. Johnson praised his "rectitude," however, saying "such men are too wise to be dishonest." He added, "I admired him very much and I thought he was interested in me." Smith, however, made one serious gaffe in his first encounter with the sensitive English boy. When Johnson was brought into the room, he said to Gerrit, "Go and shake hands with that boy, but tell him that you may be made President of the United States someday, but that he can never be." Johnson would never forget the reference to his "alienage," and would wage unremitting warfare against the laws of his adopted country which restricted the pursuit of high office to native citizens.

The proud father next took his son to see Major James S. Kip, the son of a Dutch farmer in New York City who, to the dismay of his family, had refused for years to sell his vast holdings (now Kip's Bay) and had lived on to a ripe old age before turning them into much-needed cash. Kip, like Jacob Brown, was also a dealer in potash which he sold to Bryan Johnson. Shortly after his son's arrival, Bryan bought a 6-acre apple orchard from Kip, and inadvertently involved the boy in his first, and last, brush with the law. Finding some young apple stealers in the orchard, Johnson rushed out to defend his father's property, and clouted one of the intruders with a stick. He was served with a writ of assault and battery by the town's leading lawyer, Erastus Clark, but the case never went to court. Bryan never forgave Clark for serving a writ on his young son.

Kip, a major in the Northern New York Militia, often invited young Johnson to the "general training" exercises held in the vicinity of Utica. These were largely ceremonial affairs climaxed by banquets "which constituted a great annual harvest for the chief tavern keepers of the locality." One of the most glamorous of these reviews took place on the grounds of a Georgian mansion (still one of the area's architectural landmarks) at Oldenbarneveld, now known simply as Barneveld. "It was a place of peculiar elegance for the period in question," wrote Johnson, and belonged to Colonel Adam Gerard Mappa, who had built his house in 1800 on land that had once been part of the 16,000-acre estate presented to Baron von Steuben by the state of New York. The young Johnson, still an unaccomplished horseman, greatly amused Mappa and Kip when he was unhorsed by a clothesline stretched in the yard of the tavern where the evening banquet was held.

Not many days went by before Johnson was introduced by his father to Colonel Benjamin Walker and his wife, the undisputed leaders of Utica society. Like Johnson, Walker had been born in England, but had come early to America and become one of the heroes of the American Revolution. A close friend of George Washington's, and aide-de-camp to Baron von Steuben, who named him coheir to his estate near Oldenbarneveld, Walker arrived in Utica after the Revolution as manager of the estate belonging to the Earl of Bath. Walker's exploits—his language, his extramarital adventures, and his prowess at eating and drinking—were a legend throughout New York State. Bryan Johnson was on familiar terms with Walker and was a frequent visitor at his house, and his son was much impressed by the colonel's "easy style of living and address," a quality he ascribed to "the conceded social superiority he possessed over all his associates—although his education was not classical." Although Walker's portrait, painted by Trumbull, would grace the rotunda of the Capitol in Washington, Johnson seems to have been more intrigued by Mrs. Walker.

She was a large woman and well graced her position, though she had an unfortunate propensity to drink, and was occasionally very sensibly affected thereby. On such occasions her husband would either not perceive her condition, or imagine others could not perceive it, for his conversation and conduct to her continued to evince the highest respect and affection. She, however, once came to my father's house in so bad a condition that, on the opening of the street door, she fell into the hall, and the servant who opened the door and did not know her came in and said a drunken woman was in the hall. She professed to be sick and was placed on a bed when after a sleep she became well and went home.

Speaking of Mrs. Walker's size, Moses Bagg reported that Baron von Steuben always referred to the couple as *le petit Walker et sa grande femme*. Johnson's final word on Walker was that he was "the first person in Utica who owned a coach, and for several years he was alone in that luxury."

Perhaps the oldest wooden house in Utica still standing in the 1970s was built by an Englishman, William Inman. It was the birthplace of one of Inman's sons, Henry (1801–46), the American portrait painter and founder of the American Academy of Design. Two other sons who also attained national prominence were also born there—Commodore William Inman (1790–1874), a naval hero during the War of 1812; and John Inman (1805–50), a distinguished editor of the New York *Mirror* and the *Columbian Magazine*. Johnson described the Inman house as looking like "the country residence of a gentleman," and apparently went there often to visit the Inmans.

The language [Mr. Inman] employed in conversation was far superior to any I had ever heard before, and I derived, unbeknown to him, much improvement from hearing him converse, as he was often a visitor at my father's store and [I] also visited frequently his house. I believe he was not classically educated, but report said that his father had been a steward to some nobleman in England, and he might thus have acquired the use of language to which I have referred. He had, also, a better knowledge of English literature than any other person I had ever known, and he occasionally adverted to books which I was thereby induced to read, and which otherwise I might not have known. My unacquaintance with useful books was the most obstructive difficulty I encountered in my efforts at self-instruction, and the literature I acquired was by only my fortuitous acquaintance with instructive books.

Another source of "instructive books" was the lawyer, Nathan Williams, with whom Johnson some years later would begin his study of law. Williams, a firm believer in the classics, maintained "the old Fort Schuyler Library" in his law office, and Johnson described his indebtedness to him:

> Out of this library I read much, and I remember especially Rollins' *Ancient History* and Plutarch's *Lives.* Only one volume could be taken out at a time, and its return was imperative at the end of one or two weeks. He was naturally an austere man, but behaved toward me with the utmost kindness . . . permitting me to sit in his office and read from his extensive law library, and receiving from me no compensation. . . . I was present on an occasion when his official duties required him to ask a young married lady whether the deed she had signed was executed by her without any fear of compulsion by her husband. She laughed and said that she was not afraid of her husband. "Then, Madame," replied her questioner, "you have not learned the first duty of a wife, which is to fear her husband!"

A dinner party given by his father introduced Johnson to Francis Bloodgood, the lawyer whose son, Simeon DeWitt, encouraged Johnson to write his autobiography. The party gave Johnson another opportunity to provide a "true copy" of himself. During the dinner news came that Bloodgood had been appointed County Clerk, and Major Kip told the boy to tell Mrs. Bloodgood about it, and she would give him a kiss. "I was as bashful as a girl, and afraid to carry the intelligence lest I should receive the reward. . . . I left the room, but did not bear the message. What the French call *mauvaise honte* had always greatly afflicted me . . . and I am not now emancipated therefrom."

Among the residents of Oneida County at the turn of the century was a tribe of Montauk Indians who, with the intrusion of the white man into their part of Long Island, fled into the interior of the state and changed their name to "The Brothertons." One of them, George Peters, ran afoul of the law in Fort Stanwix (now Rome, New York) when, he "murdered his wife by striking her on the head with a wooden club." He was sentenced to be hanged in Utica, and the reluctant executioner was Sheriff Charles Brodhead, whose recent appointment had been opposed originally by Governor De Witt Clinton on the grounds that he was a bachelor (according to Johnson, Clinton remarked that he "disliked a man who didn't boil his own pot"). Johnson attended the execution and reported it with the same attention to detail he had lavished on the hanging of Parker, the British mutineer.

A large crowd of people of both sexes and all ages were assembled near the gallows, anxiously awaiting the appearance of the convict. He was at length seen approaching from the jail, dressed in a white shroud and having a halter entwined around his neck, and guarded by several constables and some militia. The whole marched slowly towards the gallows, where the criminal finally took his stand on a platform which constituted the drop. The sheriff now uncoiled the rope, and leaving one end attached to the neck of the prisoner, hitched the other end to a large iron hook on the gallows above the head of the poor wretch who was to be executed. "Dominie" Kirkland, as he was familiarly called, an Indian missionary of long standing and much celebrity, officiated as the spiritual comforter of the criminal, and stood along side of him on the platform, praying in the Indian language. Several Indians were near, and I think they sang a psalm in their native language. The prisoner's arms had been pinioned in the prison, and when all the ceremonies had been properly performed, a white cap which he wore on his head was drawn over his eyes to obstruct the view of his face. The clergyman kept praying, but on a given signal moved cautiously from the drop while still speaking and as if to give no notice of his movement to the criminal—when the drop suddenly was let fall and the execution terminated with a few death struggles. The crowd instantly dispersed, and I rode home much affected by the sad but interesting ceremony.

Dominie Samuel Kirkland was the founder of Hamilton College, which stands on a tract of land near Clinton, New York, given to Kirkland by George Washington in gratitude for his work among the Oneida Indians.

Many years later, in his political allegory, *The Philosophical Emperor,* Johnson would ridicule "the squeamishness of legislators"

who abolished public executions, and now inflict all such punishments privately, lest the sight should stimulate to crime by creating in the beholders a desire to be hanged. The taste for hanging may be acquireable as well as a taste for tobacco . . . I have seen four capital executions, and at each exhibition felt an increased horror against being a principal in a like exhibition: but tastes are proverbally different. I have never succeeded in liking tobacco.

A number of Johnson's sketches of early Uticans provide a kind of "Spoon River" galaxy of small-town saints and sinners in rural America in the early 1800s. There was, for instance, Dr. Alexander Coventry, who was asked to attend a woman who had lost all of her previous children at birth. "The usual physician had left home and Coventry was called for in the emergency. He found the family greatly alarmed, and the husband asked him for his instruments, but he exhibited his hands, and said they were the only instruments he ever used, and after a short time, a living child was brought into the world to the astonishment and delight of the parents." Coventry also had a unique method of collecting fees. Meeting a young man who owed him money, Coventry informed him that he looked sick, grasped the young man's pulse, and said "You are a bad fellow and have treated me ill, but I will not see you kill yourself. I advise you to go home and go to bed, for you have a high fever." "The fellow was young and vigorous, but he immediately became livid with fright . . . gasped for breath and staggered into a chair till the doctor became also frightened, and laughing, told the fellow nothing ailed him, but he wanted to frighten him for not paying his outstanding account."

The Irish in Utica, said Johnson, consisted of "the usual diggers and ditchers." Their leader was one Dowdle "with an abundant brogue." Dowdle's forte was digging drains, and he had another Irishman as partner. In the matter of fees, Dowdle always made the first approach, and when the fee was called too high, his partner would come and lower the figure. Then the two of them would go to work together on the job. Another worthy arrived from Ireland bearing the title "Captain," which he said he had earned in the British army. His name was Aylmer Johnson, and his wife, said Johnson, "was also Irish, but she was quite lady-like in her dress and address." The "Captain" was fairly successful at card playing, but eventually went to the poorhouse and revealed that he had never been anything but a common soldier. Johnson commented, however, that "his education and manners were not unsuited to his pretensions of having been a Captain."

Another village character who intrigued the young Johnson was a blacksmith, said to have been an expert lock-picker in England, who had been transported to America "for the unlawful exercise of his skill." Johnson, losing his key one night, went to the blacksmith and arranged to have a new key made without his father's knowledge. Since it was a "secret job," however, the fee was five dollars which Johnson, in protest, paid off in installments. Gurdon Burchard, the village saddler, also attracted Johnson with his formula for managing a wife, which consisted in rudely denying her such small pleasures as putting flowers in her vegetable garden. Before long, said Johnson, "his will was undisputed." (Johnson later used variations on Burchard's method in several of his stories published in the *Knickerbocker Magazine* in 1850.) Johnson also took note of Cheeney, the bricklayer, who "was rather feeble of intellect" as a result of having once been hit by lightning while holding his trowel aloft; a cockney barber who, while dressing a customer's hair, would call to his daughter, "Sophie, *eat* the curling tongs!", and a pipe-smoking old Englishwoman whose habit began the rumor in Utica that all Englishwomen smoked pipes.

There was also a seafaring man who came from England about the time Johnson arrived, and built a house near Utica modeled after a ship's cabin. He was "honest and respectable" at first, but soon contracted a habit "of gross intoxication."

> In this condition he came one night to my father's house, and after staying till late at night and the weather being dark, my father offered to see him home, but he evidently feared my father would leave him after going part way, and he refused to go unless I should go with him. I consented, and he took my arm and I steadied him as well as I could through the deep muddy road and left him at his door. He died not long after this, and my father called on the widow. She was standing near the open coffin and weeping bitterly, and wringing her hands. She said to the corpse, "You poor wretch! You will never abuse me any more!" Such is the faithfulness of women under great provocations to the contrary.

There were other more substantial citizens of Utica whose lives have been duly chronicled by local historians, but Johnson, with his didactic turn of mind, often ignored the intimate biographical details, viewing them more as characters in a morality play, and object lessons for posterity. Among these was John Post, who was an old man when Johnson arrived in Utica. He was a fur trader like Peter Smith, and kept a store next door to Bryan's which soon made him a small fortune.

> He was of Dutch extraction and his wife was also Dutch. She had the reputation of being a witch, and a young man who lived with my father stood in much fear of her incantations. But Post had two daughters who were far more bewitching than their mother, and the oldest especially was a very pretty and lively girl and, as she possessed attractions from her father's reputed wealth, she was not without many admirers. Among them was a young man by the name of Giles Hamlin, a clerk in a neighboring store, and they were eventually married. Mr. Post had about this period . . . kept his store more from habit than occupation, but Hamlin was deemed a very expert merchant, and he induced his father-in-law to take him as a partner and to recommence business on an enlarged scale. Post in an evil hour consented, and

Hamlin went to New York and purchased on Post's credit a large stock of new goods. Hamlin's ambition consisted in transacting a wholesale business, and he soon sold all his stock to small dealers in neighboring settlements, and received in payment the promissory notes of the purchasers. He again went to New York and returned with a still larger supply of goods, and these also were soon sold on credit. The business flourished as long as the New York creditors were willing to part with their goods on credit, but eventually they called for payment, and this necessitated Hamlin to call on his debtors, but they were unable to respond. All the money Post could raise was applied in vain to appease the demands of the New York creditors, and ruin soon became apparent to Hamlin. In this emergency, Utica was alarmed in the middle of a winter night by a sudden outcry of fire and, as fires were unusual, the alarm was great. Everybody rushed from their beds, and the whole village was bright with the fire from Post's store. . . . My father's store was adjoining the burning building, and both structures were of wood, but as much snow was on the roof, my father's store was saved with some loss of wheat and flour scattered by attempts at their removal, but all that pertained to Post was destroyed. . . . Many persons suspected incendiarism as a convenient finale for the new firm, which now became avowedly insolvent. Post behaved honorably and sold all his lands to secure some preferred debts, and became in his old age divested of all the property for which he had faithfully labored. . . . Much commiseration was felt for him, and he and his aged wife and children withdrew from Utica on to a small farm, and nothing remains of him in Utica but a poor street called by his name on lands he once owned.

Moses Bagg an early Utica historian, author of *Pioneers of Utica,* added one amusing detail to Johnson's description of John Post. In the course of trading with the Indians for furs and ginseng root, Post frequently invited twenty or thirty of them to stay overnight in his kitchen, and since there were no other inns in the area, a few white visitors also dropped in for a place to sleep. One of these was a Frenchman traveling for the Caster Land Company, and Bagg gives the following entry from the unidentified vistor's journal: "Mr. Post keeps the dirtiest tavern in the State of New York, which is not saying little. Following the custom of the country, the linen is changed only on Sundays, to the misfortune of those who arrive on Saturday; and I therefore resolved to sleep on the couch they gave me with my clothes on. The common table had little to my relish, so I was obliged to live on milk—a proceeding which shocked the self-esteem of Mr. Post." Bagg, sensitive to disparaging remarks about Utica, commented: "Such unmeasured denunciations must surely be imputed to the prejudices of an

over-polished and dainty Frenchman, illy fitted to cope with the privations of a new country."

John C. Devereux, Utica's first elected mayor and the founder of
one of Utica's prominent families, occupies many pages in the annals of
the city, but Johnson's sketch of him, possibly because he later became a
rival of Johnson's in the banking business, may have a slight touch of
malice in it. Devereux had been a dancing master before coming to
Utica, and had tried hard to conceal the fact. Johnson thought him
"more French than Irish," and that he dressed "with unusual care." He
reported that his father, Bryan, delighted in asking Devereux for the
names of various steps performed at dancing parties, but Devereux
always pleaded ignorance, causing Johnson to comment, "Men seem
frequently to be ashamed of what constitutes their chief glory."

Like many Englishmen arriving in America with Chateaubriand's
image of the "noble savage" firmly implanted in their minds, Johnson
found the local Indians disappointing—"they assimilated in appearance
so much to the gypsies I had seen in England." However, one particular
Indian did attract him—the great Mohawk chief, Skenandoah, who
lived with the remnants of his tribe at Oneida Castle, some fifteen miles
from Utica. Skenandoah was reputed to be well over a hundred years
old. He had been a drunkard in his early years, but had been reformed
and converted to Christianity by Samuel Kirkland, who also taught the
chief English and turned him into a valuable ally of the Americans
during the Revolution. After his death in 1816 he was buried beside his
benefactor in the cemetery at Hamilton College. "A visit to Oneida
Castle," wrote Johnson, "was not complete without calling on Skenandoah, the head chief of the tribe. He was tall and dignified, bearing
himself as if conscious of his high position among his race. . . . He was
dressed like an Indian and lived in a low small wooden house. He was not
superior to receiving presents in money, and it was usually given by the
visitors and accepted by one of the women, several of whom were around
him." Like many other Utica merchants during severe northern winters,
Bryan Johnson was accustomed to extending credit to Indian purchasers
and waiting for payment until the spring when the Indians received their
cash annuity from the government. Bryan occasionally sent his son to
make the collection at Oneida Castle, and there Johnson once met a
Frenchman named Deferrier who managed the financial affairs of the
Mohawks. He was struck by Deferrier's Indian wife and their children—
one of whom "essayed the dress and customs of the whites, and was
admitted into white society." The experiment "of trying hard to be a
white man," Johnson reported, was not a success.

In his later years, Johnson's children and younger friends must have asked him many times about the "privations" of life in the little village at the beginning of the century. British travelers, especially such women as Frances Trollope, Mrs. Basil Hall, and Lady Emmeline Wortly were aghast at what they found in the villages of central New York State— particularly when they contrasted their physical appearances with their illustrious names. Lady Wortly, for instance, confided to her diary: "On our road to Niagara tomorrow we shall come to a great many high-sounding places: Rome, Syracuse, Egypt, Athens, Geneva, Utica . . . a noble line of places indeed . . . if their actual state, circumstances, and proportions harmonized with their pretentions." Mrs. Hall took one look and announced, "There is a strange jumble—to begin with, Utica!" And a male traveler, Captain Frederick Marryat, was downright bitter. "I do detest these old names vamped up," he wrote. "Why don't the Americans take Indian names? They need not be so very scupulous about it; they have robbed the Indians of everything else!" Even New Englanders were scornful of what they saw in "the wilds of upstate New York." The Reverend John Taylor of New Hampshire called Utica "a mixed mass of discordant materials," its churches "feeble," and its people heathenish. Johnson, however, was more charitable, though like Mrs. Trollope he was sometimes spleenish about the "domestic manners" of his fellow townsmen.

> Our food, consisting in part of fine poultry, was superior to the food I had been accustomed to, and fresh butcher's meat was plenty at all times, with good bread, butter, and cheese. Even groceries were abundant, including loaf sugar and good teas and coffee. They were all to be purchased, but we often had to go to the neighboring village of Whitesboro to purchase loaf sugar and green tea, the common kind used by country people being brown sugar, and a species of black tea called Bohea, which came in large chests of some 200 pounds weight, and was, I suppose, inferior to what often went by the same name. In traveling, the country taverns had often no other than such Bohea tea and coarse brown or maple sugar, with dark ill-made bread and fresh meat, principally beef steaks, that by long keeping had acquired a musty taste. I found, however, the manners of the people worse than the food. The habit of loud eructation was prevalent to an extraordinary degree and was occasionally practiced rather ostentatiously I thought, or at least with an entire unconsciousness that it was offensive. Another prevalent habit was the absence of the ordinary use of pocket handkerchiefs, and the supply of its place by a practice too disgusting to particularize. Both these practices were found in men more than in women. . . . Swearing was much less prevalent than I had heard it in England, and it was more confined to men than in England. Obscene

conversation among men at their social feasts was probably a fault of the age in question and it was the ordinary source of mirth and good fellowship. I was admitted early to such gatherings and often felt abashed almost beyond endurance by the songs and stories that made the reciters desired company. The withdrawal of the women from the dinner table was the signal for the commencement of these orgies, in which the oldest and most respectable would usually take the lead, and among whom I could name persons who are still venerated as departed jurists, doctors, and civilians. On one of these occasions two gentlemen, the foremost of the meeting, sang, and the one who was vanquished was to give a supper to the victor and his friends. The meed was to be accorded by the company to the song that was most licentious. In all such gatherings madeira wine was the principle and often the only beverage, except occasionally hot punch, and the great point of all the company was to make as many intoxicated as practicable. The mode consisted in drinking toasts in bumpers, from which no one was excused except on the penalty of singing a song or telling a story. As I was a boy and admitted on such occasions to my father's table only in courtesy, I was not a party to participate in any of the foregoing ceremonies, and when I became of sufficient age to be an actor in such scenes I never accepted any invitation thereto, but occasionally an ordinary gathering for other purposes would degenerate into a carousal, and I would always eject from my mouth into my pocket handkerchief the wine I was compelled to take, and then wring out the wine on the carpet under the table, and I am not aware that the act was ever detected. . . .

The social habits that I have described pertained to the best society that Utica afforded, and it included names that yet live in the highest respect. Whether similar habits of licentious speech belonged to farmers and other laboring people I know not, but people of leisure and polish that I met from any quarter seemed to be familiar with such practices, and I attribute them to the strict practical chastity which I believe marked the period, and which possibly sought a compensation in the license of speech. As far as I could judge, chastity of conduct was far more generally practiced in America than in England, and any deviation therefrom was deemed a public offense which a whole neighborhood would resent, especially when implicating married persons.

The city boy from London often wondered at how quickly and easily he became transformed into a country boy. "The possession of horses by my father, and which I could at any time ride, pleased me greatly," he wrote. "Even the garden attached to my father's house was a new kind of possession to me, and deriving therefrom cucumbers, melons, and other fruits became a source of enjoyment to me." When

Utica's Justice of the Peace, Talcott Camp, took him pigeon hunting, however, Johnson's pigeon-keeping days in London came back to him, and he balked at any further blood sports. When the boy lamented over a pigeon he had wounded, his companion "deemed my lamentation quite curious if not absurd." From Camp, a recent arrival from rural Connecticut, Johnson got his first lesson in the phonetics of New England speech. "It consisted in pronouncing *change* as though written *charnge*, *suger* as *sooger*, and *Thomas* as *th* is sounded in *thumb*."

Johnson's memory of the woods around Utica brought on other, more serious thoughts as he looked back over his life:

> The woods around Utica encouraged in me a habit of solitary reflection unusual in boys of my age, and I frequently resorted to the woods with some book, as Pope's *Homer,* Dryden's *Aeneid,* or Ovid's *Metamorphoses,* or some other book of poetry, and sitting on a stump or fallen tree, would enjoy the book heightened by the novelty of my position. I ought to have gone to school to prepare myself for entering college . . . but some domestic circumstances weighed with me sufficiently to resist leaving home, and no school existed in Utica that I felt sufficiently humble to attend, though I might probably have derived therefrom useful instruction.

Johnson deeply regretted his lack of formal schooling, and felt himself particularly deficient in spelling and etymology—defects which compelled him "continually to resort to a dictionary." Despite long struggles with Murray's *Grammar,* he admitted that he was more than twenty years old before he "properly understood the etymology of words so as to consult a dictionary understandingly." Looking back over his earlier writings he felt that his laborious efforts to acquire the rudiments of syntax, grammar, vocabulary etc. had "made them sophomorically ornate at an age when regularly educated men are simple, natural and mature." He added, however, not without some pride, that "an education self-acquired conduces probably to originality of conception, while regularly educated persons repeat current ideas rather than originate them."

Johnson's early days in Utica were by no means devoted exclusively to roaming the woods, reading, and being escorted about the country by his father's entertaining friends, for shortly after his arrival Bryan put him to work. Despite his lack of training he soon began keeping his father's books, tending the store, and traveling on his father's business. He was also put to heavier tasks such as "moving potash barrels, unheading them for inspection and heading them up again, and in loading, weighing, and unloading wheat." Johnson often stayed up all night tidying up the store after the ten P.M. closing hour, but he confessed that early rising "was a habit I never acquired throughout my life." Running a store in early Utica also required keeping a sharp eye on the customers and suppliers:

> The wheat we purchased was hoisted into a room adjoining the store, and lowered through a canvas pipe. One day a man from whom we had purchased a load soon returned with another load. After paying him for this also, a man in my father's employ saw the fellow attempt to refill his bags from the pipe, and no doubt the load we had just paid for was obtained the same way. We would have had him arrested, but before we could obtain a constable, the man drove off and escaped. Utica contained but one constable, and he was often traveling over the country—the county embracing at the time what are now Lewis, Jefferson, and St. Lawrence counties, and even more territory in other directions.

Bagg relates that young Johnson "wielded a considerable influence over his father" in business affairs, and that as a result "more money was realized in the last years of Mr. Johnson's business than in all the former." Bryan had not done badly on his own, however. When he first opened his store his chief competitor was a firm known as Kane and Van Rensselaer down the Mohawk in the village of Canajoharie.

> This trade was stopped by my father to such a degree that Kane and Rensselaer moved their establishment to Utica. Their store was near the Mohawk, and as their business kept declining, they would hail the boats passing down the river with wheat and potash to ascertain to whom the freight belonged; and the answer was to Bryan Johnson of Utica; and, as the boats returning up the river loaded with merchandise would, when hailed, answer in the same way, they resolved to go to Utica and share in the trade. The rivalry thus produced continued in unabated force while my father remained in business.

Despite the expansion of his father's business after his arrival, Johnson was uneasy in the role of storekeeper. "I desired," he said, "to accumulate a sufficiency of money that we might live without business, for I nourished a notion that country shopkeeping was not an elevated employment. I probably received this impression from England, and from the romances that had constituted most of my reading, and had tinctured me with undue aspirations and expectations."

Bryan had made many of his major purchases of goods from an Albany wholesaler, and by the time he was nineteen, Johnson was conducting all the Albany negotiations himself, making frequent trips to the state capital where for the first time he began, among other things, mingling with his own age group—so that "my evenings were spent very agreeably and profitably." The young men, he said,

> were all superior to me in literature, having received a college education, and whether they discovered the defects of my education I know not, but I was unwisely anxious to conceal my inferiority, and I thought they gave me credit for more learning than I possessed. One reason for their mistake proceeded from my having acquired in England topics of conversation that were not usual in America, and a personal refinement superior to the standard then prevalent in America. Nearly every person seemed to take an interest in me, while my own consciousness of defects distressed me, though I was ambitious to be esteemed.

Johnson was particularly pleased that these young men "took much interest in introducing me to their female acquaintances," and one of the most obliging in this respect was a precocious youth named John Howard Payne, whose opera *Clari; or, The Maid of Milan* would be performed some twenty years later at Covent Garden in London, featuring a song called "Home Sweet Home" sung by Ann Marie Tree. At the time Johnson met him he was a student at Union College in Schenectady, and the editor of a college newspaper called *Pass Time* to which Johnson managed to obtain a number of Utica subscribers. Johnson and Payne corresponded for several years until Payne went off to New York, where he acted in the Park Theater, and later to London, where he played at the Drury Lane, and later produced some sixty plays for the English stage. "While he was in Albany during my visits," wrote Johnson, "he very deservedly eclipsed me." Johnson was deeply mortified when several of Payne's friends looked him up in Utica and found him working in his father's store.

Sometime in 1803, hearing that goods, "could be bought more advantageously in that city than in Albany," Johnson went to New York, bearing a letter of introduction to Henry Beekman, a young man of property, "very sedate in his manners and very gentlemanly," who lived in a Broadway boardinghouse. With Beekman, Johnson saw his first New York theatrical production at the Park Theater. It was called "Have a Wife and Rule a Wife," and featured the great Philadelphia actor Thomas Cooper, whose Hamlet and King John had recently been acclaimed as "transcendentally excellent" by New York critics. Johnson "deemed the acting of Cooper very fine, "but when I first saw him come on the stage as a stolid booby who was to become the convenient husband of the lady he was to marry, I was so much a novice in acting as to be astonished when I was told by Mr. Beekman sotto voce that the actor was Cooper whom I had heard so much applauded."

Some of Beekman's friends tried hard during his stay in New York to acquaint him with "the curiosities of the city," but once again, as Johnson noted, his "invincible shyness more, I fear, than any moral principle, kept me from harm in these excursions." The young man returned to Albany by sailing sloop, and the trip left a lasting impression on him:

> When the time came for my return to Utica, an advertisement appeared in the papers that a steamboat was to leave in the evening from Fulton Street to Albany. This was the first I had ever heard of a steamboat, though on my way down I saw lying in the river at Albany a curious looking vessel which I now suspected was the steamboat in question. I had queried what the vessel was intended for when I saw it at Albany, but as I concluded it was a machine for dredging the river I asked no questions. I inquired of Mr. Beekman whether I had better take a passage in the steamboat to Albany or in a sloop that was to sail at the same time. He advised me to take the sloop, the steamboat being a new experiment and the wind promising a short passage by sail. I accordingly embarked on the sloop. It sailed about an hour in advance of the steamboat. We had a fair and good breeze at starting but the wind soon lulled and the steamboat passed us. We saw it steam along and I began to regret I was not on board, for it was soon out of sight while we were drifting along with the tide. When the tide became adverse we were compelled to drop anchor and wait for the returning tide. We kept creeping along in this way through our whole voyage, and before it finally came to an end the steamboat again passed us on its return trip from Albany, and passed us again the third time on its return trip from New York. This was the last of my sloop experience on the Hudson River though, with the usual buoyancy of youth, the long voyage was not wholly unpleasant. Several passengers were on board and we amused ourselves by landing at the farmhouses to obtain milk, butter, and chickens while the sloop was at anchor, and occasionally in our small row boat some of the passengers would pull up the nets in the river and abstract some fine shad, which we all well relished from the piquancy occasioned by the mode of their obtainment.

Back in Utica, restless after his adventures in New York, Johnson anxiously awaited his twenty-first birthday and the "expiration of my minority" which would take place in 1807. Since his father never demanded his presence at the store "except as the employment pleased me," he began a heavy reading schedule and turning out a few literary pieces of his own, some of which were published anonymously in the *Utica Patriot,* and illustrated, Johnson said, the truth of a line he had read in the *Spectator,* "whatever contradicts my sense I hate to see, and never can believe." He also completed a five–act tragedy "after the manner of Shakespeare," but was discouraged from doing anything with it by a New York actor who told him that only plays which had been successful in London would attract an American audience.

Public diversions were few and far between in Utica, but in 1805 the first traveling circus came to town, and while Johnson gave no details, he said of it, "I believe in no portion of my after life I ever saw an exhibition which pleased me so much as this." According to Bagg, the main feature of the show was a "live elephant" billed as "the largest and most sagacious animal in the world." The advance announcement also stated, "She will draw the cork from a bottle, and with her trunk will manage it in such a way as to drink its contents to the astonishment of the spectators." Johnson's pursuit of recreation also produced the usual narrow escapes from disaster to which boys are prone—or as Johnson put it, "instances when I came near bringing my existence to a termination." One of these involved a pumpkin with a candle in it which had been placed in a field at night as a target by some boys armed with muskets. Johnson went to investigate, thinking it might be an *ignis fatuus,* and heard "the whistling of a ball as it passed near my head." On another night, after the store had closed, Johnson ventured on the Mohawk for some ice skating, and braked just in time to avoid a patch of deep water. In writing of the latter incident he recalled, "I have a mole at the bottom of one of my feet, and when I was a child I was often told it was a sign I should be drowned." The incident also brought forth the confession that throughout his life, whenever he expected an important letter, he carefully avoided stepping on "the joints which unite the flagging that leads to the post office—in order to insure that the news would be favorable." Slavery began early in the area which became New York State, having been introduced in 1626 by the Dutch West India Company; and by the 1640s it provided much of the labor supply for Dutch landholders along the Hudson and Mohawk valleys. When the British took control of the territory thousands of new slaves were brought in by the Royal African Company, and by 1746 there were some 9,000 adult slaves in New York—the largest work force in the colonies north of Maryland. In Utica many of the more well-to-do citizens, including Bryan Johnson, used them in their households as well as in their shops and on their farms. As early as 1777 a bill was passed at the first State Constitutional Convention proclaiming that "every human being who breathes the air of the State shall enjoy the privileges of a free man," but no efforts were made to enforce it. The importation of slaves was banned by the state in 1785, and in 1779 it was decreed that all slaves born after July 4 that year were to be freed. Slaves were still readily available in Utica, however, when Johnson arrived, and the first item in his letter file was a bill of sale, dated April 23, 1802, made out to his father for "a certain Negro wench named Hester, about the age of 21 years, and also a Negro wench child of about the age of four years— daughter of aforesaid Hester named Jude." The sale was made "in consideration of the sum of $150." Of Hester, Johnson wrote: "The female, after faithful service as cook, died of consumption. While lingering, we were informed by her black attendants that she could not die because she was lying on a feather bed, and they requested that it might be removed. . . . As this request was not complied with, they took her out of bed and laid her on the floor where she died."

Johnson also described the deaths of three other blacks in Utica:

One of our neighbors owned a black woman with an infant, and on the master greatly offending her, she ran to the river, and drowned herself and infant. I saw the body when taken from the water, and her arms were clasped in death so as to retain the infant. A Negro boy who also was a slave came to death in a singular manner. He was addicted to amuse himself and others who would look at him by walking on his hands in the street with his head down, and his feet in the air. He was seen in this position one day with his head in an open barrel near his master's house, and, as his feet kept moving about in the usual manner, persons supposed he was performing his usual tricks, but as his feet eventually subsided and the boy remained in the barrel, some person went to him and found he was drowned, the barrel being half full of water. Whether he came to his death accidentally or by design was never known, but probably he fell in by accident, as he was always playful and apparently happy.

Johnson himself would become the owner of a slave shortly after attaining his majority.

On the third Tuesday of May 1805, Bryan Johnson took a step which meant much to his nineteen-year-old son. At ceremonies held in the Court of Common Pleas, "in the schoolhouse near the gaol," Bryan was made a naturalized citizen of the United States. His father's object, wrote Johnson, "was to naturalize me without any personal act on my part, and thus to assimilate me with native citizens—the law naturalizing the minor children of all persons who should become naturalized. He accordingly wrote the following certificate on the back of his naturalization paper: 'I hereby certify that at the time I became a Citizen of the United States, my son, Alexander, was under twenty-one years. Witness my hand—Utica, August 17, 1805. Bryan Johnson.' "

CHAPTER 3

1805–1811

Coming of Age

FOR ALEXANDER BRYAN JOHNSON the most important event of the year 1807 was his twenty-first birthday, marking, as he put it, "the termination of my minority." In the ten years since his arrival in Utica, Bryan Johnson had accumulated a fortune of "rising $50,000 which was then deemed ample"; and to his son, at least, the business of storekeeping was no longer appropriate for a gentleman of means who moved in the society of the Walkers, the Inmans, and the Williamses. He prevailed upon his father to sell the store and retire. But first, he seized an opportunity to prove his own mettle as a full-fledged Yankee trader.

In 1807 Thomas Jefferson, stung by British interference with American shipping in the course of Britain's war with France, instituted his ill-fated Embargo Act, imposing a ban on all exports to the British— a kind of self-blockade which, until its repeal in 1809, nearly destroyed the fledgling nation's shipping, mercantile, and planting interests. Sometime during the late winter of 1808 at the Lake Ontario port of Oswego, New York, a federal marshal seized a cargo of potash destined for Britain, and put it on auction for American bidders. A number of Uticans immediately readied their sleighs, and among them was young Johnson, driving his father's sleigh and accompanied (perhaps to his subsequent advantage) by the deputy federal marshal, who was to serve as auctioneer. Johnson in his old age described the journey and its outcome with no little pride in his youthful commercial sagacity:

> The sleighing was good, and when we arrived at the village of Whitesboro we met several other sleighs full of persons from different places, all known to me and destined also for Oswego to compete for the purchase of the ashes and a few other articles that had been seized with them. The weather was exceedingly cold, and as all the sleighs kept

together, the travelers stopped at every public house on the road to warm, and usually most of them to take a drink. The houses were, however, exceedingly few, and erected chiefly as taverns for the accommodation of travelers, and principally built of logs. One house was rather famous. It was at Oriskany, and kept by one Parkhurst, who had collected and kept for sale many bullets, scabbards, bayonets, gun barrels, soldiers' buttons, and other relics of the battle of Oriskany that had been disastrously fought with the Indians by General Herkimer many years previously. The next noted station was at Camden, where my sleigh stopped to bait our horses, and where I and the deputy marshal obtained dinner. We found a fine large fire of logs in the barroom, and around it were several women who stood warming themselves, and they were also travelers. The marshal offered to bet me a glass of cider that he would walk up to the women and place his hand in a very indecent position on one of them. I accepted his bet, thinking he would not dare to perform the action, but he walked up and fairly won the bet though probably the woman was wholly unaware of the trick, though apparently startled at the pretence of fire by which he effected it.

The road we traveled was for a large part of the way through a dense forest, but the track was good, except that the snow was so deep that when we met a sleigh moving in an opposite direction we had to stop, and each sleigh was tilted on its side so that neither should be forced off the beaten track and become buried in snow. The horses in passing each other would sometimes be forced, one or more, off the track, when the one off would flounder in the snow and with great difficulty be again brought on the solid beaten road. We saw along the path tracks of snowshoes worn by Indians in traveling, and as they were the first I had ever seen, I could never have imagined what had caused them, had I not been informed, especially as the word *shoe* conveys no idea of the article. The road would have been impassable without snow, but with that addition we found good traveling except occasionally in hollow places, where a running water kept the snow melted and made the passage difficult. We saw some tracks of deer but we met with no living animals, the frequent travel on the road probably keeping them from showing themselves. . . . We eventually reached Oswego and put up at the only tavern in the place. . . . It was wholly unprepared for our reception and, though it furnished us with sleeping accommodations, we had to wait breakfast in the morning till a messenger returned who had been despatched to Salt Point for bread and other provisions.

The party found the barrels of potash in poor condition, and all but Johnson agreed to bid upon them as a group in order to lower the price. Johnson refused to join the combine, charging that the quantity was too low for such a division, and outbid the others, betting one of them a beaver hat that he would clear a $500 profit when he sold the potash back in Utica. He won his bet handily, but never received his beaver hat. However, he reported that the transaction gave him great satisfaction "as being the first enterprise of my own conducting."

For a time, at least, Johnson regretted having persuaded his father to sell the store which had launched them both on the road to success in America, for Bryan, still in his prime, was a poor candidate for retirement. He embarrassed Johnson—and the new proprietor—by returning to the store for hours at a time in the belief that his presence attracted his old customers. He also depended greatly on his son for companionship, and the two spent hours together, walking the streets of Utica and the paths along the Mohawk. Moses Bagg, writing shortly after Johnson's death, described the pair as he remembered them from his early youth:

As they walked the streets, the father, a hale, vigorous and fresh old gentleman with exuberant silvery locks, leaning on the arm of his slighter son, both dressed with extremest care, and the former especially conspicuous by his short breeches and silk stockings—the costume of a then expiring generation—they presented a picture never to be forgotten by one who beheld them. . . . Up to the middle of life his [Bryan's] temper was hasty and his manner sometimes gruff, and thence arose the waggish soubriquet, "Old bear and cub," by which they occasionally went. To compare the father with the son . . . I would say that the father was more genial, more vivacious and more impulsive; the son was more equable, more self-reliant, and more cultured.

Idleness was even less attractive to the twenty-two-year-old Johnson. His father's almost total dependence on him for companionship, and his lack of other responsibility, began to tell on him.

I kept much aloof from other company, and indeed, had not one other companion. This was partly owing to the duty I felt toward my father, and partly to my being the only idler in the village. . . . I thus nurtured a habit of seclusion to which I was always prone, and which has been a feature of my whole life. This monotony was unsuited to my age, and I eventually became dispirited and hypochondriac. I imagined I should not live long and felt symptoms of several incipient mortal disorders.

Among the latest and most fashionable cures for "incipient mortal disorders" at this time was a trip to Saratoga Springs or to its neighbor seven miles away, Ballston Spa, whose "chalybeate" waters were guaranteed in the advertisements of the day to cure most ailments, including "depraved appetite, habitual costiveness, and cutaneous eruptions"; while the billiard tables and glamorous young ladies were well known for their palliative effect on hypochondria. Johnson chose Ballston Spa which, though less populous, had a reputation for greater elegance.

Bryan Johnson saw to it that his son went off to Ballston in style. He ordered a one-horse chaise built by Utica's best carriage maker, handsomely painted, and equipped with a roll-back leather top. Bryan also provided his son with an extra horse to be ridden by a black servant in livery. Johnson described his departure and arrival:

> The weather was bright, warm, and every way delightful; the roads were dry and even, and I was full of life and youth to relish whatever should occur. Most persons would have suffered from want of a traveling companion, but I was accustomed to be alone, and amused myself by my own observations and reflections. My servant rode behind at a respectful distance, and took care of the horses when we had to stop for refreshments, and to be otherwise useful to me. Our road towards Schenectady passed in many places close to the Mohawk River, and in one of these positions we passed a loaded boat which the boatmen were pushing forward against the current by setting poles placed against their shoulders. The captain of the boat was one Ira Carey, who had long boated for my father, and when he and his men saw me driving along in my present state, they commenced a shout of ridicule which somewhat disconcerted me, but I made no reply and was soon out of reach of their impertinence without having apparently noticed them. . . . On my arrival at Ballston, I found good accommodation at the Sans Souci, which was a very large wooden structure and the only house of entertainment there at the time. It was full of company who devoted themselves to gaiety and pleasure.

Despite his initial bravado, his black servant, and his custom-built chaise, Johnson was a lost soul amid the glamor and the fripperies of the Sans Souci. The expense staggered him, and he quickly learned the truth of the local saying that "people went to the Sans Souci and returned *sans six sous.*" Equally intimidating were the fashions and habits of the hotel's clientele.

> Many of the guests had their own carriages with which they drove around the vicinity, though the roads were sandy and soft. I had never

before seen such a collection of elegantly attired ladies. The meals were taken in a common hall and the guests who had servants were waited on by their own. Many of the guests were from the southern states, and were attended by their slaves, and I was waited on by mine, while persons who were dependent on the servants of the house fared poorly in the general scramble at dinner, where all were expected at a given hour. The time for other meals was more optional with the guests. My usual timidity kept me secluded from the persons around me, though I saw many beautiful young women with whom I would gladly have associated, and whom I admired only by sight. . . . I would have given anything for some friendly person to introduce me to the ladies I admired, and I kept thinking some person ought kindly to have seen my want and taken me by the hand, but my solitariness seemed to repel everybody from me, and I felt discouraged and distressed. . . .

At Ballston I saw for the first time a billiard table, and among the players one most skilful was a West Indian gentleman whose hand from dissipation or some other cause was exceedingly tremulous, and yet he would strike the balls wherever he desired them to go. I stood often to admire his skill, but the game possessed no attractions otherwise to me, and I have never played it. I saw at Ballston some black wet nurses who were nursing beautiful infants of their southern mistresses, and the contrast between the color of the infant and the breast it fed on made me wonder how habit could induce such a practice, though perhaps the southerners would wonder equally that prejudice should prevent northern mothers from adopting a like aid. Most persons liked the Ballston water, and the spring was resorted to usually in the mornings. I tasted it but I could not drink it, the taste assimilating with me to the taste of ink. Card playing was said to be practiced to some extent, and other means of improper dissipation, but they were probably conducted rather secretly for I saw none of them, and I only heard of their existence casually afterwards.

It is obvious that Johnson's father and mother had hoped their son would meet some eligible young ladies at Ballston, and that he himself had a similar objective in mind, but after several sets of guests had arrived and departed, he finally gave up and took his leave "without having made a single acquaintance male or female." He hated to go straight back to Utica, however, and decided on "a circuit around the City of New York." This, too, was a fiasco. The weather was hot; no "places of amusement" were open, and he had no friends in the City. He stayed long enough to recruit his horses and hurried back to his family in Utica, ashamed to admit that he had made "no new acquaintances." Back in Utica with his parents, Johnson's restlessness increased,

and having seen how the other half lived at Ballston, he began casting
about for a respectable way to increase his fortune. An opportunity soon
presented itself in the person of Colonel Lawrence Schoolcraft, the
owner of a large glass factory near Albany. Window glass was a scarce
commodity in the new nation, and was considered difficult to manufacture, but Schoolcraft, according to Johnson, "was accustomed to
relate some periods of the moon and other natural phenomena to a successful prosecution of the works, and all which secrets he kept pro-
foundly to himself." When the colonel proposed establishing a factory
near Utica, Johnson became a small shareholder and was elected one
of the directors at three dollars a day. The other directors included
Watts Sherman, then a merchant in Utica, and John Stewart, a rich
lawyer of Utica. A charter was obtained from the legislature, and the
factory was erected in the town of Vernon, some fifteen miles from
Utica. Johnson journeyed there in his chaise several times a week to see
how the work was proceeding.

The success of the company soon encouraged Peter Bours, a young
Utica merchant "abounding in enterprise and activity," to set up a rival
company. Bours also obtained a charter and, with the financial support
of such persons of note and enterprise as his father-in-law Colonel
Walker, began the manufacture of glass on a tract of land just north of
Utica. The company flourished; with Bours' "great vigor and by continuous boasting their stock became a kind of South Sea Bubble with
sales reported at a hundred percent advance." Seduced by the prospect
of the money to be made in glass, but anticipating reluctance on the part
of the legislature to charter a third glass company in Oneida County,
Johnson joined forces with two former clerks of his father's, and turned
his eyes to nearby Ontario County. He drew up a petition to the legislature setting forth in glowing terms the great advantages the county was
to derive from a new glass manufactory.

After some intensive canvassing in Ontario County, Johnson obtained the necessary subscribers to his petition, and returned to Utica.
By chance, his fellow passengers in the stage from Canandaigua were
two gentlemen en route to Albany—a young lawyer named John Greig,
of Canandaigua, and General James Wadsworth, a rich landowner from
Geneseo. The former became a lifelong friend of Johnson's and a partner in most of his subsequent business enterprises. Impressed by the
young Utican, Greig and Wadsworth promised to promote his efforts in
Albany with the legislators, one of whom happened to be Greig's father-
in-law.

After polishing up his petition and regaling his family with his
successes in Ontario County, Johnson set off for the State Capitol and

the first of many subsequent appearances before the legislature. He checked in at the city's "best hotel," and then hurried to the Capitol building to present his petition. The Speaker at the time was General William North (1755–1836) who, along with Colonel Walker, had served as aide-de-camp to Baron von Steuben, and later became coheir with Walker to the von Steuben estate. He was appointed Adjutant General of the Army by John Adams, and also served as a United States senator, preparing the initial report that eventually made the Erie Canal a reality.

Johnson was impressed by the fact that North wore "a cocked hat while he presided, and all the other members were uncovered." Concerned though he was with his mission, Johnson was intrigued by the ritual of American democracy in action. He had hoped his bill would come up immediately, but "some debate would arise and consume the whole day." Johnson filled in the time, however, by "obtruding" himself on various members of the Assembly and explaining his bill. As he listened to other peoples' bills being debated endlessly, he was particularly struck by two of the legislators, both of whom he described as "illiterate. . . . but possessing strong native sense and oratorical fluency." These two inevitably took opposite sides on each question and "therefore happily neutralized each other's efforts." He noted, however, that the Assembly, "composed principally of very plain men" listened more attentively to these rough-hewn "illiterate" politicians than they did to the more polished "professed orators."

Johnson's bill finally got through the Assembly and moved into the Senate which was largely dominated by De Witt Clinton, a close friend of Johnson's Utica neighbor, Francis A. Bloodgood who assured him that his bill would have no trouble. Johnson was deeply impressed with Clinton: "He was in the prime of life, in the height of his political power, and the Senate obeyed him as implicitly as courtiers obey an absolute monarch. The consciousness of power gave a dignity to his deportment, and he seldom spoke by way of debate, but only uttered a few words to indicate what he desired, and usually all debate thereafter became silenced, and a vote in the way he indicated became a matter of course."

All went well with the bill at first until, as Johnson wrote, "an event occurred that much delayed it." The "event" involved a debate between Clinton and an English-born property owner from Otsego County named George Clark. Clinton made a remark offensive to Clark who immediately challenged him to a duel—a challenge delivered to Clinton by James Lynch, a young lawyer from Rome, N.Y., Johnson described what happened the next morning:

Mr. Clinton arose in his place . . . and complained that a gross breach
had been committed . . . by a challenge having been delivered to him
for words spoken in debate, and he moved that the president issue a
warrent to bring the offenders, Clark and Lynch, before the Senate to
answer for their contempt. Mr. Clinton had a slight impediment in his
speech when excited, but it seemed merely to give greater energy to
what he uttered, and on this occasion as he spoke the veins visibly
swelled with indignation in his broad and alabaster-looking forehead.
An immense commotion followed the announcement, and the motion
was agreed to without any opposition. . . . Clark and Lynch were
soon found and brought into the Senate, where Clinton accused them
in a most scathing speech. . . . I believe the Senate committed Clark
to prison for a certain term, and Lynch was permitted to apologize and
to be reprimanded in open session. . . . I heard Lynch apologize the
next day, and I heard him reprimanded, but all I recollect is his flushed
countenance.

Passage of Johnson's bill took two weeks, and arriving back in
Utica, he promptly had second thoughts about it—thoughts that brought
back all the symptoms which had sent him to Saratoga Springs. "I began
to regret," he wrote, "that I had disturbed my quiet by an enterprise
that required great and untried efforts, and whose success was uncertain." He added, "I returned home with the charter . . . and was
less than twenty years old. I had no good reason for involving my
peace and fortune in any novel enterprise. . . . Emotional trouble at
this period of my life affected me with nausea and an entire absence of
appetite, but at a later period, the same kind of trouble produced a
painful sensation of the heart, a literal heartache."

While Johnson was alternating between fear and hope, he was
introduced by Colonel Schoolcraft at Vernon to the latter's seventeen-
year-old son, Henry Rowe Schoolcraft, who under the tutelage of his
father was already an expert on glass manufacture, and full of un-
bounded enthusiasm for Johnson's proposed adventure in Ontario
County. Impressed by the precocious youngster's appearance and skill,
Johnson hired him at a thousand dollars a year as superintendent of the
Ontario Glass works should it ever materialize. Again, though he did
not know it at the time, Johnson was rubbing shoulders with an American
whose fame among his contemporaries was to outshine his own by far.
Schoolcraft, shortly after parting company with Johnson, joined the Cass
expedition into the upper Mississippi Valley, and became one of the
foremost authorities on the Indians of the Western States. Among his
many books were *A Residence of Thirty Years with the Indian Tribes*

on the American Frontiers, published in 1842, and dedicated to
Johnson.

Johnson returned the compliment with a highly laudatory review
of the book, probably for a Utica newspaper, and reprinted as the last
essay in *Understanding Our American Union* (1859). The review began
by calling attention to Schoolcraft's dedication, and recalled the glassmaking episode, and Schoolcraft's role in it.

For the moment, despite his enthusiasm for his new superintendent,
Johnson's chief preoccupation was the raising of capital to get the
enterprise under way. He decided on an initial issue of one hundred
shares of stock at $250 each, out of which he would receive twenty
shares for his services. In addition he reserved sufficient shares for himself to ensure his hold on one-fourth of the total. His Utica friend,
Nathan Williams, took ten shares, but the remainder was to be held for
residents of Ontario County; and in the spring of 1810 Johnson went
off to Geneva, where his new friend, John Greig, had arranged a dinner
party—"inviting thereto such persons as he supposed would be stockholders." Johnson described his plans and extolled his new superintendent's skills to the gathering, and by the end of the evening the
stock was subscribed. He returned to Utica well pleased with himself,
but was back in Geneva within a few weeks, accompanied by Schoolcraft, to look for a factory site. One was found almost immediately—a
270-acre tract on the shores of Seneca Lake, surrounded by "fine timber
to fuel the furnaces, and with a beach frontage to supply abundantly
beautiful white sand." Schoolcraft drew up plans for a unique factory
community with the furnaces and the administrative offices surrounded
by carefully laid-out streets lined with small houses for the workmen.
While Schoolcraft remained in Geneva to supervise construction, Johnson, as part of his contract with the other directors, went off to find the
heat-resistant stone needed for the furnaces, the proper clay for the
crucibles, and, most important of all, the scarce glassblowers to man the
factory. It turned out to be a far more arduous assignment than he had
bargained for, since the stone Schoolcraft wanted was in Connecticut,
and the clay and the glassblowers were mainly in the vicinity of
Philadelphia.

For several succeeding months Johnson spent much of his time in
overland stagecoaches, rattling down narrow roads, and putting up with
primitive overnight accommodations along the way. The lonely, intro-
spective traveler had many bad moments on this trip, but his observant
eye missed none of the novelties of the American scene unfolding
around him. In Connecticut he found the Yankees friendly "beyond
what was common in other places." A Mr. Bull in New Hartford whom

he met by chance invited him for tea and escorted him to a stone quarry where he found the stone he had been told to look for. It was laden with garnets, and Johnson experienced a momentary thrill until he was informed that their market value was low—though he filled his pockets with them to take back to Utica. One of the New England novelties that impressed him most was the behavior of the schoolchildren who lined the roads as the stage passed by.

> As our stage passed along the road, all the children would either bow or courtsey, and I always bowed in return, though such a recognition seemed not common to the passengers. In passing schoolhouses on the road during any intermission for recreation, they would emulate each other in their obeisances, and sometimes a whole row of children would arrange themselves for the ceremony, and they seemed to enjoy it as if conscious of the performance of a duty.

Johnson was also intrigued by the scarcity of people in Connecticut. At one point, after crossing the New York State border, his stage drew up to a post office, and the expectant postmaster rummaged through the stage looking for mail until he heard the driver announce that "there was no mail for the whole state of Connecticut." At Andover, Johnson was mistaken for a clergyman. "It was not the first time," he said. But the incident that most impressed him occurred when a gentleman boarded the stage for a short run and, after hearing Johnson's story of the Geneva glass factory, handed him $250 as an advance on $2,500 worth of stock. The stranger later went to England, but sent in his installments regularly by mail until the amount was paid up. Johnson commented:

> We should be surprised now at such conduct in a casual traveler, but at the time people came to America under an impression that they were in a new country where little was known, and where every new venture was followed with success—just as when I left England for America I received from good-natured friends various receipts for the manufacture of sealing wax, Duffy's Elixir, and other simple things by which they thought a fortune could be made in America.

Having procured the desired stone and arranged for its shipment to Geneva, Johnson went off to Pennsylvania after a brief return to Utica. There he found the clay he needed, but the glassblowers were another matter. Since most American glassblowers were of Dutch extraction, Johnson had hired a Utica Dutchman to accompany him. On his arrival in Philadelphia, Johnson took time to observe some of the attractions of the city:

> I strolled around the city and was attracted to Peale's Museum, the first institution of the kind I had ever seen. I was much delighted with the exhibition which included the skeleton of a mastodon. I believe it had been exhumed in Kentucky. It was the first that had been found, and I had never heard of it. The bones were placed together and they stood on a platform in the natural figure of the animal, and which seemed to me several times larger than an elephant, while for the sake of contrast the skeleton of a mouse stood on the same platform. . . . In the evening a lecture was to be delivered on chemistry, illustrated by experiments, and as I had never seen anything of the kind, and had but an indifferent conception of chemistry, I attended and saw the production of water by the combustion of oxygen and hydrogen, and various other experiments with gases. From this lecture I derived much instruction, and I was thereby subsequently enabled to read with understanding a course of chemical lectures that I purchased for the purpose.
>
> On my return home to Utica, I found my glass blowers had not yet arrived, but in due time they came on in two stage coaches and I boarded them at Bellinger's tavern till I should arrange to take them on to Geneva. I found them a most ignorant and turbulent set of drunkards who, conscious of their importance to me, took every conceivable advantage. They ran up an extravagant bill at Bellinger's for wine. The number of bottles I had to pay for was enormous, . . . but I knew of no way but to indulge them, lest they should return to Philadelphia in disgust. After a few days, I procured stage coaches and sent them on to Geneva, thinking that Schoolcraft, who was himself a Dutchman and brought up with such people, would know how to manage them. I followed in my own chaise. . .

Johnson's stay in Geneva was hardly auspicious. During his first night in a boardinghouse a female traveler died, and the next day Johnson was moved into her room. Suspecting that the landlord had not even changed the deathbed sheets, Johnson, "greatly shocked," demanded another room much to the annoyance of his host. Out at the factory the next morning Johnson found the workers' houses constructed and occupied, but since the stone for the furnaces had not arrived, the men, not yet reunited with their wives, were restless and drinking heavily. Johnson, still convinced that Schoolcraft should cope with his fellow Dutchmen, drove off to make his first visit to Niagara Falls some 120 miles away. Traveling alone rarely bothered Johnson, but he found the endless stretch of forest depressing and "the vast solitude of Lake

Ontario rather awful." Buffalo, as yet unnamed, was not much more than a small collection of farmhouses, and the churning Niagara River had to be crossed by ferry. Arriving at Table Rock, he crawled out to the edge, but "the distance below looked so terrible that I crawled back affrighted." Like many later travelers he was disappointed in the Falls, "surprised that the world should not furnish some fall greater than what Niagara appeared." On the Canadian side he met up with some English officers and felt a slight twinge of nostalgia for his native country.

Returning to Geneva after a few days, he found his superintendent still struggling to maintain peace among the idle workers, and the boy's anxiety communicated itself to Johnson, who, finding nothing he could do to improve matters, went back to Utica and tried to forget the factory. There was no escaping the flood of anxious letters from Schoolcraft, however, and Johnson was soon on the road to Geneva again.

> I kept alternating between Utica and Geneva at intervals regulated by the letters I received from Schoolcraft. We were too much dependent on him to make our intercourse very pleasant, his letters to me being very often very complaining of the difficulties he encountered with the workmen. Complaints invariably grow with the habit of complaining, and they eventually became almost the whole substance of our correspondence. I deemed my reputation identified with the success of our project which I alone originated and had carried thus far, and being ever morbidly emotional, I suffered beyond measure anxiety for its result, and I would willingly have made any pecuniary sacrifice if I could have relieved the anxiety which afflicted me.

Johnson preserved no samples of his correspondence with School-craft, but there is a letter on file at the Geneva Historical Society which makes it clear that by the end of December 1810 Johnson's nerves were at the breaking point. It is one of the few letters outside of his own family file in which he addressed a recipient by his first name, and the phrasing of his initial question is highly uncharacteristic.

> Dear Henry,
>   For God's sake what is the matter with you all up there at Ontario? Formerly every letter I received was full of good tidings and fair prospects, and now since you got into operation, every letter is full of gloomy news and dismal forebodings. Your father will go up and have this business settled. In the present state of affairs, should anything happen to this furnace, I am convinced there will be no more money, and we should sink a laughing stock to our enemies, a dis-

appointment to our friends and a disgrace to ourselves. It is already known that there is something wrong at the factory. You have had all the credit of getting us into operation, and they would be as liberal in their censure should it be destroyed. It is impossible for you to separate yourself from its fate. What the directors complain of is that you evince carelessness in the concerns and interests of the company. Let me persuade you not to relax your steady diligence . . . but preserve your integrity at all events; and depend upon it, when your father goes up, all will be settled to the satisfaction of all parties!

There is evidence that the young man had indeed relaxed his "steady diligence"—at least during the 1810 Christmas season. Among his papers in Geneva is a letter in verse, written a few days after Johnson sent his reprimand, to a friend who had invited him to a party "in our back room." Schoolcraft replied:

> You invited me, Jack, to come down as a guest,
> Where the friends of gay Bacchus all join in a feast;
> But the bearer got drunk and so I was not there,
> For he gave me the note the day after the fair. . . .
> Yes, I missed all the merriment, jollity, fun,
> Which flows from a song, a droll story or pun,
> But my wishes were with you which ever will be,
> Your welfare, your happiness and prosperity.

The climax of Johnson's unhappy venture into glassmaking came one day after a clumsy glass cutter named Wiltsie, of Utica, was dismissed for having broken much of the glass he was attempting to cut. One night as Johnson stood in his doorway, Wiltsie's wife walked by and made an "ill-looking face" at him. The next morning he found a stone had been thrown through his bedroom window; and on the following night he was nearly hit by a brick through the parlor window. He ran out into the dark and grappled with the assailant long enough to recognize him as the disgruntled Wiltsie, and had him arrested the next day.

This was the last straw for Johnson. He went to Geneva and "proposed to the directors that they should purchase my shares of stock, my residence in Utica making it particularly inconvenient to attend their meetings." The stock was sold, he reported, "without any pecuniary loss," but also "with no pecuniary remuneration for all my trouble and exertions."

A somewhat different account appears in an article published in the Corning Glass Company's *Journal of Glass Studies* (Vol. VI, 1964) entitled "The Ontario Glass Manufacturing Company." The author, Mrs. Jenena Rappleye, states that in November 1810, the directors "voted to remove Mr. A. B. Johnson from the office of Secretary."

On May 1, 1811, they passed an additional resolution "to serve notice on A. B. Johnson who hath neglected to pay $10.00 on each share subscribed by him . . . shares which shall be forfeited to the company with all previous payments made thereon amounting to $1500." The fact is also recorded that Schoolcraft was discharged on December 23, 1811, and that he sold his shares to the company a year later, returning to Vernon to work for a time with his father. The factory was destroyed by fire that same year, and a foreman was killed in the blaze. It was rebuilt and operated with some success for a number of years, being very profitable during the War of 1812.

Thus ended Johnson's glassmaking venture. If, in his words, "the anxiety and labor I had undergone told severely on my sensitive organization," bringing on a recurrence of his earlier neurasthenia, still he was able to assert stoutly: "I had succeeded in establishing the manufacture of glass, and had thus satisfied the ambition which induced me to commence the undertaking."

CHAPTER 4

1811–1812

War Years in New York and Washington

IN THE EARLY SUMMER OF 1811, Johnson, smarting as a result of the Geneva debacle, and dubious over his prospects in Utica, proposed to his father that the family pull up stakes, and move to New York City where their capital might be invested more advantageously, and the young man's opportunities for a good marital "connection" might be improved. Leah was apparently not consulted, but the devoted Bryan having done well by his own "American dream" in a scant fifteen years, was now inclined to turn over the reins to his trusted only son. Within twenty-four hours a buyer for their house had been found, and a bill of sale drawn up. However, a few nights later father and son took their customary stroll about their property, and as Johnson tells it, "the house and its trees and grounds never looked so beautiful" to both of them. Reluctantly, largely in deference to his father, Johnson persuaded the buyer of the house, a close friend, to destroy the bill of sale, and it was agreed that Johnson should go off to New York alone to improve the family fortune—with no strings attached to the date of his return—the only proviso being that he should spend at least part of each summer at home in Utica.

Bryan's faith in his twenty-five year old son knew no limits, and the young man went off to New York with $16,241.37 of his father's cash to be invested as he saw fit. Stopping over in Albany, he reduced this sum by about $7,500, buying a hundred shares of stock in The Albany Mechanics and Farmers bank which proved to be "very lucrative and safe." Johnson took with him a young slave named Frank given to him by his father. Frank, wrote Johnson, "had always been treated as kindly as if he were a white," and was taken along, he confessed, "partly for convenience and partly for the éclat of being waited on by my own servant."

On arriving in New York he put up at 9 State Street, "a very beautiful location, and in an elegant house belonging to Cary Ludlow, Esq., but kept as a boardinghouse by his tenant, a Mrs. King." The price was "at the time the highest in New York"—$12.00 a week for bed and board, and half price for Frank.

Johnson's hosts and fellow boarders, he was pleased to note, were socially well connected. Ludlow, who with his wife and a granddaughter occupied all the second story of the house while the rest was taken by Mrs. King and her boarders, was a retired banker of some eminence, and his wife was "a fine looking, lady-like woman." Johnson, however, was especially attracted to the granddaughter Matilda, who was secretly said to have been an illegitimate child of one of Ludlow's deceased sons. She was "even said to have been the daughter of a West Indian Creole, and she was born in the West Indies." Johnson "thought her beautiful with her fair skin and dark auburn hair," but, he added, "I never had any reason to believe she was as much pleased with me as I was with her." In addition to the charming Matilda, there was also a Miss Heyward, the step-daughter of another boarder, Henry Cruger, "a beautiful girl of some sixteen years" who, it was said, would eventually inherit "a large property." Johnson was fascinated by the Ludlows and the Crugers, but lamented his inability to break into their charmed circle. They were, he wrote,

very aristocratic people, and acquainted with the best society of New York, and I perhaps unreasonably thought they might have introduced me to some of their acquaintances, but they never did, and my natural shyness was so inveterate that I made acquaintances with difficulty of such people as I desired for associates, resolutely refraining from consorting with people whom I deemed undesirable acquaintances. My conduct in this particular was formed in England, where such notions were common. One of our boarders, a young man who traded in the city, noticed this trait in me, and he one day remarked to me, rather reproachfully, that I refused to visit some places where he knew I had been invited, and would have been made welcome, and that I wanted to visit where I could not get invited. I refused to admit the latter part of his remark, but I felt it to be true.

New York had much to charm a young man from a country village. His room, he recalled, was in the third story, having a window fronting on the Battery. The Battery was then the pride of New York, and the most fashionable resort for promenaders of both sexes, with fine shade trees. . . . The ground was traversed with good gravel walks, and at one end of the plot was a flagstaff and signal station . . . and thither merchants would go and employ spy glasses to descry the signals of approaching merchant vessels.

Whenever he had a communication for Utica, Johnson would await the departure of one of Robert Fulton's steamboats and wander down to the docks, where he almost always found a passenger willing to transport a letter to the well-known Bryan Johnson of Utica. He also became formally acquainted with Robert Fulton.

On these occasions I almost uniformly saw Fulton standing on the dock till the departure of the boats. . . . I remember his saying to me that he had just had a Franklin stove put in his bedroom and that by placing it in advance of the fireplace, he made a great saving of heat that would otherwise have ascended the chimney. His manners were affable, and he greatly pleased me. I was never at his house, but I often saw him walking Broadway with his wife on his arm. She was a tall woman like most of the Livingstons in her family.

Among the many wonders of New York in 1812 was an alleged perpetual motion machine which had been put on exhibit by an enterprising Philadelphian. It had been widely publicized, and Johnson, who had resisted the attraction for a long time, finally decided to visit it. On approaching the hall he was passed on the street by "several gentlemen who seemed very excited," and among them was Robert Fulton. The cause of the excitement, Johnson discovered, lay in the fact that practical-minded Mr. Fulton, after a brief investigation, had discovered that the alleged perpetual motion machine was actually being operated by a man on the floor above turning a crank which, through the means of a carefully concealed cord caused the wheel below to turn. Johnson felt that if only he had possessed Fulton's assurance, he could easily have discovered the fraud himself.

Matrimony was obviously much on Johnson's mind at this juncture, as his father had hoped it would be, but he proceeded cautiously. "The only expenditure I indulged beyond good clothing and respectable boarding and lodging was an occasional visit to the theater, and I went thither frequently from my want of other opportunities of seeing the ladies of the city." His other objective was to put his money in places where it would do the most good. After numerous consultations with New York brokers, he had soon accumulated shares of stock in the Mechanics Bank, the Merchants' Bank, and the Union Bank. On the advice of one of his friends he also purchased a few notes issued by merchants, including several of John Jacob Astor's, but these somehow made him nervous—"caution being one of my strongest characteristics"— and he sold them off quickly "making only about $9.00 by the transaction." The stock purchases depleted his cash supply, but letters back to his father in Utica quickly brought the expected response, and Johnson settled back to watch his fortune grow.

Another fellow boarder was General Bloomfield, Commander of the Port of New York and the former governor of New Jersey, who had sheltered Aaron Burr before the latter's flight to England after the fatal duel with Alexander Hamilton. Johnson found Bloomfield "very affable . . . but with some defect of teeth which made him sputter while eating and caused the position near him at meals to be not desirable." Far more unsettling to Johnson, however, was an announcement Bloomfield made during the breakfast hour one morning in June 1812.

War with England had long been the topic of the newspapers and of general conversation, and men were divided on the question according to their political proclivities, especially during the early part of 1812 when a presidential election was to occur in the fall. Mr. Madison was the president in office, and De Witt Clinton, then Mayor of New York and political autocrat of the State, was the prominent opponent of Madison. Both were nominally of the same party, but like all partisan struggles, the measures of Madison were deemed all wrong by the Clintonians, while all he omitted to do were the measures deemed necessary for the public welfare. The great practical question of the time was the conduct of France and England, who were then at war with each other, and between them American interests were made a shuttlecock which both knocked from one to the other. To fight both belligerents would have been what both merited, but the government inclined to fight only England, as she, by searching our merchant vessels and impressing thereon on the high seas all persons deemed subjects of Great Britain, presented a more popular object for war than any mercantile aggressions of France.

The results of war were widely discussed, and a general impression prevailed that on the declaration of war a British fleet would bombard New York and lay it in ruins. I inclined to this belief, and as I had invested in New York banks near $17,000 not believing war would be ventured on by the government, I resolved that should war occur I would accept the first loss and immediately sell my bank stock.

Thus stood circumstances, when one morning while we were partaking of breakfast a servant informed General Bloomfield that a person at the street door desired to see him on government business. The general immediately left his seat and went out of the room. He was absent but a few moments when he returned with a letter in his hand from the Secretary of War, and he said to us, "Gentlemen, I have to announce to you that war exists between the United States and Great Britain." The excitement was great at this announcement, and it seemed as wholly unexpected to all of us as if war had never been talked of.

Word of the declaration of war spread rapidly throughout the city. At 11:00 A.M. Mayor Clinton, accompanied by members of the Common Council, "called on General Bloomfield to concert measures for the protection of the City, and to place on the General the responsibility of providing for the common defense."

When the news came, Johnson's first concern was with his investments, and ignoring a friends advise to go to Boston and "take some time for deliberation," he rushed off to Wall Street, sold off his stocks at a loss, and deposited the cash in a bank, planning to draw it out at the first sign of a British bombardment or invasion. He handed the teller six one-thousand-dollar bills, but after leaving the bank found that the equally panicky young clerk had mistaken them for one-hundred-dollar bills. Rushing back to the bank, he found it closed, but managed, after some frantic door pounding, to get in and have the mistake rectified. When he returned to his boarding house in a mood of exultation, he jokingly handed his landlady two thousand-dollar notes, and watched with horror as she threw them into the fireplace. Johnson retrieved them undamaged, but was haunted for the rest of his life with the notion that his rather elderly and unattractive landlady thought he was "tempting her virtue with so costly a bribe."

Meanwhile, despite all predictions to the contrary, no British fleet appeared in New York harbor. The fortifications thrown up at the Battery and on the other approaches to the city seemed to make it secure. To Johnson's chagrin, the price of stocks, instead of plunging, gradually began to rise. "I had the mortification," he said, "to find that had I delayed my sale I might not have encountered any loss." He also grew more and more anxious about his money remaining idle while his expenses "were proceeding onwards at the rate of about $1,260 the year."

Still, Johnson was enjoying life in New York, and he regretted the promise he had made to spend the summer with his family (Johnson wrote "to spend the *summers* with them," and may have expected at the time to settle permanently in New York). The summer of 1812 grew very warm, however, and he decided to return to Utica—"though the change was excessively repugnant to my inclinations, and I felt like a prisoner returning to his prison." His father was waiting for him at the foot of Genesee Street when his stage arrived and greeted him enthusiastically—while Johnson "endeavored to appear as cheerful as I could."

Johnson's depression over his failure to make his money grow in New York was short-lived, for shortly after his homecoming he learned the legislature had authorized a new bank in Utica, and that its directorate would include many respected old friends including Major Kip, and his neighbor, Francis Bloodgood. They promptly invited the Johnsons to purchase stock, and father and son subscribed $25,000 ($10,000 to be paid down), convinced, Johnson explained, that investment in an inland bank was far safer than any New York enterprise—"it being exempt from the danger of invasion which I feared in New York."

Having thus put his idle money to work, Johnson devoted the rest of his summer to reading, and the pursuit of eligible females.

As I was their only offspring my parents began to prevail on me to become married. I had no desire that way nor any great disinclination, but my habits were retiring and my diffidence painful, and I had no evidence of being agreeable to the few young ladies that were acquainted with me, though I found that their mothers were not disinclined to me. Indeed, in my intercourse with the mothers my diffidence was less, and I therefore appeared to better advantage than with the daughters. Utica contained a few young ladies and I rather forced myself to visit them. I called a few times on Mr. Arthur Breese, whose eldest daughter . . . was a beautiful girl some seventeen or eighteen years old. Mr. Breese had expressed to my father a wish that I should visit his family but our intercourse was very cold and formal and in no way calculated to please a young girl who was governed by her feeling and not by her intellect. The last visit I made to the family, a proposition was started that I should accompany the young lady in a walk, or to perform some errand. When we got into the street the evening was rather dark, and I proposed that she should take my arm, but she refused, and swinging her arm said she could walk better in that way. This silenced me, and as soon as we returned to the house, I took my leave and never repeated the visit.

Miss Malcolm, a sister of William Malcolm who had been private secretary to John Adams during his presidency of the United States, and who subsequently married a daughter of General Schuyler of revolutionary fame, was also in Utica visiting her brother William who then lived there. She was an exceedingly blooming young woman, of large luxurious form, but young, gay, and witty. She was as forward as I was retiring, and no two persons could be less calculated for each other than we were, and for me to think of any courtship in that direction would have been preposterous, and I never attempted it, though I fully appreciated her beauty and she seemed as fully to appreciate my awkwardness and inexperience. Two other young ladies I occasionally visited. They lived with Jeremiah Van Rensselaer whose family was long the most fashionable in Utica. Both were nieces of Mrs. Van Rensselaer. The elder was Miss Cullen, a relation of William Cullen Bryant of New York, the poet, and the younger was Miss Lawrence. Some two years only constituted the difference in their ages, and both were young and handsome. Miss Cullen was supposed to be admired by Mr. Van Rensselaer's brother, James, whom she subsequently married, and her manners were so sarcastic and cold that I never fancied her. Remarking to her one day, from lack of other conversation, that I had already some grey hairs in my head, she said, illnaturedly I thought, "If you suppose that will recommend you to young ladies you are greatly mistaken." This shocked my sensitiveness and I could not forget it. Miss Lawrence was more amiable, but she seemed preoccupied by a young doctor of Utica . . . and I have always noticed that ladies favor physicians. I was once dancing with this young lady while she was eating a cake. She bit off a piece and handed it to me, saying she supposed I would deem it the sweeter from its having been bitten by a young lady.

As the summer ended with no advancement in his career as a suitor in sight, Johnson "gladly prepared to return to New York." This time, however, he was better armed, for his friend Major Kip, aware of the young man's lack of success in Utica, had given him a letter to a Miss Rainteau, a cousin of his wife, assuring him that the girl was one he "could not fail to admire." Kip warned Johnson, however, to shave off some of his whiskers before descending on her—"the whiskers being of extra size for the period in question." Johnson would have nothing to do with such advice, noting, "I soon began to admire my whiskers in proportion to their singularity, and I parted with none of mine." Arriving in New York he dutifully presented himself to Miss Rainteau and her mother with his whiskers intact, and found that the former's appearance "fully equalled Kip's representation." Mother and daughter seemed "prepossessed" in his favor, probably, he surmised, as a result of a direct communication from Kip, but Miss Rainteau struck him as a bit young. "At that period of my life," he philosophized later, "youth, like common honesty, possessed no special attraction, and my intercourse with the young lady never advanced beyond ceremonious calls."

Johnson returned to his former lodgings on State Street, "it having quite a home aspect," and found some newcomers at Mrs. King's table. He was, as usual, intrigued by the free and easy ways of New Yorkers:

> I found at my boarding house Commodore Lewis, to whom the President had assigned the command of all the gunboats lying in New York. He was middle-aged and had a reputation for great courage, and his deportment and conversation conformed to this reputation, and possibly were the origin of it. He left our house one morning and took his fleet up the East River, and he returned the next day having captured a small English armed vessel, whose commanding officer he brought to our house as a prisoner of war. The captive was a young man, and very polite to all our lady boarders, and I was astonished at the familiarity he soon established towards those of them with whom I was always under some restraint. He found out their Christian names, and they found his, and their intercourse was soon conducted under those appellations, as though they were brother and sisters, while I, instead of profiting by this experience, only felt disgusted at the mutual freedom.

Johnson became somewhat more involved with another picaresque figure at his table, a former British army surgeon who had fought with Wellington in Spain and Portugal and was later exiled for some unexplained misconduct. The Englishman got off to a bad start with Johnson when he showed him an invitation to dinner he had received from another exile, a former British peer living in New York. The surgeon was asked to bring "Smoke Jack" with him, and Johnson, realizing that "Smoke Jack" was none other than Robert Fulton, was incensed. "I thought," he wrote, "that the nickname evinced the habitual contempt of titled people toward the untitled." However, the surgeon possessed "great conversational powers," and Johnson became the target for some of his more intimate revelations. As a matter of fact, at one point he persuaded Johnson to assist him in his pursuit of a "widow of wealth" by having him compose a "very pathetic poetical effusion" which he passed off as his own production. "What became of the whole matter," Johnson added, "I never heard."

Idleness did not seem to weigh heavily on Johnson during the early months of his second year in New York, and he spent his time "principally reading" at a bookstore on nearby Broadway which had a well-stocked reading room. For his young slave, Frank, however, his master's inactivity produced unfortunate results. Johnson had attired him in "drab livery, scarlet cuffs, a scarlet collar and a gold band around his hat," but with all his finery, Frank had little to do but polish his master's boots in the morning, wait on him during meals, and lay a bedroom fire in the evening. Far more susceptible to the temptations of the city than Johnson, Frank fell into bad company and bad habits almost at once.

On first hearing of one of Frank's escapades, Johnson struck the boy with a "small rattan cane" which he habitually carried. It was a light blow, but in retelling the story for posterity, he drew the inevitable moral. "His being a slave," he wrote, "probably induced me to strike him, though it ought to have restrained me by reason of his helplessness." Frank's carousing led to a severe cold which gradually grew worse, and Johnson had him placed in a Broadway hospital. On one of his frequent visits, Frank told him the doctor had assured him he would die since he had "been very wicked." Johnson sought to remonstrate with the Doctor but he had disappeared, and the next morning Johnson found Frank's body in the "dead house" lying in an open coffin with some shavings under his head. Johnson never ceased reproaching himself for bringing the boy to New York, and Frank was the last slave Johnson ever owned.

In describing his efforts to make up for his deficiencies in formal education, Johnson gives the impression that he regarded his heavy reading program largely as an attempt to acquire that background in belles lettres possessed by the assured young men he had met at Union College and in New York. His bookstore reading included Spenser's *Faerie Queen* and Ariosto's *Orlando Furioso*. Back at 6 State Street, however, he encountered an elderly Scot named Bell who, noting the young man's interest in bank stocks, lent him Adam Smith's *Wealth of Nations* and Lord Lauderdale's *Treatise Concerning the Nature of Value and Capital*. Suddenly Johnson found himself lifted out of the fanciful past into a world that was relevant to the teeming present of an America struggling with its uncertain economic future. He told what happened after he read these two books:

> This reading much enlarged my knowledge, and as the war made financial topics very prominent general speculations, and as a suspension of specie payments by the banks became apprehended, I commenced elaborating my views on these subjects, and the result grew into a thin octavo volume which G. & C. Carvill published for me early in 1813 under the title of *An Inquiry into the Nature of Value and Capital: And into the Operations of Government Loans, Banking Institutions and Private Credit,* with an appendix containing "An Inquiry into the Causes which Regulate the Rate of Interest and the Price of Stock."

Johnson's *Inquiry,* while its title was borrowed from Lauderdale, was in many respects a highly original and even daring work, though, as in the case of most of his later publications, the author alone seems to have had any notion of its true worth. In fact, not until the mid-twentieth century would economic historians echo Johnson's own certainty that he had indeed turned in a remarkable performance. "The book," wrote Johnson,

> attracted some attention and received a few notices from the press, some of whom supposed it had been instigated by the Government. But the success was not as much as I expected or as the book deserved. No one knew I was writing it, and its appearance seemed to surprise the few people who knew me only as an idler. I sent a few copies to my friends in the country, but I made no other efforts to bring the book into notice, and perhaps this cause operated in the little notice it obtained. Enough copies were sold to pay the publisher for his undertaking, and this was something in its favor at the time of its publication. . . . The most notable thing about the book was, I think, its production by a young man of less than twenty-seven, living in New York without business employment, and possessed of an ample fortune to pass his time as his pleasure should dictate, and with no compelling motive to write, but to be useful in a new and abstruse investigation.

Johnson's *Inquiry* was a brash book for a nineteenth-century American to write—especially a young man so concerned with "safe" investments and so cautious with his own money. But as Johnson contemplated the borrowing spree which accompanied the War of 1812 and which so alarmed conservative banking circles, he remained unruffled by it.

> Government borrows from individuals five millions of dollars. They do not require this sum for the purpose of accumulating, but for the purpose of expending. The borrowed money is therefore returned to the people, who not only have it returned to them, but they also retain the government securities which they were given to represent it. The national capital is therefore increased to the amount of the government securities, which increased capital the nation may continue to use as borrowed capital, by paying the stipulated interest for it.

Not even the country's vast Revolutionary War debt perturbed this early "New Dealer." "The new capital," he wrote, "was employed in multiplying the object of man's desire; in stimulating industry, and in rendering its efforts more productive—so that the profit far exceeded the interest charge." The alternative method of increasing taxation would have been destructive, he added, "for any taxes beyond those required for minimum government functions . . . would tend to reduce activity." Finally, in addition to these "Keynesian" foreshadowings, anyone skimming over the terse propositions which begin each section of the *Inquiry* will be struck, perhaps, by vague intimations of certain theories also propounded years later by Thorstein Veblen. "An object of capital must be an object of desire." . . . "The business of life is to procure objects of desire." . . . "Man's gratification will be restricted only by his means." . . . "His desires will increase with his means." . . . "A man seldom gets rich by individual labor." . . . "Our desires cause the production of capital." . . .

Alexander Bryan Johnson, in short, had thoroughly adopted the hearty optimism which would dominate much of the economic thinking in his country for many years to come.

As Johnson's own capital increased, most of it back in Utica safe from British incursions, so did his "objects of desire." New York had whetted those desires, and stored away in his trunk was some unused capital which it was now time to put to work. Utica might be a provincial outpost on the Mohawk, but men like Colonel Walker and Nathan Williams were well connected throughout the land, and commanded the attention of the mighty—even along the Potomac. Impressed by Bryan Johnson's son, they had sent him off from Utica armed with letters of introduction, including two rather special ones addressed to James Madison, President of the United States, and Albert Gallatin, the formidable Swiss-born Secretary of the United States Treasury.

Late in the fall of 1812, having sent his book to the printer, Johnson left New York on the "slow and tedious" road to Washington. A few years earlier, Gouverneur Morris had written of that city, "We need nothing here but houses, men, women, and other little trifles to make our city perfect." Johnson echoed this when he wrote, "I was prepared to find Washington a large space with scattered habitations, and it answered that description." New York friends had recommended a boardinghouse to him—"the best in the city"—and Johnson found it suitably adorned with "several senators and representatives, with much other respectable company."

He lost no time in presenting his letters. En route to the office of Albert Gallatin, on the day after his arrival, Johnson dropped off at the House of Representatives to watch the new House Speaker, Henry Clay—"rather a young man of upright and slender form"—get the session underway. He also stayed to hear Josiah Quincy of Massachusetts—"particularly designated to me as an able debater"—present a bill to equalize the pay of executive secretaries. From the House he went on to Gallatin, running over in his mind what he might say to him. Gallatin made things easy at first, inquiring "in an evidently foreign accent" into the health of Nathan Williams; but when it became Johnson's turn to initiate a conversation, Gallatin did little to smooth the young man's passage.

> As I wanted to say something to remove the awkwardness of a first interview, I said I had just come from the House of Representatives and had heard a very interesting debate. He desired to know the subject, and I told him it was to equalize the salaries of the several secretaries. I expected he would sympathize with my motive in alluding to this topic, but instead of that, he coolly replied that he could not conceive where the interest could lie in such a debate, the measure being of no other consequence than to end an invidious distinction of a trifling sum in the pay of the several secretaries, and of no consequence to anyone.

Gallatin was telling Johnson in no uncertain terms that the salary of the Secretary of the Treasury was not a proper subject of discussion. Johnson realized his *gaffe* too late. "To this embarrassing rebuke I replied as well as I could that the importance grew out of the position of the persons treated of by the bill. After a few moments I withdrew."

Johnson's next letter of introduction produced far more satisfactory results.

> From Mr. Gallatin's office I went to the White House to deliver my letter to President Madison. A black servant in livery opened the street door, and on my desire to see the President, he ushered me immediately into a small room furnished with a writing table and a few chairs, and departing, said the President would appear shortly.
>
> I seated myself and waited but a few moments, and in walked the President. He was small in stature, though I thought his head was large. He was dressed in black and his hair was slightly powdered. I arose on his entrance, and he asked me if I had ever been in Washington before, and where I boarded. His manners were very easy, and his age seemed near sixty. Soon the door through which I entered was again opened and in walked a very plain farmer-looking man. He said he was passing through Washington and thought he would call and pay his respects to the President. Mr. Madison arose, shook hands with him, saying he was happy to see him and desired him to be seated. This

new visitor gave me an opportunity to depart, and I left the house as I had entered it, and I was interested with the simplicity of my visit.

Several days after this agreeable visit with the President, Johnson received a message from the White House inviting him to dinner "at a given day and time."

I duly went to the dinner where I found several other guests. After a short time in an anteroom, dinner was announced, and on entering the dining room Mrs. Madison took the head of the table, and Mr. Madison sat at about the center of one of the sides, and his private secretary sat at the foot and carved. I am not sure whether the guests took seats assigned to them, or took seats promiscuously. I knew none of the guests, but the President recognized me by name. We were waited on by black servants in livery, and the little conversation that occurred was principally topics connected with late news of the war. Some of the guests during the dinner drank wine with Mrs. Madison as was then the custom and thought polite, and she tasted her glass in response. Mrs. Madison was a full contrast to her husband in size, being as much larger than ordinary women as he was smaller than ordinary men. She was probably at least fifteen years younger than her husband, and performed with ease and grace her duties at the head of the table. I think people said she was the daughter of a person at whose boarding house Mr. Madison had once lived at Philadelphia. I could easily obtain positive information on most of the topics of which I am in doubt, but I write merely my own recollections, and the labor of certainty is not my object. After the dessert Mrs. Madison left the room and she was the only lady at the table. The gentlemen rose when she withdrew, but again seated themselves, and after a short time all withdrew and I returned to my lodgings.

For some reason, Johnson seems to have been resistant to the charms of the famous Dolley Madison. He would have been pleased to know that Dolley Payne Todd, widow of John Todd, was indeed the daughter of Mrs. John Payne, keeper of the boardinghouse in which both Madison and his Princeton classmate Aaron Burr once lived for a brief stay, and that it was the notorious Burr who had introduced Madison to her.

Social life in the Madison White House was decidedly informal, featuring a "drawing room" every Wednesday night to which "acquaintances of the President and his wife went without special invitation," and Johnson attended one of these.

I slightly powdered my hair, as I found it was practiced by several persons, though I thought it unbecoming to me. The reception room was crowded with visitors. The proper etiquette for visitors was a small *chapeau de bras* which was carried under the arm, but those who had none, and I was one of that number, carried their round hat under the arm also, the arm encircling the crown. I had made several acquaintances among the ladies and others at Washington, and I had become somewhat celebrated by composing for them poetical charades. They were handed around probably from want of better excitement, and Mr. John Randolph who was at the time a representative in Congress and in the height of his fame had, I was told, praised one of my charades that was shown to him. I saw at this levee Miss Mayo, who subsequently became the wife of Commodore Decatur, and afterwards of General Scott. I was introduced to her and, as I conceived a charade that I wanted to make on her, I asked one of the waiters for pen, ink, and paper, which he brought me, and when he brought it I wrote the charade and handed it to her and she received it goodnaturedly.

Soon after I had been in the reception room, a young man of my boarding house, asked me to introduce him to Mrs. Madison, and I accordingly took him to a lady whom I supposed was Mrs. Madison, but she was a Mrs. Latrobe. . . . She saw my embarrassment and kindly remarked that the same mistake had often occurred. She was much like Mrs. Madison in figure and she seemed to imitate her dress which was rather conspicuous by wearing a turban surmounted with a plume of high ostrich feathers. . . . Among the company present were a few Quakers, and they kept their hats on, which gave no offence as it is supposed to be the custom of Quakers and perhaps their religion. During the evening ice creams of different kinds were handed round by servants several times, but no music attended and the company departed at about eleven o'clock. Mr. Madison stood in the center of the room when the company was assembling, and to shake hands with him on entering seemed part of the etiquette. Mrs. Madison was seated with the ladies, and most persons on entering the room went and bowed to her.

The Madison "drawing room" was entertaining enough, but Johnson found "a more select company" at a party given by the French ambassador, M. Sérurier. "We had an excellent supper," he reported, "but at which no person sat, but each helped himself as he chose. The spoons and forks were gold, and the china was rich and beautiful, while the eatables were of the choicest kind, but all were cold." It was here that Johnson had his first encounter with the glamorous Madame Bonaparte, the former wife of Jerome Bonaparte, whose brother, Napoleon, had so brusquely terminated that much talked-of marriage. Elizabeth Paterson Bonaparte, the daughter of a rich Baltimore merchant, had preceded Johnson into the world by seven years, and would outlast him by ten. She was, commented Johnson, "rather luxuriantly embonpoint." Obviously fascinated, he seems to have managed to appear in her presence on several occasions during his stay in Washington. At the embassy party, he noted, "she received much attention from the Ambassador and his attachés." Had Johnson felt equal to the challenge of pursuing her, he would have found that her regard for "pecuniary advancement" and suitable social connections surpassed his. While in London during a husband-hunting tour in 1814, she wrote her father urging him to be more careful in his criticism of her to her friends in Baltimore.

> Everyone who knows me has heard that your wealth is enormous. In Europe a handsome woman who is likely to have a fortune may marry well, but if it gets around that her parents are dissatisfied with her, they will think she will get nothing from them, and, if she had the beauty of Venus and the talents of Minerva, no one will marry her. . . . The reputation of your fortune would be a great advantage to me abroad, and I am sure you cannot object to my having the honor of it, provided you keep the substance.*

Johnson returned from the embassy affair well pleased with his success at charades, and his meeting with Madame Bonaparte, but as so often happened, he had his moment of embarrassment. A fellow boarder expressed the pious hope that he had paid his respects on leaving the party to Madame Sérurier, and Johnson went to bed aghast at his omission—only to find the next morning that there was no Madame Sérurier.

Well-established by now as a young man about Washington, Johnson, with his hair powdered, went off to another party, this one given by André Dashkoff, the Russian chargé d'affaires. The Russians and the French were vying with each other to impress the citizens of the young Republic, and in comparing their achievements, Johnson concluded that "everything was served up in at least equal splendor" by the Russians. He also noted that Dashkoff had an attractive wife—"very fair, with light hair, and still a young woman of easy and familiar manners." Dashkoff would be less impressive later, however, in his attempt to persuade Secretary of State James Monroe of the advantages of St. Petersburg over Ghent as the site for the peace conference that ended the War of 1812.

* Eugene Didier, *Life and Letters of Madame Bonaparte* (New York, 1879).

The high point of the fall season was a great naval ball to celebrate an American victory at sea over a British frigate, and Johnson attended, sharing in the jubilation as the British ship's flag was ceremoniously laid at the feet of Dolley Madison. "She looked very regal," he thought, but the impression was dulled somewhat when she strolled around the room on the arm of a newspaper editor, Mr. Gales, "an Irishman, not very gentlemanly-looking." For all their gay exuberance, however, Washingtonians were watching with anxiety the progress of Napoleon's advance into Russia, concerned no doubt over the painful inadequacies of Madame Bonaparte's ex-husband, Jerome, whose inertia was helping the Russians make good their retreat. "Of Napoleon's ultimate success, however," wrote Johnson, "no person hazarded a doubt, and on his success depended must of the success of the United States." America's surprising victories at sea were another subject of conversation at the parties Johnson attended.

"At the beginning of the War with England," he wrote, "nearly everybody supposed that our little navy would be swept from the ocean by England, but that on land we should constantly be victorious. The reverse of these expectations became realized, and we were more successful at sea than on the land." Two years later, Washingtonians would be made painfully aware of this as they watched their city burn; but in the winter of 1812–1813, just before Madison's second inauguration, Washington, said Johnson, was a town "where people sought amusement like the visitors at a watering place." According to Johnson, his own boarding house was a "focus of gaiety" during that anxious period, with a clever Scotsman, later suspected of being a British spy, setting the social pace. One of his many accomplishments was to lie on his back on the floor and spring to his feet without using his hands, a trick which won him some tidy bets. He also collected on another wager by tying himself into a burlap sack, and racing a fellow boarder who carried on his back a portly Congressman from Johnson's home district. Johnson considered the exploit highly undignified and was pleased when Madam Bonaparte's small son got in the way of the contestants and temporarily halted the demonstration which was eventually won by the doughty Scot.

On March 4, 1813, Madison took the oath of office in the House of Representatives. Johnson arrived early to secure a seat in the gallery where he "could see and hear the great pageant of the day."

At about twelve o'clock a discharge of artillery announced that the President-elect had left the White House and was approaching the Capitol. He came in a carriage, when cannon again announced his arrival. The chamber of the House was not filled to any great extent, and in that I was disappointed, but on the entrance of the President many persons attended him. He took his position behind the Speaker's table and seated himself in the Speaker's armchair, while overhead where he sat was a canopy and the national emblem of a carved spread eagle. Around the President were some of the Judges of the Supreme Court and some of the executive secretaries. I noticed also Attorney General Pinkney who seemed uncommonly well-dressed and in the early meridian of life. The President soon from his seat arose and Mr. Pinkney presented to him the Bible, while the Chief Justice pronounced the oath and the President kissed the book. The inauguration was hereby ended, but the President drew from his pocket and read, rather rapidly and not very loud, his inaugural address. He read with much emphasis, but though I was near the words were not distinct to me. He handed the manuscript to some one after he had read it, and several who were on the platform near the President shook hands with him. They all then retired, following the President to his carriage and accompanying him in other carriages to the White House where a levee was held for all who chose to come and pay their respects to the executive. The cannon announced the President's utterance of the oath, and the firing continued till he arrived at home.

Johnson, too, joined the throng at the President's "levee," and after shaking hands with Madison, paused for a chat with his wife. "I said to Mrs. Madison that I had missed her presence at the inauguration, and she replied rather solemnly that her feelings would not permit her to be present on such occasions, and I made as appropriate a reply to her indicated emotions as I could conceive at the moment, for such a reason for her absence had not occurred to me."

The next day Johnson, with most of his fellow boarders, took off for separate destinations, Johnson intent on a brief stopover in Baltimore on his way back to New York. He reflected that his Washington visit had been a profitable one, and that he had made some valuable acquaintances. "They were, of course, with people of both sexes."

In Baltimore Johnson put up at Barnum's ("then a celebrated hotel") with two of his Washington friends. The two young men were well known in Baltimore society, and Johnson was ill at ease—feeling "too much like a stranger in a strange place, and without the confidence and boldness that I should with all propriety have felt. . . ." Johnson imitated their manners as well as he could. "Among the extravagances I imitated," he wrote, "I had a barber come and shave me while I was lying in bed in the morning before I got up—a practice I had never before heard of." Among those who had come to Baltimore was the tricky Scotsman from the Washington boardinghouse who was being banished to Frederick, and Johnson was promptly importuned by him for a cash loan. Johnson, however, "had witnessed too many of his tricks," and kept his money.

After passing a few pleasant days in Baltimore, Johnson returned to his New York boardinghouse. "The locality was particularly interesting to me as the residence of the granddaughter of Cary Ludlow [Matilda] of whom I have already spoken. I liked her very much," Johnson confessed, "though I never intended to marry her, nor gave her any reason to view me in the character of a suitor—for against that character my intellect, for a particular reason, restrained me and controlled my feelings." In spite of this alleged indifference, he was shocked one morning to hear at breakfast that the young lady had eloped in the night with a Lieutenant Shubrick of the U.S. Navy. "My fellow lodgers judged properly my feelings toward her, and they probably expected that I should evince disappointment, but this I strove to avoid, and I endeavored to believe that I ought to rejoice at her marriage rather than regret that she was no longer reserved for my amusement."

With Matilda no longer "reserved," Johnson changed his residence to 5 Broadway, a large house facing Bowling Green which had been used by General Washington as a headquarters during the Revolution. Here he found an old friend, Eliza, a natural daughter of Colonel Walker and now the divorced wife of the Marquis de Villehaut, who, after the fall of the French monarchy, had fled to America and opened a shop near Utica, purchasing many of his goods at wholesale from Bryan Johnson. Madame de Villehaut was "quite a Frenchwoman in her manners and language," and Johnson found her fascinating despite the numerous visits she received from General Moreau, another French exile living in New York. The two annoyed Johnson by conducting their conversations in French, and Johnson was much relieved when the dashing soldier finally went off with his wife to join the Russians and the Austrians in their war against France. Moreau's New York house, with all its furnishings, was put up for auction, and Johnson attended the sale where he saw "for the first time some Astral lamps." He also marveled at the furnishings of the bedchamber.

The bedstead was peculiarly elegant, the footposts being carved female figures which were gilt. According to the usual arrangement of French bed chambers, a small cot bedstead was in the room and which was supposed to be the General's, and it was placed on a line with the large bedstead, so that the occupants of the two beds lay with their heads so as to constitute a literal meaning of the French *tête à tête,* as I supposed.

Johnson revealed very little about his relationship with Madame de Villehaut, but there may have been something more than casual friendship in the offer she made him one day at their Broadway boardinghouse.

Madame de Villehaut designed to return to Paris the next Spring, and she much urged me to accompany her, saying that she could be of essential service by introducing me into French society, of which her acquaintance was extensive and of the best description. I was strongly inclined to accept her offer and I wrote to my father, and he urged me by all means to go, but I knew it would be a great privation to him and my mother, and a source of anxiety to them, and I decided not to go.

Although Johnson thus decided to forego the romantic possibilities of a season in Paris with this intriguing exotic from Utica, he remained in touch with her after her return to Europe, acting as "agent for her funds in America." Afterwards, as the wife, and later the bereaved widow, of another Frenchman, Colonel Michel Combe, she appeared again in the autobiography.

Having refused the tempting offer of Madame de Villehaut, and by now seriously disturbed over his lack of progress in affairs of the heart, Johnson set out in earnest to make up for lost time in New York. He had made "several pleasant acquaintances among the young ladies of the city" whom he visited

more with a view to matrimony than from any lighter motive. In this particular I wished to gratify my parents, and I sympathized in their general desire that the family should not become extinct by my death. I felt also a degree of painful isolation in possessing no relative in America but my father and mother, and my habits were not social enough to supply the absence of kindred. I could no doubt have easily married, but I felt the want of family influence more than the want of a mere wife, and I was fastidious in the connection I sought. I visited frequently the family of Charles Clinton, the brother of De Witt Clinton and the nephew of Vice President Clinton. Charles lived in New York, and held the office of Clerk of the Southern District of the State. He was pecuniarily poor and his habits of temperance were not good. In all my visits to the house I never saw him, but only his wife and two marriageable daughters. The house was much frequented by young men, and those of rather a fast character. I fancied the young ladies thought that their own social position could elevate sufficiently all they admitted to their society. They passed a portion of the year at Newburgh, the original residence of the family, and I twice left New York to visit them for a short period at that village. Their house was on the bank of the Hudson just opposite Fishkill Landing, and as I was standing with them on a species of projection from the rear of the house, we saw on the Fishkill side a splendid curricle or phaeton driven by a gentleman. They told me it was Mr. John Peter de Windt, and that he was soon to be married to a granddaughter of President Adams. This was the first time I had ever heard of the two parties alluded to, and with whom I was soon thereafter to become connected. I remember looking at the equipage and the rider and thinking him highly favored. I never had the least reason for supposing that either of the Clinton young ladies suspected I had any object in my visits to them, or that either cared for me in the slightest manner, though the younger once or twice accompanied me to the Park Theatre, and once accepted a ticket from me to the great Dutch ball given in New York in honor of the evacuation of Holland by the French, a ball gotten up by the natives of Holland and called the Orange Ball.

New York, during the war years, was evidently overrun by aggressive young men in pursuit of beauty and wealth, and the sobersided youth from upstate was no match for them. One of the families he visited was that of a Mrs. Deveau, mother of two "handsome and fashionable" daughters whose "beauty was of the French style—dark hair and eyes."

They lived in Beaver Street and were much admired by a crowd of young men who flocked around them, and whose attractive manners and conversations made me feel conscious of my inability to compete with them. My visits were rather formal than friendly, though I admired much the beauty of the ladies, but my admiration was like that of a connoisseur in admiring a beautiful picture—an admiration of the intellect and not of the feelings.

There were other eligibles, but Johnson was unable to impress them, laying his failures to a certain "fastidiousness of youth which made few that I saw satisfactory to both my taste and my judgment, though I knew several that would satisfy these disjointedly." He described his impasse in his usual analytical fashion:

I never sought money as an ingredient in a wife, though I certainly should not have rejected it in connection with other ingredients that I desired, and though I was, I now think, too diffident of my own position, appearance and qualifications, I felt that to some whom I knew a more ardent attention on my part would not have been disagreeable, but they failed to present all the requirements that I was solicitous to obtain.

Although "thus engaged in what might be termed wife-hunting," Johnson found time to read several "instructive books," among them *Observations on Man* by David Hartley (1705–1757), one of the founders of the "Associationist School" of psychology. He apparently began now for the first time to explore the mystery of words and their effect on human behavior—a mystery he would confront head-on years later in his major works in the field of language philosophy.

> I longed to know all the powers of the human mind, and I conceived that I could attain my object by abstracting from a dictionary all words that named such powers—as, for instance, *judgment, reason, wisdom,* etc.—with their definitions. I even made some attempts at such a selection of words, when I found that I was only attempting to compile a new dictionary, and that probably some powers existed to which no name had been attached.

Such thoughts as these, however, were probably peripheral at this stage, for he was also toying with other notions of more immediate concern to an adopted citizen of a land currently at war with his native England.

Britain's arrogance in seizing from American vessels all seamen of English birth, and his own passionate partisanship for the American cause, led Johnson to reflect on the question of expatriation—by which he meant the right of new Americans, whatever their origin, to renounce the privileges and liabilities of citizenship in the countries where they were born for those of their new country. His interest was heightened one night during a dinner in New York with a high American naval officer and his old friend, Arthur Breese, of Utica. The officer remarked with some heat that "all Englishmen were damned cowards." Johnson let the remark pass, but Breese warned the officer, "Take care, Commodore, Mr. Johnson is an Englishman!" Johnson accepted the guest's apologies lightly, but he was disturbed by what Breese had said, "as I deemed myself an American"; and on returning home went to work on an essay which he entitled *An Inquiry into the Natural Rights of Man as Regards the Exercise of Expatriation*. It was published in New York as a 20-page pamphlet "By a Gentleman of the City of New York." Johnson wrote later that he had "retained no copy of the work, and probably no copy is extant." A probably unique copy, however, was

brought to light in 1967 by one of his many descendants, Bryan Johnson Lynch, of Barneveld, New York. The title page carried a dedication
"To All the Adopted Citizens of the United States."

Johnson's theme was a timely one for many Americans of English
birth who shared his feeling of "awkwardness" in favoring the American
cause during the War of 1812. His purpose was clearly stated in his
introduction:

> The United States being engaged in a war with that foreign nation
> which is the birthplace of many of its citizens has induced the author
> to submit to the public some thoughts he has long entertained of the
> rights individuals have of leaving the country of their birth, and as-
> similating with another nation. His object is to rescue the character
> of such persons from the obloquy which he thinks an unjust prejudice
> casts on them when they espouse the cause of their adopted country,
> in opposition to that of their nativity.

Johnson developed his argument in the form of a dialogue between
a king and a former subject. The King begins with practical matters by
complaining that the exodus of artists and laborers is causing a drain on
the resources of talent in the mother country. The Subject responds with
a terse Johnsonian answer: "Raise the price of such skill and labor to
their worth in other countries." The King then tries an appeal to
patriotism, asking, "But does not every good man love his country?"
This permits Johnson to launch into an analysis of "the nature and rise
of that principle which we call 'love of country,' " and he does so with
the same remorseless objectivity which he would later apply to marriage
and religion.

"Our love for any particular place," he wrote "arises from certain
circumstances of pleasure which that place was the theater of." Thus,
"we like the particular district in which we were born better than any
district in the nation, and we generally like the particular village or place
of our birth better than any part of that district." In the beginning we
incline toward "a prejudice against foreign communities," but as we
travel and become educated, we lose these early prejudices. As a result,
"I doubt not that an inhabitant of the frozen regions of Lapland does, in
consequence, feel a greater love of country than a refined man of civilized society who has encompassed the world for his instruction and
amusement." Returning to those "circumstances of pleasure" which
cause some men to love their native heath, Johnson posed the problem
of the man whose recollections "bring to his mind scenes of unhappiness

and trouble," and who discovers a new home which, "by its climate, by its institutions, by the cheapness of the means of life, by the facility it presents for acquiring property, or by the political liberty it allows," contributes "more to his pleasures and comforts than his native country." The answer, for Johnson, was a simple one, namely to "go where you please, and where it pleases you." Finally, when the King raises the question of a man's right to take up arms against his native country, Johnson was no less forthright. "All control assumed by a government foreign to his residence is an assumption of power operating against his natural rights . . . which he may justly resist with all the means of which he is capable."

In the beginning of the summer of 1814 Johnson again returned to his family in Utica, fully intending, it appears, to go back to New York in the fall. His family greeted him warmly, and Johnson tried to appear pleased to be home. "The necessity of appearing happy," he confessed, "kept me for some time without exhibiting any symptoms of ennui which usually oppressed me at exchanging the bustle of New York for the solitude of Utica." This time, however, Utica had a surprise in store for him.

I passed much time in walking with my father who almost constantly accompanied me, and in one of our walks up Genesee Street we passed a school house somewhere near the present location of Grace Church. The school had just been dismissed and among the female scholars I observed one whose bright appearance, mature but slight form, and auburn hair greatly interested me. Her dress was very simple, but still sufficiently unique to denote not an ordinary personage. As we passed my father bowed to her and I asked him if he knew her. He said she was a granddaughter of President John Adams and a niece of his old friend Justus B. Smith of Hamilton, New York—some thirty miles from Utica. I knew Mr. Smith, and that one of his sisters had married Charles Adams, the son of President John Adams and the junior brother of John Quincy Adams, but I had no knowledge that any branch of the family resided in Utica. My father said this young lady had removed to Utica for the benefit of her education, and that she was living on the hill with her widowed mother, Mrs. Adams, who was keeping house with the mother's maiden sister, Miss Nancy Smith, a lady some thirty years old. I had often heard Justus Smith in his visits to my father talk of purchasing articles to carry home with him to Miss Adams, but I supposed he alluded to the wife of his brother, Col. William S. Smith, who I knew had married a daughter of President John Adams while he, the Colonel, was Secretary of Legation to Mr. Adams, then minister plenipotentiary at the Court of St. James.

The marriage of Justis Smith's sister to Charles Adams I had never heard of, nor of the existence of the young lady we had just met. My father judged accurately that I was pleased with the appearance of Miss Adams, and he proposed that we should walk to the house, and he would introduce me to the family. I gladly assented, and we proceeded onwards up Genesee Street till we came to the residence. It was a white-painted snug cottage house, with a garden and a small orchard attached, and including some six acres of land. We knocked at the door and were admitted into a parlor genteelly furnished, and we found in it Miss Smith to whom my father introduced me, and who received us very kindly, knowing the intimacy that existed between my father and her brother. We failed in seeing either Mrs. Adams or her daughter, and after remaining some time we took our leave and departed.

The next evening Johnson returned alone to the Adams household, where Miss Smith introduced him to Mrs. Adams and her daughter. Johnson seems to have been somewhat tongue-tied at first, but finally managed to recall some mutual acquaintances in New York, and thus "relaxed the awkwardness of a first visit."

The young lady seemed to be engaged in some needle work, not suspecting that my visit related in any way to her, and I am not sure that I addressed any conversation to her or she to me. I made several such evening visits, and as frequently as I thought could be proper, and eventually I came to address some conversation to the young lady. My conversation was always of a grave character, and as little adapted to the taste of a young lady as can be imagined, and I deemed the thought preposterous of assuming the character of a lover to one whom I thought much my superior. Besides, the aunt remarked to some remark of mine that Miss Adams had left at Quincy a very dear friend, and that she therefore felt indisposed to the gaiety of Utica. I inferred that this dear friend was necessarily of the male gender and that it betokened she was already engaged, and I hastily concluded to no longer continue an unavailing intercourse, and therefore told the ladies that I intended to return shortly to New York.

Johnson's initial overtures must have been ambiguous, to say the least, for during a later visit he somehow discovered that "Miss Smith supposed that my visits were designed for her, and at her age she necessarily regretted my proposed return to New York." Bewildered and chagrined, Johnson reported his failure to his father, exclaiming, "I might as well think of marrying the Princess Charlotte of Wales as Miss

Adams!" His father, however, assured him that he could marry Abigail if he really wished to. The problem had by now become a matter for the whole Johnson family, and the next day his mother, Leah, went to tea with Mrs. Adams and Miss Smith, and announced firmly to the former, "My son very much admires your daughter." Johnson related the denouement of this story in this fashion:

Mrs. Adams was, of course, much surprised, and also Miss Smith, as they said my conversation was always directed to them and not to the young lady. Miss Smith at once recovered from her error, and behaved in the matter with great kindness. They both told my mother that they would impress the young lady with my views, and that being acquainted with my character they would further my suit all in their power. The next time I went to the house I was most embarrassingly left alone with the young lady, but I took courage to declare my intentions, and thenceforth became a regularly accepted lover, and after an acquaintance of some ten weeks we were married by the Rev. Henry Dwight, the Presbyterian minister of Utica, of whose church my bride was a communicant. I belonged to the Episcopal Church, but in deference to the wishes of my bride I made no objection to the Presbyterian ceremony. We were married on the evening of the 23d of October 1814 at the residence of my bride, and with no company present but my father and mother and Mrs. Adams and Miss Smith. Great fees were not usual to clergymen at the time, and I gave to Mr. Dwight $25, which sum was deemed liberal, and I sent the same sum to my own minister of the Episcopal Church. The marriage on the side of bride and groom was purely intellectual. I had no reason to expect that the feelings of my bride were her impelling motive, but I took care that she should not take the step reluctantly from the persuasion of others, and I told her that if the act was not wholly voluntary on her part I would so arrange as to take the blame of its nonaccomplishment at any expense to my own feelings. She replied that she had no objections to the marriage except she thought herself too young. I saw that she fulfilled to the uttermost all that I ever desired in a wife, and that I could not fail to love her, and that, with her good sense as evinced by even the marriage to me under the circumstances of the case, and with the kind conduct I meant to pursue towards her, she could not fail from acquiring all the affection that a wife ought to feel towards a husband. Eventually no two people ever lived together with greater mutual affection and domestic happiness than we experienced. At the time of the marriage she was sixteen years, one month, and fifteen days old, and I was twenty-eight years, four months, and twenty-four days old. Her mother had, I found subsequently, consulted Col. Benjamin Walker as to my character, and he said I possessed only one fault known to him, and that was too much fondness for money, but this Mrs. Adams deemed in my favor, as she had seen in her own family the bad consequences of an opposite character. In looking back, as I often do, at this event of my life, I feel constantly abashed at the sad diffidence with which I conducted my courtship, and which satisfies me that the embarrassment is misplaced that young men usually feel on the manner in which they shall ask the question of their acceptance or rejection, for a predetermination usually exists to accept or reject, and it will not be changed by the mode in which the proffer is made.

As a footnote to Johnson's acount of his courtship and marriage, it should be noted that Abigail's aunt, Miss Nancy Smith, who assumed initially that the young man's attentions were directed toward her, will turn up with unremitting frequency in the Johnson memoirs—first as Nancy or Ann Smith, and later as Ann Masters, the third wife and ultimately the widow of Judge Josiah Masters of Schaghticoke, New York. As Nancy Smith she lost her first encounter with Johnson gracefully; as the lugubrious and often scheming Ann Masters, however, her entrances and exits into his life would be somewhat more dramatic.

CHAPTER 5

1814–1819

Early Years of Marriage

JOHNSON AND HIS BRIDE were not to be alone on their honeymoon, for Sarah Adams decided to accompany them. They were married on a Sunday, and the next morning, with Sarah, they departed on a visit to Abigail's grandparents, the venerable John Adams, second President of the United States, and his wife, Abigail, for whom the young bride had been named. Their plans called for a return to Utica via New York City, after which they were to move in with Bryan and Leah Johnson, who "occupied a large house," along with Abigail's mother and Miss Nancy Smith (the latter, happily, "concluded to live apart" at the last moment and moved in with her brother, Justus Smith, of Hamilton, New York). Johnson described the trip and his encounter with the Adams family:

My father had arranged for our traveling by hiring of Jason Parker a light coach to be drawn by four horses. The coachman was to provide for himself and horses, and they were to take us wherever we wanted to go and to return with us to Utica, abiding my directions as to progress and time. Jason Parker was a stage proprietor, and was to furnish us with fresh horses at different stages of the route, and the compensation was to be eleven dollars per day. Thus equipped and with plenty of money in my pocket, we left Utica after breakfast on Monday morning, October 24, 1814, at about eight o'clock. On coming down Genesee Street we met Susan Breese, a schoolmate of my wife, but a few years younger. She knew of our arrangement and was waiting to be the first who should hail my wife as Mrs. Johnson. This she accomplished, and with laughing and good will we drove along and eventually left Utica behind us. The weather was delightful, the roads good, and a more happy party could not be found. We arrived at Amsterdam the first night and stayed there till morning, reaching Albany the second day. A proverb says two persons are company, but three are a committee. This is strikingly true of a bridal tour, and the license of our new feelings was somewhat sobered by the presence of a third person of matronly and dignified deportment, and these Mrs. Adams combined strongly. She quoted for our edification the couplet of, I believe, Thompson, to the effect that

> The most loving pair, every day they live,
> Will find something to pardon and forgive

but I much wondered what I could ever find in my blooming young wife that needed to be forgiven.

After I know not how many days of delightful travel we reached Boston, and while we were thinking where to put up, my wife suddenly caught sight of her uncle, Judge Thomas B. Adams, third son of the President. He saw her as soon as she saw him, and coming up to our carriage, she introduced me to him. He was strikingly fine-looking, about thirty-eight years old, and resembled much a rather portly English gentleman. He had heard of our marriage, and after cordially greeting me and his sister-in-law Mrs. Adams, he recommended us to a boarding house in the city, while he went forward to Quincy to announce our arrival. . . . In the afternoon we left Boston for Quincy, the residence of President Adams.

His mother-in-law, Johnson learned, had last left the Adams household under less than happy circumstances. After the death of her husband, Charles Adams, a not very successful lawyer in New York City, she had taken her two daughters, Abigail and Susan, to Quincy and moved in with their grandparents, who were also housing their son, Thomas Adams, and his wife and several children. "In so mixed a family," wrote Johnson, "discords occasionally arose between the two daughters-in-law in which the grandparents could not fail to become entangled." Sarah, at some point, had moved to Utica with Abigail leaving Susan in Quincy. "My mother-in-law had not visited Quincy since this event," Johnson explained, "and she indoctrinated me with the opinion that, as our bridal trip to Quincy was spontaneous on our part, we ought not to locate ourselves with President Adams, but go to a boardinghouse kept by a Mrs. Black." The next morning when the travelers reached Quincy, they went directly to Mrs. Black's, and in the afternoon Johnson and Abigail took a stroll over to the Adams house, where they learned that, despite the warmth of their reception, the former President and his wife were "much hurt at the independent step we had taken" in putting up at a boardinghouse. Johnson apologized as best he could, but "resisted a change in location—which they no doubt attributed to a proper cause."

The next morning the Adamses drove up to Mrs. Black's in a "handsome English chariot" to invite the visitors to dinner, and Adams found his new grandson-in-law deep in a book entitled *The Dignity of Human Nature,* written by one of Johnson's old teachers at the school on Finsbury Square. The President was pleased to find the young man so engaged.

> He said he had a pretty large library of his own, and that I should be welcome to take therefrom any books I might select. He could say with St. Paul, "Silver and gold have I none, but such as I have I give unto thee." I replied that I had already taken from him in my wife much more than I deserved, and that I could not think of depriving him of any books.

Johnson also learned during this meeting that Adams "had not been consulted as to my marriage, not having heard of it till it was consummated." Adams pointed out gracefully, however, that this was not the first time he had been uninformed in such matters, for the same thing had happened when his own two sons, Thomas and John Quincy, were married—"though Mrs. John Quincy Adams turned out to be a very fine woman." (John Quincy Adams, at this time, was in Russia as Minister Plenipotentiary from the United States.)

Johnson's first impression of his famous grandparents was briefly recorded:

> The President was a handsome old gentleman not much under eighty years old, but hale and vigorous in mind and body. His wife was several years his junior, but rheumatism and age had distorted her figure so as to make her appear hunchbacked. She was very keen in her intellect, with a vivid sense of propriety, which she feared would be violated with our lodging at a boarding house.

At dinner that afternoon, Johnson had an opportunity to observe the Adams family in action, and noted some "singularities" in their behavior:

Early in the afternoon we all went to dinner. No strangers were present. Judge Adams and his wife were on the party and my wife's sister, Susan Boylston Adams. She was very handsome and about the age of eighteen years, with exceedingly easy manners and ready wit. Several kinds of wine were on the table and I understood they were of choice qualities. The house was brick but quite old-fashioned, the beams appearing overhead as the ceiling. The furniture was rich but also apparently old, and I noticed as a singularity to me that the President was always spoken of in the third person—as, "Where is Sir?"—"Sir told me to go with him, etc."—and Mrs. Adams was called "Marm" and spoken of by that title when she was referred to. I understood it was a New England fashion.

Johnson did not dwell on the food he was served, but another visitor to the Adams household, the English journalist Henry Bradshaw Fearon recorded in his *Sketches of America* an awesome account of a similar feast at the Adams' table:

As the table of a "late king" may be amusing, take the following particulars: first course, a pudding made of Indian corn, molasses, and butter; second, veal, bacon, neck of mutton, potatoes, cabbages, carrots, and Indian beans; Madeira wine, of which each drank two glasses. We sat down to dinner at one o'clock. . . . For tea we had pound cake, wheat bread and butter, and bread made of Indian corn and rye. Tea was brought from the kitchen, and handed around by a neat serving girl.

Abigail Johnson and her husband were feted by her childhood friends in "a round of delightful amusements," one of which featured "dancing, music and singing, with Susan playing the piano," and Thomas Adams performing "some comic songs very happily." Accompanied by the Adams family, Abigail and Johnson took tea at the country home of Josiah Quincy, whose debating ability Johnson had admired in Washington. The young man was particularly impressed with the account of one of Quincy's prize cows whose prodigious milk output was attributed to the fact that the animal was fed skimmed milk. Johnson's inevitable embarrassing moment occurred when Mrs. Quincy asked him what he did for a living. "When I told her I had no profession, but lived without business," he wrote, "it seemed to injure me in her estimation, though I expected from my early English associations that it would produce a contrary effect." Later excursions also involved him in other small social predicaments. A visit to a naval vessel named the *John Adams,* during which the escorting officer kept removing his hat, left Johnson confused over whether he should follow suit (he did), and some of his trips alone with John Adams confronted him with similar dilemmas.

He invited me one forenoon to take a drive with him. When we came to the carriage he told me to get in, but I, under a mistaken politeness, said I would get in after him. He then told me that Louis XIV of France was about taking a drive and told some person who was to accompany him to get in, but the person said "after your Majesty." The King, accordingly, got in but immediately shut the coach door, and ordered the coachman to drive on, leaving the astonished gentleman standing in the street. I apologized as well as I could for my mistake, but I felt grateful that I had a French courtier of the Great Monarch as my precedent. On another occasion I accompanied Mr. Adams in his carriage to a great cattle show or fair some miles from Quincy. He was received with much honor, on which he took off his hat and walked some distance bareheaded. Here again I knew not how to act. If I pulled off my hat also as I walked at his side, I feared the act might be construed into taking a part of the honor to myself which I knew was intended for him alone. I believe I uncovered, though I was much embarrassed from unacquaintance with the proprieties of the occasion. On our way home, we alighted at a tavern on the road and obtained a sort of lunch or dinner, and again my simplicity misled me, for I thought I ought to pay for my own meal, but this seemed to offend Mr. Adams, who remarked, "Mr. Johnson, I suppose you do not mean to affront me." I assured him I was innocent of any such intention, and he paid the whole bill.

Other moments with John Adams, however, brought out the Boswell in Johnson (a role he urged on his sister-in-law, Susan). When he told the ex-President about a new college named Hamilton which had been founded near Utica a few years earlier, the old political enemy of Alexander Hamilton replied testily "that they had better have called it Bathsheba College"—a comment Johnson did not attempt to clarify. He heard Adams explain that he and Thomas Jefferson "were never rivals for the presidency, but the rivalry was between Jefferson and Hamilton." Johnson was also delighted with the old man's story of how he had once run across a "John Adams Street" in London, and was much disappointed to learn it had been named after "the famous architect who had constructed the Adelphi Building." Other Adams stories came to Johnson secondhand. On one of his excursions he met a "plain farmer-looking man," the President's brother, Peter Adams. Noting that the man's two sons were also "plain farmers," he questioned Abigail about them, and was told how, as a little girl, she had once been rebuked by her grandfather for not paying due deference to "Brother Peter." When Peter came to call one day, Abigail announced him as "Mr. Peter Adams," and was warned, "Never let me hear you again call him Mr. Peter Adams, but Uncle Peter!"

In nearby Boston, the Adams name opened one door after another for the young bridegroom. He was escorted through the famous Athenaeum, with its 18,000 books and assorted curiosities, by the founder and curator, noting especially John Quincy Adams' library of 4,000 volumes kept during his residence in Europe. He and Abigail also visited the studio of Gilbert Stuart, where they found the artist at work on one of his five paintings of John Adams—probably a copy of the original life portrait done in 1798 in Philadelphia.

> He had completed all but the drapery, and had long held it in this condition from a repugnance to paint drapery. I was surprised to see the tremulousness of the artist's hands, induced, as was supposed, from a habit of excessive stimulation. He also took snuff in an immoderate quantity and was not overly clean with it. He offered to make me a copy of President Adams portrait for two hundred and fifty dollars, but he said his daughter would make me a copy for fifty dollars and it would be as good as he could make—the difference being only in the imagination of the purchaser. The fame of the artist gave him no little interest to me and he was communicative and obliging.

The Adams house contained several portraits by the English painter Copley. One was of John Adams' "uncommonly beautiful daughter," Abigail Amelia, who had married Colonel William Stephens Smith, the brother of Sarah Adams. Nearby was another Copley portrait of Colonel Smith, a former aide to General Washington, whom Johnson had met in Utica. On one occasion John Adams found his guest examining two miniatures in the parlor, and identified them as "portraits of your Uncle, John Quincy Adams, and his wife." When Johnson remarked that he thought the lady handsome, the President replied drily that "she had made her husband an excellent wife."

The two weeks in Quincy passed quickly, and on the day before the departure Johnson walked alone to the local cemetery, where he saw "a long line of granite gravestones denoting the successive generations of the Adams fathers from the first who arrived from England." The next morning John and Abigail Adams paid a final call at Mrs. Black's, and Johnson was again warned by the President "that when I should again visit him to no longer indulge in the independence of putting up at a boardinghouse, but to come immediately to his house."

Johnson promised faithfully that he would "offend no more in that way," and the party said farewell, taking Susan with them as far as Boston for a day of shopping. The next morning the trio left Boston for New York, but the travelers had not counted on the fact that their New York bank notes were discounted at 28 percent in Massachusetts, a fact which had considerably depleted their funds. Reluctantly they turned back to Boston for the night, and set out the next day directly for Utica without notifying the family in Quincy that they were still in the neighborhood. When they finally reached home, Johnson, recalling the Adams' sensitivities, sent off a note to them explaining his sudden return to Boston. The reply from Quincy indicated that he was correct in doing so, since news of this had reached them. It also made clear, however, that he had been warmly received into the Adams clan, and that the clan's patriarch intended throughout his few remaining years to keep an eye on the young couple, who would soon be adding new bloodlines to the Adams genealogical tables. "We heard of your return to Boston from twenty quarters," wrote Adams. "Though there was something at first a little mysterious about it, yet we all conjectured the motives, the consultations, and ratiocinations that produced it, and unanimously applauded them all." Adams had just learned from a Boston newspaper that Johnson was one of his "brother authors," and said, "I cannot blame you nor Abby, but I have a complaint against her mother that she did not give me some information of that important matter." On the subject of Johnson's first book, he wrote, "value is a subject than which you could not have chosen any more important to the prudence of this country." There was a special message for Abigail:

Tell my lovely hussy Abby—"What!", says Abby, "why does my grandpa descend from his dignity to apply such a vulgar word to me?" Hussy, tell her, means housewife, and I hope she will know how a pot should be boiled, and a spit turned, as well as to know how cakes and puddings and pies and tarts should be made.

Abigail Johnson also received some advice from her grandmother as she prepared to settle into the role of a Utica housewife. Mrs. Adams wrote her from Quincy:

Do you think, my dear girl, because you are married, that you are to lay aside your pen, and neglect your correspondents? No! No! You ought to be stimulated to greater exertions, for your fancy is now to keep at home, where all your joys and sorrows are to center. There you have ample means to be satisfied, with a partner whose character all tongues pronounce truly estimable. I consider it a great happiness that it has been your lot to be thus connected, and I presume your husband will find you what Solomon called a good thing, and that you will do him good all the days of your life. For through all the vicissitudes of life, and after fifty years of experience, I can say with Milton,

> Hail, wedded love! Mysterious law,
> Perpetual sunshine of domestic sweets!

May you ever find it such. Present me affectionately to your parents, aunt, and to Mr. Johnson.

In his letter to Johnson, John Adams had wished that Johnson were acquainted with his old friend, Adrian Van der Kemp of Oldenbarneveld, a few miles north of Utica, and had ended with the observation, "Utica is becoming a city on a hill. You will have an opportunity of seeing our great generals."

The Dutch patriot and scholar, Van der Kemp, was soon to become a close friend of Johnson's, but the "great generals" Adams referred to never materialized. The occasion for their coming to Utica was to have been the court-martial of General James Wilkinson, a member of that military establishment of which George Dangerfield, in his *Era of Good Feeling,* wrote: "Its senior commanders were old, and to age they added inefficiency, or, in the case of General Wilkinson, a settled habit of corruption."

Acting as Adjutant General for the Army during the trial was to be Martin Van Buren who had already arrived in Utica, and whom Johnson described as "a rising young man." As the advance party began to arrive in the village, Johnson received another letter from John Adams in which the old patriot waxed lyrical about Utica's impending days of glory—with more, perhaps, than a smattering of irony. "Nothing," he said,

will be wanting but a poet to make your Utica as famous as Ithaca, the kingdom of Ulysses. Homer could easily make out of Wilkinsons, Dearborns, etc., Agamemnons, Achilleses, Ajaxes, Nestors, or what he pleased. As the news journal of Utica is likely to record facts that hereafter may be the materials of a new *Iliad* or *Odyssey,* I shall be much gratified with the numbers you are so good as to give me hopes to receive. Who knows but Wilkinson, who has suffered as many persecutions as Cato, who had advertised Harper and John Randolph for cowards, may be reduced to such a state of indignation at the disgraces of his country, her injustice and ingratitude to him, as to fall upon his sword, and become as famous or notorious as Cato? Let no one see this but yourself. I can neither speak nor think about our public affairs anything but rhodomontade and bagatelle.

Adams also urgently requested that Johnson and Abigail pay a call on Madame Deaborn, the general's wife, who had preceded her husband to Utica.

Everything was set for the event which was to turn Utica into "a city on a hill," when suddenly the entire proceedings were shifted to Troy, New York. According to Moses Bagg, the town was "robbed of the glory" of the Wilkinson trial "by the covetous spirit of the Utica landlords," who refused to give special rates to the visiting dignitaries. Bagg also condemned certain leading citizens for the "slighting treatment" they accorded many of the notables, and among the guilty ones may have been Johnson who failed to entertain any of the dignitaries— "for I feared our accommodations to receive company were not as good as I feared the parties might expect."

Of the war itself, John Adams had written that it would be "long, bloody and, for a time, disastrous"; but, he added, "the furnace of affliction purifies." Actually, the war was closer to its conclusion than Adams knew, and the internal opposition to it, especially in New England, was fiercer than he supposed, for on December 24, 1814, an American delegation headed by John Quincy Adams signed the Treaty of Ghent.

Utica had been the scene of no military engagements during the War of 1812, though it provided some sixty volunteers to the Army and Navy—including Nathan Williams, and several other close friends of Johnson's. The chief hardship inflicted on the village stemmed form its location on the main route to the St. Lawrence, making it a bivouac station for thousands of soldiers and sailors marching toward Canada, and also for returning troops and their few British prisoners after the failure of the campaign. According to a diary kept by Johnson's physician, Dr. Samuel Coventry (quoted extensively by Moses Bagg), the troops swarmed through the village and the surrounding countryside ransacking stores, forcing their way into taverns and hotels, and "robbing orchards, potato fields and hen roosts," being caught occasionally by their officers and "whipped with the cat." The worst offenders were companies of artillerymen from Massachusetts. "They were dissatisfied with their rations," wrote Coventry, "and had left almost one hundred sick and disabled along the road—nor did they approve of the invading of Canada." Coventry also indicates that a number of captured British officers were well entertained in Utica homes.

News of the war's end did not come until after Jackson's victory on January 8 at New Orleans, and Johnson's account of what happened in Utica was anticlimactic: "The news reached Utica during the winter, and we drove in a one-horse cutter at night to see the illumination which took place very generally in our houses. The cutter belonged to Nancy Smith who had come in from Hamilton where she then resided. I had at the time no horses myself."

With his flair for dramatizing hometown happenings, Moses Bagg added a little more color to the story of the Utica celebration than Johnson did:

> It promptly took its part in the joy that attended the declaration of peace with Great Britain, the first hint of whose coming reached the village in this wise: a stranger dropped one evening into the bookstore of Asahel Seward, and remarking that he saw a newspaper was printed there, he left a printed slip which he said he had no further use of, and which might be of use to the editor, and then took his departure. The stranger had business in the neighborhood, the issue of which depended on the issues of the War. Desirous to complete it, he had ridden post haste from Albany, and had reached Utica four hours in advance of the mails. The slip he brought with him as an extra, announcing the fact that peace had been made. Mr. Seward repaired at once to his printing room to direct that the news be put in type, while his clerk stuck a few candles in the windows. By the time he reappeared an excited crowd had gathered about the door, frantic to know the particulars. Despite the apprehensions of some that the stage on its coming might not confirm the intelligence, the few candles at the store kindled up others, and soon lit the town in a spontaneous blaze. A more formal and thorough illumination was made a few days later when, with scarce an exception, every house was lighted, and the streets were made brilliant with rockets and fireballs.

In the middle of the Adams letter concerning the Wilkinson trial there was a passage which Johnson omitted from his autobiography. As he had noted in the account of his meeting with the Josiah Quincys, the Adams circle cherished a high New England regard for steady employment. John Adams was blunt about it.

> Your want of a profession is a serious misfortune. If I had your fortune and your head, I would study law, physic or divinity or merchandise

or land jobbing (I will not say or stock jobbing) rather than be idle and without an object. "Il est plus difficile de s'amuser, que de s'enrichir." You may depend upon it, he is the most unhappy man, who has nothing to do. Whether he be rich or poor, high or low, if he has no plan, he is never easy on horseback, or on foot, in his carriage, or his walk in the woods, in his parlor or his study, on his sofa or in his bed, in his chair or on his couch. As the mind and body are made for action, the most implacable and inexorable enemy of human happiness is ennui. I wish the English language had a neat and well-sounding word to express it.

During the spring of 1815, still without a profession, but with his investments providing him an adequate income, Johnson made a down payment on a large and imposing Georgian house on Genesee Street, near the brow of a hill overlooking the Mohawk Valley. The house, he wrote, "had a great reputation for the care with which it had been constructed and the many novel conveniences it was said to contain"— though he admitted, somewhat proudly, that he had purchased it "without ever seeing the inside" (the house was razed during the 1920s to make way for the gold-domed Savings Bank of Utica). Abigail, by this time, was expecting her first child, and the new house remained vacant, Johnson feeling it would be wiser to remain with his parents until the birth occurred. A boy named John Adams Johnson arrived on October 3, 1815, and was hailed with great-grandfatherly joy in Quincy, Massachusetts. "Your favor of the 4th," wrote John Adams,

has diffused a glow of joy in our obscure village where dear Abby was popular. I most sincerely congratulate you both, and your father and mother, and her mother, to all of whom this event must be very pleasing. By the description you give of the young gentleman, he will be fit for a merchant, a farmer, a statesman, an admiral, a general, or whatever Providence shall please. Do you take care to make him a scholar, for without this, although the false trumpet of fame may sound him out as a great man, he can intrinsically be good for nothing.

You have given him a name that has sometimes sounded in soft music, but much more frequently with harsh discord. Whether it will be most beneficial or prejudicial to the child is very uncertain. In all events my devout prayer to God for his blessing on the offspring and the parents. My first great-grandchild is no more. The description I had of it, though I never saw it, gave me pangs at its loss that I shall not forget. May heaven spare you and me from such another affliction.

Adams added a postscript: "To alleviate a little the solemnity of this letter, tell Abby she has done her duty, and deserves well of her country.

And I hope soon to have the same applause to bestow on Caroline [his granddaughter, Caroline De Windt, of Fishkill, New York]."

The addition to the family, along with certain domestic difficulties which had been simmering for some time in the combined Johnson household, hastened the move to the new house on Genesee Street. Up to this point Johnson had carefully concealed his feelings toward his mother-in-law save for a few hints in connection with the honeymoon trip, but now he put it quite plainly: "The effect," he wrote,

> of two families living in one house became annoying to me. My father and mother were devoted to me and my wife, but their views, feelings and conversations were not congenial to Mrs. Adams, my mother-in-law, nor were her views, feelings, and conversation congenial to my father and mother. The consequence was unpleasant complaints, in which myself and wife were unconsciously compromised more or less, and my father and I found the best alternative was a division of the families. All our property belonged to him, but he readily conceded to my views and gave me the money to make the purchase. . . . He also gave me money to procure furniture, and I went to New York and purchased such articles as we concluded to be necessary.

Without further ado, Johnson moved his family into the new house. With them, however, went Sarah Adams—along with "two female servants and a boy to take care of a single horse and light carriage." Bryan and Leah remained alone at their house.

Having stabilized his domestic arrangements (or so he hoped), Johnson began seriously to consider what John Adams had called his "want of a profession." Fortunately, at this time the state of New York was looking for two directors of the newly chartered Bank of Utica (the state in granting the charter was authorized to make two appointments in addition to those voted by the stockholders) and, through the influence of his friends Kip and Bloodgood, Johnson was chosen to fill one of the vacancies. Though it was not a steady, or remunerative, job it provided, said Johnson, "my first practical insight into banking which subsequently occupied a large share of my life." Since the bank was "very profitably conducted," the directorship also conferred upon the young appointee a high degree of respectability.

Johnson took his new duties seriously, but soon grew restless over the fact that his investment of talent and time in the bank's affairs was not producing any substantial income. One day, reading back into the state's banking history, he came across an interesting story about the beginnings of the Bank of Manhattan in New York City. Its founder,

Aaron Burr, had originally chartered it as a company whose purpose, ostensibly, was to provide the city with "pure and wholesome water." Inserted into the petition for a charter, however, was a sentence which read,

> It shall and may be lawful for said company to employ all such capital as may belong or accrue to said company in the purchase of public or other stock, or in any other monied transactions not inconsistent with the constitution of this state or of the United States, for the sole benefit of this company.

This single sentence made it legally possible for Burr to turn his "pure water company" into the Bank of Manhattan, and, wrote Johnson, "the trick was highly esteemed for its smartness, and Burr derived therefrom boundless admiration." If Burr could do it in 1800, something like it might be done in 1816; and since the state, under pressure from existing banks, was unwilling to grant any new bank charters in Utica, Johnson set out to improve, if possible, on Burr's formula.

> Unfortunately, I became seduced by the general false appreciation of Burr's stratagem, and from a mistaken ambition more than any other motive, I without communicating my design to any person drew a charter for an insurance company to be established in Utica, and so worded its powers as to authorize banking much more explicitly than Burr's charter. I called it a bill to incorporate the "Utica Insurance Company" with a capital of $500,000. The bill was an entire curiosity for the fullness of its powers when once suspected, and for their entire concealment when unsuspected.

Johnson, proud of his ingenious plan, finally shared it with Kip and Bloodgood, who were feuding with the cashier of the Bank of Utica, and they agreed to join the "Utica Insurance Company." Armed with letters from this influential pair to Martin Van Buren and other powerful Democrats in the Albany legislature (the letters stressed the fact that the bearer was "so modest and shy" that he might need "particular attention"), Johnson departed for the State Capitol where he sat nervously for several weeks waiting out the "usual almost interminable delay."

> While the bill was being read by sections in Committee of the Whole its meaning seemed so glaring to me that I wondered anybody could avoid seeing it; but the meaning of words is in the intellect of the hearer, and

they, suspecting nothing but an Insurance Company, saw nothing more. After its passage through the House it went in regular order to the Senate where again after many days of delay it was read by sections in Committee of the Whole. Mr. Van Buren happened to be chairman of this committee, and as he was a very astute lawyer and much prided himself on his acuteness, I felt the bill to be in danger as he read aloud the sections, and each one had to be voted on separately. But here again no amendment was proposed, and the bill finally passed through all the proper forms and became an act of legislature.

I was careful to say nothing to any member explanatory of the bill but let it speak for itself, and after its passage I obtained a certified copy from the State Department and went home deeming I deserved as much fame as Aaron Burr, but I never performed an act that I have so much regretted. I was deceived in its character by the absence of proper ethical knowledge in my education and associations.

Flushed with success, but with an uneasy conscience, Johnson returned home, called together Kip, Bloodgood, and John Yates, a brother of New York's Governor Yates and a "lawyer of much repute," and the four men opened the books for subscription to capital stock, which was bought up eagerly in Utica and other nearby towns. Kip was made president, while Johnson became secretary, treasurer, and cashier. Among the many directors, in addition to Bloodgood, were Bryan Johnson and Nathan Williams.

Meanwhile, as the Utica Insurance Company commenced circulating its bank notes, the opposition rallied.

Van Buren, now attorney general for the state, applied for an injunction to stop the company's banking operations, and Johnson empowered Nathan Williams to argue the company's case. Kip, "a skillful lobby member," was sent to Albany with $5,500 in "secret service money with which he was to do as he pleased, and never account for the expenditure." Despite Kip's efforts, however, the legislature amended an old "restraining law" preventing individuals from banking, extending it to apply to corporations as well, and providing severe penalties for infractions. With Van Buren's suit for an injunction still pending, and the amended restraining law to go into effect in August 1818, Johnson persuaded his directors to halt all banking operations at once. Having wound up the company's banking operations, Johnson turned next to the insurance phase of its program which, although profitable, had been "entered into as only a necessary compliance with the charter." All policies held with the company were transferred to the Eagle Fire Insurance Company of New York City. "Fortunately," said Johnson, "a fire occurred shortly after the transfer and the loss, some $1500, fell on the New York Company."

During these years, two more sons were born—Alexander Smith Johnson, on July 30, 1817; and Bryan Johnson, on April 30, 1819. John Adams, now eighty-three, saluted the latter's arrival in these words:

> Although it is always a pleasure to be informed of the multiplication of my posterity, that pleasure is always attended with a degree of anxiety for their future fortunes. This anxiety I, however, constantly alleviate with hope that they will all be good for something—good sailors and soldiers, good carpenters, good farmers, good tailors, good clothiers, good shoemakers, good woodcutters, or good something or other. The world is wide enough for them all; let them labor and be virtuous.

J. Q. Adams returned to America in the summer of 1817 to become James Monroe's Secretary of State. The Johnsons, returning from a visit with the John Adams family in Quincy, stopped overnight at a tavern in Albany, where Abigail, who had not seen her uncle since she was a small child, thought she saw someone who looked like him "as far as she could remember his appearance." Johnson checked with a servant, and found that it was indeed J. Q. Adams, and that he was traveling with his wife and his niece, fourteen-year-old Mary Hellen, who was being brought up by the family. After a pleasant family party that night, Johnson went to church the next day with his newly met in-law, and was surprised to find that the Secretary of State "seemed entirely unknown to the audience." On the following Monday, having received an invitation from Adams' niece, Caroline De Windt, Johnson and Abigail accompanied the Adams family by boat to Fishkill, New York. The next morning, the Johnsons, the Adamses, and the De Windts all paid a visit to West Point.

> We started in a sloop soon after breakfast, and after a pleasant sail arrived at our destination. A suggestion was made that the arrival of Mr. Adams should be announced to the garrison that he might be received with an artillery salute, but he declined and preferred to land unannounced. On landing we went to a tavern, but the arrival of Mr. Adams became known, and the officers of the garrison came to pay their respects to him. Soon after our arrival, and accompanied by some officers of the garrison, we all started on foot to examine the ruins of Old Fort Putnam on a hill overlooking the river and commanding it. This was the fort which Arnold had agreed to surrender to the British, and lying on the bank of the river was an immense iron chain which

at Arnold's time crossed the river and obstructed the passage upwards of ships of war. Little remained of the Old Fort but the trenches around it, and I recollect something of what looked like an old oven. The fort was not situated at the summit of the mountain on which it stood, and when we were about returning, Mr. Adams was missed from the party, and after much hallooing we found he had struggled to the highest part of the mountain. His wife said to me, "I knew he would not stop till he got to the top." I thought she meant to prefigure his future elevation and the tendency of his character, and such I have no doubt was her meaning. She was a lady of the most elegant manners I had ever met. She made you feel wholly unconscious of her superior position. It was the display of an art I had never seen practiced with equal success. I was traveling under the embarrassment of having to carry on my back my little son who was too young to walk the whole distance but whom I disliked to leave alone at the tavern, and I wished him, moreover, to see the Fort as something to be remembered in his lifetime. I was, therefore, glad when our party became again all collected and we were once more housed at the tavern. We found all the military students collected in arms to perform their evolutions before Mr. Adams, and after this review we were conducted over the buildings and saw all that was deemed worthy of inspection. We again embarked, and again Mr. Adams refused to receive a parting salute, saying that his visit was not official but merely accidental.

On our return to Mr. De Windt's we found assembled a large company of the neighboring gentlemen, and an elegant dinner of which we all partook with good relish from our forenoon excursion. In the evening, several ladies arrived and more company, and a dance and supper graced the occasion. Mr. Adams danced a waltz with his niece, Mrs. De Windt, and I thought he danced very gracefully. He seemed in very good spirits and, as he was sitting in a circle with several elderly gentlemen who were not dancers, he related several anecdotes of public persons and events. In telling one of these stories which related to a duel, he was very expressive in gestures as well as in words, and after he had ended my little son, who had been a very attentive listener, said to him, "Tell it over again." Mr. Adams laughed and said it was the highest compliment of the kind he had ever received.

The next day we separated, Mr. and Mrs. Adams and their niece going towards New York, and my wife and I and child towards Utica. Mr. Adams was a very early riser. While I was staying with him at Albany, I had got up very early in the morning to make arrangements for our day's journey, and I found him in our private parlor busily writing, and with the table covered with packages of letters and other documents. When he saw me he collected them together and replaced them in a large trunk which seemed to be specially prepared for such a use. He was habitually playful in his conversation, and took my little boy on his back and ran round the room with him.

The death of Abigail Adams took place on October 28, 1819, a short time after the Johnson's last visit to Quincy. Mrs. Adams had not seemed well while they were there, and at one point had called her namesake to her bedside for a long conversation on family matters—a conversation "unfortunately interrupted by the entrance of another member of the family about whom the conversation principally related." The next morning, without having the conversation resumed, Johnson and his wife departed. Mrs. Adams died at seventy-four, and Johnson entered the full transcript of her will into his autobiography. In it, Mrs. Adams left her granddaughter $500, a clay-colored gown, ten dollars for a ring, and half of a laced muslin gown.

During the spring of 1819 Johnson took inventory of his assets to date, and his prospects for the future. The picture was encouraging. In totaling up on May 1 he found himself worth $55,000.10, with his income during the previous year amounting to $4,157 as against "family expenses" of "not over $1800." These figures included the expenses of his father and mother, "for we deemed as one both our property and expenses, never caring in whose purse the property was, or from whose purse the expenses were drawn." It pleased Johnson to know also that he could "show how every dollar was acquired," and that his expenses had been kept so low. With regard to the latter, he had noted in his work on *Value and Capital* that most people "spend money to produce pleasant reflections . . . probably derived from a desire for superiority"; and, anticipating Thorstein Veblen's theories about the leisure class, had argued that although people would rarely set about accumulating useful objects such as a "vast supply of blankets when they weren't needed," they would accumulate "diamonds, laces, or other articles which may, in one sense, be termed useless." Johnson felt no need for conspicuous consumption, and he presumably saw to it that Abigail lived by the same philosophy. What he did want, however, was respectability and "a reputation for success," and to date, aside from some success as an author, and his marriage into a distinguished family, the latter goal had not been fully reached—particularly in the Ontario Glass Works and the Utica Insurance Company. As he looked around at his friends in Utica, especially at the lawyers among them, it occurred to him that the law might be a guarantee of both respectability and success—though at the age of thirty-three it would be important to find a shortcut around the usual seven-year apprenticeship.

To put his plan into action, Johnson wrote first to Chief Justice Ambrose Spencer of the State Supreme Court, asking how he might circumvent some of the requirements, especially those in classical studies. Spencer informed him bluntly that the rules were "inexorable," but recommended his consulting Judge Jonas Platt, also of the State Supreme Court, on the subject. His letter to Judge Platt produced more encouraging results. Platt felt that Johnson's clerkship could be reduced from seven to three years, and offered to "make the proper order" if Johnson could persuade Nathan Williams to offer him a clerkship in his law office. Williams took him in immediately as a privileged clerk, and Johnson was able to "consult my own pleasure as to the time I should spend in the office, and in all else that I chose." Even though he would be thirty-six before he could practice, Johnson consoled himself with the thought that Alexander Hamilton had also "commenced his legal studies as late as I did."

In Quincy, John Adams cheered the news of Johnson's decision, writing, "It is an heroic enterprise at your age, with a wife and three children, to enter on the study of law—the most crabbed of the whole circle of the sciences—but I heartily wish you success." In the next mail from Quincy came a complete plan of study which Adams had followed as a law apprentice some sixty years earlier in the office of James Putnam in Worcester, Massachusetts—along with a piece of advice he had been given on his own admission to the bar: "Let the law be your object, rather than the gain of it. Pursue the gain enough to keep yourself out of the briars, but the law, the law must be your principal pursuit." Adams added a final note: "The path of the lawyer is now a turnpike strewed with flowers, and scented with aromatic roses. In my time it was a rugged, rocky mountain, the ascent to which was encumbered with thorns and brambles."

CHAPTER 6

1819–1822

Debut as a Banker and Some Old Family Ties

J OHNSON PURSUED HIS APPRENTICESHIP with Nathan Williams vigorously, taking a special interest in the question of usury laws. In the midst of his studies, however, he received a letter from John Greig, the old friend of his glassmaking days, and now president of the Ontario Bank in Canandaigua. The Ontario Bank had sometime earlier established a branch bank in Utica, and Greig offered Johnson a directorship in it. "We consider it extremely important," he wrote, "to receive the services of gentlemen of your experience, influence and independence, and I shall think better of my stock when you engage in the management of the branch at Utica." Johnson accepted the offer, "having no supposition that my acceptance would interfere with my legal studies." On assuming his new duties, however, Johnson found that the Ontario Branch Bank post was by no means a sinecure. Ever since its founding, under its cashier, John Lothrop, the bank had been in trouble, with its directors failing to provide ready capital "to meet the growing necessities of the institution." In addition, one of its directors, charged with delivering some bank notes to New York City, "was cheated and lost the money." Lothrop had also placed a thousand dollars in notes in the hands of a local tavernkeeper, who absconded with it and subsequently "became notorious as a forger and swindler." All this had happened before Johnson became a director, but the bank's future was by no means certain, and Johnson was kept busy looking into its operations and reporting on them to Greig. Within a few months, Greig suggested that Lothrop be removed as cashier and Johnson take his place.

The problem of removing Mr. Lothrop provoked a lengthy correspondence between Greig and Johnson, and this "delicate and very

unpleasant business" was finally solved by keeping Lothrop on as
cashier, and placing Johnson over him as president. No sooner was
Johnson installed, however, than he began to regret what he had done.
The bank's total capital was a mere $125,000; its notes were selling at
a high discount rate in New York, and in Utica "nobody would take
them." His salary of only $1,000 per year seemed to promise more
trouble than it was worth. There was one consolation. He was not risking
any of his own capital—that tidy sum which guaranteed him a "certain
and permanent independence." When word got around that A. B. Johnson was now in charge, Utica merchants began taking Ontario bank
notes at par, but for a while, at least, this distressed rather than pleased
him, for having discovered just how shaky the bank's foundations were,
he began to doubt his ability to "justify the expectation founded on my
efforts." Nonetheless, he decided on a bold experiment.

> Instead of borrowing money, I thought if I could set the bank in oper-
> ation, it would resuscitate itself. I accordingly issued a new set of bank
> notes, and to designate them from the old I signed the new notes with
> red ink, and I gave notice that the red ink notes would be paid on
> presentation and that all new deposits would also be paid on demand,
> but that the old deposits and the old notes I required some little time
> on before they could be redeemed, but in the meantime they would
> be accepted in payment of all demands due to the bank. The project
> succeeded well. The new notes were taken everywhere with unbounded
> confidence, and new deposits were made freely, till in not many weeks
> the Bank was again in full operation and we could redeem both the
> old notes and deposits as well as the new.

Despite his success, Johnson, looking back over his life, added this postscript, "I cannot, however, help regretting . . . that some more important business had not been within my grasp, and on which I could
more beneficially to myself and others have expended the energies that
I bestowed on the Branch."

Johnson had been "much rejoiced" at the birth of his third son,
Bryan—the more so, he felt, from having, himself, "long been an only
child." His parents were devoted to their grandchildren, but especially
to the eldest boy, John, who spent much of each day with them, often
going on long walks with his grandfather. One day in late November
John showed symptoms of a cold, and Johnson kept him home. He sent
for a doctor who prescribed "a simple herb tea," but a fever developed
along with breathing difficulties. The doctor diagnosed the disease as
croup. A few days later, on November 29, Johnson faced the first of his
ordeals over the loss of a loved one, and as would so often happen in the

future, his grief was coupled with gnawing doubts as to the skill and wisdom of the attending physician. He wrote, "I had never seen death till then, and I was shocked and unmanned. I clasped my poor father in my arms, knowing his anguish exceeded even mine but, alas, how powerless is man under such an infliction. My wife exhibited more self-possession than any of us, though she felt the loss as keenly as we, but she was better organized to support it, and had moreover a religious support of which we were deficient."

His five-year-old son, the father recalled, had been "a beautiful boy" whom he had taken "unwearied pains to instruct in literature, and to infuse into him all kinds of knowledge that I possessed, and of which I deemed him capable." John, he said, "had already a little knowledge of Latin, knew something of arithmetic, could read and write a little"— knowledge which had been imparted "by conversation while at playful exercise" rather than "by sedentary study." The death Johnson said, "was a blow to my father that he never recovered."

The Ontario Branch Bank, under Johnson's guidance, prospered, but the parent bank in Canandaigua began to experience difficulty, thanks to a cashier who was, said Johnson, "wholly unfit for the emergency." Johnson recommended a replacement, Henry Gibson of New York, who had formerly been cashier of the Manhattan Branch Bank of Utica. Gibson, who was to become one of Johnson's closest friends, accepted the offer and quickly put the bank back on its feet.

With both banks now flourishing, Johnson resumed his law study, "desirous of prosecuting it to its conclusion." He also found time to renew his interest in intellectual and philosophical matters, spurred on by a lenthy correspondence with Samuel L. Mitchill, a celebrated New York physician and scientist, whom Johnson had met during his stay in Albany while petitioning the charter for the Utica Insurance Company.

In addition to his fame as a physician, Mitchill (1762–1831) was known to his contemporaries as a "living encyclopedia" and a "chaos of knowledge." He studied medicine in Edinburgh, was admitted to the New York State bar, and served as a negotiator for the purchase of Indian lands in western New York. In 1792 he occupied the Chair of Natural History at Columbia University, also teaching courses in "Antiphlogistic Chemistry," and engaging in numerous acrimonious scientific controversies with the British chemist Joseph Priestley. At the turn of the century he was also ardently promoting the waters at Saratoga Springs and Ballston Spa, and lecturing on the geology of the Hudson River Palisades. From 1801 to 1804 he served as a U.S. congressman, and for the next four years as a senator. Among his few unsuccessful ventures was his campaign to get Congress to adopt the name "Fredonia" for the entire United States, a campaign which resulted in the adoption of the name by at least a dozen American villages, although it never became the name of a country until it appeared as the name of a mythical state in a Marx Brothers motion picture during the 1930s.

As a result of his correspondence with Mitchill and his readings in Mitchill's *Journal,* Johnson sent him two scientific studies of his own composition—one on the nature of sunbeams, and the other containing some "Thoughts on Population." With regard to his piece on sunbeams Johnson wrote:

> I thought heat was not derived from them as from a heated body, for in that case no object could be heated by them beyond the heat of the sunbeam itself, whereas an object exposed to the sun accumulates a greater heat than the sunbeams. I therefore assumed that, as water gives out a latent heat when it combines with quicklime, so sunbeams consolidate with the object on which they strike, and thus liberate the heat that kept the sunbeam in its original condition.

Mitchill acknowledged Johnson's paper and commented that he "wrote like a gentleman of sense and reflection," adding, "I love original and independent observers." He rejected Johnson's theories, however, and referred him to his own thoughts as published in *The Medical Reports of 1803.* Here Mitchill had announced his theories on "calor and caloric"—which persisted in the world of "natural philosophy" (now called physics) for many years, and perpetuated a confusion between the terms "heat," "energy", and "temperature," which, according to some physics teachers, persists among students to this day.

Johnson's next paper for Mitchill was more successful. "In examining the statistics of population," he wrote,

> I thought I discovered a relation between the increase of any given set of men in society and the space which they occupied on the earth's surface, those who occupied the most space increasing most in population, while those who occupied the smallest space increased least. I prepared tables illustrating the principle, drawn from authoritative consensuses of different states and places.

Mitchill was delighted with Johnson's statistical approach. "I am glad," he wrote, "you have undertaken an inquiry into the facts afforded by our Fredonian states." The article by Johnson appeared in Volume III

(September 1820) of Mitchill's *Journal*. His interest in this subject was undoubtedly prompted by his reading of Thomas Malthus' *Essay on Population,* first published in 1789, and also possibly, by some of the writings of Condorcet, the French philosopher whose theories were later attacked by Malthus. Johnson disavowed Malthus' pessimism, and joined later critics who held that Malthus failed to take into account the development in transport, colonization, and agricultural production which would take place in the nineteenth century.

Johnson ran into a dilemma when he tried to account for the "natural law" that governs the relationship between space and population. Like Malthus, he was skeptical of "laws of nature" as partaking of the miraculous, but, he said, "It is not more miraculous that nature should regulate the increase of man than that she should regulate the sex into which the increase is divided." He then went into an extended analogy involving a small Connecticut fishpond, whose owner "had made many efforts by feeding and other expedients to increase the stock of fish, but if they increased beyond the apparent ordinary stock, the surplus would die."

In line with his later support for the annexation of Texas, his faith in "internal improvements" such as the Erie Canal, and his expansionist philosophy in general, Johnson argued that the most effective way to increase America's population was to "spread it over as wide a surface as practicable, and the people thus diffused will increase far beyond what they will in more confined locations." John Adams, to whom Johnson sent his essay several years after it was published, was very much a man of the old world, however, and wrote Johnson: "Your speculations upon population are ingenious and required considerable thought, but for my part, I leave the whole subject to the duty and inclination of mankind and womankind to obey the precept: increase and multiply."

Johnson had hinted, in his account of his New York reading program, that he was deeply interested in words and the nature of language itself. Unlike his concern with sunbeams and population, however, this was to be more than a passing fancy. "The great and permanent study of my life," he wrote, "has been language with reference to its meaning in something other than words." He could not recall when or how it all began—"because I recollect no period in my life when subjects leading to this ultimate undertaking were not present with me." There may, however, be a small clue in his statement that "it grew out of an investigation by me of the power of our separate senses, and which power I evolved by a species of demonstrations founded on the distinction that exists in nature between sights, sounds, tastes, feels, and smells." He continued,

Everything seeing informed me of, I denominated a sight;
everything hearing informed me of, I denominated a sound;
everything tasting informed me of, I denominated a taste;
everything smelling informed me of, I denominated a smell;
and everything feeling informed me of, I denominated a feel.

These investigations led to the notion that

more senses than one seemed to inform me of the same thing. I could
see a candle and I could feel a candle, and this contradicted a theorem
I had demonstrated that no sense could inform me of what any other
sense can inform me of. Apparently two senses informed me of a
candle; hence I was led, unpremeditatedly, to investigate the meaning
of the word *candle,* and so of other words, and eventually of language itself.

One book that may have prompted these initial investigations of
the powers of the separate senses, which in turn led him into the realm
of linguistic analysis, may have been David Hartley's *Observations on
Man.* Modern philosophers have pointed out Hartley's concern with
"physiological psychology," and his theories about the association of
ideas, which he supported with a detailed analysis of the functions of
sight, hearing, taste, etc. These studies often led the British philosopher
to speculate on the associative aspects of language, and on the tendency
of humans to make different uses of the same word—speculations which
Johnson was to elaborate upon in *A Treatise on Language* (1828) and
The Meaning of Words (1854).

Johnson took pains to point out that these studies of his did not
interfere to any great extent with his preparation for the law and his
work at the Ontario Branch Bank.

These and other speculations interfered less with my law studies and
with my banking than most persons would imagine, for I carried
them on at intervals of business; and the moment any call of business
interrupted my study, I intermitted the study and attended to the business—so that business and study became a relaxation of each other.

In the fall of 1820 John Adams, with whom Johnson had kept up
"an uninterrupted correspondence," was invited to serve at the age of
eighty-five as a delegate to a convention called to revise the Massachusetts Constitution. He spoke only once at the meeting to defend in a

feeble, halting voice the need for a property qualification for voting as against universal suffrage. Johnson congratulated the old man on his appointment to the convention, but, if he read Adams' remarks, he kept silent about them, for within a few short years he would be speaking out strongly for universal suffrage (excluding women, of course). In reply to Johnson's congratulatory letter on his appointment, Adams dismissed the honor as "a gratification to my feelings and a spontaneous evidence of the kindness of my fellow citizens." Just before his appointment, Adams had sent Johnson a copy of his *Defense of the Constitutions of Government of the United States* (1787), and Johnson had expressed great admiration for it. "I think I can say without vanity," replied Adams,

> that it contains a greater number of and variety of solemn warnings against the dangers of republican governments, in every form and shape in which they have ever existed, than are to be found in every work, ancient or modern, now extant. It was written for that express purpose, as a warning to the people of France, as well as to the people of America; and I hope it will be so to the South Americans, as well as to all Europe. The South Americans have got it translated into Spanish and are endeavoring to copy its system. The Germans have translated it into their language, and they may derive some benefit from it if they please, but whether the people of Europe or South America have any common principles upon which they can unite, or any common intelligence capable of adopting and persevering in any regular system, remains to be determined.

Johnson, he hoped, was "pleased with the study and practice of the law," and with the "rapid growth of your city to opulence and grandeur." (Utica by then had a population of about 3,500.) This reference to "opulence and grandeur" brought back memories to Johnson of the rigors of a Utica household in those days.

> In December of this year (1820) I commenced the use of a stove in my house, which I bought of one Pocock for $39.68, probably including the price of putting it up. Previously to this time our firing was in open fireplaces where we burnt large quantities of wood on andirons made of brass and iron. The cold during the winter was at times so intense, as to prevent me from signing my name to banknotes that I occasionally brought home to sign at night. I have sat at a small table by the fire, and had my inkstand on the hearth so that the ink would boil, and before I could take up a pen full of ink to write with, the ink in the pen would be frozen. Still, being accustomed to no greater means of warmth, the inconvenience was not particularly grievous.

The use of stoves which then began in our region meliorated this difficulty, and enabled us to become more comfortable during the cold of
winter, which was more intense than it has been in subsequent years.

Another son was born to the Johnsons on February 28, 1821, and
the family named him John Adams Johnson after their dead first-born.
The announcement brought a wry letter from the old gentleman in
Quincy.

The name you have given your child will not be of any injury, though
it will do it little good, for notwithstanding the disposition you speak
of to do justice to that name, yet it never was and never will be much
beloved or esteemed in this country; I fear it has been too much
slandered and abused in writings that cannot all of them perish. It is,
however, a heart-felt satisfaction to me to find that my principles,
systems, and writings are now respected in the world, adopted and
spreading, because I believe them calculated for the benefit of mankind. As to me, they are of no consequence, for I shall very soon
follow your departed beloved son, and meet him with his great-grand-
mother and a crowd of other relations and friends who have gone
before me, where slander and panegyric will be heard no more. Tell
Abby not to despair: there is time enough for daughters.

New York State was about to revise its constitution, and Johnson
took an active interest in the proceedings. The new draft constitution
contained a provision that no person not a native-born citizen would be
eligible to run for governor. Johnson felt much "aggrieved" at this
clause "as it excluded me—I being only a naturalized citizen." He saw
it as "repressive of any political aspirations I might ever entertain, how
unlikely soever was my chance for any such distinction as that of
Governor." As Nathan Williams was to be a delegate to the Convention,
Johnson wrote him a long letter, drawing to some extent on thoughts he
had expressed in his essay on "Expatriation."

"Only one consideration," said Johnson, "can make the amendment
tenable—the duties are too confidential to be entrusted to a native." He
then turned to history. "In Europe," he asked, "did the first George
sacrifice England to Hanover, or the third William subject it to Holland?
Did Bonoparte favor Corsica, or does the French blood of Bernadotte
detract from the interests of Sweden?" Pursuing the argument, perhaps
fallaciously at times, he added, "History furnishes not merely no
instance of evil from the government of a foreigner, but the supposition
proceeds from a false view of human nature."

Next Johnson tackled those "evils" which might be derived from the adoption of the amendment. "It will create," he said, "a humiliating inferiority in adopted citizens, and remove from them a source of emulation. Never expect, thereafter, a great statesman from that portion of your population!" He added, "'Remember that ye yourselves were sometimes aliens, that the language of a foreign father lingers upon the lips of many even of your Assembly, and bears testimony that his land is peculiarly the asylum of strangers." Recalling his own situation he assured Williams, "I possess no friend, correspondent, or known connection in any country but this." Finally, Johnson questioned the operation of the Convention itself. "I know not," he wrote, "who is to arrest the pending evil. It has already been enacted without debate, and perhaps because it was not debated, but yet I hope that naturalized citizens will find a champion on the convention, and, if successful raise to himself a monument that shall endure."

Williams was impressed by this "interesting communication" from his law clerk, and promised to "bring the subject distinctly before the Convention," adding, however, "I find on consulting with some very respectable members that the subject is not without its difficulties." Just how vigorously Williams pursued the matter in Albany is not known, but when the offending amendment was retained, he informed Johnson that the failure to defeat it was "mainly attributable to Rufus King," the powerful and socially prominent U.S. Senator from New York, and former Federalist candidate for the presidency in 1816. Johnson complained, "I felt aggrieved by the amendment because it took from me a right that I previously possessed . . . and the prohibition repressed all tendency in me to enter into political contests."

Strictly speaking, up to the date of the Williams' letter Johnson could say that he had "no correspondent" abroad, for he had not written to his own relatives since a letter in 1801 announcing his safe arrival in New York. However, his father, Bryan, with whom he shared so much, had been in touch with his "connections" in Europe, and his son was surely aware of it. It was Bryan who began the correspondence.

The first family letter which is preserved in the Johnson Collection is from Bryan's older brother, William, who called himself Jones and was living in Copenhagen. It is an answer to one of Bryan's. It is dated 25 April, 1815, and (except for punctuation) is here reproduced in its original orthography:

In answer to your kind letter dated July 6th Last I have the pleasure of informing you that I and all my family are in Good Health Excepting my Wife Who died about five years ago. You may naturly suppose

I was happy to Hear of your and families Good Health and prosperity after So many Years Silence. as for our family in England, I never heard from them since I Left it So that I can give you no intelligince about them at present. I keep a Shop in the Grocery Line whereby I make a tollarable livlyhood. I have suffered much by the great fire which happened here about 20 years ago which I make no Doubt you must have heard of, and now this late and tidious War, the Bombardment of this City, and the Burthen of Taxes have been great obstructions to my Prosperity. however after many narow escapes of intire ruin, I ought not to complain, having had it in my pour to establish my Son William Who is married and has 4 Children in the same Line of Business as my Self. Both my Daughters are with me and I have got 2 Sons by another Woman, one of them, 16 years old, has a great desire for Country Life. if you should think propper, I would Send him over to you, if you would have the Goodness to assist him a little in the farming Line. He has already been accustomed to country Life, Having had a Little Farm myself Which I now have Sold. I make no Doubt it would answer Extremely well, if your Son had any fancy of seeing this part of the World, to send Him here with a Cargo of Coffee, Sugar, Rice, Rum, fine Flour, and Dye Woods, all productions Which generally are Brought here from America, and in return to take Hemp, Iron, and Sailcloths, Whereby Great freights ar made. . . . I Shall be Glad to hear from you by the first opportunity. my Son William and both my daughters Join With me their Love to you & all your Family, remaining Dear Brother your Constant Well-wisher.

One can only conjecture at the sudden outburst of family feeling that impelled Bryan to write after so many years of silence (like Alexander, he seems on his arrival in America—in his case in 1797—to have cut off all communications). Perhaps the leisure forced upon him by his retirement from business, the limited companionship with Alexander now imposed by the young man's marriage and new preoccupations, and the sentimentality of advancing years, all combined to encourage his nostalgia. One can also wonder why he chose to write to William, whose letter (even granting his difficulty in writing) expressed no great intimacy of feeling. Probably Bryan was really trying to get information about his brother Jonathan, with whom he had been much closer. But he had parted from Jonathan in anger, and may have been stubbornly refusing to make the first conciliatory move.

At almost the same time, Jonathan's son, Solomon, another Jones, was attempting to get in touch with Bryan and his family. In a letter dated from London, 2 August 1815, Solomon wrote to a Mrs. Mary Kempton, the wife of a sea captain, in New York, answering hers of 12 May (he had been on the Continent on business, he said, or he would

have written sooner). He confessed his disappointment with her letter
from America: "I expected you would have mentioned my Uncle, Aunt,
and Cousin's name in your letter. I hope *they are living and well*. If it is
not too much trouble, I should be glad to be informed if they are living
and in health."

Mrs. Kempton evidently forwarded Solomon's letter to Utica in
August 1815. Bryan's answer, dated 20 November, reached Solomon
18 January 1816, and he answered 7 February from London that
Bryan's letter:

> much surprised us all, as we had every reason to believe from so long a
> silence that yourself, Aunt Leah, and Zalick was no more. As to Zalick,
> I am much astonished at, as I had every reason to expect to have heard
> continually from him from the time he left England. For yourself
> there might be some excuse, you having left my Father not on friendly
> terms, but Zalick and his Mother parted on the best of friendship with
> the whole of my family, and wrote us on their arrival in America,
> saying they would never neglect writing, consequently there could be
> no excuse. However, let us lay all that of one side and forget of the past.

Zalick, of course, was none other than Alexander Bryan. This pet
family name is a phonetic rendition of the German *selig,* meaning
blessed. In a later letter to Johnson, Rachel, Solomon's sister, said that
he and Solomon were namesakes, and that *Zalick* and *Solomon* were
the same name. (Solomon's father, Jonathan, in a begging letter to
Johnson, complained that his son Zalick "uses him ill.") The name
Solomon, however, is not German, but from the Hebrew word for *peace.*

Despite the long lapse of time, Solomon achieved an immediate,
almost startling, intimacy. He was sorry to hear of Bryan's poor
health—"this complaint of yours the piles have been long standing
before you left England," etc. He had been married for eight years to a
Miss Daniel of Bristol whose father, Phinias, once owned a shirt manufactory in Philadelphia, and had four children. His sister, Rachel
Robinson, had been very unfortunate, her boy Edwin dying in March.
To distract her, her father had taken her and her eleven-year-old
daughter, Kitty, to the Continent, where they were living in Brussels.
Rachel's marriage to Robinson had been annulled three years ago, since
"Robinson never paid her the attention she was entitled to" (some years
later Rachel explained to her cousin Alexander that she discovered
Robinson had three children by another woman). Solomon, himself, had
been abroad during the recent wars (the Peninsular Campaign), and
until recently had been the owner of three ships. He was glad to hear

from Bryan about his uncle in Copenhagen ("We have *not* corresponded"). Finally, one learns that Bryan, although retired, was still interested in business activities and had inquired about the export to the U.S. of "diamond sparks" (probably diamonds for use in glaziers' tools), but these were scarce and expensive, and Solomon could not send any. However, he would like to be of service to Bryan and Zalick, and would ship any article that might be suitable for the American market.

As these and other letters were arriving from the family abroad, A. B. Johnson, of course, was embarking on his marriage to an Adams, and launching his career in Utica as a lawyer and banker. Not until 1824, with the death of his beloved father, would Johnson break the silence he had maintained in spite of the promise he had made in 1801 to keep close to his "loved ones at home."

In short, A. B. Johnson was most assuredly aware of his "connections" abroad—connections who were also trying hard to be "friends" and "correspondents." It is difficult to imagine, among other things, how, when he came to transcribe the letter to Williams into his memoirs, especially in the careful editing of his "fair copy" from the rough draft, he failed to note this blatant discrepancy. When, a few years later after his father's death, he finally begins his own correspondence with overseas relatives, it will become painfully obvious how important it seemed to Alexander, a young man on the rise in Utica, to conceal the existence of "Zalick," and Zalick's "connections."

CHAPTER 7

1822–1823

Dialogue with John Adams

O N JANUARY 18, 1822, Johnson was admitted to the bar after what he considered an easy examination by a committee of three lawyers appointed by the State Supreme Court. The examination was followed by a "convivial" gathering at a nearby tavern with the examiners and the candidates indulging in "the usual drinking of the period"; but Johnson avoided the celebration—"as my superior age [thirty-six years], I thought, excused me." After obtaining the license form at the cost of one dollar, paying another dollar to the licensing clerk, and still another to "the crier who administered the oath," Johnson returned home a full-fledged lawyer. His father gave him a front room in his own house for an office, and Johnson acquired a tin sign painted "A. B. Johnson, Attorney at Law." The results of his three years of study, however, turned out to be depressingly anticlimactic. "I also got printed a quantity of cards to the same effect, and sent them around to all from whom I expected business, but I was soon undeceived by being told by many persons that they must give their business to poor young men who needed it, and that they could not give it to me. All my efforts brought me but one client."

Meanwhile, Johnson had announced to John Adams his admission to the bar, adding, apparently, a reference to some writing he was doing. Adams replied at once:

I thank you for your favor of January 23 and am very glad to hear you have persevered to the end of your course in the study of the law, and particularly that Abigail was wise enough to encourage you in your pursuit. This I esteem in her a great merit and proof of prudence deserving imitation by all her sex in encouraging their husbands in all manly studies and business, and there is none more so than the law.

I advise you to commence the practice immediately and to pursue it with attention and ardor upon the most honorable and virtuous principles.

The subject of your literary design you have not mentioned, but whatever it may be, I should make it entirely subservient to my practice at the bar. In many books there is some labor, much anxiety, and more obloquy, as I have found by woeful experience, and no profit.

Concerned about his failure as a lawyer, and the adequacy of his income for a growing family (he had just, for $141.50, bought his wife a piano—one of the first to be seen in Utica), Johnson grew restless over his salary at the now-prospering Ontario Branch Bank, and accordingly wrote John Greig, asking for a raise of $500, which Greig granted immediately, making his annual salary $1,500. Looking back over this request for an extra $500, Johnson philosophized:

The employment was highly respectable, which added much to its value in my estimation, and its duties were pleasant and afforded me leisure for my literary pursuits, and a comfortable office wherein I could write, etc., though I now look back with some regret at the small pecuniary use to which I employed the most active portion of my life. The banking business operated as a sedative to my activity, and kept me quiet. What would have been the result of my activity if not thus quieted, I cannot judge.

While Johnson was straightening out his own affairs during the spring of 1822, he received a melancholy letter from his wife's aunt, Mrs. Ann Masters, the former Nancy Smith who, after his marriage to Abigail, had gone off to live with her brother in Hamilton, New York. Following her marriage to Josiah Masters, a county judge, she had moved to Schaghticoke, New York, where she had borne her thrice-married husband a son and daughter. Her letter described her husband's illness which was keeping her in "a constant state of the most alarming solicitude," but since cheerfulness was "absolutely essential to keep off his complaint," she was suppressing her anxiety. "Thus," she said, "while my soul is agonized, my countenance wears a smile." Shortly thereafter, Johnson heard from Master's nephew that the Judge was dead, and that "Aunt Masters is so much overcome as not to be able to write, nor even to set up [sic]." Mrs. Masters recovered quickly, however, and in a letter to Johnson informed him that on her promise to take care of his children, including those by previous marriages, Masters had left her an estate worth sixty thousand dollars—"minus twenty thousand in debts." She begged Johnson to come to her, to act as an executor, and "to explain every important point, and to be encouraged and supported by your approbation." Johnson and Abigail went to Schaghticoke, and found Ann Masters living in "a spacious house . . . attached to one of the largest and best farms in Rennsselaer County." Johnson gave her "such advice as I deemed useful," and, though deciding not to serve as an executor, "retained the power to act at a future day should she deem it necessary." The lugubrious and meddling Ann Masters, though he did not know it at the time, had now permanently involved Johnson in her private affairs, and herself in his.

In November Johnson appears to have told John Adams of his lack of success as a lawyer and of his decision to pursue a literary career in addition to his banking activities. Aware of Adams' advanced age (he was now 87), and also, perhaps, holding some notion of gathering material for a memoir, he seems to have asked Adams for copies of some of the ex-President's writings which he did not possess. Adams replied on November 30, 1822:

A paroxysm of ill health which has confined me to my chamber for several days has prevented me from sooner acknowledging your favor of the 11 inst. I sincerely wish it were in my power to comply with your request by sending you copies of all my writings which have been printed. They have been so dull that they have fallen abortive from the press and have never made much fortune in the world. Louis XV of France is reported to have had one hundred and six children, but I believe he never kept a register of the wives and daughters that produced them. Probably he never saw ten of the children in his life. My little literary brats have been scattered about the world with as little caution. Many of them I have never seen since they were born. I have not a copy of the greatest part of them, and duplicates only of the enclosed. The volume of *Discourses on Davila* is out of print. From 1809 to 1812 or 1813, I wrote some account of my conduct under the Commission for Peace and my Embassy to Holland, but I have not a copy of them at my command. They were originally published in the *Boston Patriot*. My son says he cannot conceive how you can write upon the "Philosophy of Human Knowledge" without having something metaphysical in it. How much fame you may acquire by your book, I know not, but I venture to prophesy that you would make more profit by arguing one cause at the bar, or filling one writ in your office, than you or I shall make by all the books we have ever written or may write. American books do not sell in America. With my best love to Mrs. Johnson and all the family.

The question posed by J. Q. Adams about a book on "Human Knowledge" without "something metaphysical in it," apparently provoked the brash rejoinder from Johnson which John Adams refers to in the beginning of his next letter. It also gave Adams an opportunity to indicate that he, too, knew something about philosophy and philosophers. "If I agree with you," he wrote, that "human knowledge ceases where metaphysics commence," I must acknowledge that I am indebted to metaphysics for the knowledge of this truth. After reading Locke and Malebranche, Berkeley and Hume, Clark and Leibniz, Condillac and Baxter-Stewart and Brown have produced a pretty clear conviction of it.

Adams, in this letter could not resist a sly dig at Johnson for his neglect of his law practice:

> Your propensity to writing perhaps prevents you from having as many writs as you wish. I am pretty well informed that you have business as a lawyer, and might have more if you were more easily and constantly to be found.
>
> There is hardly a poet to be found who has not been made a poet by grief, mortification, poverty and hunger, and I never knew a lawyer who became eminent in his profession without the stimulus of want. You are too happy to be a laborious lawyer, with a lovely wife and five children [Adams was in error, there were at this point only four], venerable parents and an independent fortune. What motive can you have to be a drudging pack-horse as I have been, and as your Uncle, J. Q. A., has been and still is?

Referring again to Johnson's request for copies of his own writings, Adams continued:

> If my life and writings should ever be worth enquiring for, I know not what way anyone can take to pursue the investigations. I have destroyed no papers but anonymous letters and letters from madmen. I shall leave all my papers entire, I hope, but the huge mass of them will present such a bundle of weakness, and error and petulance, that I shudder at the thought of them; but I have one consolation, that they will present no crimes more than the Emperor Napoleon says he committed.

Adams concluded, "We are all well, as is, excepting the incurable distemper of age. I hope neither this letter nor yours are last words."

The letters between Utica and Quincy were now being exchanged on an almost weekly basis. The remark about Johnson being hard to find (Adams' informant is not known), caused Johnson to note in his memoirs that Abigail had denied the charge and had said that "with a diagram of Utica before her, she could point to the very spot I was in at any period of the twenty-four hours." Johnson says he relayed this testimony to Quincy in his next letter—along, apparently, with many questions and observations on the past and the changing times. Adams replied in a jocular vein:

Your letter of the twenty-sixth of December just now received has thrown me into a kind of frolicsome mixture of gaiety and gravity which has raised my spirits. I am glad you are so fond of Swift. I know of no man who has exhibited stronger proofs of a sound rational mind and profound information on one hand, or of wanton fun on the other; even his indecent drollery is instructive and even moral. Voltaire is another such compound of wisdom and folly, whose writings may be read by prudent persons with great pleasure and profit. They are vastly more improving to me than the solemn pomposity of Hume and Gibbon.

I am very glad Abby always knows where to find you. I wish I always knew where to find myself. Your Albany Grecians have most unexpectedly dragged me into the newspapers, and I am in danger of being involved in an endless controversy about the honor of making the loans in Holland, and about the honor of furnishing Robert Morris with funds for supporting his banking systems and other financial operations. Your New York Knickerbockers may justly boast of the services rendered by their mother country to our country, more than she has ever had credit for or ever will; for the two nations of England and France and the Anglomanes and Francomanes in America have conspired together to throw it into the background, and bring into oblivion the friendship of Holland to the United States of America.

The letter books of General and President Washington are sacred mysteries not yet revealed to the world; whenever they shall be I am persuaded they will do no dishonor or discredit to his character. I shall never live to see the time. What can the matter be? What a rattling, and cackling and clattering, there is about the future Presidency, two years hence! There seems to be four wild horses tugging at the Presidential chair, to draw it at the same time East, West, North and South. It seems like a conclave of cardinals intriguing for the election of a Pope, everyone under the influence of some crowned potentate, or like the election of a King of Poland by Palatines, each in the pay of Russia, Austria, France, Prussia, or England. This system will last as long as God pleases. You will think this letter the ravings of dotage, as indeed it is. Now I have the last word, and you have the power, if you please, of getting the last word of this.

Johnson, aside from his concern with the New York State Constitution, had shown little interest in politics, but it would have been difficult to avoid the subject in any correspondence with John Adams at this time, for the latter's son was one of those "four wild horses tugging at the presidential chair." The other three were Andrew Jackson, a westerner, with Henry Clay and William Crawford representing the "southern interests." The "clinking and clattering" was to end in the failure of all of the candidates to win a majority, with the prize finally going to John Quincy Adams after a historic vote in the House of Representatives. John Adams' reference to the "honor of making loans in Holland" and the "honor" of aiding Robert Morris, the great financier of the American Revolution, was occasioned by the frantic efforts of John Quincy Adams' opponents to discredit him by sniping at his father's record. At this point, Adams' Utica correspondent, pleased by the length and intimacy of the letter from Quincy, began to preserve copies of his own part in the correspondence, thus making it easier to place the replies in context. A number of Johnson's letters provoked some gentle irony from the Quincy patriarch—irony which, in some cases, may have escaped the younger man. For example, in a letter written in February 1823 Johnson, still a bit of an English snob, had remarked to Adams:

> When you were in France, negotiating the treaty of independence, I believe you lived some part of the time at Passy, in a house of LeRay de Chaumont. The elder, or rather, I believe, the only son of that gentleman had occasion a few days since to converse with me on some business, in which he was led to speak particularly of various pots and kettles in the manufacturing of which his father is engaged on his property at Le Raysville. The fine and strongly marked French features of the son led me to imagine so forcibly the situation of the family when you knew them in France that I could not repress a smile when I thought how curiously our country revolutionizes the feelings and manners of Europeans.

Adams did not share Johnson's amusement over a French aristocrat's preoccupation with pots and kettles. "I lived for some years" he replied, "in the basse cour de Monsieur Le Ray de Chaumont, that is the ancient Hotel de Valentinois, a spacious palace at Passy. Yet Mr. de Chaumont was not above manufacturers in cotton or in stone. I hope his son and grandson will succeed in their iron manufactories and in all their other interests." In the same letter Adams took a rather light-hearted view of Johnson's passion for great books. "Of making and reading books," he philosophized, there is no end, and therefore it is hardly worth while to make a beginning, except for the necessary purposes of common life. I never have been afraid of a book. . . . Excepting a gratification of curiosity, I know not whether they have ever done me good or harm. They have made little alteration in my natural sentiments, opinions, or feelings. You would be surprised perhaps at the catalogue. Hobbes and Mandeville have found a perfect antidote to their poison in Bishop Butler, Doctor Clark, Doctor Tillotson, and twenty other writers. Voltaire, Rousseau, Diderot, Delambert, Frederick, King of Prussia, and Baron de Grimm have found a complete confutation in the contemplation of the heavens and the earth. The primitive world of Court de Gébelin, Bryant's Mythology, Dupries' Universal Religion and Volney's new researches into the history of ancient nations have not converted me to their system of philosophy.

Sir William Jones's works have excited a curiosity for oriental literature which can never be gratified. I wish our missionaries would import and translate Sanscrit and Persian books. We should possibly learn something useful from them that we do not know which might somewhat abate our bigotry. I would not advise you to indulge so wild a passion for reading as I have done, though it has neither done me good or harm, except as medicine for ennui.

In his next letter, John Adams continued in this vein.

I will pursue an idea suggested in my last. I do sincerely wish that the mandarins of China, the Brahmins of Hindustan, the priests of Japan and of Persia, could be influenced with the same zeal *de propaganda fide* as the Roman Catholics and Calvinists of the day are for propagating their creeds and ceremonies. I wish they would form into societies, open their purses, contribute their diamonds, pearls, and precious stones as liberally as our people do their treasures, for the translating their sacred books into English, French, Italian, Spanish, and German, and send missionaries to propagate them through all Europe and all America, north and south. We might then know what the religions really are of the great part of the world. We know as little of them now as of the religion of the inhabitants of Sirius the Dog Star.

But, *sobrius esto,* Stop! Pause! Let us consider what would be the consequence—what would our Christian theologians, from the Pope to Zinzindorf, Swedenborg, Wesley down to Mr. Moffit, say of these learned priests if they were to appear with their Brahma, and Veda, and Zoroaster, and Confucius, entering among their parishioners and congregations, and zealously laboring to make converts among them! Do you think these reverend gentlemen would be tolerant enough to permit them? Would they be content to preach and write them down, or would they try to inflame the civil power, or raise its arm of flesh and strength to drive them out?

Johnson returned Adams' compliments, and launched into an enthusiastic disquisition on prejudice. "I admire your liberality," he wrote Adams:

It is a noble characteristic of our nation that it possesses religious toleration. But I am so cynical that I attribute this blessing less to a spirit of enlarged philanthropy than to a partial necessity. If any denomination of Christians had been sufficiently numerous to control, I fear they would not have had charity or philosophy enough to tolerate dissenters. We find that the constitutions of many of our states authorize an exclusion from honors, etc. of those who disbelieve in revelation, and the liberality of some states attends to Protestants only. If any man is void of prejudice in these matters I claim to be he. As a Christian I would be glad to see all mankind Christians—nay, Presbyterians; but so long as they will not, I should rejoice to see everywhere a toleration in which the mosque and the synagogue, the pagoda and the church, should be harmoniously located alongside of each other. I would contribute this moment to the erection of any one of them if any persons were desirous of worshiping therein. And now, Sir, I have said more on this delicate subject than I ever said before, for I hold to a maxim that of such matters I may think often but speak seldom. I treat a man, in relation to his prejudices, as I treat him in relation to the corns which afflict his feet. I know that few men are without corns. They may not be on this toe or that, but so long as I am not apprised on which they are, I fear to press against any. Except for this, I would venture a few remarks on some other prejudices, for I think we have civil as well as religious prejudices. The whites exclude the blacks from offices of honor and profit, nay, in many cases from the right of suffrage; the rich act in some degree the same towards the poor; and native citizens the like to citizens who are only naturalized. And I believe from my heart that the blacks, the poor, and the naturalized, would exclude the whites, the rich, and the natives, if they were equally able.

But prejudices do not end with governments and religions. They enter into our families, accompany us to bed, and meet us when we rise up. I will particularize only two of this description, and that because I am much under its influence. When we see, say, a young woman, that is related in the second degree to an ancestor who has signalized himself in the creation of an empire more extensive than Caesar's and more practically free than that which ever entered into the imagination of an Utopian, and who, after enjoying its greatest honors, is contented in a little village with the plain life of a country gentleman, and who at an age to which few men attain can amuse himself with the light conversation of his neighbors, and with writing pleasant letters, we cannot help feeling, towards a young woman so connected, a degree of complacency beyond what her attractions, however great, could otherwise excite. This prejudice will, I hope, live forever—and my wife says, Amen.

Johnson's pleasant conceit about Abigail brought a cheerful "Amen" in return from Adams, and a compliment on Johnson's "liberal philosophy and the large scale of your religion." He did not, however, share the Utican's enthusiasm for the Presbyterians. "The Presbytery," he wrote,

have too much authority in matters of faith, like that which is claimed by the Episcopal Church, And the doctrine of both are too Calvinistical for me, as well as too hierarchical. I believe I go the whole length with you in your expansive benevolence in religious matters. I have immortalized my name to a motion in our late Convention in this State that "all men of all religions, behaving peaceably and submitting to the laws, should have equal privileges, civil and religious, in society." The Convention did not agree to my motion, but I am the more proud of it for that.

You sport very pleasantly with prejudices, and with great reason, but I believe you have stronger and earlier prejudices in favor of the blooming charms of your Abigail than for the fading laurels of her withered old grandfather.

In Voltaire's works you will find an inexhaustable source of entertainment. You will find chaff and trash, and froth and filth. These you will despise and pass over but if you think fit to amuse yourself even one moment with these you will find sparkles of wit. No man ever lived who had so much wit as Voltaire. His wit has attracted readers in all nations, and it has enabled him to propagate the spirit of toleration in religion more than all the other writers in the eighteenth century. He was a Napoleon in Literature. It seems as if Providence made it a rule never to give us a great man capable of doing us great good, without vices, follies, and extravagances which occasion what we call great evils. The progress of a great man through the world scatters desolation at the same time it bestows great blessings. A future state will set all right. Without the supposition of a future state, I can make nothing of this Universe but a chaos, notwithstanding its stupendous magnificence, and apparent sublime order. Next to Voltaire in wit and trash is Dr. Swift.

For Johnson the exchange of letters with John Adams was becoming something more than a means of collecting samples of the wit and wisdom of the second President of the United States. He was also using it as a kind of literary self-improvement exercise, matching his philosophy and style against that of the old gentleman in Quincy, trying to outdo him at times, and delighted, certainly, to be told that he had "sported pleasantly" with an idea.

In one of his replies to a letter from John Adams Johnson apparently felt called upon to defend his allegiance to the Presbyterian Church which he had joined after his marriage to Abigail. "In attaching myself to a church," he wrote Adams, "I did not scan doctrines but discipline. . . . to become a Presbyterian in this region is like a formal notice to the world that your conduct and conversation are to be more rigidly correct than that of ordinary men: that slander, irascibility, misanthropy, uncharitableness, revenge, dissipation, covetousness, etc., are not to be indulged in or secretly practiced in any instance."

Johnson's smugness on this issue was too much for John Adams, and he sent back an immediate and irate rejoinder. "Of all the whips, spurs and bridles," he wrote,

> those of the priests are the most detestable, and those of the Presbyterians are not much better than those of the Episcopal hierarchy, and none of them are much better than those of the Whydah, Ashantee or North American Osages and Cherokees. I set at defiance all ecclesiastical authority, all their creeds, confessions and ex-communications. They have no authority over me more than I have over them. I value more your maxims than all their bulls. I thank them for all the good advice they give me and am willing to pay them for it; but I choose to judge for myself whether it is good or not.

Having delivered this stinging manifesto, Adams abruptly changed the subject. "What think you of the present state of the world?" he asked.

> What think you of the steamboat navigation of the Ganges, the Nile, and the Niger—especially the Mississippi, the Missouri, and the Columbia? Have you read Major Long's *Expedition Up the Rocky Mountains?* But especially what do you think of the conspiracy of kingcraft and priestcraft against human nature? What think you of that mighty member of Mr. Worcester's Peace Society and his modest claims on the North American coast on the Pacific Ocean? I shall not long contemplate these dismal prospects, but I advise all who are to live many

years to collect themselves and prepare their hearts and their minds for the worst.*

Johnson dropped the subject of the Presbyterians in his next letter to Adams. As for Worcester, Tsar Alexander, and the other "dismal prospects" that disturbed Adams, Johnson reminded Adams that there were plenty of problems to worry about right in Utica. "I know fifty men in this village," he replied,

who would divest the remaining inhabitants of houses and lands if it could be effected by simply taking possession after the manner of the Emperor of Russia. We have at least ten husbands, and as many fathers, who possess no authority beyond their own hearths, and who rule there more despotically than it ever entered into the head of Alexander to desire. Even our boys seem infected with the same spirit, and I have thought that a Quixote or a Hercules might find more adventures than he could easily achieve if he were to walk our streets and attempt to correct the different acts of injustice that the children of nine years commit towards those of six. I hope our neighbors, the fowls and fishes, the quadrupeds and multipedes, conduct their intercourse with more self-denial, but I every day observe facts to make me doubt the truth of the position. I will venture to even say that a microscope would exhibit in the nose of Alexander heroes as active and ambitious of territory as the Emperor himself. What then is to be done in this world, which we cannot mend?

Johnson concluded these speculations by noting that the King of England, like Adams, had "just presented his nation with the gift of a valuable library. I hope," he added, "he will imitate you still farther, and the farther the better."

Adams' letters were becoming briefer. In his next, dated May 10, 1823, he recommended two biographies of Napoleon by O'Meara and

* Noah Worcester (1758–1837) was a New Hampshire Congregationalist minister and founder of a magazine, *The Friends of Peace,* which began publication in 1818. His major literary work, a pacifist tract entitled *A Solemn Review of the Custom of War,* was translated into several languages when it appeared in 1814, and attracted the attention of Tsar Alexander I of Russia whose "International League of Peace," or "Holy Alliance," caused Worcester to write numerous flattering articles about him. When the "mighty member" began to make threatening gestures toward the northwest coast of America, however, Worcester denounced him as an "enemy of peace." The Tsar's "modest claims on the North American coast" were all but forgotten shortly after Adams' letter was written, when new boundary lines were set by treaty.

Las Casas, placing the French leader far above Alexander, Caesar, Nebuchadnezzar, and "Zinges" Khan. "As a legislator, a hero and a conqueror," wrote Adams, "he was greater than them all, and a much better man." Adams dismissed Johnson's grievances against Utica, saying he knew "little about its inhabitants," though he was concerned about their political learnings in the forthcoming presidential election. "I understand," he wrote,

> they are good friends of the southern interest and much good may their political faith do them. I presume they have a reasonable quantity of New York antipathy to New England. I hope, however, they will be blessed and become a great city. Even my grandson, De Windt, is seasoned with the spice of contempt for New England and a reasonable admiration for the southern statesmen.

Adams was quite right about the growing sentiment in the Utica area in favor of "southern interests," and also on the matter of the "antipathy to New England." The majority of Utica's more influential citizens were lining up with Crawford against John Quincy Adams, and the old New England power structure, strongly Federalist in its sympathies, was being diluted by a new breed of tradesmen and entrepreneurs more recently arrived from New Jersey, Pennsylvania, and New York City, along with working-class immigrants from Ireland, Wales, Germany, etc., who had been lured by growing industry and construction work on the Erie Canal. The New Englanders, whom James Fenimore Cooper accused of "converting that district of country into an Eastern colony," were losing their grip—and so was the magic name of Adams. And although as Dixon Ryan Fox had noted in his *Decline of Aristocracy in the Politics of New York* (New York, 1965), "it was not considered elegant to be a democrat in Utica," Jacksonian democracy was on the march, and the Federalist castle of Oneida County would soon crumble before the onslaught.

Johnson quickly read O'Meara on Napoleon, but confessed in his next letter that he skipped over the pages that described the Battle of Waterloo out of "a morbid sensitivity which makes me avoid any recitals that attack my feelings." However, on the matter of Utica's politics, he replied carefully to Adams' questions:

> You advert to the politics of our village. It, as well as our whole state, is at the present much under the influence of Mr. Van Buren, our Senator in Congress. He possesses showy talents, much ambition,

caution, and management, and with all a good moral character. He went to Washington the fall before last for the first time, and with a mind unbiased in relation to the question of president, and determined to preserve a neutrality until he should be able to satisfy himself which is the strongest candidate. He has found his neutrality to be difficult, and I think he evidently leans towards Crawford. Our state will probably be regulated by his management, though in a caucus at Washington there will not be a unanimity of votes among our delegation. I am not, however, very deep in politics. To obtain in this region a popular office requires a personal management for which I feel neither qualified nor disposed. But I am in this matter wholly yours and so you must consider me in most things.

Whether or not Johnson's final statement in this letter was hypocritical, or merely simple deference to his grandfather-in-law, is a matter for conjecture, but the fact is that within a very few years Johnson would emerge as one of the staunchest of the Utica Jacksonians, and a firm upholder of the "southern interests."

This was the last of Johnson's intimate exchanges with John Adams for some time to come, and from now on his focus would shift to the new presidential candidate, John Quincy Adams, who was soon, largely by default, to become president. A possible reason for the ensuing silence from Quincy appears in a letter Johnson received in September from Abigail's sister, Susan B. Clark, who was staying with her grandfather at the time. John Quincy Adams and family, she said, had arrived earlier from Washington and "since then there have been few leisure moments." Besides, there was the incident of the Cunningham letters. In Susan Clark's words:

At present, public and private attention has been arrested by the explosion of the long threatened mine, which is to blow up all Mr. Adams' claims to the next Presidency. I allude to the correspondence between my Grandfather and the late William Cunningham, which has just made its appearance in print. These letters were written under the strictest injunctions of secrecy. They disclose the real characters of many individuals whom the public have been accustomed to idolize, and my Grandfather never intended to wound the feelings of their connections by a disclosure.

This Mr. Cunningham, in a fit of insanity, destroyed his own life, and the letters have fallen into the hands of the political enemies of both father and son, and they have given them to the world, perfidiously violating the engagements of fidelity which were made at the period of the correspondence. It is said the public are already disgusted with this breach of confidence, and that the effects resulting from the disclosure will be totally different from what has been anticipated by the Crawford party. I send you a newspaper with the first number of the "Remarks upon the Correspondence." The writer has enclosed two numbers to my Grandfather, "with the sincere hope that the pain which cannot but have been occasioned by gross breach of trust in the publication of his private letters may be, in a great degree, diminished by the veneration which it will call forth for the greatness of his public character, and the anxiety which it will disclose for the happiness of his remaining years."

Johnson added a footnote to Susan Clark's story of the Cunningham letters.

Thomas Jefferson, on the above occasion, made a happy use of it by writing to President Adams that he heard of the publication (his name had been freely used therein), but that President Adams might be assured he had never read a word of the publication and never would.

The historic letter from Jefferson to which Johnson refers, (and of which Adams himself exclaimed, "The best letter that was ever written. . . . How generous! How noble! How magnanimous!") concluded as follows:

It would be strange indeed if, at our years, we were to go an age back to hunt up imaginary, or forgotten facts, to disturb the repose of affections so sweetening to the evening of our lives. Be assured, my dear Sir, that I am incapable of receiving the slightest impression from the effort now made to plant thorns on the pillow of age, worth, and wisdom, and to sow tares between friends who have been such for near half a century. Beseeching you then not to suffer your mind to be disquieted by this wicked attempt to poison its peace, and praying you to throw it by, among things which have never happened, I add sincere assurances of my unabated and constant attachment, friendship and respect.

Despite the excitement in Quincy, and the ties that bound him to one of the "four wild horses" in the forthcoming national election, Johnson seems to have retreated, for the time being at least, back into his "very small circle"—a circle about to be enlarged by the birth of another son, new civic and domestic responsibilities, and a spate of correspondence with those all-but-forgotten "connections" he had left behind in Europe nearly a quarter of a century ago.

CHAPTER 8

1823–1824

Public and Private Events

WILLIAM CLARKSON JOHNSON, born July 16, 1823, was named after the recently deceased son of Sarah Adams' sister, Belinda Clarkson, and there is no record of any correspondence between Utica and Quincy concerning his arrival. Johnson did, however, inform Mrs. Clarkson of the event, hinting in his note that Abigail had not weathered her fifth confinement as well as usual.

Shortly after the boy's birth, the village of Utica joined in the mighty celebration that attended the opening of the Erie Canal, and Johnson, who had "assisted in the construction of the work by supplying several of the contractors with funds," joined the throng gathered along the route between Utica and Rome as De Witt Clinton and other public figures "passed in boats along the whole completed line, receiving ovations from the shore in almost continuous jubilation." The scene Johnson watched was enthusiastically described in a letter to the Albany *Advertiser* by "two gentlemen from Utica":

A boat had been prepared at Rome, and as the waters came down the Canal you might mark their progress by that of this new Argo which floated triumphantly down the Hellespont of the West, accompanied by the shouts of the people, and having on her deck a military band. The Governor and a company of friends were received on board by the band with a roll of the drum. From bridge to bridge, from village to village, the procession was saluted with cannon, and every bell swung as with instinctive life. At Whitesboro, a number of young ladies embarked, and heightened by their smiles a scene that wanted but this to make it complete.

Johnson rose to the occasion with a letter to De Witt Clinton in Albany—a masterpiece of Johnsonian panegyric which must have impressed the vain and wordy New York governor. "Permit me," he began, "to share the excitement which your metropolis is so laudably experiencing, and to mingle with the collected gratulations of a great city the feeble voice of a distant and obscure individual."

After this sonorous beginning, the cadences continued to swell:

> Unfortunately for the present festive occasion, the theme of our rejoicing is too sublime to admit of exaggeration and its consequences are too diffuse for fanciful extension. Nay, the most sober detail of truth is in danger of meeting with incredulity: I lately saw on the canal the conveyance by a pair of young and small oxen of a raft which weighed more than 196 tons, yet I can scarcely credit my own relation, and I would not venture to make it where canal navigation is unknown.

Nothing could stop Johnson now. Metaphor and simile gushed from his pen in tribute to the two great wonders of the age—Fulton's steamboat, and Clinton's Canal:

> One, like Leviathan, makes the sea as a pot of ointment, and unites nation to nation; the other, like Behemoth, drinks up the rivers at a draught and connects city to city. The first, with all the vigor of manhood, and with more than the fabled efficiency of Hercules, is subduing the monsters of national prejudice and enmities; the other, with the retired graces of a matron, is clothing her household in scarlet, and binding together the busy members of a great family—at once the cause of all life and all the pleasures with which she is surrounded.

Johnson ended his letter with the prophecy that Clinton would "transmit to posterity a fame as durable as the land you have enriched."

De Witt Clinton replied gracefully, praising both the letter and its sender, and suggesting that Johnson was perhaps not quite as "distant and obscure" an individual as he claimed. "Your very obliging and well-written letter," replied the governor, "was received with great satisfaction. The favorable opinion of enlightened men has always been cultivated by me with peculiar solicitude, as at once the evidence and the reward of merit—and from my knowledge of your talents and acquirements, I have no hesitation in ranking you in this class."

Johnson was now worth, he calculated, exactly $72,516.47; and as a gentleman of means and influence, he began to take a proprietary interest in elevating the cultural and intellectual tone of the community, as well as in its economic welfare—being careful, however, to avoid commitments that might involve major financial risks. In the late fall of 1823, for example, he proposed to President Henry Davis of Hamilton College that the trustees of the college raise $20,000 to establish a law professorship for his old friend, Judge Jonas Platt, offering to contribute to the cause an unstated sum himself. Davis, hard-pressed for funds to keep his struggling, eleven-year-old institution afloat, countered with the suggestion that Johnson lead a fund-raising drive in Utica for that purpose—an offer Johnson rejected on the grounds that he had "no leisure time." Henry Gibson, cashier of the Ontario Bank in Canandaigua, also suggested that Johnson lead a money-raising drive in Utica—this one to obtain subscribers for stock in a branch canal to connect Canandaigua with the Erie Canal. Johnson replied that he was not interested in any effort which would "discomfort me with solicitude," but sent a check for $50 to Gibson as a personal contribution. A somewhat ironic acknowledgment from Gibson greatly embarrassed Johnson, who said later, "I see an absurdity in my offering $50 as a contribution to such an undertaking."

As 1823 drew to a close Johnson, however, did find a good and inexpensive cause to which he could contribute time and effort, and one which he felt would broaden Utica's intellectual horizons: namely the Utica Lyceum. For some years now, Johnson had been reading in British publications of the rise of such organizations as The London Institute for the Diffusion of Science, Literature and the Arts, and The Glasgow Mechanics' Institution—both founded by Dr. George Birkbeck, a Scottish reformer and educator. Some two years later, a New Englander named Josiah Holbrook, of Millsbury, Massachusetts, would issue a manifesto in the January 1826 issue of the *American Journal of Education,* calling for the establishment throughout America of "Lyceums" modeled on these British prototypes, but A. B. Johnson and his fellow Uticans had already anticipated Holbrook. John Adams in a letter written to Johnson in 1824 expressed the hope that "the Utica movement" would spread.

Johnson was elected president of the new organization in February 1824, and on the fifth of that month he delivered his inaugural address. It was a tribute to "natural philosophy," which he defined as "whatever the senses can discover." People, he pointed out, may differ in their ability to use their senses, but "the eye of the true natural philosopher dignifies all that it discovers, and his ear converts to melody the croak of the boding raven, or the midnight screech of an ominous owl." To the "natural philosopher," he continued, "the globe is a widespread

theater, and all which it inhabit, actors that administer to his enjoyment."
He exhorted the new Lyceum to work at the "discovery of phenomena,"
and to make "a correct discrimination between the truths of nature and
the creatures of men's imagination."

Among those who missed the speech was John Adams' friend
Adrian Van der Kemp, whom he had urged Johnson to meet in his letter
concerning the Wilkinson trial. Johnson sent Van der Kemp a copy of
the address, and thus began a correspondence which for many years
would provide Johnson with the kind of witty and intelligent criticism
he could respect. Van der Kemp acknowledged Johnson's address,
calling it, "correct, luminous, and, as far as I can discover, unexceptionable." He added:

> If a Cato revived, if Newton's and Leibnitz's steps are pressed, and
> your country benefited by it, Utica shall claim the glory in our western
> parts, and the name of A. B. Johnson shall not be forgotten. You have
> done your duty. You will not rest till you have reached the top of the
> arduous scientific rock, always keeping in mind that, though rugged
> and steep, it is the rock of salvation.

Van der Kemp, as he often did later, had a reservation. He didn't like
that "boding raven."

Simeon DeWitt Bloodgood also sent a long letter to Johnson
congratulating him on his achievement at the Utica Lyceum, and Johnson replied with a dissertation on the subject of "praise":

> Praise is, however, salutary only where the receiver is too strong to be
> subdued by its inebriation; in which case praise, like a vanquished
> demon of romance, becomes a faithful slave, and enables the recipient
> to defy fatigue and dissipate aversion in the creation of some fabric that
> will overlook the earth and peer above the clouds. Praise is new to
> me, but I hope it will never be a stranger to you; for I am confident
> that you can merit the reception of it and bear its stimulation.

Johnson, himself, viewed his first appearance in Utica as a public
savant with modest pride. What pleased him about his speech was its
brevity. "The discourse," he said, "could no more have been made
large than a miniature could be made large. "This remark," he added,
"will apply to most of my writings, and they should be so understood
by the readers of them."

On a cold late winter night in 1823 Bryan and Leah Johnson,

accompanied by Johnson, Abigail, and some of their grandchildren, went to hear an "amateur oratorio" at Trinity Church in Utica. They were attracted to the event by the fact that James Henry Hackett, a local storekeeper and a member of Trinity's congregation, was to perform, along with his wife, "an admirable vocalist," and his sister, Mrs. Sharpe. Hackett, a graduate of Columbia University with a talent for the stage, had come to Utica a year before Johnson arrived, and had established a not very successful grocery store and wholesale outlet for earthenware imported from Scotland. As an actor, his forte was imitating the great stage figures of the period, particularly Edmund Kean; and, together with his wife and sister, he provided Uticans with their first semi-professional entertainment, thus securing, in Hackett's own words, "immediate passport for myself and wife into the best society." It was to be Hackett's last performance before leaving for New York, where he made an unsuccessful attempt at importing Holland gin, but later, "yielding to a natural talent for the stage," became one of New York's best-loved actors, especially in the role of Falstaff. John Quincy Adams became a friend and admirer of Hackett's, and there is an exchange of letters between the two in Hackett's *Notes and Comments Upon Certain Plays and Actors of Shakespeare With Criticisms and Correspondence* (New York, 1863). At one point during his New York career, Hackett was persuaded by Adams to play Lear—which he did, with disastrous results. He also became the founder of America's first theatrical family. His son, James K. Hackett, born in New York, appeared in the 1920s in such post–World War I plays as *The Better 'Ole* and *Out There*.

The Johnson family arrived early at the church to be sure of getting good seats, but found the door locked. Johnson described the incident:

> The weather was very cold and we knocked at the door to obtain admittance, but were told the door was not to be opened till a time which had not yet arrived. . . . The Rector at length came to the door and opened it ajar, to ascertain what the knocking meant. We spoke to him and told him we wanted to be admitted; but as soon as he learnt the purport of the knocking, he rudely shut the door again and excluded us. We felt indignant at this incivility, and my father said he would not wait, but would return home. Soon after he had gone, one of his servants came in haste and said my father was taken quite ill. I immediately started to go to him, and as our family physician lived by the way, I made him go with me. When we arrived my father had partially recovered, but he was still laboring for breath. I forget what remedies, if any, were applied; but the same symptoms recurred, and

occasionally they would seize him at night while he was asleep in bed, and he would have to start out of bed to avoid suffocation. Thus continued his condition till the twelfth of April 1824 when he died.

Shortly after his bereavement Johnson drew up a carefully detailed account of his father's last moments—a practice he would continue after many subsequent deaths in his family. He omitted none of Bryan's final symptoms, and reported fully on his father's medical history during the last years of his life. Woven into the painful narration, however, were details that provide a touching memorial to this early Utica pioneer, who was always, he said, "as affectionate a father as ever lived."

> At noon my son Alexander dined with him, and I visited him for the last time between five and six o'clock in the evening. He was always fond of talking to my children, and the last speech he made me about them was to inform me that Alexander had dined with him, and that he had to give him a cent before Alexander would consent to have his shoe tied. My father then found the other shoe was untied, but Alexander refused to have it tied till he received another cent.

Johnson spoke of his father's character, stressing, of course, his abstemiousness:

> He was a man of excellent judgment, of great activity of intellect and of profound knowledge of man. . . . Up to the middle of his life, his temper was irascible; but within the last twenty years he acquired a complete control over it, and I saw not any disposition to anger. He was very abstemious and scarcely ever tasted any drink stronger than table beer made at home. His principle and usual drink was water. Wine and spirituous liquors he never touched unless he sometimes drank a class of currant wine of his own making. Tobacco he never used in any form, and he was invariably truthful.

His father's death, said Johnson, "wholly unmanned me," adding, "I had during my whole life taken his advice on all subjects and scarcely considered myself a man—so dependent had I always felt on his counsel." An attendant took from Bryan's body the "gold shirt-sleeve buttons that he had always worn" and gave them to the son, who "took them as the last gift of my father, and I have worn them myself ever since, as a perpetual memorial of a loss never to be supplied." Johnson also gave locks of his father's "snow-white hair" to several of his friends, and placed on Bryan's tombstone the following epitaph:

Here lies Bryan Johnson, the lamented father of Alexander B. Johnson. He was a native of England. His mercantile enterprise gave Utica its first impulse. For paternal affection he had no equal; for knowledge of the ways of men no superior. His life was abstemious and cheerful, his death instantaneous, on the twelfth of April, 1824; in the seventy-fifth year of his age, and in the vigorous possession of all his faculties.

Johnson's statement that he was "wholly unmanned" by his father's death was exaggerated, judging from the variety of his activities during the next few months, but there is no doubt that his relationship with his father had been, as one of Johnson's obituary writers put it, "beautiful and affecting." There was, however, an aftermath of Johnson's bereavement that is of special interest.

Reference has been made to Johnson's failure to keep in touch with his relatives overseas after promising in 1801 to remain close to them; and also to his disconcerting denial of their existence in his letter on the rights of naturalized citizens to Nathan Williams. Johnson remained silent on this subject in his autobiography save for one or two ambiguous references; but privately, perhaps even clandestinely for a while, he began, after his father's death, a voluminous correspondence with his overseas family. His most revealing exchange was with his cousin Rachel Robinson.

At some point just before or during Bryan's last illness, Johnson received a letter from Rachel telling of her mother's death and imploring him to write about his life in America. The letter began, "Dear Cousin Zalick." Johnson did not answer immediately, but when his father died he wrote her of the event. In May 1824 he received a reply with "Zalick" omitted from the salutation. After commiserating with him on his loss, Rachel quoted him as asking for more news of "myself and the incidents of my life"—and she proceeded to provide it. She was living in Brussels and had entered into an export-import business which had been successful at first, but was now languishing. She had established a connection with the royal family in Brussels, and enclosed a poem she had dedicated to Queen Frederika Wilhelmina. She hoped to found a school "to teach the English and the French language, but there were certain difficulties," having to do with her religious affiliation. From this point on Rachel's letter was heavily censored by Johnson, with black ink lines drawn through key phrases. For example: "My ——— ———, the tenets of which I so publicly and proudly adhere to, would not, I think be an obstacle to such a plan, though that part of the country which is not Catholic is pretty ——— ———. How are such ——— ——— in the United States?" The letter ended with an expression of Rachel's love for Leah, "the companion of my own dear mother." She added wistfully, "I think of their little amusements, of their card parties, of their visiting—and my tears fall. I say with you, 'these things are strange.' You too, my cousin, have your own cares—a 'gray-haired man' of your age!"

Johnson wrote again, enclosing a silhouette of his father, several locks of his own and Abigail's hair, the epitaph he wrote for his father, and copies of two of his speeches. "All of these precious relics," Rachel wrote a few weeks later, "were deposited with some letters from my mother, and some blades of grass from the ground that covers my Edwin." She enclosed two locks of her own hair—"fair samples, as you requested, cut from different parts of my head." In answer to his demand that she tell him "pretty exactly the effect time has had on me," Rachel went into considerable detail. One can only conjecture as to what else Johnson's own letter contained, but it must have touched a sensitive nerve, and one full page of her reply is again heavily censored. What emerges in part, is this:

> With what sentiments of pain did I observe your reference to ———.
> ——— Where are you, my cousin? Where is the reasoning youth I once knew? . . . But you, my cousin, possess a solid edifice whose foundations are laid on stone! Is it possible you have ——— quitted it for one raised on rolling sands? Or do you dwell in the tottering structure that it may screen you from the torrents of ——— which even your Republic appears not exempt from? But in that case, my cousin, it is purest hypocrisy. . . . Oh how painful is the labyrinth of doubt in which I am as regards your ———!

Johnson remained silent for some time after receiving this outburst, for in Rachel's next letter, written eight months later, she said:

> I know not how my last letter was received by you—that long oration of my opinions, or whether the friendship so many years latent and so recently called forth has been proof against my animadversions on what in you I think is blamable; or whether it can no longer be agreeable to you to correspond with one who differs from you in ———
> ———.

Despite his silence and her doubts, Rachel persisted. Her "pecuniary situation had deteriorated," and she had no money to care for her father, Jonathan (Jonathan appended a note in which he listed his various needs). She had heard of the election of John Quincy Adams, and assuming he was Abigail's father, added, "I congratulate you on being so closely connected with the person who is at the head of your Republic." She also enclosed an essay she had written entitled "Nature of the Atmosphere," and asked Johnson to present it for her to the new President. On the cover of her letter Johnson wrote: "Rachel Robinson— begs for her father."

Shortly thereafter, Rachel acknowledged a "kind" letter from Johnson and thanked him for its enclosure—a "bill on Havre for 261 francs for the use of my father." Despite her gratitude, however, she could not help referring once again to the forbidden topic. "I will, as you suggest," she said, "advert to the topic no more after telling you in truth and bitterness of my heart that your explanation has given me much pain." She added, as a family news item, that their mutual cousin, Sally Jonas, had two daughters. Johnson inked out their first names.

In subsequent letters Rachel tried hard to spare her cousin's feelings, but on the one or two occasions she forgot herself, she was as outspoken as ever. One gathers that Johnson brought the subject up again himself, however, for in one letter she wrote, "If you want me to unbosom myself to you entirely, write so to me . . . at present I can only tell you that be the cause virtue, enthusiasm, ambition, infatuation, or madness, the desire of pecuniary gain which your ——— ———and under which my ———." The rest is hidden under heavy ink. Several years later, after Johnson had sent her a copy of his *Treatise on Language,* she told him sadly, "If it were not for that ——— ——— to which conscientiously and according to my opinions I could not give currency, I would have your book printed in England and take on the expense and hazard of it myself, but as it is, it cannot be." In most cases, from this point of her indiscretions were mere slips of the tongue, as when she began a news item with, "On our return home, a young gentleman of our ——— religion. . . ."

As the correspondence continued, Johnson unburdened himself more and more to Rachel; and among other things, he seems to have complained about Utica and the "primitive manners" of its citizens. Rachel replied, "I cannot think Utica is the sphere Nature intended you to move in with all your philosophy. Lay your hand on your heart and ask if it be so." She also began to hint that he would be better off back in England or on the Continent.

Rachel's appeals for money began to disturb Johnson. Accordingly, he asked a friend, Eleazer Gidney, a Utica dentist who was going abroad, to call on Rachel and her father and look into their social and financial status. Gidney's account of his visit indicated that they seemed to be quite well off. Shortly before getting Gidney's report he had received a frantic appeal from Rachel for a hundred pound loan—"the last half hour has brought me a citation from the bailiff for the payment of house rent"—and Johnson now wrote and curtly informed her of Gidney's impression, omitting, as Rachel noted bitterly, his usual salutation, "My dear Cousin." Rachel reacted violently. Mr. Gidney, she wrote, was misled by circumstances. She had just formed "a second engagement" with an apparently affluent Mr. Vernimmen, though she still used the name Robinson for commercial purposes. When Gidney arrived she had introduced Vernimmen to him as "Mr. Robinson." She used the sub-terfuge, she said, because she knew that Gidney would "report on the kind of connections you had in Europe on his return to Utica." She concluded caustically, "It is not very likely that we would draw aside the veil which hid our ——— ———."

Mr. Vernimmen disappeared from Rachel's story, having reneged on his promise to become converted to Judaism and to marry Rachel—but not before fathering a daughter, Sophia.

The exchange of letters between Rachel and her American cousin continued. Hers were often abrasive, and would have added a dissonant and much too personal a note to the story Johnson wished his family to hear. His admiration for her, and his dependence upon her as an occasional outlet for his frustrations were obvious, however, and there were several tributes to her—one of them referring to an incident which took place during this period. Rachel sent him a play she had written which had been turned down by a London producer. Johnson thought it "very well written," and sent it on to the manager of the Park Theater in New York, who rejected it (and later lost it) with the com-ment, "Plays not having been first played in London with decided success are only a drug with us, and only produce trouble without profit." Johnson related this, he said, "as an item of the literary history of the time," but he identified Rachel only as "a female cousin of much culture and intellectual originality."

Johnson missed the daily walks and consultations with his father, and their sudden ending "obstructed my endeavors to come to any con-clusions in matters which involved much responsibility." As he made note of this he vowed that he would "never cast such an impediment on his sons," but would "throw the conduct of each on his own understand-ing." There was one immediate domestic problem, however, in which Johnson was forced to "come to conclusions"—a problem Johnson precipitated when he moved his widowed mother into the already crowded house on Genesee Street. As Johnson put it, the presence of Sarah Adams and Leah under one roof brought into play "the immutable law" which defines the "ill adaption of one house for more than one family." Johnson had faced the same problem earlier when, after his marriage, he moved his family and mother-in-law out of Bryan's house because of difficulties between Sarah and his parents. This time, however, with Leah a widow, the incompatibility between the two older women became even more evident, and Johnson no longer had his father around to talk things over with. One can only guess at the sources of the friction, but obviously Leah's ways were not Sarah's ways, and Sarah's were not Leah's.

His own mother, said Johnson, was a "uniformly cheerful and rather jocose woman, the most tender mother that nature ever exhibited." Sarah Adams, on the other hand, was proud, independent, haughty, and undoubtedly sensitive over her financial dependence on her son-in-law. Leah's devotion to her son amounted almost to an obsession—"she seemed to regard herself," he said, "as living only for me and my benefit . . . her affection for my children was equal to her affection for me." Leah fussed over him. She was "painfully solicitous" about his health, and "constantly inquiring into the sufficiency of my wearing apparel." She was also concerned about the money he spent on her, and became "painfully cautious in her expenses"—setting an example, no doubt, that Sarah, who had deemed his "fondness for money" a good thing when Abigail married him, must have found galling. Sarah was a product of the new world, married into a family that had helped to shape it. Leah was a newcomer of uncertain origins, speaking English still with difficulty, intimidated by the crudities of a frontier village, and thrust into a dry Presbyterian world which placed a premium on respectability, and which scorned the card playing which Rachel said Leah enjoyed, and the gossip and light-hearted laughter of her own kind. "She loved America and the Americans," wrote Johnson, "but she loved England and Englishmen better." When she first came to Utica, he wrote after her death, she occasionally "rode some miles into the country," but later "she rarely left the house except to walk to church or to my office." He added, "I believe she never saw either of the two bridges that cross the Mohawk River in our city."

When Sarah Adams died, Johnson wrote gently and circumspectly about her, but, reading between the lines one can sense some of the sources of conflict. "Her piety," he said, "was always ready to display itself where she deemed it might with propriety, and without giving offense. The neatness of her person was always conspicuous, together with an order and precision in everything that came under her management"—and one may assume that many things came "under her management." Any faults she might have had were charitably explained by her son-in-law. "Her figure and deportment bore the semblance of haughtiness," he said, "but I believe it arose from a timidity of address. She always intended to be humble and meek." She avoided "demonstrations of affection," but she could rise to any effort "necessary to the service of her friends." To her grandchildren she was "affectionate and monitory," and for Johnson himself "she would have at any time done any service that she could imagine would have been acceptable."

At first Johnson "bore the disadvantage without complaining—though the evil was nonetheless constant." Within a few months, however, he realized that his mother would have to move out, and that when this happened, Sarah must go, too. He sent her a formal note. Leah, he admitted tactfully, had long been a "source of uneasiness and irritation" to Abigail, and the situation had become so "destructive to the peace of my house" that he had accordingly "made arrangements to remove her to her former house," adding bluntly "and you too must find some other place of abode." A few days later, after what must have been a painful scene with Abigail, Johnson had a change of heart, and wrote again to Sarah. "Abby thinks," he said, "we can all live together with a sufficiency of comfort. . . . I never intended to impute any fault to any person . . . and thought my proposals were for the benefit of the whole." Sarah moved out without bothering to reply. However, she carefully preserved his two letters, plus a letter he had apparently sent to her sister, Ann Masters; after her death, he came across them clipped to a long letter of her own to Abigail. Before filing it, he made this note on the margin: "This may be a copy, and the original may have been sent—though I doubt it." One can be almost certain that Abigail did receive the letter, for it seems unlikely that Sarah would have let so much injured pride and such noble words of resignation go to waste. Sarah described Johnson's letter thus to her daughter: "[It] shows no solicitude or inquiry as to your Mother's health or happiness—and I feel it my duty in justification to myself to inform you that your husband desired me to change my abode—he has sacrificed, he said, his happiness for ten years to gratify you. What gave rise to this I did not think proper to inquire." Then, indicating that Abigail had asked her privately to return, Sarah chided her, "My dear child, how can I recede from my promise? Are you not willing to make one sacrifice for his comfort?" And, in what must have been a practiced style, she concluded:

> I must separate from all I hold dear in life, but this separation, my dear, can never break the tie that binds me to you and yours. I should be lessened in my own estimation—also degraded in yours—should I return to his house uninvited. He has wounded me at an advanced

period of life without any provocation on my part. I have never raised my voice against him since I have been under his roof. . . . Kiss my dear children for me.

Johnson commented dryly that "the separation was best for all," and that it continued "forever thereinafter." Leah returned to her old house with a female servant, while Sarah "took rooms as a boarder with a widow lady." Johnson visited his own mother every day until her death, and called on Sarah "frequently." Peace was restored to the Johnson household.

CHAPTER 9

1824–1826

A Public Figure

J OHNSON, ABOUT TO BE ADMITTED to the State Supreme Court as a counselor-at-law (although during his three-year probationary period as a lawyer he had yet to handle his first case), was becoming a public figure in Utica, and the favorable reception accorded his February 1824 speech at the Lyceum encouraged him to accept an invitation to deliver the annual Fourth of July oration held at the Presbyterian church. Bored with the patriotic effusions he had listened to over the years, he departed from the usual orthodoxies. His first target was prejudice: "a demon which the virtuous mistake for virtue, the patriot for patriotism, and the bigot for zeal." Prejudice, he said, "has arraigned man against man . . . by the tinge of his skin, or the slighter difference of accidental location." He wished, he said, "that our various constitutions might shed their manna . . . not on a sect, nor a color, not a nativity, but on all men who dwell within their boundaries." Later in the speech he reverted to the theme of "color," mocking the government of Santo Domingo for excluding from public office those who "possessed not the degree of blackness which was requisite," and praising an organization which sought to "transport a portion of our native population to regions where privileges that we have denied await acceptance" (he would reverse this appraisal of the American Colonization Society with a vengeance in a later speech).

The burden of his address lay in his attack on laws that denied naturalized citizens the right to seek office. In an excess of enthusiasm, along with some careless documentation, he suggested that in selecting a President Americans might consider "from France, a Lafayette; or from Germany, a Steuben; or from Poland [sic], a De Kalb." What must have startled his audience even more, however, was his bold assertion that "not even the acknowledgment of a belief in God is relevant to a man's capacity for public office." Johnson's conclusion was simple and eloquent. The one shining example among all the constitutions of the United States, he said, was that of Vermont, where "we discover not the term white, nor freeman, nor landholder, nor citizen—but simply every man! I love that plain and comprehensive word!"

Despite Johnson's fears about his bold speech, only two correspondents took issue with him. One was Van der Kemp. "Foreigners coming here to an asylum," he wrote "ought to seek for an asylum, for peace, tranquility, security. It is enough if their children become American citizens. It is a weakness to amalgamate them with us." The other dissenter was Ann Masters. "To the best of my recollection," she wrote, "it was the introduction of foreigners into power at Athens that first sapped the foundations of their liberties." She assured Johnson he would feel differently if he were a native-born American, and added, "but all the privileges you feel the want of, you have the consolation of knowing your children will enjoy."

Shortly after his Fourth of July effort, Johnson accepted another speaking engagement from the Utica Lyceum. His subject was "Eloquence." He had obviously read rather widely in the works of the Scotch rhetoricians Hugh Blair and George Campbell, and was well versed in the writings of Samuel Johnson. He shared the distaste of the first two for tautology and "pleonasmus," and he praised the latter for always using "the right word." Where Campbell and Blair illustrated their cardinal rhetorical sins by citing lines from Swift, Addison, Bolingbroke, etc., Johnson made Henry Clay his chief target. When Clay, for instance, spoke of "hopeless despair," Johnson reminded his audience that "hopelessness adds nothing to the meaning of despair"; and when Clay complained about the "languor which now prevails," Johnson remarked, "If a languor prevails . . . it prevails now. The present tense of the verb renders the 'now' superfluous." Finally Johnson descended on Clay for another sentence. "It is like the atmosphere which surrounds us," wrote Clay, "all must inhale it, and none can escape it." Johnson, with lofty scorn, orated, "One of these assertions is superfluous. Nay, if I were severe I might insist it is pleonastic to say that atmosphere surrounds us. Circumambiency is as inseparable from the definition of the atmosphere as fluidity is from a definition of water." "Verbosity," he added, "is the most insidious foe which a speaker has to contend with."

The highest art of the speaker, Johnson declared (using a favorite phrase of Blair's) "is the ability to produce the *nice distinctions* of which language is susceptible"; but he warned against overdoing imagery and other "niceties" of speech, for "this art is like poison: its abuse consti-

tutes the extremity of evil, but a medicinal application of it is the per-
fection of skill." Johnson praised Samuel Johnson for his use of the
"right word" which helped the author of *The Rambler* to avoid "the
verbosity with which unskillful authors are overwhelmed." Johnson
concluded with the warning that eloquence is hard work.

Johnson printed this address, as he had the others. A copy went
to Van der Kemp who, though approving in general of the speech,
caught him up on the statement, "man is destitute of extrinsic ornament."
"Permit me now," teased Van der Kemp, "is man by nature destitute of
extrinsic ornaments? Are you acquainted with Apollo of Belvedere?"
Johnson also sent a copy to De Witt Clinton, who was also trying hard
to establish a scholarly reputation for himself—though in such august
circles as the American Academy of Arts and the Phi Beta Kappa
Society of New York. Clinton replied enthusiastically: "The literature of
our country is under great obligation to you for the part you have taken
in its promotion." Johnson was overwhelmed, and promptly dispatched
one of those high-flown acknowledgments which, as he had confessed in
the introduction to his autobiography, had been "much tinctured by the
reading of Swift and his contemporaries who often tried to make their
epistolary correspondence mutually pleasing to the self-love of the
correspondents."

Johnson seems to have taken little interest in the 1824 presidential
race. It was not until after John Quincy Adams' inauguration in
February 1825 that Johnson took any notice of it—and then only in a
roundabout way in a prim letter to John Adams, congratulating him on
"the consummation of the most exhalted parental hopes" (it is interesting to note that J. Q. Adams, after hearing of his election also wrote his
father describing the victory as one "upon which I can only offer *you*
my congratulations"). One reason why Johnson ignored what had become a family affair was the fact that he was absorbed in what he later
called "the great and permanent study of my life"—an investigation into
"language with reference to its meaning in something other than words."
He began to shape his ideas "into a course of lectures, as more likely to
excite attention, and also enabling me better than any other mode, to
make intelligible the abstruse topics I discussed." The first lecture, which
is called "An Introductory Address," was delivered at the Utica Lyceum
on February 17, 1825.

This lecture, as Johnson gave it to that small gathering of the
faithful in Utica, stands, with some minor changes, as "Lecture I" of the
twenty-nine lectures which make up *The Philosophy of Human Knowledge; or, A Treatise on Language* (1828). It was the only one he
actually delivered orally, and was printed as a pamphlet in Utica a few

weeks after it was given. One wonders what it was like that night when the already prosperous young banker, a storekeeper's son, former glass-maker, proper Presbyterian, husband of Abigail Adams stood up and revealed what he had really been up to during the past few years. Johnson spoke of his own misgivings years later when he wrote, "I still view these studies in the same way. They have been unfortunate, and cheated me out of a life which, had it been employed in ordinary pursuits, would have yielded me more tangible and satisfactory results." He said the same thing more gracefully in his opening remarks to the Lyceum:

> It is my misfortune to possess a strong inclination for abstruse studies. Its indulgence has diminished my convivial enjoyments and employed the ardor which at my age, is usually expended in political discussions—vociferous in the defense of rights not invaded, and vindictive in the redress of wrongs not inflicted. It has driven me from the sagacious whispers of the counting house, and the loquacious war of judicatories, to an unambitious avocation which, whilst it affords the conveniences that our plainess renders essential, enables me to gratify my unenviable propensity.

Johnson then set the stage carefully for his initial exploration of the phenomenon of language. "Man exists in a world of his own creation," he began.

> He cannot step but on ground transformed by culture, not look but on objects produced by art. The animals which constitute his food are unknown to nature . . . his virtues, language, actions, sentiments, and desires are nearly all factitious. Stupendous in achievement, he is boundless in attempts. Having subdued the surface of the earth, he would explore its center; having vanquished diseases, he would subdue death. Unsatisfied with recording unperishably the past, he would anticipate the future. Uncontented with subjugating the ocean, he would traverse the air. Success seems but to sharpen his avidity; while facility augments his impatience. Thus restless, it is important to know the extent of our powers that we may not dissipate strength in designs for which our facilities are unsuited; or attempt practicabilities by incompetent methods. This knowledge is the philosophy I propose to discuss.

One of the "incompetent methods" with which man has to work is language—a human creation "whose excessive exercise constitutes the folly of wisdom, and the wisdom of folly." Out of man's language "come propositions which govern our philosophies, but these propositions are only as valid as the words from which they are created. . . . We have overlooked the most important characteristic of language, that every word possesses as many meanings as it possesses applications to different phenomena." Johnson then turned to one of those many analogies which would bolster his argument in the *Treatise*. "Words," he said, "may be compared to music: "When a Briton listens to a certain tune of Handel, the notes distinctly articulate "God save great George the King"; but when an American hears it, the notes articulate "God save great Washington." Hence the difficulty in understanding a strange doctrine. The words will constantly excite old opinions, though the speaker intends new." As a result of the deceptions inherent in language, Johnson continued, metaphysics is "full of puerilities . . . modern philosophy is a dreary host of ambiguities . . . every science is encumbered with propositions which are hostile to the information of our senses." Mankind, he argued, has continually identified "erroneous conclusions with indisputable truths. Whatever contradicts the former, we deem incompatible with the latter." Thus, every man "possesses some metaphysical system which he has imbibed, he knows not how and credits, he knows not why. Its incomprehensibility renders him sensitive to its preservation. It is an unfortunate child, whose very idiocy endears it to his feelings."

Having challenged a variety of sciences and philosophies ("Locke's *Essay* presents no page that will not bear an expunction of a quarter of its words with benefit to perspicuity"), Johnson warned his audience that "the perverted estimation of language is so habitual that you will be constantly liable to misapprehend my remarks." He added, however, that if he should happen to succeed in his purpose, "the success will ultimately accomplish a great revolution in every branch of learning."

The lecture must have lasted a good two hours, and at its conclusion Johnson was "respectfully requested to continue the discourse as soon as convenient." Johnson, however, never appeared again before the Lyceum, fearing, he said, that "the topic could not be made interesting to a promiscuous audience like that which in our village could alone be gathered." Only friend Van der Kemp was able to muster a comment on Johnson's performance. "The name of A. B. Johnson," he wrote, "shall be re-echoed in time." What was perhaps the last word on Johnson's "Introductory Lecture" at the Lyceum, however, was written several years later by Timothy Flint in his review of the *Treatise on Language*. "What an audience must that of the Utica Lyceum have been," he wrote, "to have patiently followed this gentleman through his acute, and fine spun, and sometimes darkly woven disquisitions." And what an incurable optimist Johnson must have been to launch his linguistic "revolution" at the Utica Lyceum.

In Johnson's account of the next three years, he made but few passing references to his "abstruse studies." Among them was the statement that they frequently "soothed me into inaction"—and by "inaction" he, of course, meant writing. On the "action" side, however, it was also a busy time. There were tempting opportunities to augment his growing fortune, new civic enterprises, forays into the many reform movements that were sweeping Utica, quarrels with fellow Presbyterians, some unwanted social activities foisted upon him by "consanguinity," and two important deaths in the Adams clan.

Shortly after the Adams inauguration, Johnson's banking partner, John Greig of Canandaigua, was preparing for a European trip, and Johnson made his first overture to the new President, requesting letters of introduction for Greig to use abroad. Adams rebuffed him, calling his request "contrary to a usage which has been uniformly observed since the existence of our Government." Johnson apparently made no reply, but noted with annoyance that Greig was "a gentleman of wealth and much social distinction." He then wrote to Abigail's cousin John Adams Smith (the son of J. Q. Adams' sister), who was serving as chargé d'affaires in London while awaiting the arrival of Rufus King, Adams' new ambassador. Smith supplied the introductions. In a curious aside Johnson wrote that he had always assumed that Smith had "obtained his appointment through the influence of President John Adams," but that when he mentioned this to the Quincy patriarch he was told it was De Witt Clinton who pulled the necessary strings. Johnson then proceeded, with a touch of malice, to relate a story about "some trouble" Smith was in when he got the appointment.

> He had been engaged to a daughter of Peter Smith . . . the father of Gerrit Smith . . . but when he went to New York to purchase his wedding suit of clothes, she by a sudden inconsistency and probably to despite her father, ran away with Walter Cochran and got married to him after a brief acquaintance. Mr. Cochran was twice her age or more, but he was a gentleman of gay and brilliant manners. He drove a light carriage with two horses driven tandem, which was then unusual and deemed particularly stylish. He said jocosely that he was going to Peterboro to marry the "Empress," as he laughingly called Miss Smith, and nothing was greater than our surprise when he returned to Utica with her as his wife. [Mr. John Adams Smith] took tea with us at my father's house after his appointment and I thought he assumed an unnatural gaiety to conceal the chagrin of his disappointment, which was sufficiently recent to be remembered by all with whom he associated. Miss Smith, who jilted him, was deemed a great fortune, her father being the richest man in our vicinity.

Prior to Greig's departure, Johnson suggested to him the joint purchase of "the village and surrounding property of Little Falls" about twenty miles west of Utica on the Mohawk, and then owned by Edward Ellice, a member of the British House of Commons. John Bleeker, of Albany, was serving as Ellice's American agent. Like others of the disappearing tribe of British investors in American properties, Ellice had clung to the practice of leasing his land rather than selling it, but Americans were moving in fast, and Little Falls was particularly attractive—with its water-power potential, and its locks affording access to the upper Mohawk and the newly completed Erie Canal. Ignoring Bleeker, Johnson and Greig wrote directly to Ellice, who seemed "anxious to sell," but Bleeker was in touch with the state legislature in Albany which had been attempting to pass "unfriendly legislation" against Ellice. He induced several members of the legislature to make him an offer higher than Johnson's, and they got the land, much to Johnson's chagrin—since it turned out, Johnson wrote, "to be a highly lucrative purchase." Johnson blamed his withdrawal on his "habitual extreme caution" and his "mood of inaction."

Shortly after his arrival in England, Greig was attracted by British advances in the field of life insurance, a business that didn't get under way on any large scale in America until the middle 1840s. He wrote Johnson urging him to procure from the state legislature at its next session an act of incorporation of an American company, promising he could "easily obtain capital for it" on his return. "You have no idea," he wrote, "the extent to which it is carried on in this country!" Johnson, however, was not interested, blaming his reluctance to act on his "indisposition to interfere with the certain acquisition of my property from the process of accumulating my income." He also referred again to his literary preoccupations. One also recalls, however, Johnson's shock at the gambling he saw as a young man at Ballston Spa—and life insurance struck him as out-and-out gambling, fraught with dangerous consequences. It was, he would announce in an 1851 essay, "The Relative Merits of Life Insurance and Savings Banks," a lottery which paralyzed a man's effort by promising to "care for him in sickness, bury him when dead, and provide for his widow and orphans." One who labors to purchase life insurance "cannot command the energy he would feel if he were laboring for present affluence." It was also "unfavorable to domestic purity." In this connection he cited instances in England where "mothers had murdered their infants to obtain some petty sums which certain clubs bestow for funeral expenses," to which he added the tale of a Londoner who "killed with strychnine his wife's sister after inducing her to insure her life largely for the benefit of his wife." And in a fable called "The Lunatic Asylum at Boresko," published in his *Encyclopedia of Instruction,* he would equate the life insurance practices of the unfortunate inmates with "communist and socialist schemes, phrenology, hare-brained religions, animal magnetism, and kindred modern disorders." Boreskans believed the moon is made of green cheese, and they also believed in life insurance.

On July 13, 1824, after an absence of forty years, the Marquis de Lafayette arrived in New York aboard the American ship *Cadmus* to begin his triumphal tour through the states of the Union he had helped to create. "He was like a father among his children," wrote James Fenimore Cooper after the New York reception, and his "children" shouted their love for him wherever he went. The first stop after New York was Boston, where a great arch spanned Washington Street proclaiming, "We bow not the neck, we bend not the knee/But our hearts, Lafayette, we surrender to thee!" At Harvard, young Edward Everett climaxed a two-hour oration with "Welcome Lafayette, thrice welcome to our shores—friend of our fathers and of our country!" And out in Quincy, John Adams held an "affecting reunion" with his old comrade. Johnson was not certain whether it was John or John Quincy Adams who suggested that the great Frenchman, if he got to Utica, pay a visit to his granddaughter Abigail and her husband. A few days later, unaware that this honor might soon befall them, Johnson and Abigail set out for Philadelphia by way of Albany to visit Abigail's aunt. Their night in Albany coincided with a brief stopover by Lafayette, who was en route back to New York, and the Johnson, peering from a hotel window, found the parade of welcome "very affecting and the enthusiasm very contagious." Arriving in Philadelphia they were put up at the Mansion House Tavern, where they were ensconced "very elegantly" in a parlor and bedroom especially decorated to receive the general, who was expected in that city two weeks later. They moved out to suburban Kinderton a few days before his arrival, but came back to the city to witness the parade to Independence Hall, headed by Major General Jacob Brown, and an escort of 150 veterans of the Revolution. Despite the fact that Brown was the old friend who had escorted him from New York to Utica in 1801, and later aided him in his early banking efforts, Johnson failed to make himself known, though he seems to have been a little wistful about not doing so. "Had I made my presence known to him," he wrote, "I could have figured in the procession, but yielding to my natural shyness, I took special pains not to be seen by him."

Several weeks later, Johnson's and Lafayette's paths crossed again, but this time a friend intervened and they became acquainted. The friend was Philip Hone, mayor of New York City, and the meeting took place in one of the city's museums. On being told by Hone that Mrs. Johnson was the granddaughter of President Adams, the general was "very courteous and polite," but there is still no indication that any invitation was issued to come to Utica. When the general was finally received in the Johnson house on Genesee Street, the arrangements were made, according to the Utica *Sentinel and Gazeteer* for June 14, 1825, "by particular request of the President of the United States [John Quincy Adams]—Mrs. Johnson being a niece of the President." Johnson described the affair with typical understatement, proud, no doubt, of the contrast between his own quiet little family reception and all the cannonading, saluting, weeping, hailing, and farewelling that went on in the city streets.

> We were informed of his intention to visit us and we invited a number of our friends and neighbors to our house that they might see him. He was received by our village authorities at Whitesboro, and escorted by them and a large number of carriages to Bagg's tavern at Utica, where he was addressed in a set speech by Captain William Clark, who was president of the village corporation. Captain Clark read his address at the entrance of Bagg's tavern, and he was much disconcerted in the reading and pronounced it brokenly and badly. The General in reply spoke extemporally and fluently and, of course, in a very courteous strain. After resting for some time, a procession was formed and the General was escorted to my house, where I introduced him to the company, and he took some refreshments that we had prepared for the occasion. We cannot help associating with great historic actions some corresponding notion of the appearance of the actor, but nothing extraordinary was seen in Lafayette. He seemed a quiet, self-composed gentleman. What struck me as most noticeable in him was a very low tone of voice in speaking, and a very light and slow tread as he walked. Of course our conversation was all commonplace. I introduced all my children to him separately, and he in a paternal manner placed his hand on the head of each one, as they were all young. I had a silhouette of Baron Steuben and I showed it to the General, who professed to recognize therein the Baron, whom he had known during the American Revolutionary War. Numerous persons, Indians and others, who had been in the American Army under his command, were generally recognized by him wherever he met them after they announced their former position. How much of this was mere courtesy no man can tell, but it greatly pleased all who were thus recognized. After staying with us some half hour or longer, the General withdrew and joined the escort that was waiting for him and returned to Bagg's Hotel. As he passed out of my house and down the steps he professed to admire the distant scenery, and said, complaisantly I supposed, that it was very

beautiful. A man whom everybody is striving to honor and please cannot help feeling amiable to everybody and everything. This was the last time I ever saw the General.

Johnson does not seem to have participated further in the general's strenuous reception in Utica, and was probably glad to have missed the scene of his departure. The Frenchman was loaded onto a packet boat, renamed the *Lafayette,* which was drawn along the canal by three white horses in "elegant style." Twenty-one-gun salutes were fired, and Uticans "rent the air with loud and continuous cheering" while small boys threw flowers down on their hero's head from the Canal bridges. At one point, while the general "presented himself to the people and answered their congratulations with bows and expressive gesticulations," a young Indian leapt into the packet from a bridge shouting "Where is Kayewela . . . I must see Kayewela!" Lafayette's faithful secretary, Lavasseur, explained in his Journal that "Kayewela" meant "Great White Father," and added, in a sentence worthy of his countryman, Chateaubriand, "The lithe young Indian leaped to the bank ten feet distant and immediately disappeared."*

During the summer of Lafayette's visit, Abigail became concerned over her grandfather's failing health and in August 1825 traveled to Cambridge with Mr. and Mrs. John Lothrop to attend a Harvard commencement presided over by President Kirkland, Mrs. Lothrop's brother. From there she went on to Quincy. A letter from her indicated that despite John Adams' poor health there was no slackening of the social pace at Quincy. There were also some reassuring words to her husband concerning his place in the hearts of the Adamses.

> . . . On Saturday, sixteen strangers were here, some from South Carolina, Virginia, and other places. There is not a day without two or three. We had Count Vidner and the Baron Niedersteller the other afternoon—the former is an Italian Count and the latter, the Prussian Charge d'Affaires to the United States. . . . I saw the Baron at the Commencement. He recognized me immediately, and I was honored by a bow almost to the ground. Grandfather said, in a room full of company, that he was proud of his granddaughter Johnson, and he should be happy to have her stay six months instead of one. Our friends all enquire very kindly after you. Those who have not seen you are very anxious for an opportunity of becoming acquainted, and those who

---

* Quoted in *The Lafayette Memorial,* published by the Utica Chapter, Daughters of the American Revolution, Utica, 1925.

have will be very happy to see you again. Mr. Josiah Quincy has given me a piece of crystalized salt for you and hopes to have the pleasure of a visit when you arrive.

Nearly a year later, Abigail's low-bowing friend, the baron, called on the Johnsons while enroute to Niagara Falls, bearing a letter of introduction from De Witt Clinton. Abigail was recovering from the birth of her sixth child, and her nervous husband was left to cope with the visitor.

I endeavored to entertain him as well as I could, but I was always too shy and formal to make myself agreeable. I felt as though I had not very well fulfilled the intentions of Governor Clinton in not inviting him to dinner, but I never gave a dinner party in my life, with only one exception, I believe, and that much later in my life. The difficulty was in my habitual shyness and consequent awkwardness.

As soon as John Lothrop returned to Utica to carry on as cashier in the Ontario Branch Bank, Johnson departed for Quincy to join Abigail and bring her back to Utica. He found John Adams much more feeble than he had expected.

He could not go up and downstairs from his bedroom without the assistance of a man servant. The tremor of his hands prevented him from feeding himself, and a servant stood by him and placed in his mouth what he was to eat. He still contrived to drink without assistance. He used a silver mug holding about a pint, and clasping it with both hands he would get it to his mouth but with difficulty. I was sitting with him in his room, and I remarked that I did not see much change around me since my last visit. He replied, "Mr. Johnson, there is one great change." I enquired what. He answered, "They all speak so low in addressing me that I cannot understand what they say." His niece (a Miss Smith) who was keeping house for him said, "Sir, the change is in you, for you cannot hear us as well as formerly." But he persisted that the fault was not in his hearing. He asked me to read to him some newspapers that were lying on his table, and I read accordingly. After I had read all that I supposed would interest him, I said as much, but Miss Smith told me I could read again what I had read and it would seem new. His intellect was not otherwise impaired, nor his interest in surrounding objects.

Ten months later, John Adams died, and Johnson recorded the event.

On the Fourth of July, President John Adams departed this life. We might have known that the period of his death was near, and especially from the circumstances in which we saw him the previous fall, but death is usually a surprise and we were surprised and shocked. His uniform kindness had endeared him to us both, and to my wife he stood more in the relation of father than of grandfather.

The old President's last day was far more graphically described by Abigail Johnson's sister, Susan B. Clark, in a letter, dated July 9, 1862, to the Johnsons. In a long recital she recorded the details of Adams' last moments. "I said to him," she wrote, "Grandfather, do you know what day it is? It is the Fourth of July, Sir, the fiftieth day of Independence. 'It is a great day, it is a good day,' was his reply." Then Susan reported the dying President's last words:

> The family was all assembled in the chamber, and as Thomas and myself were writing on the bed, we heard him whisper, "Thomas Jefferson survives." [Jefferson, it will be remembered, died on the same day.] Cousin Louisa asked him if we should send for Mr. Whitney [Adams' clergyman]. "No," he said, "I pray for myself, pray for all of you. Give my love to Mrs. Johnson and her children." The last words he spoke were to me, struggling for breath, "Help me, child, help me." "I wish I could, Sir," was my reply.

Carried away by the solemnity of the occasion, Susan added an apocalyptic passage which was undoubtedly original with herself:

> At the moment, as if to render the scene more awfully impressive, a clap of thunder shook the house. A few minutes after the weary spirit was at rest, a splendid rainbow arched immediately over the heavens. It was a sublime sight! Amidst the joyful acclimations of thousands when the entire country was celebrating their great jubilee, the spirit of the Patriot ascended to God who gave it. What a wonderful event! The hand of the Almighty was visible in it!

Johnson made an abstract of Susan Clark's letter, omitting certain family references, and sent it to his friend A. C. Dauby, editor of the Utica *Observer*, who published it immediately, noting with pride the subject's close connection with Utica's "distinguished citizen, A. B. Johnson." Johnson also sent Van der Kemp a copy, and received an effusive note of thanks in which the old Dutchman recalled proudly "the friendship with which I was honored by your beloved grandparent."

Abigail Johnson was left a hundred dollars by her grandfather's will, but it was dependent upon the sale of certain lands administered by Josiah Quincy, and though Johnson's letter files contain numerous references to the proposed land sale, it never seems to have materialized Johnson's final tribute to his distinguished grandfather-in-law may sound anticlimatic after the intimacy between them over the past decade, but it was typical.

He had often said to me that the smallness of his income prevented him from entertaining his visitors with the hospitality he desired. But we may well admit the integrity which his small property evinced. After exercising through life the greatest prudence and economy his position would permit, he died leaving only about $40,000.

CHAPTER 10

1826–1828

Varied Preoccupations

JOHNSON WAS NOW SPENDING LONG HOURS in his office away from his bustling household working at his ledger books and, after hours, at those "abstruse studies" which would shortly give birth to *The Philosophy of Human Knowledge; or, A Treatise on Language*. Readers of this work will find numerous references to a new acquisition he made at this time, Abraham Rees' four-volume *New Cyclopedia or Universal Dictionary of the Arts and Sciences, Biography, Geography*, first published in London in 1802. The publishers of the 1822 American edition had just gone out of business, and imperfect sets of the work were being offered as lottery prizes. Johnson broke a long-standing rule against gambling and bought a lottery ticket, which won him one of the sets. Fascinated by the work, but uneasy over his method of obtaining it, he invested $150 in a complete set "bound in boards" which, he said, was "a great bargain . . . and afforded me much amusement and instruction throughout my life." Johnson often took issue with his *Cyclopedia*, however, calling it on one occasion "a succession of verbal deductions from artificial definitions"; and in the twelfth lecture of his *Treatise*, for example, he cited its definition of "matter" as "an extended, solid, devisable, moveable, passive substance, the first principle of all natural things." He argued, "Matter is not these *words*—they constitute the verbal meaning of the word *matter*." Nevertheless, the work was to provide many of the illustrations and analogies which would embellish his philosophical writings, and was doubtless the source of many of the scientific experiments he used to illustrate his philosophical propositions.

Among Johnson's business, literary, and family preoccupations, there was also the church he had so staunchly defended against the verbal onslaughts of old John Adams. His faith in organized religion as a necessary fixture in man's life would never waver, and years later, on his deathbed he would assure a visitor, "I would not knowingly employ any young man who did not regularly attend church." At this particular moment, however, his relations with the local Presbytery were subject to severe strain, and he was finding it difficult to conform to their "rigidly correct" standards. His first brush with them came when he journeyed on a Sunday from Albany to Utica via canal boat. Shortly thereafter he received a delegation from the Session at his home, and was enjoined to explain his Sabbath travels. "Such surveillance," he wrote, "I had not expected when I left the Episcopal Church, and it somewhat annoyed me—but it was common at the time referred to." A few weeks after this incident, Johnson was visited again by a committee and invited to make a substantial contribution to the construction of a new brick church to be designed by the famous architect Philip Hooker. Family pews were being offered for pledges of $2,000 each, and the committee, headed by a Utica lawyer, John Bradish, assumed that their leading banker would want to head the list of subscribers. Johnson offered them $150—with or without a pew. Bradish was stunned, and informed Johnson that if he couldn't do better than that, he might as well "give nothing at all." Whereupon Johnson gave notice that he was "not to be dragooned into subscribing more," and that he would cheerfully "accept Bradish's alternative." Later that day, as Johnson passed Bradish's office on his return from the bank, the lawyer stepped outside and invited him to enter his office and "pray with him." As Johnson recalled the event, "I told him I would not come in for that purpose, and went home for dinner." Grudgingly, the Presbyterians accepted Johnson's $150, but a real showdown will occur some years later.

Johnson and Abigail continued their regular worship with the Presbyterians, despite these contretemps, and shortly after John Adams' death, Johnson was made president of the Union Tract Society, a mildly ecumenical Protestant group formed to disseminate religious pamphlets among the unconverted. Within a few months after assuming office, however, Johnson became aware of "curious sectarian distinctions" within the organization.

> The tracts of our Society kept for distribution were first subjected to examination by a committee representing the various sects of which our Society was composed. One of these occasions a tract narrated a sea voyage . . . and the account stated that a child was born during the passage, and that on the eighth day the infant was baptized. This tract was objected to by our Baptist representative who could never consent that such a tract be placed in the hands of children who were

taught that baptism could be administered only to adults. If the tract had said that the infant had been sprinkled, he would not have objected, but using the word *baptism* made it objectionable, and the tract was therefore not admitted into our collection.

Johnson's doubts were shared by others in central New York State. Residents of Lebanon, in nearby Madison County, for instance, were perturbed by an order issued by New York's Secretary of State J. V. N. Yates, requesting the systematic use of Tract Society material in the common schools. A legislative committee was formed to investigate, and the request was declared illegal on the grounds that certain sects, mainly the Presbyterians, were using the tracts to further their own special interests—in the case of the Presbyterians, Sabbatarianism.

At about the time Johnson was officiating at the Tract Society, he also accepted the presidency of the Oneida Evangelical Society. Again, his later comments leave one wondering why he persisted in involving himself in causes for which he had little real sympathy. The Evangelical Society did, however, bring him into the periphery, at least, of one of the most violent religious upheavals in American history, the great Oneida Revival which, in turn, directly or indirectly, was a catalyst for many other New York State social and spiritual eruptions: the Utopian experiments of John Humphrey Noyes and Thomas Lake Harris at Oneida and Brockton, the Anti-Abolitionist riots in Utica, Mormonism in Palmyra, the Women's Rights movement in Seneca Falls, Spiritualism in Hydesville, Millennialism in Dresden, Anti-Masonry in Batavia, temperance movements, and the countless other "ultraist enthusiasms." The Evangelical Society, which Johnson headed briefly, was a cooperative effort on the part of the Utica Protestants to build up their lagging congregations, this time by providing funds for itinerant evengelists who followed in the wake of Charles Grandison Finney, the most eloquent of all nineteenth-century American "soul winners."

The Oneida Revivals swept over Utica like a forest fire in 1826. Johnson's own pastor, the Rev. Samuel Aiken, reported to the Oneida Presbytery that "places of worship were thronged, and the stillness of the sepulchre reigned, broken occasionally by a deep sigh from some heart that was writhing under the condemning influence of divine truth," and posters appeared on the streets announcing Finney's presence "By Command of the King of Kings." Aiken fixed the total number of converts to his own church at "one hundred souls," and estimated that four hundred were brought to other Utica churches within a few months.*

* Noah Coe, *A Narrative of the Revival of Religion in Oneida County* (Utica, 1826), p. 24.

Johnson attended a number of Finney's sermons, and was undoubtedly impressed. In a passage from a letter to one of his children (later included in *A Cyclopedia of Instruction*) he described a Finney revival:

> A protracted meeting is in progress here, and it occasions much religious agitation. Many persons deem the leading preacher a miserable ranter; but as he always collects large audiences, I expected to find him a man of some genius, and, on hearing him this afternoon, my expectation was realized. Some people cannot endure a minister unless he preaches the doctrines which they approve; but I can be pleased with a fervent and ingenious discourse, when its doctrines accord not with my views of orthodoxy.

Among the many manifestations of revivalist zeal he must also have noted were the daily exhortations in the Utica press. A favorite device of the *Western Recorder,* for instance, was a "Spiritual Barometer." It had a scale ranging from 70 above zero to 70 below, and demonstrated the "progress of sin and holiness." On the downward scale, one progressed as follows:

> 0   INDIFFERENCE
>   Family worship only on Sunday evenings.
>
> − 10   Private prayer frequently omitted.
>   Family religion wholly declined.
>
> − 20   Levity in conversation.
>   Fashions however expensive adopted.
>
> —30   Luxurious entertainments (company).
>   Free Association with worldly minded.
>
> − 40   Love of novels.
>   Theater, cards, etc.
>
> − 50   Continued parties of pleasure.
>   House of God forsaken.
>   Much wine, spirits and other strong drink.

And so on—down to—70, "Disease and death." One knows little about the frequency of Johnson's prayers, but aside from occasional carelessness about the Sabbath, a few trips to the theater, and a number of obviously worldly—minded friends, he seems to have avoided the sub-zero temperatures.

In the autobiography, Johnson recaptured little of the frenzy of the Oneida Revival which prompted him to accept the presidency of the Evangelical Society. Looking back upon it, he seems to have had no regrets over the fact that, like the Tract Society, it was short lived.

> Finney's imagination being exceedingly active and his language very descriptive of what his imagination conceived, I several times went to hear him, and this probably induced the institutors of the Society to elect me its president. I was informed that the principle objective was to create a fund for his benefit, and as I deemed him original and talented, I accepted the appointment. As, however, was usual in such cases, after existing nominally for about two years, the Society became extinct . . . though during its existence it answered the purpose for which it existed; nor were we without some good fruits.

As Finney carried his message into the larger cities, the controversy over his methods grew to national proportions. Among other things, there were vociferous objections to "female prayer and exhortation, loud groaning, speaking out or falling down in time of public or social worship," and Johnson, again looking back, also seems to have been disturbed by these "ultraist" excesses:

> . . . it usually created, wherever practiced, much discord in private families by exciting in some of the members thereof an enthusiasm which interfered with domestic harmony towards other members of the family who remained unexcited. Several such cases arose in Utica between husband and wife, parent and child; and the parties became the town talk. A conversion of the recusant individuals was in some cases openly prayed for in the churches, and their names made public to the increased disgust and indignation of the aggrieved individuals. A person who has never witnessed such scenes in a small village can hardly conceive the extent to which such practices occurred at the time in question.

Ten years later, just prior to his graduation from Geneva College (now Hobart College) in 1839, Johnson's third son, John Adams Johnson, had his "religious sensibilities very much awakened" during a flury of student revivalism, but there seems to have been no "interference with the domestic harmony" of the Johnson family.

Johnson concluded his account of Utica's "moment of delirium" with a letter from Finney thanking him for his part in promoting the "good fruits" of the Oneida Revival. Funds raised by the Utica Evangelical Society, said Finney, had been "instrumental in rescuing the church and society at Stephentown, Pennsylvania, from the brink of ruin . . . they are about settling a young man of whom they speak in highest terms." Finney's gratitude, and Johnson's labors in his behalf (restrained though they were), may well have had something to do with the fact that Johnson was never prayed for "by name." It may also have staved off (for a few years) his ultimate break with the Presbyterians in 1834.

Johnson recorded one final episode indirectly connected with the Revival in an account of the efforts of the Oneida Institute to extract a contribution from him. In 1827 George Washington Gale, noting the effects of his theological discussions with Charles Finney, expanded his efforts to train young ministers, and launched a seminary in Whitesboro, New York (now a suburb of Utica), which he called the Oneida Institute. Using a gift of $2,000 from the Oneida Presbytery, Gale purchased a hundred-acre farm, and began his first year with twenty students, increasing his enrollment to seventy by 1830. The Institute offered courses in Latin and Greek along with studies in Hebrew. Its most unusual feature, however, was its program of manual labor. Each student was required to work three and one-half hours per day on the farm, with the farm profits used to defray the salaries of the teachers. The success of Gale's experiment attracted Theodore Weld away from Hamilton College, where he was entered as a student, and later led Weld to found the "New York City Gentlemen for Manual Labor Schools," whose manifesto, written by Weld, attracted national attention and led eventually, in part, to the founding of Oberlin College in Ohio, which Finney served as president from 1851 to 1866. Gale's Institute became a hotbed of New York State Abolitionism under the leadership of Beriah Green, who will appear later in Johnson's memoirs. One of its more notable achievements was the admission of several black students, among them Henry Highland Garnet, who graduated with honors in 1840 and became, with Frederick Douglass, one of the great militant black leaders of the abolitionist movement.

Johnson disapproved totally of Gale's manual labor program, saying that "persons who intend to follow sedentary occupations became unfitted therefor by laborious habits while young. To this defect I attributed the sudden breaking in health of many of our clergymen."

Looking back across forty years on the alarums and excursions of the 1820s, Johnson gave the impression that he had remained relatively aloof from it all. The letters he faithfully transcribed, however, sometimes gave him away, and it seems obvious that his detachment was "as of the present writing" rather than a reflection of his real involvement at the time. This was apparent in his treatment of the Revival, and it is no less obvious in his approach to another enthusiasm of the period, namely aid to the Greeks in their revolt against the Turks.

On the night of December 30, 1823, Utica's libertarians gathered together to hear speeches and pass resolutions in behalf of the Greek cause. Later a benefit was staged, with a concert and the reading of poetry. "The whole civilized world was aroused to sympathy," says Moses Bagg, "and Utica was moved to do something in behalf of the sufferers." Like some more recent American Aid gestures, this one went awry, and Johnson's good friend, Jonas Platt, recently appointed to the State Supreme Court, found himself in difficulty.

To supplement the nationwide grass-roots effort Congress authorized the construction of two frigates for sale to the Greek insurgents. However, construction costs soared far beyond expectations, and the Greeks suspended payment. Platt was named to head an arbitration board which, after protracted hearings, found no evidence of fraud—and one of the ships was finally handed over to Greece. Platt, meanwhile, was accused in the national press, and by some of his neighbors in Utica, of taking an exorbitant fee as arbitrator—seemingly at the expense of the heroic Greeks. Johnson at once came to Platt's defense in a strong, carefully worded letter, which reviewed the entire episode and concluded that, "in view of the magnitude of the case" and the temper of the times, Platt's fee had been entirely justified. Platt was deeply moved by these opinions from a "discerning and impartial judge," and thanked Johnson profusely. Reflecting on the event, Johnson marveled at the "acrimony" of the controversy, and at the passions stirred up, mainly by the clergy, over the perfidy of the Turks.

> In reflecting upon the Crusades . . . as recorded in European histories, I had always supposed they belong to a phase of society with which we had no sympathy; but the feeling in favor of the Greeks as against the Turks revealed the ancient spirit in a remarkable degree; and no doubt, had our government desired, we could have raised large armies to fight the Turks. . . . We had a meeting in Utica, presided over by a clergyman, and large funds were collected to aid the struggle.

According to Bagg, the "large funds" amounted to $164.57.

Charles Adams Johnson, a fifth son, was born on April 3, 1826, and Johnson was pleased with the increase in his family, saying that he "could not have too many children." He would have "preferred a girl," he added, "but males are more favored by providence than females . . . whose destiny depended more on the husbands they might marry than on any deserts of their own." Abigail was not "so well pleased with this increase, but she had a noble constitution . . . and bore her fate with as much patience as I could expect." That summer Johnson presented her with a secondhand "closed coach" which cost him $342, and a pair of new horses and a harness for $319—extravagances he excused on the strength of his latest capital count of $83,481.57. The following winter he also purchased a two-horse sleigh, and at the same time treated himself and Abigail to riding lessons given by one "West, a celebrated equestrian," who had arrived in Utica. This last indulgence ended any ambition Johnson might have had as a horseman, for in riding about the ring with his feet out of the stirrups (West's idea) he was thrown on his back and severely shaken up. Since West "treated his female riders with more concern," Johnson let Abigail continue the course, and bought her a new $45 lady's saddle—but he himself took no more lessons.

Johnson's next attention to Abigail was even more personal. A New York artist named Dickenson, who had done a miniature portrait of Johnson in 1814, arrived in Utica, and Johnson commissioned a miniature of Abigail. Dickenson's price had risen from $25 to $40, but Johnson took the plunge anyway, and was disappointed with the results. "It seemed far less handsome than the original," he wrote, adding, "The original I had always adored, and possibly the painting's not exciting in me the feeling of the original, might have made it less truthful to me than it was. Most persons said the likeness was good, and I therefore accepted it and paid him the $40—but I still think it an unfavorable likeness."

Despite his determination not to gamble with his money, but to rely on "gradual accumulation from savings out of my income," Johnson still had an eye out for profitable investments, and made one in 1827 which ultimately netted him a profit of roughly one hundred thousand dollars. It also made many changes in Utica which, for better or for worse, may still be observed today.

One of Johnson's early partners in the organization of the Ontario Branch Bank was Abraham Varick, Jr., the nephew of Colonel Richard Varick, an early mayor of New York City. Varick had moved from New York to Utica in 1804 as an agent of the Holland Land Company, and had made a fortune buying and selling land around the outskirts of the village, as well as in various manufacturing concerns—particularly the cotton mills which brought prosperity to Utica in the late nineteenth and early twentieth centuries. At Johnson's suggestion, Varick and he formed a partnership and began to buy up lands in the western suburbs (mostly farmland) of Utica which were sold in building lots of forty by a hundred and twenty feet.

My sales were necessarily made to poor people who were willing to build small dwellings in the suburbs where they could purchase land for a small sum and at long credit; and I had the great pleasure in many cases of seeing the purchasers become affluent and respectable by the influence of possessing a homestead of their own. In some instances my purchasers were intemperate men, but they are now temperate and possess a comfortable competency. I rigidly insisted that all interest on the purchases be promptly paid, well knowing that nothing is so destructive to poor men as laxity that permits interest to accumulate against them. The principal I permitted them to pay as their convenience enabled them, and I never exacted it faster.

Today the visitor to the "Cornhill" district of Utica, an impoverished problem area of the city housing numerous ethnic groups, will cross streets which Johnson named proudly after members of his family—William, Bryan, Louisa, Leah, and Arthur. He will also find many of Johnson's heroes and friends memorialized: Clinton, Platt, Jason, Parker, and Miller, as well as a Johnson Street and a Johnson Square. As Johnson put it so succinctly in his memoirs, "My taste made me always prefer to see houses rather than meadows or gardens; and men and women rather than trees."

As the fateful 1828 presidential election drew near, Johnson seems to have remained steadfast in his loyalty to John Quincy Adams, despite the strong anti-Adams sentiment among the anti-tariff, pro-Southern interest members of the Utica business community. Consanguinity still prevailed over political issues, and Johnson's dramatic conversion to the "Jacksonian persuasion" would have to wait at least until "Uncle John Quincy" was safely out of office.

The President was too busy with affairs of state and the forthcoming campaign to favor the Utica Johnsons with many letters, but he did from time to time send on pieces of literature which he thought would interest them. One of these was a tribute to John Adams by Judge Cranch of the U.S. District Court, stressing Adams' scorn for popularity, a trait his son had inherited. In thanking the President for the memoir, Johnson added a few observations of his own. The "strongest trait" in the former President's character, he felt, was his "inflexibile rectitude":

I once remarked to him that a person in possession of power ought to appoint his friends to office, when their qualifications and claims were equal to those of unfriendly candidates. He immediately replied with a sudden energy of expression, "Private friendships have nothing to do with the exercise of public duties. If the qualifications of two candidates were so nearly alike that I could not discover the preponderance, I would reject my friend that I might be certain I was not influenced by partiality."

Two letters from Susan Clark described life in the White House in the spring before the election of 1828. The first was written to Johnson:

The drawing rooms and parties are all over with the exception of dinners which the President gives twice a week. He looks very badly. I was perfectly shocked on seeing him. He has the appearance of a man harassed to death with care, and I heartily wish Congress would adjourn and give him an opportunity of going to the North, which is the only thing to restore him. Political parties run very high. Van Buren is electioneering with all his might, and a sworn enemy of the President. I was much diverted yesterday morning. As Uncle was returning from a ride on horseback, he encountered Mr. Van Buren at the gate, and very politely urged him to stay to breakfast with him. You never saw a man more completely embarrassed than was Van Buren. "Should be very happy to, but—should be very happy—should be—." "Good morning, Mr. Van Buren," said the President, "I am sorry you won't breakfast with me," and he rode on. We were much diverted with this rencounter and it served for our amusement all breakfast time.

We lead a peculiar life here. Every one has their separate apartments, and the family only meet at meals. The three great drawing rooms below are only open on public evenings and at the dinners; but people are constantly coming to look at the house and a porter is stationed below to receive all such persons and gratify their curiosity. Aunt has a very elegant drawing room upstairs, where she receives visitors, and her own suite of rooms are connected with it. My room is the one which was occupied by General Lafayette, and is furnished in great style. We breakfast between nine and ten, dine at six and take tea at nine. In the interim every one does as they please, ride, walk, read or employ themselves as they choose. Whatever you want, you have only to ring for, and it is brought without asking any questions. French cooks, French servants and French gentlemen, render a knowledge of the language almost indispensable. The house is altogether extremely elegant, and I have been amusing myself by taking an inventory of the furniture below, for the especial gratification of my friends whose curiosity remains ungratified.

Susan's second letter dated five days later was addressed to Abigail, and is a continuation of the first, though far more lavish in its culinary particulars.

On Saturday there was a great dinner here, and as your curiosity may be no little excited as to the manner in which such affairs are conducted in this splendid mansion, I will give you a detail of them. The company, consisting of forty persons, began to assemble at five o'clock in the yellow drawing room below, where seated in full dress, is the Presidentess, Mrs. Clark [the writer] and Miss Adams [a daughter of Judge Thomas Adams]. The ceremony of introduction being over, every one endeavors to be as agreeable as possible until six, when dinner is announced. The President then takes a lady, and the most distinguished Senator, Mrs. Adams. Then follow General Macomb and Mrs. Clark; Abby and Mr. Ingersoll, the rest follow indiscriminately. The dinner service is of silver. In the center of the table is a plateau twelve feet in length, containing sixteen small gold statues, each holding two wax candles; also seven rich burnished gold baskets of flowers each supported on the heads of three graces who stand on gold pedestals. The ornament which forms the middle of the group is larger than the rest. At each end of the table is a Chinese Pagoda of sugar, and sparkling with sugar frost work. There is no fixed ceremony at table. All the dishes are in the most exquisite style of French cookery, and the servants hand them to you, so that you have the choice of everything on the table without asking or answering questions. If the meats are so disguised that you are ignorant what they are, the servant whispers the name of each dish as he hands it to you. The meats consist of four courses, with vegetables consisting of green peas, cucumbers, and string beans. The fifth course consists of partridges at the head and chickens at the foot of the table. The dessert is composed of jellies in the most exquisite forms and colors, sweet meats, ice which is made by throwing peaches or strawberries in the middle of the ice while it is freezing, blancmange made with almonds, every description of French cake, Turk's head of sponge cake, almond, custard, ripe strawberries put in calf's foot jelly while it is cooling, and which gives it a beautiful appearance. By the time this is all arranged it is twilight, and the servants with their long torches pass rapidly along, just touching the candles; and in a moment the whole room is in a blaze of light. A chandelier of cut glass is suspended over the table and contains thirty-six candles. Then come a vast variety of wines and champagnes, the circulation of which sets many a tongue in motion; and the last course consists of every kind of fruit that can be obtained, preserves, with pineapple and raspberry ices, and a variety of bonbons. Conversation flows freely. Every lady has a gentleman on each side of her, who are in duty bound to make themselves agreeable, and if she possesses a spark of intelligence or wit she can give it full play. We rise from table at about eight o'clock and adjourn to the drawing room; where coffee is immediately served and the company take leave. Abby and I generally spend our mornings together. After breakfast, we retire to our own apartments where we amuse ourselves with music, needle work and reading, or adjourn to the billiard room for exercise, it being too warm to walk out until evening. At one o'clock the bell rings, which indicates that refreshments are provided in the dining room to which all who are disposed assemble; then comes the carriage and whoever chooses takes a drive. The house is altogether magnificent, but so large that it is almost impossible to go over it in one day; the fatigue would be excessive. I wonder in your travels, that Mr. Johnson has never brought you here. At this season it is truly enchanting. We have strawberries and green peas in abundance, and the whole country is glowing with beauty."

Sarah Adams did not live to see her brother-in-law's defeat at the hands of Andrew Jackson. She died on August 3, 1828, at the age of sixty-two. Johnson described the deathbed scene, noting that Abigail, alone, was called to her bedside a few moments before death. His own role was to fulfill Sarah's request that her stomach be examined after death; and a full autopsy was performed at the Johnson house. The report, which Johnson transcribed, tells us more than we want to know about the spread of the malignancy which caused the mother-in-law's death. There is no doubt that Johnson had a pronounced streak of morbidity in his nature, as has been noted before, but the attention he paid to autopsies was consistent with other aspects of his nature. He had a relentless curiosity about cause and effect. He distrusted all theorizing until the facts were in—particularly by the doctors of his day. Cancer, he might have said, was a "unit word"—like "cholera" —not necessarily related to the specific, non-unit cancer of Mrs. Adams. She had said she felt as though her stomach "were tied in two." This was a sensory perception which Johnson, in his language works, would term a "feel"—and it was more to be trusted than the non-sensory deductions of a family doctor. Thus, when the postmortem showed that Mrs. Adams' stomach was in much the condition she had described, Johnson viewed this as "an extraordinary coincidence" that vindicated his empiricism. Sarah's will, with Johnson named as executor, left all of her personal property to Abigail, including her "gold snuff box [still retained by one of Johnson's descendants], diamond ring, watch, silver tankard and clothing, as a tribute due a dutiful child." Sixty dollars in gold, "rolled up in a piece of wrapping paper," were also found, and were passed on to another sister, Belinda Clarkson.

Johnson added a melancholy postscript to the story—melancholy, that is, from a practical banker's point of view. "Had Mrs. Adams lived a week longer," he wrote, "she would have been co-heir of one of the largest estates in New York, the estate of William Jauncey of that city, who left several millions of property, and of whom she was a first cousin and next of kin." Johnson was also troubled with misgivings over having sent Sarah away from his house.

That Mrs. Adams died thus, a few days in advance of Mr. Jauncey, I thought might never have occurred had she continued her residence with me where her comforts would probably have been more assiduously administered to than in a boarding house. The reflection somewhat troubled me at the time, and I deemed it providential punishment for not bearing longer the disadvantage of her residence with me. My motive, however, I thought good, for it was a desire not to deal differently by her than I was in the manner of dealing with my own mother who was always an object of my tenderest solicitude. I thought we might all be happier as separate families . . . but looking back I ought probably to have borne all the evils of the position as I had already borne them some thirteen years ago.

CHAPTER 11

1828

A Major Work on Language

JOHNSON'S MAJOR WORK ON LANGUAGE, *The Philosophy of Human Knowledge; or, A Treatise on Language,* revised in 1836 as *A Treatise on Language; or, The Relation Which Words Bear to Things,* appeared during the first months of the year 1828. "My book," he announced matter-of-factly, "was published in New York by G. & C. Carvill, No. 108 Broadway. It made a large octavo volume of 200 pages, divided into an introduction and twelve lectures." Since only a small handful of his contemporaries ever read the book, and even fewer grasped what he was driving at, he endeavored, as he would on several occasions in his autobiography, to explain his method and his purpose.

> The book was the result of labors persevered in through many years; and I devoted incredible efforts to condense my meaning into the smallest number of words that was consistent with perspicuity. . . . A book composed of the thoughts of other men is easily written; but to write what is original, as I suppose mine to be, required no little effort. The purport of the book is to teach men to interpret words by the unverbal things that words refer to; and not to interpret words by other words. I assumed that every proposition has an unverbal meaning, and when that unverbal meaning is found, language is properly at the end of its office. To persevere in interpreting any given word or set of words by other words is to pursue a round without end. I assumed that words are in themselves unmeaning sounds—French sounds, German sounds, English sounds; while the meaning that is unverbal is neither French, English, nor German, but some unverbal subjective something in man's consciousness; or some objective unverbal thing that our senses reveal. Nearly all preceding philosophies

went no further than phraseology. You were required to interpret the word *idea, mind, matter, etc.* into some other words, and every philosopher would inculcate a different verbal meaning; and hence all such discussions related to the verbal meaning of words. I discarded all such processes, my philosophy relating only to unverbal existences or things. I know not that to this day any person understands the above explanation in the manner I intend it to be understood, though nothing seems to me more plain, simple, and self-evident, and it must eventually come to be admitted. I assumed further that unverbal things are analysable into seven different classes—sights, sounds, tastes, feels, smells, emotions, and intellections. Each of the said classes is generically different from any and all the others. By this classification *scarlet* is a sight, *heat* a feel, *thunder* a sound, *odor* a smell, *sweet* a taste, *anger* an emotion, and *thought* an intellection. To know the particular one or more of these unverbal things that any word or proposition signifies, you must be taught by your own consciousness; each unverbal thing being alone its only proper expositor. It certainly is not the word or words that you may employ about it. To manifest the distinction between words and unverbal things is the first substantial advance ever made in metaphysical knowledge.

Johnson added that he had arranged the book in the form of lectures as "advantageous to perspicuity." He also said he had intended to devise "a set of sensible illustrations," but "never carried the conception into execution—principally from a want of sufficient external encouragement."

No "vanity press" ever drove a harder bargain with an aspiring author than the one the Carvills concocted, but Johnson seems to have entered into it with his eyes open. He unblushingly described the arrangement with his publishers:

Carvills were the only booksellers to whom I offered my lectures. The value of the work they professed themselves ignorant of, but as it is of a nature not deemed very saleable, they declined publishing it at their own risk. If they published it at my risk, I supposed they would make no effort to gain notoriety for it, and as its notoriety was alone my object, I entered into an arrangement with them that I thought would insure their efforts in the distribution of the book. I gave them the copyright; all profit was to be theirs, and if a loss should occur, I was to make it good to any extent not over a hundred dollars; and they were to call on me for this loss, if any, at the end of a year after the publication. I made no reservation of a single copy for myself, and all that I have gratuitously distributed (I should think fifty copies) I have purchased from them at a dollar to a dollar and a quarter the copy. Carvills, however, sent me six copies, intended, I suppose to be gratuitous. I have long suspected they make no efforts to get the work known, probably from the circumstance of its having cost them nothing.

One of the first copies Johnson sent to John Quincy Adams, who acknowledged it less than a month before his defeat by Andrew Jackson. Adams wrote dutifully on October 15, 1828, that he hoped to read it "when a mind more at ease than mine is at this time, and less absorbed by necessary occupations than it is now, will allow me to give it that deliberate application which a subject so abstracted and so profound requires." He had read enough, he said, "to perceive that it pursues an original turn of reflection," and he hoped that Johnson's meditations would prove "a cheering relaxation from more profitable labors in worldly affairs."

The first ray of hope that he might receive more than polite acknowledgments came when his friend Samuel Dakin sent him a draft essay on the book which he planned to submit to the *North American Review*. Dakin asked him to make any alterations he pleased, but Johnson returned it intact. "Indeed," he wrote later, "I felt that to be in any way concerned in the production of a review of my own work would constitute an indelicacy from which I shrunk." Dakin praised the *Philosophy* as "destined to produce many a salutary reform"; but the review never appeared, nor did Dakin receive a reply from the prestigious Boston magazine.

Johnson's mailing list included a number of people who he assumed were qualified to fathom the mysteries of "unverbal things," but the response was negligible. Harvard's president, Josiah Quincy, promised to give it "the attention my respect for the author demands," but never referred to it again. Benjamin Silliman, Yale's distinguished professor of chemistry and mineralogy, replied that "because of the number and the pressure of my avocations, it may be some time before I can read your work." He did offer a note of sympathy, however, for the author of a book "whose success with the public is at least doubtful." Van der Kemp had his usual polite reservations. Referring to Johnson's charge that John Locke was too verbose, he suggested that Johnson, too, might have made the experiment "of expunging with benefit to perspicuity." Finally, Van der Kemp chided Johnson for "not softening a little the doom of Spinoza—who, with all his errors, possessed a great deal of good and laid the foundation to destroy the theories of Descartes." He praised Spinoza's moral character, and suggested, "a few words of praise are a valuable remembrance." This remonstrance was occasioned by Johnson's objection to Spinoza's theory that Deity "was the first material out of which all things were fabricated." The philosopher's "verbal processes," said Johnson, had led him into an absurdity, for,

> when men find that language forces them to admit that all things were originally made out of nothing or of God, we may doubt whether language is applicable to such speculations. . . . By accumulating and arranging words, we can no more discover any realities which we have not experienced than we can, by taking thought, add one cubit to our stature.

There were two exceptions to these somewhat tedious responses. One came from Fanny Wright, known to her many enemies as "the great red harlot of infidelity," and to Walt Whitman as "beautiful in bodily shape and gifts of soul." The other came from Timothy Flint, the earnest proprietor of *The Western Review* in Cincinnati. Both recognized a revolutionary force in Johnson's work, and tried valiantly to encourage and advise him, but neither could wean him from his posture of aloofness. The former's "defect of sex," as it was called by many early opponents of women's rights, plus her radical notions, made Johnson stand off. As for Flint, he was a clergyman, and while Johnson was flattered by his encomiums, he would have preferred them to come from a scientist like Silliman at Yale.

Frances Wright (1795–1852) was born in Scotland, the daughter of a freethinker and an ardent promoter of the works of Thomas Paine. She came to America in 1818, and traveled extensively throughout the eastern part of the country, recording her impressions in *Views on Society and Manners* in *America* (1821). On her second trip to this country in 1825 she joined her friend, General Lafayette, during part of his triumphal tour, and continued to reside in America for the rest of her life. Influenced by the ideas of the British socialist Robert Owen, she founded Nashoba Colony in Tennessee for the benefit of emancipated slaves (an experiment in which she was accused of fostering miscegenation). Later, as editor of the *New Harmony Gazette,* and a tireless lecturer in northern cities, she shocked the public with her advanced ideas on birth control, divorce, free love, and her attacks on organized religion. She also became an abolitionist and, though she never played a formal role in the Women's Rights movement, a strong advocate of its principles. Her first letter to Johnson read in part:

The mistaking the sign for the thing has held and yet holds the human mind averted from knowledge, even as the mistaking the maxim for the truth; and the seeking in declamatory sayings instead of in our own sensations the rule of human life has led our feet astray from the paths of virtue, and blinded us to all the sources of true happiness. . . . We have now always to impart through the medium of words as vague and confused as the minds of those who employ them, what should be elicited to the opening faculties by practical experiments addressed to the senses. I sympathize truly with your labors, for I believe I understand both their difficulties and their value, and feel therefore not altogether unauthorized to express to you my acknowledgments as a member of the human family whose improvement you are assisting, no less than as an individual whom you have honored and obliged.

In Fanny Wright's second letter to Johnson, she said, "I feel persuaded your little work needs but to be known to make a revolution in the human mind, by causing it to detect the source of all its follies and disputes. How to make your labors known, therefore, is the thing to be considered."

Following up this practical line of thought, she asked some direct, and to Johnson, perhaps, impertinent questions. What were his arrangements with Carvill? What were they doing to promote the Book? One of her friends, she told Johnson, had tried to buy a copy of the *Treatise* from them, and the clerk, after denying its existence, had finally found one in the cellar. She suggested he arrange to send copies to her office in New York with authorization to promote and sell them, adding that her co-worker, a Frenchman named William Picquepal, might arrange to have the work translated into French and published in Paris.

Her next two suggestions, although undoubtedly wise ones, served only to confirm Johnson's impression that Miss Wright was stepping out of bounds. Fearing that some of his inferences that such concepts as "Divinity" and "Creation" were "purely verbal" might offend the prevailing orthodoxy, he had qualified his approach by exempting "Revelation," or Biblical testimony, from those truths about the nature of verbal and non-verbal things which could be adduced from the evidence obtained purely through the senses. Miss Wright, in common with many twentieth century critics of the *Treatise* felt that he had thus weakened his whole point about the nature of language, adding emphatically that his points appeared "misplaced in a work treating only of knowledge by sensation," and suggesting that they would appear to better advantage

A. B. Johnson, probably in his mid-thirties, watercolor on ivory by Carl Weinedel, 1827. *Courtesy of Bryan Johnson Lynch, Reading, Vt.*

THE BURNEY'S ACADEMY, center, in Gosport, England, which Johnson attended briefly as a boy around 1793. From *The Story of Gosport* (1965), by L. F. W. White, *by permission of S. W. P. Barrell, Publishers, Southsea, England.*

BARONESS HYDE DE NEUVILLE'S "View of Utica from the hotel September 1807" (six years after Johnson's arrival) represents the view from the front of the Holland Land Company Hotel (later known as the York House on Whitesboro Street). Col. Benjamin Walker, aide-de-camp to Baron von Steuben, and a close friend of Johnson's, was one of the earlier managers. The view looks south, up the center of Hotel Street, which served as a shortcut between the hotel and Genesee Street in the background. The water pump at the corner may be one of three installed by the village in 1805. The York House survived as a warehouse until 1966, when it was destroyed by fire. A reporter during the early 1800s described Utica as "a great emporium of European and other foreign goods with which the trades here supply a considerable portion of the country to the westward." Marshall B. Davidson, *New York: A Pictoral History* (Scribners, 1977). Drawing courtesy of *American Historical Prints, Prints Division, The New York Public Library*.

ABIGAIL ADAMS JOHNSON, probably in her mid-thirties, watercolor on ivory by Anson Dickenson, 1826. A granddaughter of John Adams and a niece of John Quincy Adams, she married Johnson after a brief courtship in 1814 which was carefully managed by Johnson's mother, Leah, and Abigail's mother, Nancy Smith Adams. The latter accompanied the Johnsons on their honeymoon at the John Adams home in Quincy, Mass. Abigail Adams Johnson died on July 4, 1836. *Courtesy of Bryan Lynch, Reading, Vt.*

JOHN ADAMS, second President of the United States, 1797–1801, oil on canvas by Gilbert Stuart. Johnson watched Stuart work on an Adams portrait during his honeymoon in Quincy, and noting how the artist's hands shook, suspected him of indulging in too much snuff and other stimulants. *Courtesy of the National Gallery of Art, Washington, D.C.*

Now THE SITE of the "Bank with the Gold Dome," the residence pictured above was the home of Alexander B. Johnson, pioneer merchant, lawyer, author, insurance man, and banker of Old Fort Schuyler and early Utica. Johnson entertained many prominent people in this house, including the Marquis de Lafayette and John Quincy Adams. Johnson bought the house sight unseen in 1815. *Courtesy of The Savings Bank of Utica.*

AN

ADDRESS

TO THE

UTICA LYCEUM,

Delivered, February 17, 1825.

BY

A. B. JOHNSON,

PREFATORY TO HIS

COURSE OF LECTURES

ON THE

Philosophy of Human Knowledge.

———

UTICA,

PRINTED BY MERRELL & HASTINGS,

No. 40, Genesee Street.

1825.

COVER PAGE OF PAMPHLET of Johnson's first lecture on language which later became the introductory chapter to his *Treatise on Language. Courtesy of Putnam Pamphlet Collection, Hamilton College Library, Clinton, N.Y.*

JOHN QUINCY ADAMS, sixth President of the United States, 1825–29. A former Boylston Professor of Rhetoric and Oratory at Harvard, Adams frequently took issue with Johnson's theories on language. Bronze bust by H. I. Browere, 1825. *Courtesy New York State Historical Association, Cooperstown.*

THIS VIEW OF UTICA by William Henry Bartlett was published in 1840. The view is to the north, with Washington Street at left and Genesee Street at right. The high ridge of Deerfield Hill, beyond the north side of the Mohawk River, forms the horizon. In the left background is the spire of the second edifice of the First Presbyterian Church, built in 1827 to the design of the Albany architect, Philip Hooker, and destroyed by fire in 1851. At Bagg's Square, at the far end of Genesee Street, is the Greek temple-like depot of the Utica & Schenectady and Utica & Syracuse railroads (later part of the New York Central). The gate posts at extreme right are those of Alexander Bryan Johnson. *Courtesy of the Oneida Historical Society, Utica, N.Y.*

VIEW IN GENESEE STREET, Utica, N.Y., engraving by John W. Barber and Henry Howe, taken from *Historical Collections of the State of New York* (1844). The view looks up Genesee Street from Bagg's Square and includes a parade of the local militia. Johnson walked back and forth daily from his home farther up Genesee Street past these buildings to his office at the Ontario Branch Bank several blocks south of Bagg's Square. The large building at the extreme right stood until the early 1970s, when it was demolished. *Courtesy of the Oneida Historical Society, Utica, N.Y.*

D. W. Moody, lithograph of Utica, N.Y., c. 1850, during the period of Utica's greatest growth. On the highland, extreme right, the New York State Asylum for the Insane, the first institution in the state to care for the mentally disordered, opened in 1834. It is an excellent example of Greek revival architecture. Right center is the Utica Presbyterian Church which excommunicated Johnson, and left center is the Episcopal Church which he later espoused. The old railroad station is lower left, with the stage coaches lined up next to it to receive passengers. The railroad was then called the Utica-Syracuse Railroad. John Street, center, and Genesee Street, left center, converge in Bagg's Square, foreground. *Courtesy of I. N. Phelps Stokes Collection of American Historical Prints, New York Public Library.*

The Oneida Institute, Whitesboro, N.Y., the first American institution of higher education to accept black students. It trained many black abolitionist leaders and was the focal point for abolitionist activism in New York State. Johnson disapproved of its "manual labor" requirements and its "radical curriculum."

A. B. JOHNSON, probably in his early fifties. From a daguerreotype. *Courtesy of Bryan Johnson Lynch, Reading, Vt.*

in "a separate treatise." She also suggested a different title, namely, *The Nature and Boundaries of Language: or A Treatise Upon Language, Showing its Use and Abuse.* Again she repeated her offer to publicize the work, and any subsequent books or pamphlets he might produce, in her magazine *The Free Enquirer;* and also "to have them read in our hall."

Johnson, who had stated in his book, "We possess a testimony within ourselves—the Holy Spirit acting on our feelings, and producing the fervent acquiescence which we term faith," firmly rejected Miss Wright's first suggestion, replying that so long as the book would be published by him, he had "essential reasons to preserve the part you propose to expunge," and that if it were to be published in French, the part about "Revelation" should be left intact. He made no reference to her suggested title change.

Some months later Miss Wright and Phicquepal visited Utica, and Johnson paid a brief call on them at Baggs Hotel, prior to a lecture she was to give there. His reaction was typical:

> I was much struck with her appearance. She was a tall and fair-complexioned woman of apparently thirty years of age, and her countenance exhibited a strongly defined perpendicular indentation between her eyebrows, that is supposed by Lavater to denote thoughtfulness, and which I had never before seen on the face of a female. She was good looking but not handsome, and somewhat masculine. Mr. Phicquepal seemed to listen with high respect to all she uttered, and he intimated that he expected to be highly edified by the conversation that would ensue between me and Miss Wright. But in this expectation he must have been sadly disappointed, for I purposely avoided all literary conversations, as I always shunned such a display, if I had felt able to enter into it, and which I never did. I excused myself from attending the lectures she proposed to give, for their character was wholly unsuited to the religious orthodoxy of Utica; and though I should have felt no repugnance to hear her peculiar tenets, my attendance would have been deemed out of character for me, and therefore I did not hear her.

It is a pity Johnson's obsessive puritanism caused him to shun this handsome, freethinking woman, one of his few contemporaries who might have brought him to the attention of that wider audience for which he yearned. Despite his coolness, however, Fanny Wright wrote an enthusiastic review of the *Philosophy* in the March 18, 1829, issue of the *Free Enquirer,* saying among other things:

A work of highest merit issued from the press of this city during the last year and while calculated to advance the human intellect by a full century in the path of true knowledge and sound thinking, we believe its appearance remains yet unnoticed, and all but unknown. This inattention, however, its enlightened author will know how to interpret.

At about the same time, Fanny Wright sent Johnson a copy of her new work, *A Course of Popular Lectures Delivered by Frances Wright* (New York, 1829). He wrote of it, "In her first lecture she spoke of my *Philosophy of Human Knowledge* and praised me highly therefor." The lecture was the sincerest form of flattery, for it was pure Johnson in content and style. It began:

Let us not be alarmed by sounding words, and let us not be deceived by them. Let us look to things. It is things which we have to consider. Words are, or more correctly, should be, only the signs of things. I say *they should be,* for it is a most lamentable truth that they are now very generally conceived to constitute the very substance of knowledge. Words, indeed, would seem at present contrived rather for the purpose of confusing our ideas, than administering to their distinctness and arrangement. Instead of viewing them as shadows, we mistake them for substance, and conceive that, in proportion as we enlarge our vocabulary, we multiply our acquirements.

Johnson acknowledged both the review and the *Lectures* in a single letter, and though it was couched in formal, third person terms, his respect for her intellect was obvious—or as obvious as he felt he could let it be without encouraging any closer association:

Miss Frances Wright will please accept my warmest acknowledgments for the very kind manner in which she has spoken of my lectures. I have read with much interest her own lecture, and while I thank her for transmitting it to me, I would say, that I see by it her commendation is valuable. I see, also, that Miss Wright is more likely to understand me than most other readers I shall obtain, and perhaps I may without insufferable vanity apply somewhat the same language to myself with reference to her lectures. I know we differ immeasurably on one essential point, and while I will not undertake the hopeless task of removing the difference, I desire to say that I yield to no man or woman in toleration. I can tolerate even intolerance. This I believe is the last degree of toleration—the Ultima Thule.

Finally, it is interesting to speculate on why Johnson got in touch with Fanny Wright. He tells us only that "Frances Wright, familiarly called Fanny Wright, wrote to me"; but it is clear that he first sent her a copy of his book. One explanation for his turning to this notorious advocate of numerous causes which he must have found incongenial may simply be that she was the editor of the controversial but popular, *Free Enquirer*. Dedicated to extreme Jacksonian democracy, it was a mouthpiece for intellectual radicals, and Johnson may have viewed it as a logical outlet for his own unorthodox notions on language. Also, at about the time Johnson's book was published, Congress was receiving a flood of petitions from prominent Sabbatarians to have post offices closed on Sundays. Fanny Wright had roared her opposition to such interference by the "priestcraft," and this was a subject close to Johnson's heart—as was her stand on the separation of church and state. Finally, she was also launching a series of attacks on the Bank of the United States which, within a few years, was to become a target of Johnson's wrath. If Johnson, then, were even a casual follower of her crusades he must have recognized a kindred soul, equipped to deal with his own unorthodoxies. He must also have known of his friend, Lafayette's, regard for her—a regard which nearly ruined the French hero's American tour when he insisted on taking her along with him, though not as far as Utica. Despite all this, however, he would certainly never have said with Walt Whitman (who heard Fanny Wright lecture when he was ten years old), "I never felt so glowingly toward any woman. She possessed herself of my body and soul!"

The Reverend Timothy Flint, whose review of Johnson's *Philosophy of Human Knowledge* was certainly the longest Johnson ever received, graduated with the class of 1800 at Harvard and shortly thereafter went into the Mississippi Valley as a missionary and part-time explorer. He later moved to Cincinnati, where he spent three years (1827–1830) as editor of the *Western Review*. He also wrote novels and short stories based on his Mississippi Valley experience. Perhaps his greatest literary success was his fanciful *Biographical Memoir of Daniel Boone*, which helped to establish the Boone legend. After giving up the *Western Review*, he moved to New York City, where he served briefly as editor of the *Knickerbocker Magazine* and wrote free-lance articles and stories for American and British periodicals. Among his numerous forgotten novels were *The Life and Adventures of Arthur Clenning* (1826), *The Shoshone Valley* (1830), and *George Mason, the Young Backwoodsman* (1829).

Apparently Johnson included Flint among the recipients of his *Philosophy,* for sometime in 1829 he received a long note from Flint thanking him for the book and promising "such a notice as my health will allow." "These are new and important views," wrote Flint, "which will throw strong light upon the origin and use of language." He chided Johnson, however, for his attacks upon natural theology. "I admit," he wrote, "that the question may recur, who made God? But we follow the division of the chain to the last link. Instinct, analogy, and the phrenological protuberances of veneration impel us to answer to the question—He who built all things is God! In other words I regret that anything was said that might be wrested to be adverse to Natural Religion. . . . I have not the honor to know you at all, but I am sure the author of this work cannot be a bigot."

Johnson noted in his autobiography that such praise "was grateful to me," adding that his readers might think, "I avow it too openly and repay it too assiduously." He presumed that Mr. Flint's praise "was yielded to me from benevolent motives," and that it was "due to my merits" rather than a "desire to please me." He answered Flint immediately—and with far more "assiduous" thanks than he gave to Fanny Wright:

> You know not how gratefully I received this morning your kind favor of the sixteenth inst. In me is an abundance of excitability, but I literally starve for lack of excitement—a mouthful of praise is a luxury to me. . . . The expectation of such a reward from the wise, the reflecting, and the liberal, was all I expected of my book; and as yet I have received too little to tempt me further in the painful and laborious occupation of book making. . . .

On the subject of "bigots," Johnson replied, "You judge correctly when you think I am not a bigot." And to reinforce Flint's conviction on that score Johnson enclosed a copy of his 1824 Fourth of July oration— a document which would serve him on numerous occasions as exhibit number one on this subject. Flint had asked him for a "sketch" of his life, and Johnson sent him the following:

> I have lived in Utica since I was fifteen years old, nearly twenty-eight years, and the only circumstance remarkable about me (though I am sorry it should be remarkable) is that all the distilled liquors I ever drank, either mixed with water or pure, would not fill a wine glass. Water is my uniform drink, and no man can have attained my age with less bodily suffering. I was either so fortunate or so unfortunate as to inherit enough property to keep me all my life from the pursuit of business; except that for about the last twelve years, I have had the principal supervision of a bank in this village. At the age of thirty-two, I commenced the study of law, and have attained the degree of attorney

and counsellor of our Supreme Court, though I have never practiced the profession. My literary education is perhaps in better keeping with the character of a philosopher, as it is entirely a result of my own unassisted efforts—at least from the age of twelve years. The remaining incidents of my life may be included in three grand events which are generally recorded in our family Bibles—born, married, and died. The first was in England, the second was to a granddaughter of the elder President Adams about fourteen years ago, and the last event is still to be revealed.

Johnson received Flint's twenty-page review in the March and April 1829 issues of the *Western Review,* and acknowledged it gratefully—without reference to any of the author's frequently stated regrets over Johnson's dismissal of "natural theology." His letter was largely devoted to the pain and futility of writing books:

> . . . I see nothing in your remarks but what gives me pleasure, except the labor of thought and wearisomeness of composition that I have occasioned you. If these exercises are as painful to you as they are to me, I strongly pray that you have a stronger motive for their performance than I have.

Flint's review was honest and, despite certain reservations based on his own theological tenets, highly complimentary. Like the *Philosophy* itself, however, the review seems to have gone unnoticed. Six years later, in a series of "Sketches of the Literature of the United States" written for the London *Athenaeum,* Flint summed up his impressions of the Johnson work in the following terse paragraph:

> This most ingenious tracing of language to its elements by investigating the sources from which words were derived, evincing profound thought, directed in a channel, as far as we know, perfectly original, the production of an opulent scholar in his closet, also fell unnoticed from a press which at present seems disposed to direct attention to nothing but the most insipid of flat novels.

Johnson's own last words on the subject of Timothy Flint sounded a note of finality: "Mr. Flint soon removed from Cincinnati to New York as to a better place for his usefulness; and after much literary labor in his new location, he died. I never saw him personally or had any other intercourse with him than the foregoing."

In concluding his account of the publication and reception of his *Philosophy of Human Knowledge,* Johnson transcribed a number of letters from unknown readers who had somehow stumbled upon the book in various parts of the country, and had recognized in him a kindred lonely voice in the American wilderness; and these letters led him to melancholy, and half-humorous, reflections. "I had no reason to believe," he wrote,

> that any of the notices above set forth and others more complimentary that I omit, were induced by any mercenary or other sinister motives, for none of the parties ever solicited any favor from me and never received any—not even to the extent of any social civilities, my habits always being very recluse so that I never gave a dinner party, and never, since my marriage, was a guest at any one that I remember. In relation, however, to epistolary commendation, I am aware that it is not conclusive of the work it praises. The best criterion of merit is the fate of a book which it receives from the general public; and thus judged my literary labors have not been successful and I have wasted my life in self-delusion. I suppose no publication can be so eccentric but it will meet with applauding readers as eccentric as the author. We had at one time living in Utica an ingenious mechanic, but we deemed him a monomaniac on the subject of steam. Finally, he left Utica and went to Troy where he found a man as crazy as himself on the same subject; and as the Troy man had money which the Utica man lacked, they began experiments on their conceived steam improvements, and soon became ruined as all sane men supposed they would. I hope, however, this case is not parallel to my publications for those who applauded them, though some of the letters received by me would seem to favor such a conclusion.

Fortunately Johnson, despite his suspicion that he might resemble the "monomaniac on the subject of steam," was not soon to become "ruined" at least not financially.

CHAPTER 12

1829–1831

Civic, Business, and Literary Demands

AFTER HER SEVENTH PREGNANCY IN FOURTEEN YEARS, Abigail delivered on September 27, 1829, some six weeks after her mother's
death, their first daughter, and they named her Sarah Adams Johnson.
Recalling the event in his old age, Johnson wrote: "The birth of a
daughter greatly pleased me. I remember walking in the fields near
Utica where I often walked, and contemplating her future destiny with
all the good views that my ever active imagination could present."

Other more immediate problems than Sarah's future were pressing
in on Johnson at this time, however. The charters of most banks in New
York State were drawn so as to expire in 1832, and bankers throughout
the state were in an uproar over "various theories, some very new and
wild" as to the future conduct of banking operations. Martin Van Buren,
the new governor, soon to be called to the State Department by Andrew
Jackson, spent most of his brief term of office on an ambitious bank
reform program which included the so-called Safety Fund plan. A board
of commissioners was established to supervise bank operations, with an
increase in state control. Johnson described the plan as follows:

Every bank was to contribute three percent of its capital to this fund,
and from it were to be paid any bank notes or bank debt that the insolvency of any bank should leave unpaid. On any such loss a new
contribution by the solvent banks was to be made till the fund should
regain its original integrity, but no bank was to contribute to the fund
more than half of one percent each year, and the fund was to be held
and managed by the State.

In addition to debates over the "Safety Fund," Albany legislators
were also investigating "branch banks," Ontario Branch Bank being one

of several such institutions in the state. Some of the legislators were in a mood to replace them with "new and independent" institutions. Johnson went off to Albany to do what he could to stop these "wild schemes." Johnson agreed to support the Safety Fund, thus pleasing the legislators who felt that his example would bring other banks into line—which it did; but he agreed to do so only if the charter of the Ontario Branch were renewed. Johnson presented his case successfully and returned to Utica well pleased with himself. "I found," he wrote, "that no person had expected the branch would have been retained, and the advocates of a new bank felt sure of its being established in its stead."

It was perhaps during the visit to Albany that Johnson became acquainted with young Millard Fillmore, a state senator from Buffalo, later to become the fourth American president with whom Johnson was on speaking terms. Fillmore had introduced a bill in the state legislature to make "atheism apply only to the credibility of witnesses in the courts, and not to their competency." Johnson promptly sent off a letter of congratulations to him. It read in part:

> The existing exclusion of infidels is unfortunately connected with political considerations which will prove an obstacle to the dispassionate consideration of your proposition; but I have long deemed the existing rule a stain upon our jurisprudence, a vestige of bigotry, and an unjustifiable infringement of the freedom of opinion. . . . I am a Christian of the straightest sect. But I will not pay Christianity so poor an homage as to infer that it needs the miserable support of any legal coercion.

Johnson's liberalism received an even sterner test on the night of July 29, 1829, when he was asked to deliver an address before the newly formed Utica Temperance Society. The temperance movement got its start in central New York during the Finney revivals, with the influx of hard-drinking "canawlers" into the region providing the horrible examples. At Hamilton College, students formed a temperance group which also embraced antisecret society agitators and later, abolitionists; while in Schenectady the president of Union College, the colorful Eliphalet Knott, would soon terrify his students with the news that they were liable to death by "spontaneous combustion" if they ventured too close to a stove while drinking alcohol. Compared to Saratoga Springs, where temperance societies were launched in 1808 when tourists began to ignore the mineral waters for tastier brews, Utica was slow to begin, but it made up for it later by launching the mother chapter of "The Order of the Good Templars," an international temperance society which soon spread into Canada and western Europe.

Johnson's address to the new Utica group was not one of his more distinguished bits of oratory, marked as it was by such noncharacteristic rhetoric as "Oh! Woe! Woe!," or, "Give it wing, O Heaven!—Speed it, O earth!" He did, however, express reservations on the subject of temperance which must have damped the ardor of the meeting somewhat. "I neither drink, nor administer to drinking," he said, "but far be from me the tyranny that would constrain others to my practices, however pure, or to my opinions, however evengelical." He continued, "I love temperance, but I love freedom more; I abhor intemperance, but I dislike intolerance more. The liberty which I possess of refraining from a drink, I would yield equally to those who wish to drink."

The orator's tolerance, however, did not extend to females who wished to join the movement. "I invoke the regard of females," he said, "but I seek not their cooperation. I have heard of female temperance societies, but I can view them only as a slander on the sex." And, forgetting, apparently, the excesses of some of his friends' wives which he had described earlier, he added, "I would dispose of female drinking as the Romans disposed of patricide—deem it too improbable to require regulation." Years later, when the Maine Liquor Law, calling for total prohibition, was being considered for adoption in New York State, Johnson reiterated his views on coercion in a newspaper article written in 1854 and later republished in *A Guide to the Right Understanding of Our American Union*. "We greatly mistake the Maine Liquor Question," he wrote,

> when we look only upon its effects on drunkenness. . . . Underlying all is the greater question of self-government; not one man governing another, but each man governing himself. Even Adam was permitted the liberty of eating the forbidden fruit, for barren indeed would have been his total abstinence had it depended on coercion.

Johnson sent a copy of his temperance address to John Quincy Adams, who used it as an excuse to thank Johnson for the many previous enclosures he had failed to acknowledge. "For a succession of years," wrote the ex-President,

> my own time was so totally absorbed with public duties that I had none left for meditation, or even for reading. . . . I perused of your publications enough to convince me that they were the productions of

a mind original in the turn of thought, and relying entirely, or nearly so, upon itself. Some of them were on subjects so abstruse in their nature, and were so discussed by you, that I could scarcely trust myself, without a deeper examination of them than I was able to give, to form a judgment upon them. They are now all at Washington whence I have not yet removed the books and papers collected during my public service there.

Adams concluded his letter with the hope that he would someday be better acquainted with the Johnson family, and that they "will all consider me as their friend and kinsman." Johnson replied with a brief note of thanks, and assured Adams that "no danger exists that my children will fail to consider you their friend and kinsman." And he added, "I am a zealous believer in the moral influence of consanguinity and the principle shall not fail in my own family from any defect, on my part, in its machinery."

Johnson's regard for "consanguinity" was never more deeply expressed than in his concern for his children's welfare. Sometime during the spring of 1829, his son Bryan, a student at a school in the Utica suburbs, apparently misbehaved, and was slapped by one of his tutors. Johnson quickly got off a note to the headmaster, Charles Bartlett, and, echoing his own father's reactions to a similar incident in Johnson's childhood, read Mr. Bartlett a lecture on corporal punishment.

Boys, whatever we may think, possess our feelings, and blows will as certainly excite hostility, mutiny, dislike and every bad feeling in them. Nothing keeps such consequences from bursting forth, but the same necessity that keeps southern slaves at their tasks. Besides, the idea is unsound in philosophy that the mind can be stimulated by blows on the body.

At about the same time, thirteen-year-old Alexander provided his father with still another opportunity to pass an object lesson on to posterity. Alexander had set out on a two-week walking tour of New England with a group of amateur geologists. When he began the journey, said Johnson, "he was very slender." However, on his return he "kept rapidly acquiring flesh, and became very fat." "I have always attributed this change," said Johnson, "to the great and unusual exertions of traveling far and long on foot, and I record it as a lesson worth preserving and as an error to be avoided." Johnson, as he had indicated earlier in his attack on Manual Labor schools, was no advocate of physical exertion.

As the new year, 1830, came around, Johnson dropped his usual caution as an investor and began to buy up stock in various banks throughout central New York. In the midst of a flurry of investments, Johnson became interested again in the question of the usury laws that prevailed in New York State and, at the suggestion of his friends Samuel Beardsley and Nathan Williams, he printed a questionnaire which he sent to "distinguished persons in various states to obtain from them information on the legal interest rates in their respective states, and of the legal penalties for taking any excess of interest . . . and also requesting their opinion of usury laws generally." The replies came in quickly, the majority arguing for retaining the laws as they were, and having them strictly enforced. From John Quincy Adams, however, he received a lengthy argument that "penal laws against usury are incompatible with the spirit of free government, unjust in principle, and inefficient in practice." Retracing the history of such laws from pre-Revolutionary times to the present, Adams told of his disappointment when a bill of his own to lessen the penalties for usury in Massachusetts had been vetoed by Governor Caleb Strong after it had passed both houses of the legislature. Adams concluded by admitting that there should be "some power . . . competent to relieve the sufferer from the obligation of bad bargains," but, "further than this, legislation should not interfere with contracts."

Johnson disagreed openly with Adams. This letter, he wrote, "showed how superficially the question of usury is viewed by men of high standing." Revealing that he was a reader of utilitarian philosopher Jeremy Bentham, Johnson attacked the latter's principle that "money is like every other commodity, and that traffic in money should be as free as traffic in other articles." The success of Bentham's *Treatise on Usury,* "under the false assumption of its foundation, is one of the curiosities of literature," he said. Later, in 1856, when a bill was introduced in Albany to repeal all usury laws, Johnson used the elaborate documentation he had acquired to publish a strong defense of those laws in the Albany *Evening Journal.* "The repeal would have been effected," he wrote, "but for my article."

While all this activity and speculation on economic matters was going on, Johnson and his family were occupying their evenings in an unusual fashion—putting together a "collated dictionary."

The public first learned about Johnson's new role as a lexicographer from a pamphlet he published late in 1830 entitled *A Plan for a Collated Dictionary; or, A Complete Index to the English Language,* designed, as he put it, "to exhibit together all words which relate to the same subject for the benefit of persons who are not acquainted with the whole compass of the language and to assist the memory of persons who are acquainted."

The *Plan* began with a rationale for a new kind of dictionary. "Our language," he wrote,

> is rich with spoils from every other, but uncollected except in the Babel of an alphabetical arrangement. Webster lists 70,000 words. These all men are supposed to know. On this false assumption is founded the alphabetical arrangement of our dictionaries. To teach us the words themselves lexicography has never made an attempt. . . . If irony were suited to so grave an evil, a lexicographer might say to students with reference to his definitions what a celebrated cookery book says of cooking a hare—first, catch it.

One can get a fair idea of what the "Collated Dictionary" might have been like from some of the questions Johnson asked and answered in his published *Plan*. What, he asked, are *cobweb, summer, spring, tree, son,* adjectively? The answers: *araneous, estival, vernal, arboreal, filial.* What are the verbs for *doctrine, naked, abscess, climate, timid,* etc.? The answers: *indoctrinate, denude, imposthumate, acclimate, intimidate.*

Another important relationship between words is that which they bear to their antonyms, and these, too, should be collated. Thus *war/peace; potent/impotent; desecrate/consecrate; analogous/anomolous,* etc.

In discussing the relationship between "affirmatives" and "negatives" Johnson takes a philosophical approach which will be familiar to readers of his *Treatise on Language*. "The blind," he says, "cannot recognize darkness, because they cannot know what 'not darkness' is. The deaf cannot recognize silence, because they cannot know what 'not-silence' is." He quickly drops these speculations, however, and goes on to further examples of words and their negatives: *laudable/illaudable;* "capable of weeping"/*illachrymable;* "capable of decay"/*indefectible,* etc.

Johnson also wanted other types of groupings. For example, under *digestion* he would place *peptic, eupeptic, dyspeptic,* etc; and under *murder: patricide, sororicide, deicide, infanticide, tyrannicide.* In short, as Johnson puts it, he sought

> a complete index to our language, so that a person who refers to any word may see all the words with which it is connected in significa-tion;—may see also how the word can be expressed substantively,

adjectively, verbally, and adverbally; may see its synonyms, its corre-latives, its negatives, and affirmatives.

Johnson described the way in which he and his family went about the work of compilation:

> I procured two blank folio books. Each is the size of a volume of news-papers. On the outer edge of every second page, the bookbinder pasted a column, cut from an English dictionary.
> Having a whole dictionary thus formed of single columns . . . I took another dictionary, and with scissors cut out, for instance, the word *abacus,* with its definition. This word purports to be "a counting table." I pasted it in my dictionary against the verb, *to count.* But abacus is also "the uppermost member of a column." I therefore cut another *abacus* with its definition from a supplemental dictionary and pasted it into mine, against the word, *column.* After a little familiarity with the labor, and with the assistance of my children to whom it was a pleasant and instructive amusement, I could generally cut out two hundred words of an evening, and place them appropriately in my dictionary.

Initially, the Young Men's Association of Albany offered to assist with Johnson's proposed dictionary, and later Johnson entered into prolonged negotiations with Lyman Cobb, author of several dictionaries and the publisher of *Cobb's Toys* and other self-help books for children. Cobb assured Johnson that his work would "soon supersede all dictionaries on any other plan." Cobb kept at Johnson for more than three years to complete his dictionary, or at least, to turn it over to him for completion, but Cobb's perennial insolvency and his insistence on getting a share of the profits frightened Johnson away, goading him into his old familiar theme, "as I never wrote for pecuniary gain, I was unwilling to hazard therein any pecuniary loss." Despite Johnson's intransigence, however, Cobb acted as his literary agent in 1835, and succeeded in placing the revised *Treatise on Language* with Harper and Brothers. On that occasion, with perhaps a touch of bitterness, he wrote to Johnson, "Messrs. H. & B. never throw the risk and responsibility of getting up and selling a new work upon the author."

Johnson finally rejected any assistance with the dictionary, pre-ferring, he said, "to devote my own leisure to the production." When he found, however, that it involved "merely mechanical labor," he abandoned the whole plan on the grounds that his time "could be more profitably employed" than in cutting up dictionaries. Eventually, he turned all of his folio books and his notes over to his son William Clarkson Johnson, who hoped someday to complete the work, but never did.

Johnson's *Plan* attracted more attention, perhaps, than any of his other published pamphlets. His friend Bloodgood wrote that he was satisfied "the work would revolutionize the lexicographical world," and asked for copies to send to London. Peter du Ponceau, himself a lexicographer, wrote from Philadelphia that the dictionary would greatly "facilitate the study of the acquisition of the English language," and reminded Johnson that his plan had once been attempted by Court de Gébelin for Latin and French, but that death "had arrested his progress." John Quincy Adams wrote a long letter to Abigail echoing, in his frequent references to Samuel Johnson, some of his own early lectures at Harvard when he held the chair of Boylston Professor of Rhetoric and Oratory. He complained that Johnson's plan was "not entirely new, bolstering his argument with numerous references to similar dictionaries in the Latin and Greek languages, though admitting that nothing quite like them had been attempted in English." Rather patronizingly he advised the Johnson family to continue the task "which has provided you all amusement," and then added some contributions of his own. Johnson had run into difficulty turning "stepmother" into an adjective, and Adams suggested "novercal," adding, "and if your husband wishes to complete his set of words from this root he may introduce the word to *novercalize,* and the adverb *novercally* in the substantives, *novercation* and *novercality.*" He reminded Abigail, however of the ridicule heaped on Samuel Johnson for his definition of *network* as "anything reticulated or decussated, with interstices between the intersections."

Those who urged Johnson to continue with his dictionary were probably correct in their conviction that this was his opportunity to make a name for himself in literature. That Johnson was more than a little wistful over his failure is obvious in the correspondence he initiated many years later with Peter Mark Roget, compiler of the perennially successful *Thesaurus.* In 1854 one of Johnson's sons returned from a visit to the Smithsonian Institution and reported to his father that he had heard news of a new English work that seemed to be founded on the plan of his dictionary. Recalling that his friend Bloodgood had sent copies of the *Plan* to London, Johnson concluded that the *Plan* had "originated the work of Mr. Roget." Johnson kept no copy of his letter to Roget, but the reply from England, while pleasant enough about any hints of plagiarism which Johnson may have dropped, was rather emphatic on other matters. Roget wrote:

I have just received your letter of the twenty-seventh ulto. by which you inform me that you had, many years ago, projected a work somewhat similar in principle to the one I lately published under the title *Thesaurus of English Words and Phrases Classified and Arranged, so as to Facilitate the Expression of Ideas and Assist in Literary Composition,* and of which an improved and enlarged edition was published about a year ago. Your work was quite unknown to me, and I shall feel much interest in perusing the pamphlet you mention as having been published by you, if I should ever be so fortunate as to meet with it, as also your more recent work on language. I have not yet received the book you speak of sending me, but I beg to thank you by anticipation. I am rather surprised that you have not met with my *Thesaurus,* for I have learned that a pirated edition of it has been printed and sold in the United States—of course without my consent or participation. To this flagrant national disregard of justice, by which English authors are much injured, I must necessarily submit. I only hope that the buccaneering editor has not introduced into the work any corruptions of his own—a fraud which I understand has occasionally been practiced and against which the aggrieved author is allowed no means of protecting himself.

In September 1831, Uticans were stirred by the plight of the Poles in their ill-fated struggle for liberation against Russia, and a mass meeting similar to the one previously held for the embattled Greeks was organized, with Johnson serving as chairman. This time the sum of $974.59 was collected, to be sent to General Lafayette, now seventy-four, who had appealed to Americans to aid the Polish cause. Johnson produced a graceful letter of transmittal to the venerable champion of liberty. It read in part:

Utica, which in 1825 you honored with your presence, and which we hope is still in your remembrance, has laid on me the pleasing task of transmitting to you $974.59 for the assistance of Poland. . . . We send the money, then, as a mere symbol of the solemn interest which Polish heroism has excited in us for Poland; and as a recognition of her enrollment in the martyrology of liberty, not, we trust, to receive a martyr's doom, but to live in everlasting glory among nations. We send it that the Poles may see also, in this spontaneous tribute of a small and remote inland village, that the great community of twelve millions of freemen of which we are a fraction, hold universally in detestation the monstrous perversion that people are the property of their government. . . . In what way our little contribution shall reach Poland, we leave unlimitedly to your knowledge and discretion. I deeming myself peculiarly happy in an opportunity of expressing to you our fondest and most cherished recollections, I remain your fellow citizen.

The General acknowledged Utica's gift in a gracious letter, which Johnson ceremoniously presented to Utica's mayor a year later when the village was incorporated as a city. In his letter of presentation, he reminded the mayor that his own father, Bryan, had "created not a little of the pristine impulse to which Utica is indebted for its eminence," and offered up Lafayette's tribute as "the best felicitation in my power to our new civic capacity." "Time," he added,

> which will soon translate to Heaven the venerable and extraordinary writer of the transmitted letter, will consecrate the relic, while even our humble efforts for liberty in Poland, chronicled by its pages, may inspire the future inhabitants of our City to sacrifice property for worthy public ends and to the favoring of universal philanthropy, which together constitute the glory of any people.

The original of Lafayette's letter was destroyed by fire many years later, but Johnson treasured the copy he had kept, and placed it in his memoir:

> The resolutions, the address, the donation of $974.59, and the letter which my American fellow-citizens of Utica have been pleased to send to me, could not fail to excite those feelings of admiration, pride, and gratitude, the more gratifying to my heart when I remember the situation of your part of the country in the years 1777 and 1794, as well as the welcome bestowed upon me six years ago in your flourishing and beautiful town. The unhappy downfall of Poland will have been known in Utica long before this answer can reach you. But while we have to mourn together over the fate of that heroic nation, and to hope the day of justice shall again rise upon them, we find some consolation in the thought that the appropriation of fraternal relief could never be so seasonable as it proves to be in their present circumstances. I have requested the American committee that had framed the first address to the sympathy of the citizens of the United States to assist me in the judicious distribution of the money entrusted to my hands. We meet every week, and there is an understanding between us, the French committee, and a committee of the Poles already arrived in this capital. Accounts of those proceedings have already been transmitted to New York. Every mark of your so long experienced affection and confidence is to me a most precious treasure. I beg you, gentlemen, to receive yourselves, and to transmit to the citizens of Utica the homage of my grateful and affectionate respect.

Johnson carefully avoided any personal references in his letter that accompanied the gift to the Poles, but he had also sent a separate note to Lafayette conveying the "kindest and most respectful regards of my self and my family." He said, "We take a deep interest in everything that relates to you; and in this we act but in unison with the whole American people." In a characteristic postscript he expressed the hope that the general would acknowledge the formal letter "without adverting therein to this private communication of mine." Lafayette followed Johnson's protocol, and in a brief personal note to Johnson assured him that "Your public and private letters have been most gratifying to me. The kindness of your own and your family's welcome on my visit to Utica are remembered with cordial affection and gratitude."

When Utica became a city, and hung Johnson's gift in its Council Chambers, it bestowed the General's name on one of its main thoroughfares.

CHAPTER 13

1831–1834

Language: Theory and Practice

SHORTLY AFTER THE APPEARANCE of the *Plan for a Collated Dictionary*, the New York State Lyceum, which Johnson had helped to organize, invited him to deliver an "anniversary address" at a convention in Utica. Casting about for a topic, Johnson decided to make another attempt to explain his thoughts on language in terms that a listening audience might comprehend. However, public neglect of his *Philosophy of Human Knowledge* was uppermost in his mind, and he devoted the beginning of his lecture to a statement on the dilemma of the serious writer in America, and the sad state of American culture in general. He called his lecture "A Discourse on Language," and readied it for the program. However, the delegates never appeared, and the event was canceled.

The Lyceum movement was a short-lived affair, a product of the first blush of Jacksonian democracy, largely dying out by 1840. For one thing, its usual program content was often well over the heads of the workingclass audiences for which it had been designed. For another, most Lyceums imposed a strict ban on political discussions, and politics was the subject people most wanted to talk about during the Jacksonian era. The Utica Lyceum withered away into a debating society called the Young Men's Association, and Johnson took no further part in it.

Although the lecture was not delivered, Johnson printed it and sent copies to his friends. Johnson took his cue, perhaps, from John Adams' earlier remark that "American books do not sell in America." Referring to his own experience, he said, "In 1828 I attempted to develop this science [of language] but the book received no praise, no censure, nor perusal." He added, "I seek not to animate the dead. . . . A period must arrive when every science must be reformed by the principles thus

188

diffused, however worthless they appeared by my illumination." He then commented on the fate of American authors in general:

> Other countries boast of their "sublimest poet," their "profoundest philosopher"; but Americans ignore their poets and philosophers. England regards us with metropolitan superciliousness. . . . We regard English authors with a provincial awe which makes us receive as oracular even their contempt of our literature.

Among the suggestions Johnson offered was the establishment of a national library devoted entirely to American writings. He then lashed out at American book reviewing, singling out James Audubon, who survived "without a pittance of encouragement from the American press," and achieved fame only after he had been "crowned with the laurels of Europe." To cap his indictment Johnson turned to the local scene. Had John Milton "written his books at Utica he would have been unknown still, even here, and not great anywhere. With us the love of glory no sooner kindles itself into a little blaze than the damp around us extinguishes it forever." Johnson made no effort to rationalize that all-pervading "damp," as did Gulian Verplanck, another New York State writer, in an address given at Union College in 1836. "There are some meditations," explained Verplanck, "so subtle and unreal, so remote from use . . . that they can find no room among the strife and bustle, the railroad noise and rapidity of this work-day world of America." Johnson knew about this "work-day world," for he was a part of it, but he could not forgive it for ignoring his literary efforts.

Johnson's friends greeted his "Discourse" with interest, and John Quincy Adams, now that he had the leisure to read "general literature," dispatched his longest letter to Johnson, ranging over a wide variety of topics. He responded first to the author's commentary on the neglect of American Literature and his suggestion for a library of native literature:

> A few days since I received under a cover directed in your handwriting, a printed copy of your "Discourse on Language" which I have read with perhaps less pleasure than I should have done, if it had contained more welcome truths. The insensibility of the people within our country, to the merits of our own literature has often been remarked, though never to my knowledge with the keenness of severity and the aptitude of illustration with which you have presented it to view. The fact is, I fear, unquestionable, and it has sometimes occurred to me that it would be an interesting and perhaps useful inquiry to trace it to its causes—at first, how far and within what limitations this neglect of native literature is justly chargeable upon our countrymen; secondly,

how much of it is attributable to a general insensibility to literature, and how much to the quality of that which our native writers produce. Your namesake, the lexicographer of Lichfield, defined *oats* as "grain which in England is generally given to horses, but in Scotland is food for man." This was deemed by the fiery Scots an insult, not that the fact was questioned, but because there was insinuated in the definition something identical between the brute creation in England and the human species in Scotland. Now, philosophically speaking, oats are just as fit for the nurture of the human body as wheat, and where the soil will produce oats and will not bear wheat, the men of the region must accommodate themselves to the less palatable meal, or import the other from abroad or starve. Thus the Irishman feeds upon potatoes, we of the Yankee land upon maize, and the Carolinian upon rice; but we all know that in all these vegetables, there is less nutritious and less palatable matter than in the harvests that wave around you at Utica. We all, I presume, prefer wheaten bread when we can get it; yet I have met with a Scot who stoutly maintained that no wheaten flour was ever kneaded into bread so delicious as the oatmeal cake, as they make it in Scotland; nor should I go far to find a Yankee preferring an Indian pudding to a loaf of the best wheaten flour that your fields could supply. Your suggestion that it would be a good purpose to collect a library composed exclusively of native literature is a good seed, even if sown in a barren soil. I cannot persuade myself that it would be impracticable to form and keep alive such a society in one or another of our populous cities; and it would be the more desirable, as the formation of large private libraries seems to be unattainable by the character of our Institutions, and we accordingly have no such thing. But a library of native literature might, among other good effects, teach us a lesson of humility. Of what would it consist? How long is it since the Aristarchus of Edinburgh [Sidney Smith] put the trumpet to his mouth and blundered out, "Who reads an American book?" If Americans can produce no books, but such as nobody will read, why should they complain that their literature is neglected? If the soil yields nothing but Indian corn, must we interdict the importation of flour? Among the reasons which retard the growth of our literature is that which I have just suggested—we have no private libraries. Gentlemen in easy circumstances and having a taste for literature collect a few books, enough to adorn the upper shelves of a mahogany bookcase with glass doors, and that is their provision for life. Those books are often works of sterling merit and sometimes merely of fashionable repute. A library— even a private library—deserving of the name requires a large space for its location. Our dwelling houses are not built with dimensions capable of holding a considerable collection of books, and although there are among us men of opulence, who build large and costly houses, I know not a single instance in which room has been found in such a house for a capacious library.

Adams also took up those portions of the "Discourse" dealing with language, which Johnson had been unable to resist dwelling upon:

Your subject, if I understand you, is the inherent imperfection of language by its undertaking to generalize that which nature produces individually. The position is perhaps incontrovertible, but is this imperfection remediable? Is not the classification of objects produced individually by nature an enlargement of the powers of language? The producing power of nature is infinite, but the mind of man is finite to conceive and still more finite to impart. Language is one of the modes by which man imparts his thoughts to his fellow men. If the scriptural account of the creation is to be taken not as hieroglyphic or allegorical but in its literal sense, God himself used language, by naming Heaven, Earth, and Sea as he created them. But the beasts of the field, and the fowls of the air, he brought to Adam, and whatever he called every living thing, that was the name thereof. Perhaps, also, the subsequent confusion of tongues at Babel, and the yet later gift of tongues to the Apostles of Christ would deserve consideration in a disquisition upon language. But if you set all this aside, and consider language physiologically and philologically, you see in it a human invention for the conveyance of thought by the tongue. I say the tongue, because that is the principal organ used to effect the purpose; and from that the word language is derived. But the lips, the teeth, the larynx, the lungs and how many other organs I know not, contribute to the operation; and the result is all communicated to the ear—the only primitive recipient of thought by language. By another invention of more marvelous ingenuity, man has devised a means of printing language to the eye, by the use of the hand. But all this is feeble and imperfect in its nature. Man has the perception only of an infinitely small portion of the objects created by God; and of that infinitely small portion he is able to convey only a parcel infinitely small, to his fellow creature man. Language, therefore, as a nomenclature of things must not pretend to cope with the infinite varieties of nature, or of the Creator but must content itself with the humbler character of a vehicle to convey from man to his neighbor, a few of his thoughts; and as it is the interest of all to multiply as much as possible the agents of this faculty, is not the methodical aggregation of many things differing by individuality, but generically identical—one of the most effectual imaginable expedients to multiply the powers of language and to enlarge the domain of speech.

Johnson could have found no fault with the early portions of the Adams letter, but the latter part, dealing with language, seems to have spoiled the entire epistle for him, for he appended a note in his autobiography saying, "I copy this long letter as due to his social position which consecrates whatever proceeds from him as the temple sanctifies all that pertains thereto." He also added a note of explanation:

> My "Discourse on Language" in no way conflicts with any of the remarks of Mr. Adams. It was designed by me simply as an exposition of the nature of language, and by no means complaining of language as it is. Language is doubtless all that Mr. Adams maintains, but the more we understand its nature, the less we shall be deceived by its inevitable generalities and other defects.

Johnson did not miss any of the innuendo in Adam's question, "Why should we persist in writing what all people persist in not reading?" He explained in his autobiography:

> I write from urgency of my inclination: as flowers bloom in the forest, irrespective of whether they shall be viewed or not. They bloom as a necessity of their organization, and I, with many more like me, write and publish as a necessity of my organization. We also possess hope which tells us that a time may come when what we write will be appreciated. If this is a delusion it is only one of thousands with which hope cheers us through life; and when we yield to its deceptive prophecies, we but yield to the nature which Providence has given to us.

He also expanded on an interesting metaphor in his "Discourse" to illustrate the demands of vanity on a serious writer, and his own consuming need for recognition.

> In my "Discourse on Language" I alluded to Martin Van Buren under the figure of a "Queen Bee." Mr. Van Buren commenced life as a law student, and after passing through various grades of honor, he at length aspired to the Presidency, which he subsequently obtained. I endeavored to show that men grow by the honors they obtain, though we are prone to suppose that honors are a consequence of preliminary attainments. I said: "Naturalists affirm that the larva of common bees is convertible into a Queen Bee by ministrations which the hive can perform. Similar transformations are produced by men on each other. I have traced the process in the young attorney [Van Buren] rough from his native village, and seen him successively transformed into the adroit legislator, the shrewd attorney general, the eloquent senator, the capacious governor, the profound head of a department, the confidential ambassador, panting, perhaps, for the presidential chair which he

may well grace and with countless partisans eager to see him seated. The man, thus exalted, seems like the Queen Bee, peculiarly endowed by nature—but I see in him nothing but the ordinary expansion of intellect and ambition, by a course of high, popular feeding.

Alvin Bronson, a friend of Johnson's, showed this passage to Van Buren, who was "greatly amused," and borrowed Bronson's copy "to read it again more leisurely."

The literary New York banker, Gorham Worth, also sent Johnson an appraisal of the "Discourse" which elicited from Johnson some astringent remarks on America's two favorite authors, James Fenimore Cooper and Washington Irving. Worth had described those parts of the "Discourse" dealing with language as "too abstract for my taste, too metaphysical for my habits of thought, and too philological for my studies." He approved of the earlier portion, however, and remarked that Irving's works were "over-rated," and that Cooper's works were "not worth reading." Worth's reference to Cooper and Irving brought forth the following:

> You speak of Cooper and Irving like an author, for authors and women cannot bear the praises of anyone but themselves. I fear I have a touch of this infirmity, for I never read any of Cooper's trash and never shall; but Irving tells very pretty stories, and I mean to add them to my stock of nursery amusements, though they will never be as popular as Jack the Giant Killer and Tom Thumb. . . .

Johnson did eventually unbend in his attitude toward fiction. He may not yet have been ready to share the enthusiasm with which, in November 1841, his son Charles, then a freshman at Geneva College [now Hobart], suggested eagerly to him, "If you are reading *Barnaby Rudge,* you will find that the *Brother Jonathan* publish it one week before the *New World!*"; and by March 14, 1846, his son Alexander was able to write him: "I am very much pleased that you have at length read Scott's novels, and that you find them to your taste. It marks a very different feeling from that you were in when you before attempted to read them." There is no doubt, however, that Johnson's dislike of fiction was almost an obsession. His friend DeWitt Bloodgood had written several unsuccessful novels, and Johnson, with considerable irony, explained his failure to him. "You have neglected," he wrote Bloodgood, "to season your novels with the sauce of cruelty, and in this lies their defect. The more cruelty you display, the better will your books create delight, but the horrors must be so natural that the reader may be able to fancy them real, or they will not answer the designed purpose." Johnson argued that man's cruelty is innate, and that the most successful fiction writers pander to his baser nature. Behind all his refinements "lurks the insatiable and unsubdued cruelty of our nature. The monster is only chained and kept in the dark, but he yearns for his food, and it is administered to him in novels and romances, through highly wrought representations of fictional cruelty." Johnson was particularly concerned about the "unmerited miseries of female youth and beauty" inflicted upon them by novelists.

> When I accidentally cast my eyes on these modern fictions and see, as in one of Scott's novels, snares preparing, trapdoors constructing to immure to destruction some beautiful and faultless woman, I as uniformly and indignantly cast from me the book, as I should an invitation from some South Sea cannibal to make a dinner with him on a human victim.

Johnson admitted, however, that "like the Roman concubines" such books afforded "an outlet to a passion which might otherwise take a more dangerous channel."

Sometime during this period, Johnson turned briefly from his literary speculations to more mundane matters, among them, stoves and railroad tracks. Over in Schenectady, Eliphalet Nott, the flamboyant president of Union College, had invented an anthracite coal burning stove. Johnson bought one, and found certain dangerous defects in it. He wrote Nott suggesting a major modification, and to his delight Nott thanked him profusely, informing him that his suggestion had "produced its effect." His proposal for "a new mode of constructing double tracks on railroads," however, was turned down by the authorities in Albany, and Johnson resolved to "hereafter leave mechanics and adhere to phrases and sentences."

Among the "phrases and sentences" Johnson produced shortly thereafter which appeared in a series of letters to Judge Ezekiel Bacon, a former Chairman of the House Ways and Means Committee under Thomas Jefferson. Bacon, a fellow Utican, had lost his religious faith, and his spiritual depressions had become, in Johnson's words, an "object of universal gossip." Bacon appealed to his church-going friend for help, and Johnson promptly diagnosed the problem as an outgrowth of an "erroneous opinion that religion must be preceded by an intellectual faith in the scriptures." Johnson's letters to Bacon were undoubtedly, in part at least, the genesis of his later book, *Religion in its Relation to the Present Life* (1841), and they are revealing examples of his life-long efforts to reconcile his religious orthodoxy with his dogged empiricism. "Should a man of your turn of mind, or mine," he wrote Bacon, "wait for such a preliminary [intellectual belief], we would never possess religion." Religion, he felt, had nothing to do with "conviction of intellect founded on evidence." For example, he said, "most sermons violate all the rules of logic and common sense by fallacious and often absurd arguments to produce a belief founded on evidence." Thus, these "tales of prefabricated miracles and other devices" lead critics to refer sarcastically to "pious frauds and priestcraft." Religious feeling, he said, "is not always present with every man, but like our other feelings, it is always exciteable."

> High health may reject religion, prosperity may reject it, tumult may reject it; but let sickness, silence and adversity visit a man, they will as naturally excite religion as they excite fear, of which religion in one of its phases is a modification, as are hope, veneration and gratitude modifications of religion in some of its other phases . . . Men may live without religion and they may live united with sects of the coldest temperaments; all possess within us the match that will burn and the mine which will explode religion-wise when we are brought under the operation of kindling appliances.

The key to religious feeling, Johnson summarized, lies in the use of these "kindling appliances." Among such he listed "kneeling, covering or uncovering the head, spreading or elevating the hands." He also recommended a "well executed solemn anthem, or a sermon or a prayer casually heard." Finally, referring no doubt to the recent success of the evangelist Charles Grandison Finney's "Oneida revivals," Johnson concluded:

> The exercise of our churches during revivals are founded on the workings of human nature, and evince no little skill on the part of our clergymen. The manner seems to be by making the audience take an active part in the services, by coming into the aisle of the church, kneeling, confessing, praying, and being prayed for and with. Our words and actions naturally excite our feelings. We can listen cooly to almost anything while we refrain from words and actions, but you know how prone every man is to become warm in debate simply from the influence of words on his feelings. . . . Your political feelings might be again enkindled if you would enter the arena, and give and take thrusts and blows.

In *Religion in its Relation to the Present Life,* Johnson would sum it all up in the words, "Would you love God, you must act and speak as though you loved him."

At the risk of claiming too much prescience for A. B. Johnson, it is still interesting to note how his theory that acting out an emotion or feeling will generate that emotion or feeling so closely parallels some of the James-Lange theory of emotions. As William James put it in his *Principles of Psychology* in 1896, "We feel sorry because we cry, angry because we strike, afraid because we tremble, and not that we cry, strike or tremble because we are sorry, angry or fearful, as the case may be." Johnson's approach to religion is also echoed in James' belief that the essence of faith is not intelligence, but the desire to believe what cannot be scientifically proved or refuted. One might also point out that Johnson was a precurser of Phineas Parkhurst Quimby and his "mind cures," Mary Baker Eddy, Norman Vincent Peale, and, of course, the fashionable Dr. Emile Coué of the 1920s who had thousands of Americans practicing logotherapy each morning by declaiming, "Day by day in every way, I am better and better."

In the summer of 1832, Utica became a disaster area in the cholera epidemic which spread inland from the Atlantic Coast. As it moved across the countryside, its arrival was announced in handbills, and entire communities fell into a state of panic. The newspapers, wrote Johnson, "were filled with cholera statistics; bills of health and mortality were posted in all the streets announcing the number of deaths during the day, and the number of new cases." Uticans whom Johnson met on the streets were fragrant with camphor carried in their mouths and pockets, and fresh vegetables considered dangerous disappeared from the markets. As the panic spread, Johnson developed a theory about the disease. The symptoms of terror, he felt, closely resembled the symptoms of cholera itself, and, in fact, not only could terror produce cholera, but "terror and cholera were identical." Acting upon this theory, Johnson promptly forbade any discussion of cholera within his family circle "as the best means of preventing the fear which the topic excited." However, one night, as they were seated in the family parlor, Abigail and the children began to recount some of the "horrid particulars" of new cases in Utica. Johnson described what happened:

> I felt the blood rush to my head, and I concluded that if my theory were true that terror and cholera were identical, then I had the cholera. I immediately said I was not well; and I rushed into the open air and began to walk, whistle, sing and dance to divert my thoughts as the best way of allaying my fear, and in this I soon succeeded and

became ashamed of having made so open a display of my weakness. But one of my sons had, in the meantime, run to our family physician. . . . He came soon, but I was reassured and quiet, but he felt my pulse and told me I had better go to bed and I should soon sleep and be well in the morning. He gave me, also, a preparation of cayenne pepper in the form of tea, and I awoke in the morning as well as ever. Finding, however, by last night's experience that my feelings were not controlled by my intellect, I concluded to leave the city with my family, and seek a temporary abode in the country.

When the Johnsons (all except his mother, Leah, who remained quietly at home) reached the "country" (New Hartford), Johnson discovered the local farmers "at work in their fields and apparently undisturbed and unconscious of cholera." This confirmed his theory that "people living detached from society were out of the influence of exciting each other by tales of death and cholera, and were consequently well." On returning to Utica, Johnson found his mother enjoying her usual good health, and ascribed this to the fact that she "lived in great seclusion, and heard but little of the sickness." His old friend Judge Nathan Williams had remained in Utica "visiting and administering to those who were taken sick," but Johnson, perhaps to assuage any guilt feelings he might have had, carefully explained in his autobiography that he and Williams were "differently organized emotionally." He also theorized that Williams escape from the cholera might have been the result of his "mingling among it and familiarizing himself thereto, and thereby preventing it from alarming him." One wonders, of course, whether Johnson might have invented his theory about terror as a means of rationalizing his flight to New Hartford; but it is also possible that he was on the track of an idea to be examined years later by, among others, Dr. Walter Cannon in such works as *Bodily Changes in Fear, Hunger, Pain and Rage* (1915), and *Voodoo Death* (1945).

CHAPTER 14

1834–1836

War with Biddle's "Monster": The Bank of the United States

THE CHOLERA EPIDEMIC WANED during the spring of 1832, and the Johnsons returned to Genesee Street to await the arrival of their ninth child, due in November. Meanwhile in Utica, as throughout the Republic, new political tensions were building, and Johnson, vacillating between involvement and noninvolvement, would soon find the choice thrust upon him. For the next few years, the philosophical errors of Spinoza and Locke would be supplanted in his category of human failures by the political and social errors of his less speculative contemporaries. Ironically, what Johnson did from 1832 to 1836 as a man of action came closer to providing him with a place in the history books than the works on language which would be acclaimed in the twentieth century.

But before entering upon the national political scene, Johnson had several local and domestic situations to cope with. The first involved nearby Hamilton College, alma mater of many of his closest friends, and, at the time of its chartering in 1812, one of the country's westernmost outposts of higher education. Throughout its first fifteen years, Hamilton had done reasonably well, serving up a classical bill of academic fare and a way of life imported from the older New England colleges. Suddenly, however, the winds of Jacksonian democracy and Charles Finney's "new measures" began to blow across the hilltop campus, and Hamilton found itself in a turmoil of student insurrection, faculty dissension—and financial difficulties. Its second president, the Reverend Henry Davis, former head of Middlebury College, who still favored kneebreeches and silver-buckled shoes, had tightened the reins on his new constituency after taking office in 1817, and for a year, at least, succeeded in maintaining order and decorum. On Christmas Day,

1818, however, he grew a little too zealous. His predecessor, Azel Backus, had promised the students that Christmas Day would be "forever a holiday;" but Davis, impatient with such un-New England fripperies, decreed that all classes would be attended until 11 A.M. that day. Hamilton sophomores retaliated by locking the classroom doors against their instructors, and later threatened to transfer to more liberal-minded institutions. The Utica trustees, several of whom had sons at the College, were incensed by Davis's rigidity and one of them said of the rebellious sophomores, "They are in our hands, and we will let Dr. Davis know that they are not to be governed like the students of a New England College."

About a year later the junior class rebelled over the dismissal of a student for obstreperous behavior in the Chapel. The trustees backed Davis by a slim majority, but acceded to student demands that the young man be given his Hamilton degree. The students found it more and more convenient to bypass Davis and take their grievances directly to the trustees, managing, among other things, to secure the dismissal of an unpopular tutor. The high point of Davis's difficulties came on November 16, 1823, when dissident students placed a small cannon, heavily loaded and plugged, outside a tutor's room on the third floor of a dormitory. The explosion wrecked the room, nearly killed the tutor, and sent fragments of iron through the roof and into the basement. The incensed president demanded that the faculty be permitted to handle the incident, but once again the trustees moved in, backed by the forces of law and order in Clinton and Utica. By 1828 ten trustees had resigned, and the student body had been reduced to nine members of the class of 1831. Davis hung on, refusing steadfastly to resign, and finally, with a new board to back him, made a slow start toward bringing the college out of what Johnson called "its declining condition." In the fall of 1832, having finally badgered the trustees into submission, and appeased the students with a few reforms, Davis belatedly submitted his resignation. Just prior to doing so, however, he launched a fund-raising drive, turning, among others, to Johnson. His first overture was in the form of an invitation to join the reconstituted Board of Trustees.

Johnson "deemed the position highly undesirable in view of the condition of the College, and refused the seat." Shortly thereafter Davis announced that Johnson had been awarded an honorary M.A. by the College, noting that the honor had been conferred "as a testimony of the high respect entertained for your character by the guardians of this Institution." This time, Johnson was even more blunt in his comments. "The college," he wrote, "had for some time previously been dispensing its honorary degrees profusely in Utica, and to persons much less deserving of such honors than I thought myself to be." He added, "I thought this proceeding indelicate under the pending intention to solicit aid from me for the College." To Davis he wrote, "Circumstances exist compatible with the highest reverence for your Institution that induce me to decline the honor thus within my reach. . . ." Davis, however, ignored the refusal. Johnson's name was duly entered in the 1832 catalogue, and appears in all subsequent alumni lists, as an honorary member of the class of '32.

The birth of Johnson's ninth child and second daughter, whom the Johnsons named Louisa Ann Smith Johnson, took place on November 24, 1832. Johnson expressed his satisfaction in later years with Abigail's proficiency as a childbearer:

> All my children were born in perfect formation and health and my wife passed through the ordeal with as little suffering as usually can attend so severe a natural event. She also nursed all her children, and generally attended to all their wants personally; though we always kept one or two nurses for general purposes.

Johnson was always impatient with the details of history and, in fact, with history itself—unless he felt he had been directly involved in it. The burning issues and conflicts, for instance, of Andrew Jackson's first term (1828–1832) went unmentioned in the autobiography, and Johnson gave no hint that he was shortly to become a fighting, passionately partisan Jacksonian, deeply involved in the President's historic struggle with Biddle's "Monster," the Second Bank of the United States. The tumultuous election campaign of 1832 in which Jackson's opponent, Henry Clay, foolishly raised the issue of the Bank's recharter, hoping to embarrass the President at the polls, was also ignored, despite the fact that Utica, perhaps more than any other upstate city, was noisy with factionalism—Whig against Democrat, Southern against New England interests, "original" against "new" Jackson men. There is only one entry in the autobiography for the entire fateful year 1833—a curious reference to a nonevent in Johnson's life which, nonetheless, does provide a vague hint that somehow, somewhere along the line, Johnson had sloughed off the obligations of "consanguinity" which tied him to the Adams clan, and had drifted slowly into the Jackson camp.

In May 1833 Daniel Webster, recipient of many favors from the Bank of the United States, and an implacable foe of Jackson, came to Utica, and Johnson was invited to a reception for him. Johnson declined the honor—"not being of Whig politics, nor ever admiring Mr. Webster's principles, though his oratorical powers were great." Johnson added, "He seems to be more of a partisan than a statesman, and indeed our great men have usually been seekers of local popularity rather than national statesmen."

Johnson's entrance into the "Bank war" came slowly and reluctantly. Before it was over, however, he had emerged as a key figure in New York State's crucial victory over the Bank—a victory that paved the way for its demise, and wrote finis to the hopes and aspirations of the old Federalists. Had Johnson cared to exploit his role in this titanic struggle he might well have emerged as a national hero. As it was, only a few "insiders" were fully aware of the part he played, and it wasn't until the 1950s and 1960s that their evidence (and Johnson's own) became available to historians.

The Second Bank of the United States was created under Madison in 1816, with many of the features of Alexander Hamilton's National Bank of 1791. Under the terms of its creation, the charter was to be renewed in 1836 and, although by 1832 there was a rising tide of opposition to its policies, there were still formidable forces working to see that the new charter perpetuated the Bank's awesome power in governmental and financial circles. Ostensibly it was a private Philadelphia corporation presided over by Nicholas Biddle; in reality, it was something else. The Bank's ties with government were profitable and, to say the least, unusual, for one-fifth of its $35 million capital was subscribed by government without interest payments. It paid no state taxes, and any competition was thwarted by congressional fiat prohibiting the chartering of any similar institutions outside of its own "branch" banks. As a sop to critics the government was given the right to appoint five of its twenty-five directors, but no federal deposits could be removed without the consent of Congress.

As the time for rechartering drew near, Biddle had as his allies the conservative Jeffersonians, the old Federalists, and a host of politicians like Webster who had received favors from the Bank. His opponents included the debtor interests of the West, who had suffered under the Bank's hard money policy, and local banking interests in the East, who were alarmed, among other things, by the Bank's immunity from the Safety Fund provisions. In the beginning, Jackson himself remained more or less neutral, deeply distrustful of all banks, yet sensitive to political realities. As the day of decision came closer, however, the President announced his decision to veto the charter bill, oblivious to Clay's threat to "veto him" if he did so. Jackson delivered his famous message charging that the bill would "make the rich richer and the potent more powerful," while Biddle denounced the veto as "a manifesto of anarchy." Even Jackson's most ardent supporters feared he would be defeated in the November election, and many of the "original Jackson men" deserted him, but Jackson carried the day. The Bank, however, with several years to go before its old charter expired, continued to give battle, forcing Jackson to play his trump card—the removal of all federal deposits. Biddle countered immediately with a policy of retrenchment and manipulation which, as he hoped it would, produced a major financial panic.

On January 16, 1834, Johnson's friend Congressman Samuel Beardsley arose in the House to reply to the powerful Horace Binney, who had spoken for three days in support of the Bank, and against the removal of federal deposits. "I, for one," Beardsley shouted, "say perish credit; perish commerce. . . . Give us a broken, a deranged, and a worthless currency rather than the ignoble and corrupting tyranny of an irresponsible corporation!" Two weeks later, while the turmoil was at its height, Beardsley wrote Johnson a grim warning, pinpointing local New York State banks as the target of Biddle's reprisals. "I am firmly persuaded," he said, "that if money can be used so as to injure them, it will so be used. . . . The United States Bank can use millions to effect such an object, and it will not be restrained by any feelings of justice or mercy. . . . Its spite is against New York, and it would sacrifice millions to break down the currency of that State."

The apparently unruffled president of the Ontario Branch Bank continued to remain aloof from the fray, however, until the arrival of a letter from Thomas W. Orcutt, the cashier of the Mechanics and Farmers' Bank in Albany—a letter indicating that the crisis was coming closer to home, and proposing a measure which touched directly on Johnson's sensitive pocketbook nerve. Orcutt wrote:

> Probably no bank in the country is better prepared for the crisis at which we have arrived than is the Ontario Bank and its branch. But many friends of that bank are deeply interested in other institutions; and if the present panic cannot be arrested, it is difficult to see who can resist it. In my opinion the stoppage of one bank will be the signal for a general rush upon all specie.

Then Orcutt came directly to the point: would the Ontario Branch and its parent bank in Canandaigua contribute $25,000 each to "sustain, say, the Chemung Canal Bank and the Steuben?" His own bank, Orcutt implied, was already doing its bit for some of the others, and would do more if Johnson would also make a move. Orcutt concluded with a passionate appeal to Johnson's patriotism:

Every effort should be put forth, and no time is to be lost. There is, there can be, but one interest in the country, and that is the interest of every man. Our banks are sound, and our country prosperous, and no man or set of men should be allowed with impunity to taint with suspicion the one, or trifle with the other. These are times to require active, bold and firm minds.

Johnson moved at once, not with a paltry loan of $25,000, as Orcutt had suggested, but with a bold and imaginative plan by which the state could relieve the banks. He described it as follows:

The Commissioners of the Canal Fund had the power to create State six-percent stock for the construction of the Chenango and Erie Canals. This stock was as good as gold and silver, for it possessed a ready market in England and elsewhere in Europe. I suggested that a sufficient amount should be created and sold, and the proceeds deposited in the banks of Albany, who were the general redeeming banks of the state.

On March 15th Orcutt replied ecstatically, "The Commissioners of the Canal Fund have adopted your suggestion and the country is saved." The excitement in Albany was intense, and on the same day that Johnson received Orcutt's announcement he received a similar message from Greene C. Bronson, now Attorney General of the State and a commissioner of the Canal Fund: "The country is safe. Much has been done to cripple New York, but not a bone of her is yet broken—and will not be, if our bankers and capitalists will not give way to unnecessary panic."

But A. B. Johnson, no doubt exhilarated by the impact he was having in Albany, was only just getting started. His next suggestion to Orcutt was "that the State might also create a public stock and loan the money to those who needed assistance." Orcutt rushed Johnson's letter to Governor Marcy and other officials, who "regarded it favorably," but expressed some doubts as to whether the state legislature would adopt the measure without some pressure from the voters. Anticipating this reservation, Johnson had also suggested that a "public meeting" be organized in Utica to encourage such pressure.

The March 25th meeting called by Johnson in Utica's Courthouse was attended by "a large and enthusiastic gathering" of Oneida County Democrats. Judge Nathan Williams was in the chair, and called on Johnson for the opening speech. The politicians, he charged, "seek power now through the distress produced by the Philadelphia Bank invasion." The issue was not, he continued, whether the Bank be constitutional or unconstitutional—a necessary fiscal agent, or unnecessary. "The issue is whether the country shall be coerced to give the Bank a new charter." He then proceeded to identify the three villains in the plot: the Bank itself, politicians seeking power, and the partisan press. With regard to the latter he produced a communication he had just received from a leading New York State editor warning him that "one word from our papers here would blow your country banks to atoms." Thus, he pointed out, "we must be cautious and not attribute to [the Bank] more power than it possesses, for all its power is largely dependent upon the press and the politicians. It is but an instrument in the hands of a party . . . a party with as many names as a swindler, and which changes them as often; a party whose objects are in as constant a flux as its name, raving for war, and when war was declared, raving for peace." Johnson was here referring to the recent official adoption of the name "Whig" by the former "National Republicans"—a tactic first suggested by Colonel James Watson Webb, editor of the New York *Courier and Enquirer,* which had originally supported Jackson, but turned against him over the Bank issue.

Johnson denied hotly the Whig allegation that it was Jackson alone who was attacking the Bank, and not the people. Jackson was "but vigorously executing what the people have decreed." Then, after a lenghty eulogy of Jackson, "whom Providence has placed at the helm of State," Johnson moved to his conclusion:

> Let the people of every state call on their legislators to remove our pecuniary difficulties. New York alone has but to will what it wishes, and the wish can be accomplished. With an ability to create, at a moment and without cost, a stock that is equivalent to gold and silver, let the State not stand idly by while an infuriated enemy is ravaging the country. The ground on which the Bank advocates stand . . . will thus be removed from under them, and they will be left suspended as monuments of disappointed malice.

Less than a month after the Utica meeting, the New York State Legislature passed by a considerable majority a bill to raise $6 million in state stock, and the money raised was farmed out, through the Albany banks, to many hard-pressed bankers in the upstate area. Johnson pointed out, with obvious satisfaction, that the Ontario Bank "required none and took none"; but as one friendly newspaper put it, he had become, for the moment at least, "the Nestor of New York State democracy." The speech was printed in numerous state newspapers, including the powerful Albany *Argus,* and letters of acclaim and gratitude poured in upon Johnson. Attorney General Bronson praised the "great anti-

Bank meeting at Utica," but reserved his highest praise for the Johnson speech. Beardsley wrote, "Utica has done nobly, and the whole country is coming up to the contest in a spirit which will overwhelm all opposition." He warned, however: "You must look for attacks and abuse. You will receive them. But fear not. The ground assumed by you is correct. The people, a vast majority of them, will sustain . . . the principles you have promulgated."

As the congressional elections approached in the fall of 1834, the Bank made a last desperate effort to muster support for the renewal of its charter. As Johnson told it:

> The hopes of the Bank depended upon obtaining a sufficient congressional majority to overcome the veto; and to this end it again recalled all its loans that could be demanded and produced the most general money pressure the country had ever experienced; inveterated by the whole Whig or Federal party, who openly rejoiced at even their own personal ruin, since it evinced the necessity of rechartering the Bank. Manufacturers stopped work and discharged their workmen . . . ship owners dismantled their ships and turned loose the sailors . . . and merchants everywhere stopped payment and declared themselves ruined . . . the Bible exclamation of Rachel, "Give me children or else I shall die," was parodied by a general cry, "Recharter the Bank or else we die!"

A month before the elections, Johnson again plunged into the fray, and produced a pamphlet in the form of a "Letter" to Judge Nathan Williams. In commenting on the "Letter," which was widely distributed and reprinted in dozens of American newspapers, Johnson said, "I was not opposed to a United States Bank, but I was opposed to it in a contest which seemed to present no alternative but whether the Bank should rule the country or be ruled by the country." In the "Letter" Johnson berated the Whigs and the opposition press, extolled the virtues and the cause of Andrew Jackson, and called for a resounding defeat of the Bank advocates in the next election. Johnson added an eloquent summary of the "cruel acts" against the country perpetrated by the Bank and its allies in their "daring conspiracy to obtain, by a sort of Sabine rape, the suffrages of the people." The country beheld, he wrote, "a reversal of the common principles of human nature."

> Men rejoiced at their own embarrassments, and merchants proclaimed commerce at an end. Notes of the most solvent banks were denounced,

bankruptcy no longer excited pity, but undisguised gratification. The more meritorious was the victim, the louder was the shout of triumph. Malignity emulated death in its love of a shining mark.

Spearheading the attack, he said, was the Whig press. "The North published lies in aid of panic in the South, and the South published lies in aid of panic in the North." They even advocated a run on banks "for the avowed purpose of producing ruin. Like skillful inquisitors . . . editors directed panic with equal skill to the banks and individuals which were the most susceptible to injury." He also scored the lobbyists. "Multitudes of men," he said, "under the name of committees were pouring into Washington to intimidate the President. Legislation in Congress ceased . . . its sittings were declared interminable, and the country was declared in a state of revolution." Johnson recalled those merchants in New York who were forced to close their shops for a day so their employees could attend a pro-Bank meeting in Castle Garden. "Let them," he warned, "again close their shops and marshall their dependents, burst open again the arsenal and dragoon the New York voters—the great inquest of the nation is approaching! They who had no eye for pity, who laughed at our calamity, must be rebuked. All the interests of the State call for judgment!"

Finally, in a strong Jacksonian vein, Johnson related the contest to the restrictions against universal suffrage which were "as unjust to the merits of the poor, [as they are] prejudicial to their morals." He pointed out that "in war the country is defended on sea and land by the poor almost alone." Reverting to an old theme, he exclaimed: "Discrimination growing out of a man's race or ancestry is equally invidious. Had Satan devised a system to debase mankind he could have produced no plan more efficacious than that which estimates a man by the quality of his ancestors." The Whigs, naturally, wanted these restrictions kept, because the poor, and those of foreign ancestry, would vote for Jackson and against the Bank. Johnson ended his "Letter" with this confident note: "Jackson will be sustained! The blighting principles of aristocracy cannot be forced on us, to arrest the thrilling experiment of equal privileges to all men." The voice was now that of a full-fledged Jacksonian Democrat.

Aging Uncle John Quincy Adams had come out of retirement to join his protégé, the eloquent Edward Everett, in the fight to save Biddle's Bank, but Johnson had new friends and mentors now, among them the Albany *Argus,* which prefaced Johnson's "Letter" in its editorial column with these words,

It is with unfeigned pleasure that we lay before our readers, the eloquent letter of A. B. Johnson of Utica. . . . Mr. Johnson has touched
several of the great questions which now agitate the country with the
hand of a master. Mr. Johnson is a gentleman of fortune who has
much to lose, while he can gain nothing by bad rulers. He is a man of
retiring habits, and although he early took the side of Democratic
principles, he has never taken a very active part in politics except on
those great occasions when the country was in danger of some great
evil, either from within or without.

Attorney General Bronson wrote again, saying, "It [the "Letter"] is a
production which does great credit to your head and heart." He had
one reservation, however. In the text of the "Letter," as published in
the *Argus,* but omitted from the *American Union* version, Johnson had
written, "I shall never write or speak again on politics." To this
Bronson replied,

> Strongly as you may be inclined to a life separated from the strife and
> perplexity incident to party politics, I hold that no American citizen
> is at liberty wholly to withdraw himself from our political concerns—
> especially one who is so able as yourself to be useful in ameliorating
> the condition of your fellow men. The time may come when you will
> feel it a duty both to speak and write in defense of sound political prin-
> ciples, and then I am persuaded you will review and reverse your
> present resolution.

At the end of Bronson's letter there was a note penned by Governor
Marcy: "Mr. Bronson has read me the foregoing, and I assure you
that I most heartily concur in his high commendation."

In New York City, acid-tongued Gorham Worth wrote a lengthy
letter of approbation. Worth had been a vigorous opponent of the Jackson administration up to the point where the Bank of the United States
began its calculated efforts to create financial panic. His description of
the Bank's machinations endeared him to Johnson. "The course pursued by the opposition in conjunction with the Bank," he wrote,

> its satellite and pensioned press, produced a scene that beggars all
> description and changed or rather transferred my hatred of the Jackson
> party to that of the Bank. It was a scene of imposition and insult,
> oppression and coercion. It was a war upon the interests of the nation—
> an assault upon the independence of the people. It was a continued
> and gigantic effort to overthrow by terror and distress the government

of the country, and to erect upon its ruins a monied power capable of overawing and controlling the popular will. The brunt of the battle, as you know, was borne by this state. The blow was aimed at New York and it fell like a thunderbolt upon this city. And, what is almost incredible, the most wealthy and intelligent half of our own citizens joined hand and heart in the treasonable and suicidal crusade against their own interests and the interests of the city. For one, I can never forget the scene and will certainly never forgive the actors. Your disquisition upon the principles of the two parties is characteristic of your pen. In it is much truth, some fine and to me original views, many happy illustrations and truly eloquent passages; but a little darkened by metaphysical speculation and a learned but vain philosophy. Nevertheless you deserve well of your country and it gives me pleasure to agree with you in the main.

In berating Johnson's "learned but vain philosophy," Worth was probably referring to the latter's liberal views on universal suffrage and racial equality.

From Washington came two final accolades—one from Vice President Martin Van Buren (no great favorite of Johnson's), and the other from U.S. Attorney General Benjamin F. Butler, a close confidant of President Jackson, and of Van Buren when the latter became President. The election of Van Buren in 1834 was seen as a resounding vindication of Jackson's policy, and spelled the death of the Bank as a national institution, although it continued to have influence as the Philadelphia Bank.

There is a tragicomic footnote to the story of Johnson's crusade against the Second Bank of the United States. Biddle lost his bank, but Johnson lost his church. Biddle never found another U.S. bank; but Johnson found the Episcopalians—or rather, refound them.

Toward the end of his "Letter" to Judge Williams, Johnson, forgetful of an earlier run-in with the Presbyterians over his Sunday travels, spoke proudly of his role in persuading Major Barry, the U.S. Postmaster General, to process mail on Sunday. Barry had been under special attack by the pro-Bank factions for his stand against current regulations that the Post Office should be a self-sustaining operation with its expenditures limited to the amount of the postage received. Since governmental agencies accounted for a vast amount of the postal traffic, he argued, government should make up the deficits rather than "wrenching its postage from the hands of labor." Had Johnson confined himself to that issue he would have been on safe ground, but he couldn't resist leading up to it with the following:

Previously to October, 1830, the mails which were destined for New York, and which arrived in Albany on Saturday, had to lie there until Monday morning. A man having a note to pay on Monday was compelled to have his money in New York by Saturday. The aggregate loss of interest to the whole community must have been great. Unacquainted with Major Barry, I ventured to direct to him the evil, and immediately he answered me as follows—"Instructions shall be given to the Postmaster at Albany to put up a mail on Sundays as well as on other days. The advantages to Utica, and other towns West of Albany are most apparent, and shall be continued to them."

Johnson then proceeded to hail Major Barry as standing "eminent among the benefactors of the age."

In Geneva, New York, Johnson's old friend and former pastor, the Reverend Henry Dwight, who had officiated at the Johnson wedding, caught the passage and suggested to Nathan Williams that Johnson might come under the censure of the church "for promoting the Sunday mail." Williams passed the warning on to his friend in Utica, but Johnson paid no attention to it until, a few days later, he was called upon at his bank by a committee of two delegated by the Session "to inquire of me whether I did not believe in the obligatory character of the fourth commandment of the Decalogue." Johnson described the visitation as follows:

The committee were plain, simple men and probably they intended well, but they were all my political opponents and were, I supposed, instigated by other persons more knowing than themselves and less well inclined. I therefore said that the matter they alluded to was a political paper, and that I would not discuss a political subject with them. They departed and soon thereafter I received a formal written notice that I was suspended from the communion, and was cited to answer certain charges against me in the premises.

Johnson, "in the heat of the moment," left the church and took a temporary pew in the Reformed Dutch church of Utica, bringing his entire family with him. The Presbyterians did their best to force him to answer their citation but after some halfhearted attempts to reason with them, Johnson gave up and terminated the discussion with a peremptory note to the pastor. "I stand," he wrote,

as virtually excommunicated as I can be after the anathema shall issue from your pulpit. You say the proceedings can be reviewed by higher ecclesiastical judicatories, but denying your disciplinary cognizance of Sunday mails, and fearing also that the question which is now simple may become obscured and even lost amid forms and technicalities, I shall close our controversy. . . . Besides I possess neither health nor spirits for such litigation. This letter will terminate all the notice I shall ever take of your citation and of the whole subject. Nothing remains but for me to shield myself from this bold effort to subordinate my civil duties to my ecclesiastical relations and to publish this and my former letters, that the community may understand my position. The justice and sympathy of the public will, I am sure, disarm your proscription of all power to injure me.

Johnson noted that he passed on the entire correspondence with the Session to one of his sons, adding, "but I have avoided looking at it ever since." This correspondence has never turned up in his own or in any of his descendants' files, but it was preserved by the First Presbyterian church in Utica in a volume entitled "Church Records of Utica Session, 1822–1843."

According to these records, when the "committee of two," called initially on Johnson to remonstrate over the offending passage in his "Letter" to Williams, they approached their unpleasant assignment in a restrained and humble manner. They merely listed the complaints of the Session, and urged him to "review the subject with them and examine it prayerfully." Johnson, too, was restrained at first, pointing out that he "agreed fully that secular business should normally be laid aside on the Sabbath," but insisting that there were certain activities, like the transportation of mail, that were essential to the well-being of the community and "very proper." He asked the committee to express his sorrow to the Session that "anyone's feelings were hurt." He also promised to "examine prayerfully" the whole matter. After their departure, however, he began to brood about the affair, and several days later, on December 9, 1834, he sent off a bristling letter to the Reverend Samuel Aiken, pastor of the church. Prior to the committee's visit, he wrote, he had received a letter "from one of the most influential and conspicuous female members of your church denouncing the principles of Democracy in general, and threatening me with the wrath of Heaven." He said she had also accused him of "having boasted of my influence to induce Major Barry to violate the Sabbath" (which, in a way, Johnson did) and of having "committed an act which severs me from the charity of conscientious Christians." He had, he said, also received a letter from the "female's" son-in-law—a letter "which had been carried about by her and read in private houses." The great "clamor" that ensued, Johnson insisted, was purely and simply an excuse for attacking his political views—"the only handle by which they could take hold of me." It was well known, he said, that the church was dominated by Whigs who disapproved of his Democratic leanings.

Having made this point, Johnson expostulated:

> Let the Sanctuary be sacred from political strife. Let one place exist where men of all politics may mingle their sympathies and discover that they need each other's charities. Against your indiscriminate confusion of politics with religion, I solemnly protest!

His wrath boiling over, he then hurled the following at the Session.

> I remember no such burst of feeling was elicited even when a member of your Session some years ago confessed in open church the commission of such lascivious liberties with females as rendered him in his own estimation unsuitable for an Elder of the church. . . . I honestly believe therefore that the present clamors are political.

As to the offending passage about Major Barry and the Sunday mails, Johnson confessed he "regretted that I introduced it." He said, "I will even admit that I may be in error about my whole view . . . but until I possess more knowledge on the subject, I must continue to believe that I am *not* in error." He added, however, "If a surrender of this abstract principle shall be deemed necessary to my connection with your church, your Session may know that I shall not surrender it—nor shall I surrender any other political opinion."

Finally, Johnson warned:

> Whatever your determination shall be, the Session will greatly oblige me by refraining from *all* personal interviews with me on the subject, and even by refraining from answering this letter. I have lately been persecuted politically. . . . I am in a poor state of nerves to encounter a new enemy in a quarter where I had hoped to find peace and comfort. Were nothing at issue but my rights, I might surrender them for the sake of repose, but as a member of the freest people that ever existed, I will *never* furnish a precedent which will give the church supervision and scrutiny over the political opinions and actions of its members, and thus in the case of senators and congressmen, enable the church to control votes on Sunday mails, war, Indians, or any other political question!

The Session was aghast at the violence of Johnson's letter, and aware that it was stirring up a hornet's nest, deputized the Rev. Samuel Aiken to call on Johnson and assure him that "the object of the Committee had not been disciplinary, but a kind of brotherly move." Johnson, however, was not placated, and said he would "refuse to retract a single syllable" of his letter, demanding that it be presented formally to the entire Session. This the Session did, concluding unanimously that Johnson's letter "presented a new case entirely." It showed, the clerk recorded, "a great want of charity and Christian courtesy." It had "impeached the motives of the Session by attributing to them political prejudices . . . and virtually set the Session at defiance." Finally, the letter had "introduced disorder and misrule into the church of God," and it would thus be forced "to institute a course of discipline with Alexander Bryan Johnson." He was ordered to appear before the Session at 6:30 P.M. on the 7th day of January. Johnson replied promptly: "I shall attend none of your meetings. You may take your course, and I will take mine. I deny the jurisdiction of the Church and care not for their citation. I shall pay no attention to it."

The Session met without Johnson and drew up a peremptory set of charges and a citation which they sent to him. Johnson then sent a curt note to Aiken: "Sir: I will thank you to inform me whether the summons of your Session which I have just received interdicts me from the Communion table of your church at the coming communion on the 4th?" Aiken, who seems to have been caught in the middle of a quarrel he did not relish, replied hesitantly: "The citation does not *necessarily* preclude you from the ordinance of the Lord's Supper, nor from any other church privileges. . . . It will be easy for you to remove the ban by letting the mutual explanation go on."

Shortly after receiving this note from Aiken, Johnson ran into him on the street, and the two had a long talk. Aiken told Johnson that he felt he had "misapprehended the entire controversy," and invited him to come to a meeting of the Session and give them a chance to explain their stand in "an informal and amicable conference." Johnson, mellowing slightly, agreed to go and for the first time listened to a reading of the entire record of the Session's deliberations—including his own letter of December 9. Obviously chagrined, he announced after the reading (according to the secretary's minutes), "Had I known the result of the report of the Committee as appears by your records, I would have sooner burned my fingers than to have written my letter of the 9th." The secretary also noted that "Mr. Johnson reported his willingness to make any proper concessions." When he returned home that night, Johnson sat down and wrote a letter to Aiken saying that his letter had been written "under much excitement" and acknowledged it was not "so kind and charitable as it might have been." After receiving this note, the Conference passed a resolution to the effect that "the said confession by Mr. Johnson was deemed satisfactory, and the controversy was dropped." Johnson, however, still had some enemies in the church— among them Spencer Kellogg with whom he was engaged in some business litigation, and a "new charge" (unspecified in the record) was brought against him. Also Johnson did not relish having his apology for his letter referred to as a "confession." He promptly got off another harsh note to the Session, and this time, Aiken, his patience exhausted, informed Johnson that he would definitely be "debarred from the Communion table." At this point, Johnson penned the letter to Aiken, already quoted, acknowledging his "excommunication" and threatening to take the whole matter before the Utica public. In this connection he demanded a full transcript of all of the Session's proceedings, offering to pay for a copyist. The Session delayed complying with his request for many weeks, and when he finally received the transcript, he had had a change of heart, and settled for a letter from Aiken stating that he had been "a member of the Presbyterian church in good standing," thus permitting him to transfer to another church.

Word of Johnson's dispute with the Presbyterians spread, and thirteen of his friends (good Democrats all) published a long letter to him urging that the transcript be made public. "We are unwilling to believe," they wrote, "that one whose reputation for probity and intelligence has so long been unsuspected and confessedly above reproach, should have rendered himself obnoxious to the just censure of the religion of his own or any other communion." But Johnson had had enough. "Further agitation," he replied, "would only keep my feelings excited and no triumph could be gained by me over the offending individuals who were screened by acting as a body corporate."

Johnson was not comfortable in the Dutch Reformed church and, after attending it for a few weeks, he was invited to join the Episcopalian church by its new young rector, Dr. Proal.

> I accordingly joined his church with all my family. I had been educated in the Episcopal Church and my father and myself had at an early age been vestrymen of this church and had aided in its erection, and I now had additional reasons for preferring it, as interfering less with the personal freedom of its members than any other church known to me . . . a consideration of great value in a small, inland community where all persons of the same communion are brought in intimate relations with each other.

Johnson showed his correspondence with the Presbyterians to Proal, and the young Anglican exploded in righteous indignation. "It develops," he wrote Johnson, "an attempt at religious despotism approximating the tyranny of the Romish Inquisition . . . I could scarcely have thought that so much disingenuousness—shall I say moral obliquity?—could have been practiced in a community calling itself Christian!"

Johnson remained a staunch Anglican until his death, as did the members of his obliging family. Old John Adams, remembering his grandson-in-law's pious hymn to Presbyterian virtues, might have been amused.

CHAPTER 15

1834

Abolition, Temperance, and "Tight Lacing"

D URING THE EARLY WEEKS OF JANUARY 1834, while Johnson was being drawn into the conflict with the Bank of the United States, he also became embroiled in a controversy over the American Colonization Society, whose stated objective was "to promote and execute a plan of colonizing (with their own consent) the free people of color residing in our country, in Africa, or such other place as Congress may deem expedient." A year later he would also figure, though somewhat less publicly, in the antiabolitionist riots which focused national attention on Utica, still a community of fewer than 10,000 people.

It was no accident, as Charles C. Cole, Jr., pointed out in his *Social Ideas of the Northern Evangelists* (New York, 1954), that "it was in Oneida County, heart of the new revivals, that the strongest abolitionist conviction was found." New England had William Lloyd Garrison, Wendell Phillips, and Harriet Beecher Stowe, full of righteousness, strong on rhetoric and indignation; but central New York had Gerrit Smith, Theodore Weld, Beriah Green, William Goodell, and a host of others, all products of the Finney revival and eloquent in action as well as words. Active in the underground railroad and in smuggling abolitionist literature into the South, they also produced a determined opposition among influential Utica merchants and politicians loath to provoke the "southern interests," law-and-order men equating the fervor of the abolitionists with the enthusiasms of the Millerites, the Shakers, the phrenologists, and the Mormons. Behind them stood a restless mix of antitemperance men, laborers who feared the competition of freed blacks, and quick-tempered immigrants who had worked on the construction of the Erie Canal and wanted no tampering with their new American dream. Even the normally uninhibited Charles Finney confessed to his wife in 1834 that he "didn't think it would do to say much about abolition here [Utica] in public." Confrontation was inevitable, and the abolitionists lost no time in providing it.

Johnson had friends on both sides—among them, Gerrit Smith, at first a colonizationist and later an all-out antislavery man, and Johnson's next-door neighbor, Samuel Beardsley, a conservative on most issues except for the Bank of the United States. With his passion for staying out of trouble, it is a small miracle that Johnson entered the fray at all, but enter it he did, with resounding rhetoric and unshakable conviction—the rhetoric unsettling many of his friends, and the conviction leading him to a dilemma that would remain unsolved for the rest of his life.

During the first week of the new year, an agent for the Colonization Society, J. N. Danforth, came to Utica to raise funds and set up auxiliary branches of the Society, which had been founded in 1826 and which numbered General Lafayette and Henry Clay among its directors. Danforth launched a series of lectures at the Dutch Reformed church during the first week, and the next week moved to the larger Presbyterian church for a round of "public discussions" on colonization and the whole question of slavery. To these "discussions" came at least two of the area's most militant abolitionists, Beriah Green, newly elected president of the Oneida Institute, who had been forced out of Western Reserve College as professor of religion because of his outspoken attacks on slavery; and Alvin Stewart, a temperance leader as well as an abolitionist. Stewart, according to Johnson, had previously been "addicted to gross inebriety," but had performed outstanding services for the temperance movement—though Johnson, "from his conduct and appearance," suspected him of "using opium to supply the place of alcohol." After the meeting on the 10th, in which both Green and Stewart ignored the issue of colonization and demanded immediate emancipation for all slaves, the two men were "grossly abused" by a Utica mob and their effigies were burned at a public demonstration. Stewart's effigy was hanged, not only with placards denouncing his abolitionist views, but also with quotations from his temperance speeches. Immediately after the incident, Johnson wrote a letter to E. C. Delevan, head of the New York State Temperance Society, urging that a gold medal be presented to Stewart, and enclosing a check for ten dollars as a contribution. Delevan, however, returned the check, explaining that "fifty others would feel slighted."

Whether or not the incident triggered Johnson's decision to speak at the meeting on the 13th is not certain, but it is quite likely that it did. His own explanation for the step is almost too preposterous to be credited. "Men must feed on the food of the region in which they live," he wrote, "hence, Greenlanders eat blubber. So men must feed intellectually on topics which interest their locality. Impelled by the dearth of better intellectual topics, our Utica became engrossed by the . . . discussion, and I with others took part therein, and delivered a speech on the resolution—but against it."

The motion offered at the final meeting was: "*Resolved,* That this meeting deeply deplore the unfortunate condition of the colored population of this country; and commend to the zealous support of the philanthropist and the Christian, the American Colonization Society as the instrument under Providence which is best calculated to ameliorate the condition of the free Negro, and secure the ultimate emancipation of the slave."

George Dangerfield, in *The Era of Good Feeling* (New York, 1952), says of the Colonization Society: "Nobody commented upon the undemocratic nature of the argument that free Negroes could never improve their lot in America, or upon the curious notion that Africa was such a cultural and climatic unity that any American Negro could be happy in any part of it." But in Utica, New York, Johnson spoke boldly to these and other points for thirty minutes.

"I believe the Society and its supporters are mistaken in the moral nature of their institutions," he began. "When it states that no black men will be transported without their assent, it indulges in pure hypocrisy," for the "assent is extorted from them. We are merely soothing our consciences in saying that we colonize none but those who assent to be transported." It was a fallacy, he said, "that the blacks, being indigenous to the climate, enjoy a greater immunity from disease than the whites. Exemption from disease is not inheritable. It is a personal privilege which attaches to those alone who are born in the climate." Johnson listed the degradations experienced by the black man: "He cannot enter a church, a canal boat, a tavern, a steamboat . . . he is practically excluded from every post of honor and profit which usually stimulate other men to virtue and industry. . . . In the absence of all stimulants which excite white men to profits, I am surprised at the decency that colored people exhibit."

The clergymen present were reminded of their fondness for the injunction "Thou shalt love thy neighbor as thyself."

Is this a Commandment which expediency can annul? . . . I call on the clergymen to maintain such a doctrine if they dare. They may as well preach deism as that our conduct towards the black is not sinful. . . . The Society removes the blacks to Africa, because we insist on violating this command. The Society, thus, like a brothel, makes itself subservient to the sins of the community.

Thus far Johnson had undoubtedly pleased the militant abolitionists in his audience, but shortly, in words reminiscent of his feelings towards legislating sobriety, he turned to the rights of the southern states and their slaveholders: "Had I the power to make slaveholding appear to them so sinful as to cause them to liberate their slaves, I should feel more exalted than Napoleon; but had I the power to compel them to relinquish their slaves, I would rather die than exert it. To persuade them is a duty; to coerce them is a crime."

Johnson advocated a policy of "gradualism," insisting that the slaveholders would eventually yield to moral pressures. "Within a few years," he said, "the slave system has been greatly meliorated"; and as evidence he cited his belief that "the slaves are better clothed and fed than formerly." But Johnson's target was not the southern slaveholder; it was the hypocrisy of the American Colonization Society. "Sooner would I cast a thousand dollars into the ocean, than cast a dollar into the treasury of the Society. . . . Christianity and this Society cannot live together. Choose ye this night which ye will serve!"

Johnson published his speech but, warned by Beriah Green that some in the audience might attempt to "apply painful correction to the address," he hastily added a conciliatory foreword, which he later justified on the grounds that "my remarks were so adverse to the opinions prevailing at the time, though they are at the present writing (1865) entirely orthodox." In his foreword, Johnson took pains to point out that the author had never been "a member of any society for either abolition or colonization, and intending never to be of either, simply means to enjoy on those subjects the independence of thought and action which the laws and his circumstances in life enable him to maintain." His views, he said, "would have been presented with less pungency had not the terms of the debate precluded amplification by limiting every speech to thirty minutes." He then "disclaimed all imputation against the motives of the Society and its supporters" and praised its "highly meritorious intentions," as well as the talents of Mr. Danforth. The foreword merely compounded the confusion as to where exactly Johnson stood, and both the abolitionists and the colonizationists were irritated by the entire production. Beriah Green tried to delay the publication of the speech, imploring Johnson to "review the laws of the slaveholding states before you publish the statement that they are growing milder in their bearing on the condition of the slave." He was also "pained" to hear Johnson imply that "the colored people in this country were an idle class," asking, "Is it not high time that the condition and prospects of our colored brethren . . . should be justly represented?" Finally, Green was furious over some of Johnson's polite references to Mr. Danforth. "A more confused, feeble, unfair reasoner, I think I never heard!" he exclaimed. Johnson wrote later that he never replied to Green's letter, or altered his own remarks, but he did append a brief note referring to "a gentleman who was present at the delivery" of the speech. In it he denied that he had implied colored men were "naturally inferior to other men," ascribing the picture he drew of them to "the limited acquaintance with them his (the speaker's) secluded habits have afforded." In a final burst of goodwill, Johnson added, "That even this country (with its discouraging prejudices) possesses colored men of virtue, wealth, and literature, he is happy to possess the gentleman's assertion for believing, and the more of such instances can be substantiated, the greater will be his gratification."

Illustrating the dilemma of all who try to stay on middle ground, was a letter from Arthur Tappan, the New York Maecenas of the abolition movement, who, after reading Johnson's published speech, hailed him as "a valuable auxiliary to this glorious cause." Tappan begged him not to "disappoint our expectation and prayer that we may have your efficient cooperation," adding, "A lukewarm abolitionist is an anomaly. It is a cause that demands and receives the whole soul." Johnson objected to this attempt to polarize his attitudes, and added a note to Tappan's letter in the autobiography. "Mr. Tappan," he wrote, "seems to have fallen into the general error that no alternative existed but to be an abolitionist or colonizationist."

After the Colonization Society debates, the Utica City Council met to denounce organized antislavery agitation as "little short of treason to the government of our country." Another motion was offered to indict Beriah Green for treason, failing by only one vote. During the 1840s Johnson would speak out again on developing aspects of the slavery question in a series of essays; but with tempers boiling in Utica, he maintained, with one notable exception, a discreet silence on the subject throughout the next two years. That one exception, which he pointedly ignored in his autobiography, occurred nearly a year and a half later, and illustrates some of the ambiguities in the choices men like Johnson were forced to make at that time.

Antiabolitionist feelings flared up again in the late summer of 1835. On September 3, at a meeting held in the Courthouse, resolutions were adopted denouncing the abolitionists as "incendiaries." Johnson's friend Augustine Dauby, the editor of the Utica *Observer,* praised the antiabolitionist fervor of the assemblage as "exceeding our most sanguine hopes," and assured his readers that the abolitionists "compose but a small fraction of our community." To reinforce his optimistic viewpoint he added this piece of information:

> A. B. Johnson, Esq. expressed his desire to have his name associated with the proceedings of the evening, in testimony of his approbation of them. He had been charged in some places with being an abolitionist; but he disclaimed the charge. He had never attended an abolition meeting or been a member of any abolition society.

Dauby did not say that Johnson attended the meeting in person, and, indeed, Johnson may well have conveyed his request through a friend, but in later editorials Dauby regularly listed Johnson among the Utica "patriots."

Two weeks after the Courthouse meeting, the Oneida County grand jury met to discuss "inflammatory" publications being printed and distributed in the Utica area by the abolitionists, and agreed that "for the future quiet and happiness of this people" they should be destroyed "whenever and wherever found." Meanwhile, however, in New York City, abolitionist leaders were planning the first statewide antislavery convention. Some felt the meeting should be staged in New York City, but others argued for Utica as being centrally located and more accessible to men like Beriah Green, Alvin Stewart, and the affluent Gerrit Smith, whom the abolitionists hoped to convert from his pro-colonization Society stand. The abolitionists in Utica fell in with the idea, and it was announced that the convention would be held in their city on October 21.

The reaction of the Utica antiabolitionists was immediate and angry, though somewhat confused at first. On October 8 a meeting was held which began calmly enough with mild antiabolitionist speeches coupled with earnest statements on the right of free assembly and free speech. Just before the meeting ended, however, Congressman Samuel Beardsley, Johnson's next-door neighbor, leapt to his feet and denounced the plan for a convention. Rather than have Utica selected, he shouted, he would "almost as soon see it swept from the face of the earth, or sunk as low as Sodom and Gomorrah!" The crowd cheered, but no decisive action was taken.

On October 17, after receiving a formal request from the abolitionists for the use of the Courthouse as a convention site, the Common Council met and voted 7 to 4 in favor of the request—again influenced by the free speech argument. When they heard this news, the antiabolitionists exploded, and the next night they met in the Courthouse to denounce the Common Council's action as a "flagrant usurpation of power." Beardsley spoke again, declaiming "I would rather this building be razed from its foundation, or be destroyed by fire from Heaven, than be thus contaminated." Dauby reported the fiery session on October 19 in his *Observer,* noting that when someone mildly suggested that free discussion be allowed he was hissed down. Dauby himself announced that if the convention were held he would do his duty "manfully to prevent the meeting, peacefully if I can, forcibly if I must." The Common Council, under pressure, reversed its decision on the use of the Courthouse, and, as six hundred or more abolitionists streamed into the city on the 20th, they found no place in which to assemble but the Bleecker Street Presbyterian church. A feeble attempt was made on the morning of the 20th to prevent violence, without success. As the night of the opening of the convention drew near, Utica was in a state of near chaos. Pomeroy Jones, an eyewitness to the events, described what happened in his *Annals of Oneida County:*

October 21st, at 9:00 A.M., a meeting of citizens was held at the Court House. The Anti-Slavery Convention, consisting of 600 delegates from all parts of the State, met and organized rather hastily, at the Second Church on Bleecker Street. . . . The day had been ushered in by the firing of cannon, and thousands flocked to the city from the country and neighboring counties. At the Democratic County Convention at Hampton, October 15th, a resolution had been adopted . . . declaring that "the citizens of Utica owe it to themselves, to the State and the Union, that the contemplated convention of incendiary individuals is not permitted to assemble within its corporate bounds; that their churches, their court, academy and school rooms be closed against these wicked or deluded men who, whatever may be their pretensions, are riveting the fetters of bondmen and enkindling the flames of civil strife."

The meeting at the Court House . . . appointed a Committee of twenty-five to advise the delegates to the convention of the state of public feeling . . . and to warn them to abandon "their pernicious movements." [The Committee] then proceeded to the church attended by a large concourse of people. After considerable violence and force, an entrance was effected amid the greatest noise and confusion. The resolutions . . . were read to the Convention and then the latter was broken up amid a scene of uproar, of violence and imprecations upon the delegates who were then driven from the house and subsequently from the city. The church was locked and the key was taken, and the committee returned to the Court House.

After the church had been forcibly closed, most of the "Committee of Twenty-five" returned to their homes, but not so the tumultuous mob that had gathered in the Utica streets. The dismayed abolitionists decided to flee to Gerrit Smith's farm in Peterboro, where Smith had offered them facilities to continue their meeting, but the mob pursued them through Vernon, some seventeen miles away, overturning their carriages and pelting them with stones and mud. The group finally reached the safety of Peterboro, but meanwhile back in Utica more rioters destroyed the presses of the *Oneida Standard and Democrat,* which had been sympathetic to the abolitionists, and others made an attack on Alvin Stewart's house, but were turned away by well-armed members of the Stewart family.

In all this there is no evidence that Johnson did any more than permit his name to be used at the meeting on September 3, which denounced the abolitionists in principle, and endorsed no direct action against them. However, Dauby's obvious delight in announcing that A. B. Johnson was safely in the antiabolitionist fold, despite rumors to the contrary, indicates that Johnson, indirectly, provided some aid and comfort to the militants.

There is an interesting sidelight to this dismal story of what happened in Utica on October 21. In 1970 Professor Leonard L. Richards of the University of Massachusetts published a study of the antiabolitionist riots of this period entitled *Gentlemen of Property and Standing* (New York, 1970). The author, noting many resemblances between similar riots at the time in New York City, Cincinnati, and Utica, made a painstaking examination of the three outbreaks, focusing, in part, on the background of the individual participants in the rival antiabolitionist and abolitionist factions. Reviewing the religious affiliation, social position, occupational status, etc., of the three antiabolitionist "mobs," Richards reached the conclusion which is implicit in his title. The Utica organizers, for example, were among the city's elite—bankers, lawyers, wealthy merchants, and high-ranking state and local politicians. Thirty-four percent of them were members of Johnson's Episcopal church, while none of the abolitionist group were so listed. Richards' tables also indicate that 97 percent of the antiabolitionist group were native Americans, while 35 percent of the abolitionists were foreign-born. The name of A. B. Johnson appears in the roster of the anti-abolitionist "mob," and Richards' well-documented fact sheet on Johnson, which he kindly made available to the authors, lists Johnson as "rich, a banker, Episcopalian, vigorous and original thinker," etc. Richards' only error was in also listing him as a "colonizationist"—a possible deduction if one did not have available the record of Johnson's participation in the Colonization Society debates.

Pomeroy Jones, the Oneida County historian, in summing up

the results of the Utica episode, said, "As might have been expected, hundreds became abolitionists merely from sympathy." Among those "hundreds" was Gerrit Smith, who promptly withdrew his support from the colonizationists, and became a powerful national voice for immediate emancipation. This time, A. B. Johnson, in contrast to his experience in the Colonization Society debates, seems to have enjoyed (if that is the word) the best of two worlds. He continued a friendly correspondence with Gerrit Smith despite their numerous differences, and his letter files contain no correspondence on the Utica riot. His omission of this important event from the autobiography may be a testament to his unease, for he placed a high premium on consistency, especially where freedom of expression was concerned; and in this instance, he must have felt he had slipped badly. His fellow Uticans tried hard, on the other hand, to justify their behavior. The local newspapers, with the exception of the *Oneida Standard and Democrat,* assured the citizenry that it had "done its duty," and several of the "mob" leaders were elected to high offices in November (Samuel Beardsley to State Attorney General). The mood of self-congratulation was short-lived, however. Early in 1836 Theodore Weld, the most militant of the New York abolitionists, came back from the west to Utica and delivered a series of lectures in the church where the riots had taken place, and throngs came to hear him. By the eleventh night hundreds had to be turned away, and the abolitionists exulted over their growing numerical strength. The Oneida Institute sent its students into the streets to spread the message of abolition. By the end of 1836 Utica was firmly in the abolitionist camp, and the New York State Anti-Slavery Society held its second convention there with no opposition whatever. Johnson, however, remained aloof.

Johnson described the year 1834 as being the "most active year of my life." While he was engaged in the Bank controversy and Colonization Society debate he was also the complainant in a long and involved lawsuit against Spencer Kellogg, whom he had accused of misrepresentation in connection with a bank loan to Kellogg's brother-in-law. (The abolitionist Kellogg had been one of the Presbyterian deacons who engineered Johnson's excommunication earlier.) Johnson had also become involved in another temperance battle—this one over the question of "extending the temperance pledge from distilled to fermented drinks . . . wine, cider and beer." E. C. Delevan had invited Johnson to write on the subject for his State Temperance newspaper, and Johnson obliged with a carefully reasoned attack against broadening the pledge. "I based my argument," he wrote, "on the principle that the prohibition of wine equally with distilled spirits diluted the pledge by making dram-drinking no worse than wine drinking, and thus obliterating a useful and well-understood distinction, and making a less evil equal to a greater."

There was something almost manic in Johnson's burst of enthusiasm for good works during the early months of 1834. On February 6, for example, he fired off a letter to George McWhorter, of Oswego, who headed a committee of New York State citizens to promote the construction of a ship canal around Niagara Falls into Lake Erie. The legislature was interested in the project, but powerful forces raised the spectre of a large burden of debt for the state. This gave Johnson an opportunity to expound his theory of deficit spending which he had elaborated in his early work, *The Nature of Value and Capital.* "We are yet torpid," Johnson wrote,

> and asleep in our views and efforts in relation to public improvements by roads and canals. Our thoughts seem to regard money making as the aim of public improvements, while I deem the improvements a benefit in themselves, far superior to any money income that may be derived from them. . . . Whether the income shall ever be collected or not is of little consequence. . . . If posterity is to enjoy the Canal, posterity will not be injured by leaving to it the debt by which the Canal was constructed. . . . I care not how large a debt we contract, nor how long its payment is deferred, if the improvements be worth the expenditure by the facilities they yield to the commerce, agriculture, and other great interests of the State.

McWhorter was impressed by Johnson's broad views on the matter, and urged him "to communicate his suggestions to some of our public men who manage the machinery of the State"; and before he knew it, Johnson found himself chairman of the New York State Central Executive Committee on the Ship Canal, charged with formulating resolutions to be transmitted to the legislature. For a while it seemed that Johnson's theories might prevail, but the conservative legislature balked, and a compromise was reached authorizing "enlargement of the present canal." That any action was taken at all was credited by many to Johnson's initiative. Henry Seymour, for instance, the father of Horatio Seymour, a later governor of New York, told him, "You have started a ball which will not cease rolling till the Canal will be enlarged." Johnson added a note to this in 1861, "The prophecy has now been fulfilled." The Canal issue also gave Johnson a chance to express his hardening attitude on states' rights. Many advocates of the Ship Canal had called for federal funds, but Johnson insisted that public improvements were the province of the "separate states." Later, in an essay entitled "The Constitutional Power of Congress Over Internal Improvements," published in *Our American Union,* he drew on his experience in this discussion:

> When New York first seriously contemplated the connection of Lake Erie with the Hudson River, she felt like a child that was beginning to walk alone, and deemed the assistance of Congress as indispensable. That assistance fortunately failing her, she, first timidly, then boldly, called forth her own energies, and soon—her strength increasing with her efforts—completed the undertaking, and many kindred ones . . . and suddenly became the Empire State. And better, her example taught other states their latent energies, by which instruction our Confederacy is become intersected with canals and railroads to an extent which the General Government could not have equalled in centuries, had it possessed all requisite constitutional powers.

Johnson also made a brief foray into the question of ladies' apparel and "tight lacing." Johnson's concern was strictly over the issue of health, but he approached the subject with all the fervor of his diatribes against the Bank and the Colonization Society. He had been asked for his views by the Reverend A. G. Whittelsey and his wife, the sister of Samuel Griswold Goodrich, author of the famous "Peter Parley" books for children; and his article appeared in the couple's *Mothers Magazine,* one of the many products of Utica's growing publishing industry. "How," he asked, "shall we combat an evil of this magnitude?"

> I know of no way as that by which we combat intemperance—by total abstinence. Whether females, especially Christian females, might not by some concerted operation produce a reform of this great evil, equal to temperance reform among men [he would still not admit that women drank], is a thought that might be worth considering.

Then, in a Swiftian vein, he proposed that women should

> substitute as a far better fashion some artificial enlargement of the chest and waist by padding their dresses, and thus rendering in a short time, a conical waist as repugnant to fashion as it is to the natural beauty of the female form, and to the health and lives of its victims.

CHAPTER 16

1834–1835

Advice to the Lovelorn,
Politics, and a New Purchase

JOHNSON PRESERVED COPIES of certain of his own letters which he felt would display "my mode of thinking" and "illuminate my character for posterity." One such letter, written in November 1834, went to his old friend Watts Sherman who was in the process of wife hunting and wanted some advice from Johnson. "What kind of connection," asked Sherman, would be most desirable and expedient for me to form, and what the essential requisites are that I should seek to find in a woman?" Johnson promptly produced a long epistle to Sherman in which he did, indeed, display his "mode of thinking" on this subject.

"I would advise you," Johnson wrote, "to make wealth an ingredient in the woman you are to marry." He granted that few women "had wealth in immediate possession," but Sherman should at least seek out a bride to whom "a respectable patrimony will probably descend," for "to such a female will naturally pertain a highly respectable family and connections." Next, Johnson recommended a female "in good physical condition," and that Sherman take a careful look at her lineage avoiding "a consumptive family" or one "afflicted with madness or any other great and kindred afflictions." As to the lady's character and behavior, he advised his friend to take only a moderate interest in such matters, for "women, by their relative station in life sexually, and by their education, natural tenderness, and comparatively feeble passions, are prone to virtue, peace and tenderness." Besides, he added, "the moral qualities which a young woman reveals or actually possesses afford no criterion (or at least a very poor one) of the disposition she will display when more mature in years and under the operation of special circumstances." Of course, he admitted, the woman "could become a complete virago," but usually, "such transformations . . . proceed from faults or unskillfulness of the husband." To mold a proper wife, he con-

226

tinued, "requires a tact and skill which he can acquire only by care, judgment and persevering attention." The husbands' "general actions," he contended, are more important that his "verbal precepts," for the latter "are more productive of strife than of concord." As for the woman's "strength of intellect," it should be viewed in relation to that of the husband, and be sufficient to protect him "from pain in her social intercourse with his friends."

Having provided Sherman with a list of wifely ingredients, Johnson proceeded to disabuse him of any notion that falling in love was a necessary first step in any courtship. It would be far better for a man to marry someone for whom he has "a strong affection," but if she meets the right specifications, he need not delay his pursuit on that account. In fact, wrote Johnson, "a better course consists in selecting a woman before his feelings are much interested in her. . . . Let him marry her, and love will certainly ensue." The process, explained Johnson, was a very simple one, "for love is not the mysterious being that metaphysics supposes, but a very plain and common principle." Here Johnson returned to those "kindling appliances" he had recommended to Judge Ezekiel Bacon as a stimulus to religiosity. "You can as assuredly become in love after marriage," he argued, "as a piece of dry wood can become ignited when placed in contact with fire . . . since Providence has affixed a remarkable connection between a man's feelings and his words and actions; hence, if you desire to love a person, the love will surely come if you employ toward the person words that indicate love, and actions that correspond with the words."

Johnson would elaborate upon these notions later in the opening line of *Breviat* XLVI in his book, *An Encyclopedia of Instruction* (1857): "The feeling that causes a man to kiss his wife, he can excite in himself at any time by kissing her."

As the spring of 1835 approached, Johnson found himself once again back in the political arena, and this time came dangerously close (at least he saw it that way) to winning a seat in the House of Representatives. A presidential election was scheduled for November 1836, and Johnson was chosen as a delegate to the nominating convention to be held in Baltimore on May 25, 1835. (Jackson, obeying the two-term precedent, had declined re-election.) Johnson's invitation came, he said, from the "Republican" party, but the two names, "Democratic" and "Republican," he noted, were "about this time struggling for ascendancy," and "Democratic" ultimately prevailed—to Johnson's satisfaction. Johnson accepted the invitation, mostly to give Abigail a "journey for recreation," and "to witness the ceremony of nominating a President— which under the circumstances was equivalent to an election." The

Johnsons went by way of New York where he was to hold preliminary "informational" meetings with the city delegates prior to the Baltimore convention.

The New York delegates gathered at a private home, and Johnson was disappointed to find the meeting entirely prearranged and a "mere matter of form." The next day he and Abigail moved on to Baltimore, putting up at Barnum's—"the best house in the city." The New York delegation caucused again in Baltimore agreeing upon Van Buren as their presidential nominee, but divided over the vice-presidential candidate. Johnson did not record his own choice, but, recalling his battle with the Presbyterians over the Sunday mail issue, he probably voted for the winner, Richard M. Johnson of Kentucky, known as "Tecumseh" Johnson as a result of his claim that he killed the Indian warrior. Like his Utica namesake, the Kentuckian had waged a vigorous campaign in behalf of transporting the mails on Sunday, and had gone so far, wrote Johnson, as having his bill reprinted "on pocket handkerchiefs of a cheap kind for the communality."

The convention, held in a Baltimore church, was presided over by the former Speaker of the House, Andrew Stevenson of Virginia, and Johnson was flattered to find that Stevenson remembered him as a result of a brief introduction years earlier in New York's City Hotel. As for the proceedings, Johnson reported, "I soon found, as I had previously in New York, that my individual opinion was wholly ineffective where it conflicted with prearranged modes and decisions." He summed it all up by saying, "many speeches were made, and some resolutions were adopted."

Johnson had prepared a speech for the convention, "but finding all its proceedings to have been prearranged, and that my remarks would have been difficult to introduce," he waited till he got home and rewrote the address for a Utica audience which gathered to hear him on June 9. His address to his constituents was later published as an essay entitled "The Mode of Selecting a New President," in *Our American Union*. It was a scholarly, well-documented review of the history of the convention system from the one which chose Jefferson in 1800 up through the Baltimore meeting, and in contrast to his somewhat jaundiced autobiographical report, extolled the system as a means of ensuring the democratic process, and avoiding rule "by the smaller class, the aristocracy." Somewhat optimistically he suggested that Martin Van Buren might have turned down his own nomination had he not "felt that the Convention represented the general will of the people." The address is chiefly interesting, however, for the light it sheds on his true feelings about John Quincy Adams. Adams, he said, "was the only President who administered the office in opposition to a Convention." He added, "What a lesson we may read in this! The only President elected in opposition to a convention—Mr. Adams! He failed utterly in satisfying the country, and it lay under his guidance (not without fault of his) like Samson shorn." He then contrasted Adams' failure with Jackson's success. "We must possess not merely a competent, but a popular President—and to be popular, he must be the offspring of the democracy, brought into being at their own time and in their own way, and hence feeling a moral obligation to conform to their views of government and policy."

A delegate to a national party convention in Johnson's day stood high on the list of possible contenders for a seat in Congress, and his chances for election were excellent if his party, as the Democrats were in Utica, was in a majority. Thus, shortly after returning from Baltimore, Johnson was offered the nomination by several "active and influential politicians." He concluded not to accept, he said, because he felt he "would have to resign from the Bank if he went to Washington." In the opening of a letter to Worth, however, his reasons were more broadly stated. "With a fortune above my habits of expenditure," he wrote, "and with an employment both honorable and pleasant, I possess no desire for office; nor would I accept any that would in any probability be offered to me."

In midsummer of 1835 Johnson was also busy with other concerns—among them a revision of his *Philosophy of Human Knowledge,* which was published by Harper Brothers under the abridged title *A Treatise on Language* in 1836. Meanwhile, he was also being solicited by the *Knickerbocker Magazine,* one of the country's newest and most prestigious literary publications, for articles on any topic—"subject to your choice." Gaylord Clark, the editor, assured him that what he had read of his writings "is to my mind full evidence of what you would produce for the respectable publication." From 1849 through 1850 Johnson wrote widely for the *Knickerbocker,* reprinting most of his contributions in his *Encyclopedia of Instruction;* but for the moment he was not interested in Clark's offer. "As I never wrote for pay," he explained, "my contributions to literature were produced only when my inclinations dictated; and I found my feelings were rather perverse against writing on invitation." A more pressing reason for avoiding literary engagements, however, may have been a new financial crisis that was disturbing the country.

The whole aspect of money matters had become perfectly reversed since the contest was closed with the United States Bank. The money

of the Government when it was removed from the Bank, had been
placed by the government in the state banks and they were invited by
the government to lend freely, so as to counteract the efforts of the
United States Bank to make money scarce. The local banks of our
cities who became the chief depositories of the government were
nothing loth to use the public deposits in loans and thus to gain as
much by the use of them as possible, and money soon became abundant beyond all the known uses therefor; and by consequence men
soon became ingenious in the discovery of new uses so as to become
rich by the use of the capital that could be borrowed. The banks of
most of the states, New York included, were practically unlimited in
the quantity of banknotes they could create and issue, and hence no
limit seemed to exist to the magnitude of the currency. Real estate,
being illimitable in quantity, soon became the object to which money
was profusely directed. The national lands were bought up at every
land office till the public became alarmed at finding that the public
domain was fast being exchanged for credit in banks of whose solvency
the government knew but little. At length the government published an
order that thereafter the government land offices should receive nothing
but specie in payment for lands. The government was probably unaware
of the effect of the order, but it checked the circulation of banknotes
and sent the holders to the banks for specie. The call was gradual, but
as it increased in intensity the banks had to stop the issue of notes and
to call in their loans to provide funds for the new demand on them for
specie. Debtors soon experienced a difficulty in meeting their vastly
extended engagements. A panic soon ensued, bankruptcy became common; the banks were unable to meet the daily increasing demands on
them for specie and they eventually, one and all, had to suspend
payments.

The situation was aggravated on December 16, 1835, by a disastrous fire in New York City. Johnson's third son, Bryan, was there as an
apprentice in the dry goods firm of Lord and Bacon, and witnessed the
destruction, which included the building and warehouse of his own firm.
He reported to his father that seven hundred buildings had burned at a
loss of $25,000,000, and that "all the insurance companies are thought
to be ruined." A side effect of the fire was to increase land speculation
since, as Johnson pointed out, "money was so abundant that arrangements were speedily made for rebuilding." The land fever spread to
Utica, and local citizens began buying up vacant lots and breaking
them up into small parcels "25 feet front by 100 feet deep" which they
sold to New York City buyers "at almost fabulous prices." But when the
buyers came to see their properties, said Johnson, "they were found with

difficulty . . . often discovered in swampy ground and remote meadows." Johnson himself was caught up in the excitement, and placed in the hands of a New York broker, some 1,000 lots which he had owned for some time in Utica. The broker, however, turned out to be a "man of intemperate habits . . . and lost hold on the contract by getting drunk." Johnson, on hearing this disturbing news, set out for New York.

The trip to New York was a fiasco financially, but while there he did manage to take one daring step. He bought a wig, and the adventure produced two letters to Abigail back in Utica—letters that are rare indeed in the Johnson file. It also produced a wistfully amusing account in the autobiography of what must have been a traumatic experience. On March 16, he wrote:

> I have not as yet effected anything, nor do I believe I shall be able to. The great outcry in Utica about Utica property in this city is, I think, deceptive. I shall probably try this week and then return home. I have not yet seen Varick, for he is still in Washington. Our son, Bryan, is with me every evening. I have bought a wig, but it spoils all my beauty; and I shall not wear it till you give your judgment. Love to all the dear children, and my mother.

Four days later Johnson wrote Abigail again, telling her of the forthcoming publication of his *Treatise on Language* by Harpers, adding, "You say I may do as I please in relation to a wig. This comes too late. I must hold you to the responsibility of advising the measure. I have it on, and the Rubicam is passed. I hardly know myself. It makes my heart ache a thousand times, but Bryan insists it is an improvement." Reflecting on this crisis in his autobiography, Johnson wrote, "I am at the present day continually told that I look as I did twenty or thirty years ago, but I know they mean only that my wig looks as it did."

CHAPTER 17

1836–1837

"The Fatal Fourth"
and *A Treatise on Language*

ABIGAIL ADAMS JOHNSON died on July 4, 1836—the "fatal fourth" Johnson called it. Though Johnson did not record the fact in his account of the events of 1835, his wife had presented him in November of that year with his third daughter, Frances Elizabeth, named after his two sisters who had died when they were children—one of them before Johnson was born. The birth was a difficult one, and Johnson's doctor advised him to provide a wet nurse, but he was unable to locate one. After her confinement, Abigail told him that she "had for some time felt a pain in her abdomen," and that at one point, placing her hand on the spot, "she had felt a large internal tumor which alarmed her."

When Johnson returned from New York, he found that his wife's condition had grown worse. By early June, her doctor ordered her to wean her seven-month-old daughter, and "take to her bed." Johnson provided a full-time nurse, and brought three doctors in on the case— to no avail. On July 2 Abigail's death agonies began, and Johnson in his autobiography spared none of the details—the convulsions, clenched teeth, and the screams of pain: On the Fourth of July the militia with their music marching past the house troubled her as she seemed disposed to doze, and I went out and induced the soldiers to pass the house without music, and they kindly complied. One man kept discharging a gun near the house, and I went to him and urged him to desist which he did. . . . As night approached my wife grew restless and uttered a horrid shriek as from a sudden agony. I immediately gave her some morphine . . . and it seemed to ease the pain, and she remarked rebukingly, "Why do you palter with small doses?" . . . I stood by her bedside and about nine or ten o'clock that night while I still held her hand she breathed her last and was dead.

The cause of Abigail's death, according to the autopsy, was cancer of the uterus. Johnson kept the autopsy report on his desk for five years before he could bear to read it, but read it he did eventually, and passed it on to posterity in his autobiography. His own diagnosis gave a clue to the origins of his diatribe against tight lacing.

> In relation to the tumor and the consequent adhesions and disease, I have always attributed them to over-tight lacing. Laced corsets were not worn until some time after our marriage. A female peddler brought them to Utica, and recommended them to my wife who was becoming corpulent. She tried one on and wore corsets ever after, and I thought with increasing tightness, till disease forced her to leave them off. She was finely formed for strength and longevity, had she not thus interfered with her vital powers.

Johnson must have expressed his dissatisfaction to the doctors over their treatment, for they invited him to witness the last stages of the autopsy to prove to him "that death was inevitable," but he declined.

> I went to bed but in vain sought sleep. I got up in the middle of the night, went out into the street and walked down town. I found that no change of position procured any relief. I was left with nine children. The oldest was not quite nineteen years, and the youngest not quite eight months. . . . My wife's aunt, Mrs. Masters . . . approached me leading several of the children and directing my thoughts to them in the hope of thereby arousing me from the stupor of my grief. I loved my children with an ardor probably unusual, but my whole soul had been absorbed in my wife, who had constantly relieved me from all care of the children and of all domestic duties. She had managed everything in the house and pertaining thereto, and a new and dreary world seemed opening before me.

To his friend, Henry Gibson, he wrote:

> She constituted all my society, all my confidence, and all my unreserved intercourse. I counselled with her on all subjects. . . . I knew no more of all that related to servants, clothing, household expenditures, education of children than you know of my domestic arrangements. To never have married is probably better than any connubial state; to never have had children is probably better than to possess them, and never to have possessed life is probably better than all other states. . . . Do not advert to my topic of grief when you

write me, as anything which your kind sympathy will induce you to say will probably give me new grief.

One aftermath of Abigail's death was a letter to his cousin Rachel in Europe—the first in several years. Her reply, omitted from the autobiography, indicates that the letter must have been an unrestrained expression of misery. "Do not sink under the chastening hands of your God!" she exhorted him. He must remember his mother, Leah, "who has no expectation beyond laying her bones in a land unknown to her fathers." The letter was stern but warm, full of reminders of her own tragedies, and her reliance upon her God. Earlier Johnson would have inked out many telltale sentences and phrases, but from this time on, throughout the rest of the "Rachel" file, there is no further editing.

Young Alexander S. Johnson did not return to Yale, but fearing for his father's health, remained in Utica to continue his studies in a Utica law firm. At some point he wrote a long letter to a Professor Tully, at the Yale Medical School, describing his father's condition and asking for an opinion. Tully replied that the "depression was constitutional," that Abigail's death was only "the exciting cause of the latent defect," and that he "would probably become worse." Years later, when Alexander showed the letter to his father, Johnson commented, "No doubt I might have realized this prediction but for the vigor of my intellect which resisted successfully at last the tendency of my emotional depression." Johnson then paid his final tribute to Abigail:

> My moral education had been as poor as my intellectual, and I had not attempted to cultivate it as I had attempted to cultivate my intellect. She impressed me with religious belief and social improvement. . . . Her social position had been much superior to mine, and I admired her for her youth, her beauty, her wisdom and discretion. She was essentially and peculiarly the help that was meet for me.

Johnson began the story of his recovery with the words, "Nothing is more wonderful than man's ability to sustain himself under such an affliction as I suffered." Then he added, "The first alleviation I experienced was through another death."

The death was that of Mr. Treadway, who had married Abigail's sister, Susan. With Treadway's well-timed death, "his widow was thus enabled to live in my family and take charge of my children and domestic affairs." Susan with her young daughter moved in at once and "became, in short, the mistress of the household," permitted "to use my carriage and horses." With this return of domestic regularity, Johnson decided to divert himself by traveling, and left Utica with his son Alexander for New York via Saratoga Springs. This time he went by train, rails having recently been laid from Utica to Schenectady. Johnson found the speed "novel and surprising," faster, he thought, than it ever was subsequently. Saratoga, however, was once again depressing, and he "kept secluded except as a spectator," missing the "pleasure which flowed from female companionship." Alexander enjoyed himself but, after a few days, his restless father herded him off to New York, where they put up at the new Astor House. Johnson admired the accommodations, but found the place far too noisy. "The barkeeper hallooed to the waiters in a very loud manner when any bell rang . . . and such occasions occurred momentarily." Immensely annoyed, Johnson cut short his visit and hurried back to Utica by way of New Haven. A cold bath taken prior to his departure from New York "in a bathing house constructed at the Battery and which floated on the water" brought on acute stomach pain, however, and induced a stopover in New Haven, where a dose of morphine was prescribed for him by a local doctor. "It was the first opium I had ever taken, and the effect was pleasantly exciting to me, till its effects suddenly left me and I felt ready to faint." The return to Utica was made "with no further adventure."

The trip to New York and Saratoga turned out to be doubtful therapy, but shortly after his return home he received a letter from John Quincy Adams which did far more to take his mind off his troubles than did the Astor House. There is no record of a note from Adams on the death of Abigail, although both his wife and Mrs. Thomas Boylston Adams wrote warm letters of condolence. What prompted Adams' unusually long letter to Johnson was his receipt of a copy of the new Harper's edition of *A Treatise on Language*. The ex-President apparently gave the book his full attention and produced a thoughtful commentary, which not only displayed his formidable knowledge but also put a finger on a problem which, although Johnson never actually credited him with discovering it, was to produce radical, and some feel, unfortunate, additions to Johnson's philosophical views on language in his later work, *The Meaning of Words*. Adams wrote:

Since my arrival at Washington, I have received from you a copy of your ingenious and elaborate *Treatise on Language; or, The Relation Which Words Bear to Things* and I have read it with great care and attention, without being able to assent to many of its opinions, and particularly to that which, if I understand the work, forms the foundation of your theory—namely that sensation is the only source of human knowledge, and that every word not expressive of some sensual impression is insignificant. I must admit that the view you have taken of the whole subject is new and sustained with great meditative power, a power which I can trace neither to sight, sound, taste, feel, or smell. I read Locke's *Essay Upon the Human Understanding* at the University precisely fifty years ago. I have read it again within the last fifteen years. I read Reid and Berkeley also while at College and they left impressions on my mind, I believe, indelible while memory holds her seat. From Locke I learned the doctrine of Ideas, and to believe that there were two sources of them in the human intellect—*sensation* and *reflection.* You divide all human thoughts into six classes, assigning one class to each of the five senses, and then you admit only one class more, which you call verbal thoughts, and which include all Locke's ideas of reflection. All the words of your sixth class are significant of ideas of reflection. They are, therefore, quite as significant to the *mind* as any of the words significant of sensible existences. The word *mind* itself in your system is insignificant, it means nothing which either or all the five senses indicate. *Mind* is neither sight, sound, feel, taste, nor smell; nor is it a combination of any two or more of these. Is *mind* then a word without meaning?

I think you have not used the word *mind* at all. But besides your six classes of words, your eleventh lecture seems to me to admit another and an all important class—a class which you derive from *internal feelings.* But these are not the physical sense. They are neither sights, sounds, tastes, feels, nor smells. They are what the English poet has called "the shadowy tribes of mind." You acknowledge that they are not *usually* deemed the objects of our senses—and that is, because they are *not* objects of our senses. But they are sources of *thoughts* in our minds, as much as sensible existences; and *language* is the exponent of human thoughts—of all human thoughts, whether originating in sensation or in reflection—whether imparted to us by the senses, the memory, the imagination, or the reasoning faculty. These are all sources of *words* highly significant to the mind, without references to the senses of the earthly clod.

I must confess that the course of argument throughout your lectures, and the primary position upon which it seems to be founded, would have led me to class you among the philosophers who deny all spiritual existences and who are commonly called *pantheists.* Your fifteenth lecture has effectually guarded me against that misconception. I give unqualified credence to your declaration that it is not your intention to dispute the truths of Divine Revelation, or the doctrines of Christian faith. I believe you also implicitly when you say, that if you thought the tendency of your discourse was to unsettle in any person the religious opinions of Christianity, you would not have published it. The declarations have not only afforded me cordial gratification, as assurances of your own belief, but as they have been pledges of the purity and excellence of your intentions. They have convinced me that the error of my deductions from your reasoning is in my own imperfect comprehension of your whole system, rather than in the system itself.

Johnson answered the Adams letter, but kept no copy. He reported, however, that he "labored hard to explain" his "principal object which President Adams failed to notice—but how far I succeeded would appear to be small." The "principal object" was, of course, to show "that men should not interpret by words the knowledge they derive from their senses, but should interpret words by the sensible revelations to which words refer." He added, characteristically, "I believe I am the first writer who has attempted that mode of interpretation." However, he admitted that in differentiating between words which derive meaning from the physical senses and those which take meaning from thoughts and "internal feelings," Adams brought on some "reflections" which caused him eventually to "deem the book defective" in omitting an analysis of those words like *mind* which referred to "no sensible revelations."

What Adams really thought of his odd Utica in-law is hidden in his letter, but, as was often the case, he expressed a more forceful opinion in his private diary. On November 26, two weeks before writing the letter to Johnson, he made this entry about the *Treatise:*

It is a work of an extraordinary character, and deserving of much consideration, at least from me. It assumes the merit of a profound discovery, undetected by all the writers upon metaphysics of former ages. There is something of the Jeremy Bentham character about it. A free use of neologies—words of the author's invention, but deficient both in euphony and precision. A style deeply studied, affecting originality; antipathetic, highly figurative, and often stranded upon the commonest rules of grammar. He quotes Berkeley, Locke, Hume, Descartes, and Reid, as mere schoolboys utterly ignorant of his great discovery, and consequently committing egregious blunders, which it has been reserved to him to expose. But instead of quoting them in their own words, he gives his own version or paraphrase of conceptions which he imputes to them. He has long and perseveringly and painfully meditated his subject into a system which has unity and consistency and some ingenuity or invention. But I find it very difficult to understand him, and am doubtful whether he has really presented some new views of language, or whether his book is a mere bundle of common truisms, mystified into an appearance of metaphysical refinement.

It must have been a great shock to the former professor of Oratory and Rhetoric at Harvard to find a Utica banker writing off the works of Locke, Hume, Berkeley and others. As for Johnson, he was far more flattered by a brief notice in an obscure magazine, *The Southern Rose* published in Charleston, South Carolina. The reviewer, Johnson wrote, "seemed to apprehend my meaning better than Mr. Adams." The object of Johnson's *Treatise,* said *The Southern Rose,* "is to teach us to contemplate created things apart from words."

Johnson's *Treatise on Language: or, The Relationship Which Words Bear to Things* appeared in a series of "Lectures" broken up into numbered "Propositions," each elucidated by examples, anecdotes, and references to the writings of earlier philosophers. The reader may find it, along with a critical essay, collated with Johnson's earlier work, *The Philosophy of Human Knowledge,* in David Rynin's University of California Press edition (1947), or in a revised edition published by Dover Publications (1968). There is also a succinct summary of Johnson's main philosophical tenets by Rynin, in the 1969 edition of MacMillan's *Encyclopedia of Philosophy* (Vol. 4, p. 266–90), Macmillan Publishing Company and the Free Press, edited by Paul Edwards. Finally, for other mid-twentieth century appraisals of Johnson's works on language, together with his forays into economic theory, religion and political thought, one may turn to *Language and Value,* a series of essays on Johnson by distinguished American European and Canadian scholars, edited by Charles L. Todd and Russell T. Blackwood (Greenwood Press, 1969).

The authors will make no attempt to summarize Johnson's *Treatise* beyond what has already been written, but we would like, at this point, to pair off at least two of Johnson's "propositions" with similar statements made a full century later, by the distinguished physicist, Percy W. Bridgman.

Johnson: Proposition #24, Lecture V: *A Treatise on Language*

IMPUTING TO NATURE THE IDENTITY WHICH EXISTS IN LANGUAGE CAUSES MUCH FALLACIOUS SPECULATION.
 . . . Light *moves* from the sun to the earth, and a coach *moves* from Utica to Albany. The word *motion* is proper in both phrases; but when we deem the motions as identical in nature as in language, we are transferring to nature what is simply a property of language. The mistake is unimportant till, by virtue of the supposed identity, we attribute to the *motion* of light the concomitants of the coaches *motion.* Proceeding thus, we calculate that during one vibration of a clock's pendulum, light moves as consecutively as the coach, one hundred and sixty thousand miles.

Bridgman: *The Logic of Modern Physics* (1927):

Physically, it is of the essence of light that it is not a thing that *travels*, and in choosing to treat it as a thing that does, I do not see how we can avoid the most serious difficulties.

Johnson: Proposition #4, Lecture XIX:

OUR SENSES ALONE CAN ANSWER QUESTIONS. WORDS CAN ONLY REFER TO WHAT OUR SENSES REVEAL:
. . . When the Lord answered from the flaming bush the inquiry of Moses by saying, "I am that I am," the answer was wonderfully expressive of the nature of language . . . We may say to life, "What art thou?" and to death, "What art thou?" . . . but language can furnish no better answer than, I am that I am.

Bridgman: *The Intelligent Individaul and Society* (N.Y. 1938):

The physicist has come to recognize that it is unpleasantly easy to put words together into formal questions which admit of no possible operational check on the correctness of the answer, and in making this recognition and in learning to avoid the *meaningless* questions he has acquired an important tool in aid of precise thinking.

Percy Bridgman knew nothing of Johnson's works or even of his existence when he wrote these words. Nor did Bertrand Russell, Ludwig Wittgenstein, Aldous Huxley, I. A. Richards, S. I. Hayakawa, and other students of the philosophy of language when they began, a century after Johnson wrote his *Treatise,* to delve into the meaning of words.

CHAPTER 18

1837—1838

Domestic Woes and National Panic

I N THE LONG AND DREARY MONTHS after Abigail's death, Johnson found himself turning more and more to Rachel as a confidante. Over the year a strong bond of sympathy had been established between them, although by now they had not seen each other for thirty-five years.

To be sure, Rachel often harassed Johnson with pleas for financial help. She also peristed in her attempts to engage him in a dazzling variety of joint business ventures, even though, as she was forced to admit, "on several occasions you have declared your unwillingness to have anything to do with commercial transactions." On October 13, 1836, in one of her least happy inspirations, she told him of a "brewing establishment" available at a low price which "being properly conducted" would yield large profits, and she suggested that Johnson come to England and join her in its operation. Of his response to this suggestion, she wrote "I am glad anyhow that my brewing proposition made you relax from your ordinary gravity."

Rachel also continued unremittingly to defy the injunction Johnson had laid down against religious discussions. On October 13, 1836, speaking of Leah, she wrote: "I am greatly pleased to find my Aunt's strength still admits of her *walking* in preference to *riding*—but to Church! Heaven, is it possible!" Impenitent at her indiscretion, she added: "I shall not apologize to you for the expression of my feelings— if you and she were less dear to me I should not let such a remark escape me—therefore take it as it is intended."

In the same letter Rachel misinterpreted, possibly deliberately, a remark of Johnson's about her daughters. "You say that my position must be very disadvantageous to them." By "position" Johnson was undoubtedly referring to Rachel's position as a woman alone, using her divorced husband's name, and with a younger daughter born out of wedlock. Rachel, however, took him to be referring to religious status:

> If you mean in respect to our religious tenets, you are only right as regards the extremely small sphere of our connections—but otherwise the character of the Israelite stands on very different grounds to what it did before you left England. The march of intellect has done much— the actual Sheriff of London is a steady Israelite. The Jew is here no longer an object of odium, rather of admiration—even our theatrical and other pieces of fiction excite most interest when delineating in fascinating traits the characters of the formerly despised descendants of Jacob.

Most valuable to Johnson after Abigail's death was the feeling that with Rachel he could allow himself to express his doubts and frustrations, his sense "of dullness, of melancholy, of sadness." Rachel tried her best to buoy him up. She also tried to distract him with repeated pleas for him to visit England. She prodded him for news about his "new work on language." She rebuked him again and again for questioning divine wisdom, and suggested that his sufferings may have been a punishment for his lack of gratitude for all his blessings. When Johnson told her he was "prostrated forever" and exclaimed "What a world is this!" she reminded him that in his earlier letters, he had boasted of an "uninterrupted succession of prosperity" and suggested that his melancholy was "ingratitude toward the bounty of Heaven."

Gloomy or not, Johnson was soon forced by the financial condition of the country into a period of feverish activity on behalf of his, and other, hard-pressed local banks. Johnson began his story of the panic of 1837 in a sarcastic vein. "Notwithstanding the existing money pressure," he wrote, "our state legislature was much engaged in discussing bank questions, the currency, etc., and thus making matters worse." As president of one of the few New York banks which were still solvent, he received a barrage of letters asking for guidance—letters he answered, "giving all the advice I deemed for the good of the State." Some of his answers got into print, and were instrumental in calming the fears of his fellow bankers.

Old friends of the Bank of the United States (including, of course, Biddle himself) blamed the money panic entirely upon Andrew Jackson's attacks on their institution, and his encouragement of land speculation. Jackson himself, heading back to Tennessee after Van Buren's inauguration, saw and felt the havoc. Nashville was selling bank notes at 15 percent below par; southern planters were deeply in debt; and the sale of public lands, which had jumped to $2 million in 1836, had fallen to less than $1 million. The U.S. Treasury overflowed with unsound paper money, and Jackson's famous "Specie Circular," forbidding the Treasury to receive anything but gold and silver in payment for public land, was useless since most of his "pet" banks had no gold and silver with which to redeem the notes. One by one the country banks throughout New York State ran out of specie, and dividends went unpaid.

Johnson began his rescue efforts with a letter to David Wager, a state senator in Albany, urging the legislature to make a "thorough study" of the state's banking problems, but Wager replied that there was no one in Albany "competent to do it," suggesting that Johnson take on the task himself. Johnson did so, and published a lengthy "study" in the Albany *Argus* which was read aloud in the State Senate. Its strong defense of the role of private banks, said Wager, "has badly shaken the faith of those who were for imposing more restrictions." Meanwhile, the Oneida Bank, which had recently been chartered in Utica, and in which Johnson owned ten shares of stock, came under attack by the legislature, and Johnson was subpoenaed to testify on its methods of stock distribution. Johnson had also encouraged others to invest in the bank, but his explanation was so convincing that the investigation was dropped. One result of his testimony, however, was a decision to lodge the stock subscription money in his own bank—a measure Johnson termed "fortunate," since another bank was shortly robbed by a man who "subsequently escaped to Canada, bought a farm, made quite a village around him by his capital and enterprise, and was deemed by his neighbors as a very useful and respectable man." The issue of banning all bank notes under five dollars was revived in the nervous legislature, but Johnson counseled a "hands-off" policy, and the measure was dropped.

The first moment of real alarm Johnson experienced came when the powerful Merchants and Farmers Bank of Albany suddenly refused to receive in payment for canal tolls the notes of banks in Buffalo, Chautauqua, Oswego, and Ogdensburg. Johnson kept a portion of the Ontario Branch Bank's funds in Albany, and he was urged to withdraw them "as sparingly as possible." His letters became somewhat more frantic at this point, but he skillfully manipulated loans from other banks to shore up his own institution. By late May, however, all New York City banks suspended specie payments. In June the Ontario Branch was forced to adopt the same expedient. He commemorated the disaster by saying, "We finally joined the suspension with only the small honor of being the last bank that suspended." However, Johnson hung on. When specie payment was suspended, his bank, in common with many others, owed money to the "pet" banks for deposits made for canal tolls, and Johnson was informed by State Comptroller Azariah Flagg that he must return the money in specie, or allow the state 10 percent if return was made in paper. This prompted one of Johnson's fiercest rebuttals. "I am not sure," he wrote, "that courtesy requires more than a categorical reply. . . ."

> Were I to require any debtor of mine to pay me in specie at a loss to him of ten percent, the community would be indignant at my extortion . . . How dangerous, therefore, is the precedent which the Commissioners of the Canal Fund wish to establish—for who would thereafter deem improper in his private concerns what the Commissioners should sanction officially?

Like many former Jacksonians, especially in the banking fraternity, Johnson was becoming bitterly disillusioned with Van Buren's fiscal policies. Van Buren's fatal error, for Johnson and others who believed in a *laissez-faire* approach to the national economy, was his advocacy of the "Sub-Treasury" bill which he proposed shortly after his inauguration. This bill, prompted in part by the vast land speculation which took place during the last months of the Jackson administration, called for "locking up" large amounts of specie in an "independent treasury" in Washington, and in various "subtreasuries" located in federal mints across the country where the speculators could not get at it. The bill was supported by the radical "Locofoco" wing of the Democratic party, which believed that the financial crisis had been brought on by the issuance of too much paper money; and it was opposed by the conservative "Hunker" faction which, by joining forces with the Whigs, had elected William H. Seward to the New York governorship (Jackson later used the pseudonym "Old Hunker" in some of his press attacks on Van Buren). Although his alignment with the Whigs would expose him to bitter charges of betrayal during the next election, it was consistent with his antifederalist principles which he felt were being abandoned by Van Buren just as they had been by the supporters of the U.S. Bank.

The proposed new State Banking Bill envisaged a kind of State sub-treasury system which would compel all New York banks to keep 15 percent of their capital, or 20 percent of their circulation and deposits, locked up in their own vaults as what Johnson called "a kind of ballast to keep them upright." Johnson did some mathematical calculations and pointed out that, since the banks of the state possessed about $30 million in deposits and circulation, a total of $6 million would thus be rendered "inactive" by the new bill. In addition to the specie locked up in the vaults, however, the banks needed a working supply for their daily needs—while the fact was that they possessed only about $3.5 million in specie all told. A resumption of specie payments under these circumstances, Johnson argued, was an absurdity, and somehow the banks must find more specie "for the ballast above spoken of." However, more specie was unavailable as a result of Van Buren's Sub-Treasury plan. "Throughout the Union," he said, "some sixty millions of useless specie would be locked up—a sum far larger than the total specie ordinarily existent in the Union."

Johnson wrote to Senator White that he was "as disgusted by the Bank Bill as a patient would be at a new dose of lobelia and cayenne pepper." That his Democratic friends were supporting it did not surprise him, and he hoped they would "ride their hobby till their seats were sore in the saddle." However, he was amazed that the Whigs would mount the same hobby, since their victory in the last election had been "a living monument to the wrath of the people against such hobbies."

While the Bank Bill was being argued in Albany, a national banking convention was called in New York's City Hall to deliberate the whole question of specie payment resumption, and Johnson went as a delegate.

Since the New York Bank Bill provided for the resumption of specie payments on May 1, 1838, the main thrust of the convention was toward a national resumption on the same date. The opposition came from Biddle and the U.S. Bank, by now a state institution chartered by Pennsylvania, though still possessing a capital of over $30 million, giving it, "a commanding influence over all the delegates except those from New York." Biddle, supported by delegates from all other major eastern cities pointed to Britain's success with the suspension of specie payment. In a fiery speech to the convention, Johnson retorted that the analogy was irrelevant, and that Biddle was not "debating the true question." He defended New York's decision to resume specie payments and urged the nation to do likewise. "Let not the banks presume," he said, "to stand between the people and the lawmakers, and decide that they will not obey the laws when they deem them injurious to the people. The people ask no such protection at our hands."

Johnson argued in vain, however, and the convention broke up unable to reach a decision. "I much suspected," Johnson wrote later, "that something more than was alleged controlled the United States Bank from the resumption, and its subsequent bankruptcy evinced that my suspicions were not ill-founded." The next morning Johnson called a meeting of the New York delegation "to deliberate their peculiar position," and presented a resolution stating "that in obedience to the requirements of the Legislature, the Banks of the State of New York would resume specie payments on the first day of May; and that, hoping the result would be beneficial, the responsibility of the measure would rest with the Legislature." This bold and rebellious action of the New Yorkers aroused the *New York American* to bitter editorial protest, refering to the "pale-faced and lily-livered preamble and resolution of our banks" as the work of Mr. A. B. Johnson of Utica, "a special pet of the party and the *Argus.*" Another New York paper, however (which Johnson failed to identify), supported him, charging the *American* with acting with the sole "malignant and despicable purpose of assailing the reputed author of it, Mr. A. B. Johnson of Utica." The editor regretted, however, that Johnson had avoided, in the preamble, putting a finger on the real villain in the case—"The Philadelphia Bank and its associated presses."

On May 1 the New York Banks resumed specie payments. The other states held off for a while, but "after some time they all came into the measure." Biddle fired off his last shot, a letter to John Quincy Adams, a long-time friend of the U.S. Bank, in which he again pointed to the experience of Britain, arguing that the banks, like those in England, "should remain exactly as they are—preparing to resume, but not yet resuming." Johnson accused Biddle of failing to reflect that English banks were acting in accordance with English law, and the New York banks were acting in accordance with their own law. He returned home a hero—at least to the "Hunkers" in his party.

At this point there reappeared in Johnson's life (if only by correspondence) the glamorous exotic whom he had first known in Utica as Eliza Walker, the illegitimate daughter of Colonel Walker, and then in his New York boarding-house days as the divorced wife of the Marquis de Villehaut. Johnson may often have thought wistfully of a road not taken when he had rejected her invitation to go with her to Paris "to be introduced into French society." After saying goodbye to Johnson in 1812 she went to France, where she married Col. Michel Combe, an officer on Napoleon's staff in the Russian campaign. He too was forced to flee France, and the couple came to Utica and built a house on Col. Walker's property. With the accession of Louis Philippe to the French throne, the Combes returned to France where he rejoined the army and went off to the wars in Algeria.

On Johnson's return from the Bank Convention, he found letters awaiting him from Mme. Combe announcing the death of her husband during the siege of Constantine. Combe had become a national hero, and a statue of him, made from the cannon that caused his death, was being erected in his home town of Feurs. His wife had also had a portrait made of him, laid out in his regimentals, and enclosed a lithograph of it for Johnson, along with letters from his fellow officers describing the final battle and the hero's last moments. Johnson reverently transcribed all of the letters into his autobiography.

In one of her own letters, the bereaved lady poured out her grief to Johnson. "Alas," she wrote, "where there is no hope, resignation or death must follow"; but then, in a more practical vein, she commissioned him to "facilitate the arrival of my funds in France." A greater source of pride to Johnson, however, was another commission—to translate and publish in the Utica newspapers the stirring funeral oration "delineating the gallant conduct of Col. Combe." Johnson took the speech to his Episcopal minister, Dr. Proal, who was of French descent; but dissatisfied with Proal's pedestrian prose, he "somewhat emended it in places where I thought emendation would improve it, either in text or translation." Mme. Combe, he said, "received it with much poignancy."

While Johnson was managing Mme. Combe's Utica properties, he was visited regularly by an old woman to whom Mme. Combe had directed him to pay monthly "the trifling sum of five dollars." Mme. Combe represented her to him as "once her servant, who had been very kind and attentive." On one of her visits to Johnson, the supplicant became garrulous and "seemed inclined to give me some reasons for the money she was receiving—but I discountenanced the communication as an attempt to convert the kindness of Mme. Combe into some less worthy motive." Finally, the poormaster of Utica called on Johnson one day to inform him that the old woman was dead, and asked Johnson to pay for her funeral expenses. Johnson did so, and informed Mme. Combe of the event. Her reply must have puzzled him. "Poor thing!" she wrote. "She had given evidences of insanity long before she left my house and one day, among many other extravagancies, she said that everybody in Utica knew me to be a noted drunkard like the rest of my family. I feel obliged to you for having supplied what was necessary for her decent interment."

Johnson let the matter drop there, but ten years later, after her death, he received another caller—a gentleman from New York who claimed that the old woman was a sister of Mme. Combe and that his own wife was the daughter of another sister—all of them the progeny of Col. Walker. As proof the caller produced letters from Mme. Combe to his wife "which evinced much regard on the writer's part," and though the signature had been omitted, the handwriting, Johnson said, "was certainly Madame Combe's." Johnson retained his faith in Mme. Combe, but "a couple of legal gentlemen who became converts to his story" came to the claimant's aid, and the whole property was eventually received by him. Johnson took great satisfaction in turning down the victorious claimant's offer to reimburse him for the services he had long performed for Mme. Combe out of friendship.

Meanwhile, in the fall of 1837, another death intervened, and Johnson was once more plunged into private grief. This time it was the death of his eighteen-year-old son, Bryan, in New York City after a three-week illness. Johnson spent the boy's last days at his bedside, and saw him sink into a coma shortly after the doctor had resorted to bleeding. "It seemed to me," wrote Johnson, "that he had been murdered, and my agony was enhanced accordingly." He could not bring himself to take the body back to Utica, fearing it would only intensify his grief "with useless ceremony"; and Bryan was buried in the graveyard of New York's Trinity Church.

In a letter to John Quincy Adams, written two days after Bryan's death, there is, startlingly enough, no mention of Johnson's loss. It is a flowery, sententious paean of praise for an oration Adams had delivered in Newburyport, interspersed with laments for his own failure to achieve literary fame.

CHAPTER 19

1837–1839

Wife Hunting, Death of a Mother, and More from Cousin Rachel

AS HE CONTEMPLATED his many sorrows which neither his private writing nor his public banking activities could distract him from, Johnson, distrustful of his own resources, turned to a friend for advice. The friend, Joshua A. Spencer, had also recently lost his wife, and relayed the following wisdom to Johnson: "Though it is the greatest misfortune which can happen to a man, it is often repaired more completely than any other great evil can be; and to refuse the permitted reparation is to war unavailingly against both Providence and society." He obligingly appended a list of "several ladies with whom he had become acquainted in his numerous professional journeys." Later, said Johnson, Spencer "took pains to introduce me to three ladies . . . whom I visited a few times, without, however, the object being known to the ladies thus visited." Johnson continued the story:

> In an excursion I made to New York, I accidentally met a lady who was on a visit at the house of a common friend. I saw her there a few times and had known her several years. She was a widow without children and about thirty-five-years old and her appearance and social position were satisfactory to me. I was of an age when men are not very excitable in their feelings, and on a calm intellectual view of the subject I decided to propose marriage to her, and an opportunity therefor soon occurred. I told her that I desired no answer to my proposal till after she had returned to her own home and consulted with her mother and brother, who also were well known to me. With this understanding we parted, and I returned home to Utica, and she to her friends.

The "common friend," was Ann Masters, Abigail's busybody aunt, who divided her time between New York City and central New York.

The lady in question was a Mary Ann Smith, a niece of Ann Masters and Sarah Adams, and the widow of another Smith cousin. Johnson's proposal hardly swept the lady off her feet, but her brother and her mother seem to have applied considerable pressure on her. Ann Masters, playing the part of matchmaker with enthusiasm, was able to relay to Johnson on December 13, 1837, a message from Kinderton, the Smith estate near Philadelphia, indicating "the gratification the lady's mother and brother felt at the dawning happiness of a beloved daughter," and assuring him that "a letter from you expressive of your wishes would meet with a return agreeable to your felings." Yet, before Johnson had time to write a letter "expressive of his wishes," he received a letter from Mary Ann in which (in his words) she said that "on the consultation I had recommended, her friends decided she should accept my offer, and that she accepted accordingly."

Johnson replied immediately, offering to come to Kinderton to make the arrangements final, adding an inappropriate (and somewhat garbled) quotation from Macbeth before the murder of Duncan, "If it were well done, when it were done, it were well it were done quickly." On the same day he wrote to Ann Masters in New York telling her that he had decided upon "immediate action." However, before Ann had time to receive his letter, Johnson had received another communication from Mary Ann in which she said she feared she had written her answer "in too decided a tenor," and that he had perhaps misunderstood her intentions. Johnson fired back a chilly reply. "You say you fear," he said, "your former letter may have been misunderstood. I think it admits of no misunderstanding, and I am satisfied that I did not misunderstand it." After lecturing her on her "oscillation of feelings," he concluded, "I, therefore, submit to the altered position in which your last letter wishes us to stand."

From the correspondence which follows it is obvious that there was much backing and filling before the affair was terminated. Mary Ann's mother, it appears, was in Johnson's corner, and wrote Johnson that "nothing was needed but some further acquaintance." She also suggested that he come to Kinderton and spend some time with the family. After some of her usual prying, however, Ann Masters revealed that Mary Ann's brother was provoking so much "rage and threats in the household" that Mary Ann had left "until matters assumed a more serene spirit." Johnson, meanwhile, wrote the mother admitting she was probably right about the need for further acquaintance, adding, with an odd choice of metaphor, that he would "not falter when my judgment shall discover a proper opportunity in leaping boldly into the chasm of matrimony," but that under the circumstances he felt a visit would not be appropriate for some months. He sent a copy of this letter to Mrs. Masters in which he added that he would "not marry Queen Victoria except by her own free will." In the same letter he apparently mentioned an alternative to Mary Ann, namely Susan Treadway who was currently keeping house for him.

This message sent Ann Masters into a panic, and she replied at once, begging Johnson to wait until he had been to Kinderton, adding that Susan "is, and will be, cruel to your children." She also dashed off a peremptory note to Mary Ann, sent through her brother, demanding that a decision be made at once. Mary Ann's reply, forwarded by Ann Masters, was not preserved, but we do know that Johnson eventually went to Kinderton and that "nothing decisive ever resulted therefrom." Johnson summed it all up by writing in his autobiography, "The lady was too rich to be influenced by my property, and I was too rich to be influenced by hers—though it was large." He added, "We continued through life as friends, but nothing more, the essential question never being again propounded on either side."

Ann Master's warning about Susan Treadway apparently had the desired effect, for there is no further mention of her candidacy. However, the indefatigable Ann had a trump card up her sleeve, namely her own twenty-five-year-old stepdaughter, Eliza Masters, who, as Johnson put it, "had been an inmate of my house since the age of six or seven." Johnson wrote that he had watched her "grow to womanhood, though the thought of marrying her never occurred to me until about two months before the event." Eliza was deficient in one of the important virtues he had outlined for Watt Sherman, but this time it didn't matter. "Property she had none," he said, "but that defect in her I prized rather than disliked."

Eliza's decision to marry Johnson was a bold one, though Johnson never admitted it. She was twenty-five and he was fifty-two, with eight motherless children ranging from three to twenty-one in age. The marriage seems to have been a success, at least as far as Johnson was concerned, for he said of it, "Time continually cemented our union, and made it a source of such domestic felicity as few married people have had the good fortune to realize." The only elements of bitterness came from cousin Rachel in England and from Susan Treadway. Rachel argued that he should have delayed until after he had revisited the land of his birth. She had long hoped, she said, that with the death of Abigail "the strong tie that connected you with American interests would have been dissolved," and that Johnson would "one day return to your ancient opinions, connections and country." Susan Treadway however, was not only grieved, but deeply humiliated, especially since the whole thing had so obviously been engineered by her arch-enemy, Ann Masters. At no point did Johnson indicate any sensitivity to her feelings. He knew full well the effect the marriage would have on Susan, but failed to inform her of his plans until the morning of the ceremonies when he drafted a letter to her which began, "You will probably be as much pleased and suprised as I am that I am married." The final letter Susan received, however, began, "You will probably be as pleased and surprised as I am to learn that I am to be married this morning." He tried to soften the blow by telling her that he planned to settle three hundred dollars a year on her, in addition to the one hundred dollars he was sending her daughter, Susan—but this did not make her any less bitter. Of Ann Masters she wrote, "the malignity and ill nature which marked her conduct toward me is unprecedented in the annals of relationships."

Johnson's note to Susan must have been hand delivered at the last moment, for she appeared at the wedding with her daughter, along with Mrs. Masters and her daughter, Mag, and several of the Johnson children. After the wedding she went back to the Johnson house to "prepare it for the couple's return," and shortly thereafter on to Philadelphia. The Johnsons went, "by the cars and steamboat" to the Astor House in New York for a ten-day honeymoon, accompanied to the City by Ann Masters and Mag, though not to the Astor House.

Despite all the drama, the other Johnson children seem to have been pleased by the match, adjusting to their old playmate (whom they continued to call Eliza) in the role of mother. John Adams Johnson wrote to his brother, Alexander, in New York that his father anticipated that he "would hereafter be a happy man," adding, "if he is I shall be glad he has taken this step." John also noted that Susan Treadway had been provided for so that his father and Eliza could "live by themselves." Johnson was relieved and delighted by the reaction of his family, and especially by that of his mother, Leah, whom he reported being "much pleased" with Eliza.

Leah Johnson, who had tied her destiny to her son's since their arrival in Utica in 1801, who had followed him faithfully into the churches of his choice, and taken up her abode where he directed, died on Christmas Day, 1838, less than two months after his remarriage. Neither she nor her son was sure of her age, and they rarely talked about the past together. "She probably," he said, "had nephews and nieces in Holland, and possibly some brothers and sisters, but I never heard or knew of any." Despite the fact that she had never seen "the two bridges that cross the Mohawk," he told himself she had lived a full life, busy with her needlework and other domestic diversions. On the other hand, there are certain hints to the contrary. Two years earlier, Rachel Robinson lamented the news that his mother was "indifferent to the prolongation of life," and she had her own views as to why this might be the case—views which Johnson rendered less specific in his edited copy of her letter. Leah's condition, Rachel insisted, was "obviously resulting from a want of congeniality between herself and any object around her," adding one of those references which Johnson had carefully inked out. "There can be no sympathy of feeling, pardon my candor, and I cannot think she is —— ——, and if not, how painful must be her present condition!" And back in 1828, when Johnson apparently told Rachel of his troubles with Sarah Adams and his decision to move Leah, she had offered to come to America, despite her fear of seasickness, and "bring Aunt Leah home—away from that different house."

Rachel expressed her grief at the death of Leah in her usual passionate flood:

> Her last embrace is even now present to my memory. Do you recollect our parting in 1801? My Mother and my Brother accompanied you to the Liverpool Stage Coach. I was left at home as my feelings overpowered me. How often did I at No. 65 Chiswell Street dress her hair, how often did she in her jocose way praise my dexterity! I see her even now in the green satin quilted petticoat which we had prepared to keep her warm on her long and disheartening voyage. . . . Your Mother, my dear friend, according to my calculation, must have been 87 years old, not as you, I suppose by mistake, say 77. However, what is the difference of years in the scale of eternity?

Susan Treadway, who had been a close observer in Johnson's house, also gave some clues as to Leah's life in Utica. In her letter of condolence she wrote, "To her, I trust, the exchange is happy. Her sources of enjoyment were few, and her willingness to die has long been apparent to those who conversed with her."

Having no major causes or enterprises to keep him busy during the winter of 1838, Johnson engaged his energy with minor projects which would keep him close to home. His old friend William Maynard, for instance (the former state senator who had helped him in chartering the Ontario Branch Bank), had died during the cholera epidemic, leaving behind several indigent sisters, and Johnson organized a campaign to raise money for them. Another old friend, Abraham Varick, his former partner in Utica real estate purchases, died leaving a great deal of property to his widow and family—but little cash. Johnson got together with Henry Gibson of the parent bank in Canandaigua in an effort to buy up the property as an investment, but Johnson eventually backed out, feeling that land investments "required too much attention and effort." At the end of the year he also took on a major assignment for the Episcopal church. In December, the Episcopal Diocese of New York, which then embraced the entire state, formed a second diocese in the western portion, and Johnson was asked to become a trustee, charged with administering the funds of the new diocese. Eventually the trustees were incorporated, with Johnson as treasurer directly responsible to the bishop in New York. He performed the work "gratuitously" and boasted that "the whole fund was managed, and interest paid over to the Bishop without any loss, or deduction for postage." Later he also became the custodian of the "Missionary fund" for the Diocese of Western New York.

The winter of 1838 and spring of 1839 seem to have been relatively quiet. Johnson subscribed a hundred dollars to help buy a farm in Utica to be used as the site of a State Lunatic Asylum that had been authorized by the legislature, corresponded with old friends on various trivial matters, and apparently permitted his young bride to encourage his indulgence in a certain amount of socializing. Susan Treadway, commenting on the news she received from him, remarked in one of her letters, "I am happy to find that your wife has the power to draw you from the seclusion in which you have hitherto lived," adding, "This will be advantageous to your children, and agreeable to yourself."

In July Johnson received word from his son John Adams Johnson that he had just completed his final examinations at Geneva College and would receive his degree on August 7. John did his best to discourage his father from attending the commencement exercises. He would be "happy to see Eliza and yourself," of course, but he didn't feel the event would be "good enough to pay for the trouble of coming." John was the commencement speaker, and his speech was to be on "The Obligation of American Scholars." A year earlier, when John was to give his junior year oration, he had been even more blunt in fending off his father's appearance. "I can only say," he had written, "that if you do come, I verily doubt if I shall be able to speak at all. I already have many misgivings as to my success, and I rely on it only from speaking before an audience of strangers." Johnson and Eliza obligingly stayed away, and John returned home a few days later.

John, whom Johnson said he had "designed for the law," was sent immediately into the law office of Johnson's friend Charles P. Kirkland, as a clerk. He had wanted a tour abroad before going to work, but his father felt this might "break up his application to study," and that the travel should be postponed until after his admission to the bar. John went dutifully to work, and seemed "interested and pleased therewith." About a month after reporting to Mr. Kirkland, he arrived home one day with a headache. His father took him on a long walk along the roadbed of the Utica-Syracuse railroad, but on returning home, John went to bed with a fever, and, as his father put it, "he never got up."

Johnson described the deathbed scene nearly thirty years later with all his usual attention to detail, ending the melancholy tale with the exclamation, "My God! My God! What have I passed through, and that I still live is wonderful!" His major consolation was the presence of his son Alexander during the final moments and a letter from the president of Geneva College informing him that shortly before graduation John's "religious sensibilities were very awakened"—an experience that "may have shown fruits during his last hours." John died, as his brother Bryan had, of typhoid fever, and again Johnson had to stand by as the doctors bled him. Of his dead son he said: "Our intercourse was that of friends more than that of parent and child; and he counseled me as much as I counseled him."

In her letter of condolence on the death of John Adams Johnson, Rachel Robinson disclosed some of her own cares:

> Our situation is not the most agreeable, nor are we at all in the sphere suitable to our tastes or feelings. I wish my girls were well married, though I see no prospect of the kind, for with our religious principles there are no suitable matches for them: with low Israelites they would of course not unite, and with the higher class, the circumstances of their births would prove an obstacle. Indeed, I often think of the promise in one of the commandments of "visiting upon the third and fourth generation," and that the sin which I committed in wandering (for I have only *wandered*) from my religion, will be visited by my children not being permitted to be reproduced in their posterity. Our fathers were, you know, of the tribe of Aaron, called among us *Cohens,* and for a daughter of that tribe to err subjected the offender to the punishment of death. . . . Perhaps you believe this bigotry—yet no, you cannot, for you believe in revealed religion, though you have diverged from the common stock. You are the only being with whom I commune on subjects like these, and to you (though seas roll between us and though most likely we shall never again behold each other) I write in the fullness of my heart, for here I have no congenial mind to commune with.

Soon Rachel had more distressing news for Johnson. "I have suffered a great domestic misfortune," she wrote, *not by death*—but to me is, I fear, lost forever my dear, my beautiful Sophia! As far as worldly opinions go, she has not dishonored herself. She is married—but to one whom I can never in any way acknowledge, to one who, as an outcast from his family (a family of rank and consideration), abused my humanity, my hospitality, my confidence—for as he was in want, I fed him at my table. He proved unworthy by his base habits and general intemperance.

The young man, who was not of the Jewish faith, had entered the army, and was about to embark for India. Rachel had trusted her daughter's "strict and undeviating attention to all our religious observances," and had relied on her "affection for her mother," but she was woefully mistaken. "On June 26th last," she wrote, "my misguided girl left her mother's house, was married at a neighboring church, and on July 3rd embarked with a scoundrel for Calcutta."

Johnson's response was apparently less sympathetic than Rachel had expected, for in her next letter she wrote: "You say you cannot well conceive how such a person as the man to whom she has united herself could find a place at my table." She tried to justify her misplaced confidence in Sophia's suitor. On discovering that he was of dissipated habits, and "fond of frequenting public houses," she began "to discountenance his visits." Despite this, Sophia had run off with him, and Rachel even found herself obliged to pay back to the ship's captain the money the couple had borrowed for their passage. The marriage ended tragically, and before long Rachel wrote to Johnson:

I have lost my ever dear, my beautiful, my excellent but infatuated Sophy—yes, she is lost to me for ever! *An untimely death has cut her off—she died of cholera at a short distance from Calcutta on the 29th March last*—and her husband who led her from me died also about 6 weeks after of the same fatal disease. . . . Her husband's friends had taken him out of the Army and procured for him an excellent situation in the Assam Tea Company. . . . In all this the hand of God appears to me most evident. You know that I have transgressed our Laws—which in a daughter of the tribe of Aaron (of which are you and I) is according to Scripture to be visited with the most severe punishment. I feel myself a living monument of Divine wrath.

Rachel allowed herself to speak more freely about her religious convictions:

This week has been the time of our new year's festival—a memorial of the creation and of the covenant with Abraham—next Wednesday

(the 14th of the month) will be our great fast or Day of Atonement—
you may possibly have a recollection of it being called *Yom Kippour*—
(though as you said in a former letter of yours some years since) you
have hardly a recollection of ever having been in any place of worship.

At this time a new link was forged with Rachel when Eliza began
to add postscripts to Johnson's letters. In reply to one letter both
Catherine and Rachel added messages to Eliza. Catherine's style lacked
the tempestuous quality of Rachel's writing but had a kind of old-
fashioned elegance:

I trust my degree of relationship is not so far removed as to render
improper my addressing as *Dear Cousin* the lady who so amiably wrote
to my Mother under that appellation; and that you will believe me
when I assure you that I sincerely wish I may become acquainted, not
only by letter, but personally also, with yourself as likewise with your
valued husband, my Mother's dear and favorite relative, whose name
and youthful promising character became familiar and endeared to me
from my earliest infancy, by my Mother's frequent conversations re-
specting him. I much regret that the wide Atlantic rolls between us,
though in these days of steam navigation its immensity may be said to
have become so narrowed as to perhaps admit the hope that at some
not distant period he and you may be induced to cross it. It would be
a nice and not a fatiguing nor tedious summer trip. I should also much
like to know my beautiful Cousin Sarah, and indeed *all* my American Cousins.

In response to one of Eliza's letters, Rachel sat for a miniature,
which she forwarded with a note, "You have doubtless heard of the
Aerial ship now in progress. For my own part I have little doubt of the
success of the invention. Who knows but we may yet, one day, *fly into
each other's arms?*" Never tiring of attempting to draw Johnson back
into the fold, she concluded this letter by reminding him again, *"You are
a direct descendant of Aaron!"* Eventually Rachel ended the story of
the unfortunate Sophia by reporting to Johnson that her body, having
been disinterred in India, had finally arrived in London, and been
buried there "after much effort with the authorities of our Synagogue."

John Adams Johnson died on September 12, 1839. A few weeks
later, Johnson took Eliza, now five months pregnant, on a business trip
to Elmira, where the Chemung Canal Bank was having difficulty. Johnson looked over the bank's records, called an election, and with the aid of
proxies he had picked up around the state, replaced the entire board and

the cashier. Johnson noted mournfully that "the removed cashier was deemed a martyr by the town's people who tendered him a pubilc dinner."

Johnson then took Eliza on a tour of the Blassburg coal mines across the New York State border in Pennsylvania. At one mine they were seated in a cart pushed by miners, given an uncomfortable ride through the low-ceilinged tunnels, with water dripping on their heads from time to time, and then treated to a coarse meal of fried potatoes, pork, brown bread, and "something like tea or coffee." When they were taken to another mine, the couple decided to do their exploring by means of a map of the tunnels in the superintendent's office. The superintendent, "a gentlemanly young man," assuming her to be Johnson's daughter, provided both Johnson and Eliza with considerable amusement (or so Johnson said) by addressing her as "Miss," and "making himself agreeable to her" throughout the day. Finally Johnson "by making some remarks to undeceive him," broke the spell, and "the young man's conduct took a sudden change."

On January 22, 1840, Eliza gave birth to a baby boy, whom Johnson named Bryan after the son who had died in New York. Alexander S. Johnson, now twenty-two, wrote promptly from New York, hoping that "the little gentleman" would be a "source of inestimable comfort," and that he would "possess all the distinguishing marks of his predecessors . . . improving on their virtues and avoiding their failings." Alexander's use of his stepmother's first name in the letter pleased Johnson.

CHAPTER 20

1840–1841

Some Family Notes

THE JOHNSON FAMILY seems to have been a happy and affectionate one. Eliza established herself as the mother of her large brood, and there is no suggestion that the children of Abigail felt themselves separated (except in age) from the children of Eliza. The family letters that survive from this period are fuller than those for other years and provide a lively picture of the activities and personalities of the children—especially of the four eldest "predecessors" of the newborn Bryan—Alexander, William, Charles, and Sarah.

Alexander (23 in 1840) was living in New York City, the hard-working junior partner in the law firm of Hurlbut & Johnson. Charles (14) entered Geneva as a freshman in 1840, joining William, now a senior (17). Sarah (12) was about to be sent to Mrs. Binse's school in New York City, where she would be passionately homesick.

Alexander, as the oldest son, had a relationship with his father that was, even more than that of John Adams Johnson, "that of friends more than that of parent and child." Alexander discussed Johnson's literary ideas with him (sometimes disagreeing with him), assisted him in his publication, acted as Johnson's agent in carrying out various commissions in the city (often, those for Cousin Rachel), commented on the local and national business and political scene, and, when they were in town, kept a kindly, tolerant, but shrewdly observant eye on Charles and Sarah.

Alexander was tempted to engage in philosophical writing himself, but little seems to have come of it save a review in the *New World* of Combe's lectures on phrenology, which he sent to Johnson. In reply to Johnson's comments he wrote, "Your views of phrenology I agree with, so I shall not be compelled to argue the matter." But he felt compelled to defend the phrenologists to some extent:

Their merit consists in being the first sect of philosophers who thought it worth while to observe man by way of finding out his mental constitution. And their recorded observations of independent facts fill volumes, and are full of interest as facts to all thinking people. They are content to see the fact and to assent and bow to the potency of facts without saying one word touching the reason why or the manner how the facts are as they are.

As has been noted, Johnson had placed phrenologists in the same category with other "lunatics"—Millerites, spiritualists—and life insurance agents.

Alexander enjoyed the life of the city, and was comfortably established at "Bunker's boardinghouse," where a fellow boarder was Mr. Stebbins, a friend from Cazenovia, with whom he spent pleasant evenings, and with whom he could at least speak about home. Calls on Johnson for money were promptly complied with.

I want some money again and shall have to persecute you accordingly for $250, for which I will be very much obliged and will pay you just as soon as I get rich and able, which delectable day, alas! is not yet come, nor can I ever see the faint morning beam which should foretoken it yet shining upon me.

Alex also frequently regaled his father with entertaining social gossip in the big city, and stories of corruption and scandal in the New York business world. Apparently, he engaged in some desultory wife hunting, but complained, "it does seem to me as if all the decent women in the world were married already, leaving none behind for the unfortunate people who are not now provided for." Obviously his father had been unable to resist sending along some advice on this subject, for in one letter Alexander wrote him, "you do not seem to understand my notions. I could endure a little money as an ingredient in a wife . . . but with the money I also want a wife who shall please me." He added, "Whether I shall find one with money, Heaven only knows; at all events I am not aware of being in any special danger just now of getting one of any sort." It would be another twelve years before Alexander faced up to that "special danger."

Alexander derived pleasure from a visit which J. Q. Adams paid to New York City. On November 20, 1840, he wrote his father:

I have been cultivating to some little extent Mr. Adams, Mrs. De Windt and so on. I called on Mr. Adams day before yesterday and was very kindly received, but in a moment or two that stupid Col. Stone made his appearance with a couple of men, one of whom had been anxiously waiting Mr. A's arrival that he might have the honor of painting his portrait, which he assured us was the only thing necessary to render him happy for life. The poor man endured his affliction with great equanimity and listened and bowed in a style perfectly faultless. I was amused with the painter. Could not Mr. Adams remain in town a day or two longer? He should feel so disappointed at losing the opportunity, and might never have another. But no, Mr. A. could not stay. The painter then asked if Mr. A. could not come to Boston to sit. Yes, Mr. A. said, he would, and added, "when Mr. Durand painted me, he came to Quincy. I live nine miles from Boston, but I will come." The man then said he would come to Quincy, was very proud of the honor and so on, and departed. . . .

His lecture in the evening I attended with Mrs. De Windt. The Lord deliver me from a woman of a pure nervous temperament. Her movements are lightning-like and as difficult to follow as the doublings of a hare. When the lecture was over she rushed up to the pulpit where Mr. A. had been speaking, and crowding through all the men who were upon it went up to him, shook hands, said how d'ye do, and then came back to me remarking that she was satisfied I would not have done such a thing to see anybody. She seems to possess, however, an exceedingly cultivated mind, fine sentiments, and a good heart, and is a pleasant woman when quiet. She has been kind enough to lend me a collection of her Grandmother's letters, commencing in 1808 and continued almost weekly to 1819, which have amused and pleased me much. I find that you made quite an impression at Quincy in 1814, though the old lady could not get over not being consulted about your marriage. . . . These letters are not comprised in the published collection. They exhibit Mrs. Adams in a noble light. Her purity, dignity, affection, elevated sentiments, breathing more of heaven than earth and her patriotism and wisdom, displayed in these familiar letters, show her forth as the woman of all the world, and justify all the reverence with which her immediate descendants seem to regard her memory. . . . Mr. A. is a truly wonderful man. His vigor of body is alone enough to render him remarkable. Mrs. De Windt tells me that on the evening he left Halifax a lady requested of him his autograph. Instead of giving it, he sat up till two o'clock in the morning to write her a piece of poetry, he being to sail for Boston at four o'clock in the morning. There is gallantry for you at 73; I would not and could not do it at 23.

As a senior at Geneva in 1840, William Clarkson Johnson continued the tradition of piety and academic position which John Adams Johnson had established. He announced his intention to be confirmed, and carried out his project, hoping it would please Johnson. In January

1841 the new term began with the class studying French, Astronomy, and Latin, but William hoped they would be able to substitute "some more important study as metaphysics or modern literature in place of the Latin." He diligently read the *Treatise on Language* and the *Lectures* and thought them "excellent." "In our metaphysical forensic disputations," he added, "I have practised your doctrines and applied them to the subjects with singular success." He continued to apply them and himself with success, and was chosen to be the commencement speaker. Very strangely, he added: "Mr. De Zeng is out of town. As soon as he returns I will attend to your business. I forget the exact number of diamonds you stated you had." From which it appears that Johnson had not forgotten the Geneva glass factory (now run by a Mr. De Zeng) which he had established years ago, and that—in spite of protestations of wishing to have nothing to do with commercial trans-actions—had arranged with Rachel or Solomon for the importation and sale of some glazier's diamonds.

Charles Adams Johnson was a very different Johnson. In his Freshman year at Geneva he and a friend broke college regulations by leaving their classes for a hunting trip near Oneida Lake. This breach of discipline was compounded by frequent carrousals in Geneva's Franklin House from which William frequently returned, according to a letter his father received from President Hale, "excited, I suppose, with wine." The president also reported that Charles was doing poorly in his studies, and suggested that Johnson send him "a word of advice and warning." When Johnson passed on Hale's letter, Charles replied with a long, angry denial in a letter whose spelling and punctuation must have con-firmed his father's worst fears.

In the spring of 1841, Charles developed a mysterious fistula in his neck, and his father sent him to New York for treatment by the famous surgeon, Dr. Valentine Mott.

Johnson himself went down to New York at one point to see how Charles was progressing. His visit occasioned an anxious and affectionate letter from Eliza (the only letter from her to Johnson which survives), expressing her anxiety and affection:

I have this moment received your second letter, and am distressed about poor Charles. When you left home I thought the surgical opera-tion would be a very slight one and expected you in the cars on Wednesday. Not seeing you I began to have my fears that the operation was more serious than we had anticipated. I regret that I did not go down with you, for I might have been of comfort to you, and not suffered myself so much from anxiety and disappointment. I have

waited dinner every day, and have been sadly disappointed when the
news would arrive that "the steamboat did not get to Albany in time
for the cars," consequently no Mr. Johnson and no letter. The river
being very low this happens almost every day, but I have lived on
hope, thinking three o'clock in the morning would find you safely here.
Every night I have fastened my tape to the window blind, and retired, not to sleep, however, but to have the fidgets, for I have kept
awake the whole night waiting for morning and thinking about Charley.
. . . The children are all well and happy, devoting themselves to the
plum trees. Little Bry goes all over the house calling Papa? and
Arthur? and tries to pull William out of your seat at the table. . . .
My love to Charles and Alexander. Do come home soon to your
affectionate Eliza.

It was Sarah who caused Johnson most concern at this time. As
the eldest daughter, beautiful, obstinate, pampered, and sometimes just
plain silly, she found life at boarding school very bleak, and her letters
are a constant cry of homesickness mingled with teenage nonsense.
Alexander thought her letters "humbug," and said they filled him "only
with mirth." His visits reassured him, and he urged Johnson not to
write her "any cross letters."

Sarah eventually reconciled herself to the task of finishing her
education (Johnson assured her that a lady does not go to school after
16, and must acquire all her accomplishments before she reaches that
age), and Johnson was well-pleased with her, but he never approved of
the marriage she made. One may conclude this interlude about the
activities of the older Johnson children who were away from home at
this period with a nostalgic picture of the others at Utica, as Sarah
imagined them in one of her letters (November 18, 1841) from the
boarding school:

> I wish I was at good old Utica in all the cold and snow. If I could
> have my choice of going with you and scrubbing the kitchen all my
> life or staying here, I would choose to go home. No matter if we lived
> in a log cabin, I want to be under my own roof. . . . One of the
> girls at school had a beautiful watch sent to her from Paris. . . . I
> wish I could see you all once more, if it was only for a minute. I
> think I can see you and Mother laying there on the sofa, and Bill
> sitting in the rocking chair with his feet on another chair, and Arthur
> with his boots off, Louisa drumming on the piano, and Fanny with
> your pencil, and Bryan in all kinds of mischief.

William was at home, entered, after his graduation, as a law clerk
in a Utica office. Charles, kept in New York by his medical treatments,

did not return to Geneva, and entered Yale as a freshman the following year.

With all his bustling family and the many distractions they afforded him, Johnson continued faithfully to tend his ledger books at the Ontario Bank. He also became deeply involved in the 1840 presidential race in a manner that would place a strain upon his relations with some old friends and former allies in Utica. He was engaged in writing two more books—one an exercise in political satire, and the other a hardheaded look at religion and its relevance to the workaday world of America. He was now in his middle fifties, fretting over the passage of time, content with his fortune, but still hot in pursuit of the elusive goddess, fame.

CHAPTER 21

1840–1841

A Democrat Turned Whig

THE YEAR 1839 WAS AN OFF YEAR IN POLITICS, but the Whigs and the Democrats had been marshaling their forces in Oneida County in preparation for the tumultuous election of 1840. In 1838 the Whigs had nominated Seward for governor, while the Democrats stayed with Marcy. Seward won by over 10,000 votes throughout the state, but trailed by 1,000 votes in Oneida County. The Utica Democrats were dismayed by the Seward victory, but Johnson decided to stay away from their attempts to rally their forces. On the Fourth of July 1840 he was "flattered" by an invitation to attend a "Democratic Celebration" in nearby Herkimer, where he would doubtless have been asked to speak, but he declined it. By this time his eye was on Martin Van Buren, and the events taking place in Washington.

Johnson had prized his association with Van Buren, and the fact that he had been one of the Baltimore convention which had nominated him four years earlier. Van Buren had sent him copies of his speeches, often with a personal note attached, and had arranged, at Johnson's request, a commission in the Navy for the stepson of Johnson's Episcopal minister, Dr. Proal. "Still," Johnson wrote, "I much disapproved of Mr. Van Buren's persistent urging on the country of his Sub-Treasury System." Johnson felt that its rejection by Congress when it was first submitted should have been enough, and that by making it an issue in the forthcoming election he was "attempting to resist the will of the people." He also felt that Van Buren's conduct resembled "the persistency of the U.S. Bank to regain a charter in opposition to the will of the people." General William Henry Harrison, the hero of Tippecanoe, on the other hand, was opposed to the Sub-Treasury, and Johnson, after much soul-searching, decided to cast his lot with the Whigs, who were supporting Harrison. The battle that ensued in Oneida County over Johnson's defection goes largely unreported in the autobiography. He wrote merely that he "owed it" to his "consistency to publish the reasons which would . . . induce me to prefer the presidency of William H. Harrison, and I accordingly published my reasons under my own name."

Johnson's "Letter to the Democratic Electors of Oneida County" appeared as an "extra" edition of the Oneida *Whig*. In it he indicated he had far more against Van Buren and the Democrats than the Sub-Treasury question. He disapproved, as well, of the President's "doctrines against banknotes, state debts and public improvements," and he especially disliked the tactics of the radical "Locofocos" in the Democratic party who had rallied to Van Buren's support and had led the attack on the banks of New York State. In addition, the Whigs were making much of the states' rights issue in the South, and Johnson, despite his distaste for slavery, was impressed by their arguments. Finally, it is clear from his "Letter," and from many of his letters to the press, that he now also disliked Van Buren as a person. This would shortly be made apparent in his attacks on the "Little Magician" in *The Philosophical Emperor,* and in the sometimes vulgar rhetoric of his later diatribes in the New York State press.

The "Letter to the Democratic Electors" began in a more-in-sorrow-than-in-anger mood. He recalled his fight against the Bank of the United States, and based his argument against the Sub-Treasury bill, not on Van Buren's right to propose it, or on the merits of the bill, but on the President's insistence on reintroducing it after the people had rejected it once. This he compared to the efforts made to revive the U.S. Bank against the will of the people. Johnson also seems to have been impressed by the Whigs' boisterous campaign tactics in behalf of Harrison, praising the effectiveness of the "Tippecanoe and Tyler, too" slogan, and berating our "infatuated Democratic leaders' tendency to view Whig tactics as nothing but a bacchanalian enthusiasm for log cabins and hard cider."

Anticipating the uproar his "Letter" would evoke from Oneida Democrats, Johnson concluded with a strong defense of his duty to speak to the issue, saying,

"if persons situated as I am, who never held an office, who never sought one and never expect one, possess not independence enough to speak through the trammels of party when vital issues are at stake, we are undeserving of the blessed institutions under which we live."

Alexander expressed his approval of Johnson's "Letter," adding, "I think you have found & elegantly set forth sound, manly, substantial views of the policy of the present political conflict."

Johnson received an immediate answer to his "Letter" in a fullpage "Reply to A. B. Johnson," also published as an "Extra" by the Utica *Observer* and reprinted widely across the state. The "Reply" was signed "An Elector of Oneida County"—but it was written by James Watson Williams, the son of Judge Nathan Williams, one of Johnson's closest friends, and the former editor of the *Observer*. Williams had long been a staunch colleague of Johnson's in numerous civic enterprises. Years later he would publish one of the most eloquent and kindly obituaries Johnson was to receive.

Williams began with an anecdote told by John Selden, an English wit, about the "way country folk have of trying if a man be weak in the hams by coming up behind him and giving him a blow unawares; if he bend once, he will bend again." Johnson "bent once," said Williams, in the case of John Quincy Adams (Johnson had presumably voted for Adams, at least in the election of 1824) and was now repeating the process. He accused Johnson of "an aggravated act of political desertion," and hinted darkly that his "position as a monied and financial man and the president of an influential bank," would expose him, as well as others, to the charge "that the monied interests of the country are taking quotations from earlier speeches and pamphlets by Johnson which contradicted his present stand, including a vicious attack on the Whigs in which Johnson, with uncharacteristically lurid rhetoric, had said,

> Like quadrupeds who exhibit every spring a sort of sexual frenzy, our opponents are subject to an annual political frenzy. It is a real orgasm, approaching gradually, becoming boisterous in the later part of the summer, exhibiting its highest paroxysms during the last days of October, and subsiding early in November, leaving its subjects exhausted and helpless.

Williams concluded by saying, "I am, sir, personally your friend, but now, politically, your enemy."

Whig and "Hunker" newspapers throughout New York State greeted Johnson's defection with enthusiasm, and Johnson transcribed several of the editorials in full into his autobiography, along with letters from admiring friends. However, he was now a man without a party, and when the Whigs gathered in Richmond, Virginia, to launch their well-organized campaign for Harrison and Tyler, Johnson and Eliza went along merely as spectators.

The Johnsons were given special seating at the convention, but he "preferred the freedom of standing where I could withdraw when I became weary of the speeches." Even Daniel Webster couldn't hold him, and Johnson walked out for air halfway through his oration. What did interest him, though, was the opportunity to observe the slaves. He asked Crane to take him to an auction, but was told they "rarely occurred in the city." Johnson, however, recorded an incident that occurred shortly after their train pulled out of Richmond:

> While we were traveling our car ran off the track, which delayed us without causing any injury. A black man . . . was stooping down to aid in replacing our car on the track, and I noticed with much indignation that a young passenger kept striking the black man on the head with a cane. The young man apparently struck him in fun, and, as the poor black could not resent the injury, I felt much like interposing in his favor, but prudence overcame my sense of justice.

En route back from Richmond the Johnsons stopped off in Washington, and Johnson decided to pay a call on Martin Van Buren at the White House. The President was out of town, however, and Johnson merely left his card. He and Eliza were taken about the White House, and Johnson was disappointed in the furnishings. "The furniture," he wrote, "seemed to me more gaudy than splendid . . . in many cases the gilding was chipped off, making it look like the injured gilt frame of a looking glass."

Back in Utica, Johnson found the presidential campaign in full swing, with log cabins erected in various parts of the city, and each of them overflowing with Harrison's alleged favorite tipple, hard cider. "I never entered one of these buildings," said Johnson, "and know nothing of them but the outside." The Democrats had countered feebly with hickory poles, the symbol of earlier Jackson campaigns, but Johnson found they "had lost their charm," and did little but "excite ridicule." He was impressed, however, by the Whig parades, with log cabins mounted on wheels along with barrels of cider, and followed by men carrying banners "with numerous devices—the most 'piquant' of which," Johnson felt, was one proclaiming, "Harrison and Tyler will bust Van Buren's boiler."

Alexander in New York, was also observing the frenzy of the 1840 election, and wrote his father about it. It is interesting, among other things, for its comment on the passage from Johnson's 1834 speech which Williams had thrown back at him: "I could not but be reminded of that most *outrageous* description of the Whig orgasm you gave in one of your speeches."

The Harrison-Tyler ticket swept Oneida County as it did the rest of the country, but William C. Bouck, the Democratic nominee for governor, carried the county by some five hundred votes, although he lost the election to William Seward. In summing up the Van Buren defeat, Johnson laid it once again to "the derangement of business" brought about by the Sub-Treasury plan. He noted, however, that "the system has been retained, and after a time business became shaped to the new measure and derangement therefrom ceased." The Sub-Treasury Act was repealed in 1841 but was reenacted by the Democrats in 1846.

Alexander was sarcastic about President Harrison's inaugural address:

> We have today the inaugural of our new President, who seems to possess a very intimate acquaintance with Greek & Roman history. Is it not truly refreshing to find once more high in office, a man who still remembers & can use what he read in Goldsmith's Abridged History of Greece while at school I thought that we had got through with all such puerilities, but it seems their reign is to be renewed. . . . The rest of his address seems to me to come pretty much under the general denomination of "gammon," a word not in the dictionary, but of infinite meaning if one only understands it, & not at all to be translated into other words.

Johnson, as he became more and more involved in the national political scene and watched the power struggles being enacted in Washington, decided shortly after the election to write a satirical allegory dealing with the Jackson, Van Buren, and Harrison administrations. He chose the allegorical form, he said, "supposing that everyone was disgusted with the old mode of literal discussion." He also hoped "to make the book diverting, irrespective of the instruction I intended to convey." After he sent it off to Harpers, however, Harrison died, and Johnson was forced to revise the ending with the help of Alexander who went to work at once. It is evident from his correspondence with his father that he was largely responsible for the revision which toned down Johnson's enthusiastic appraisal of Harrison and gave much more credit to Tyler. Alexander also read proof on the entire book, and carried on the negotiations with Harpers (whom he referred to in one letter as "The Harpies"), hoping, no doubt, that his father would, for once, have the book properly distributed and publicized. Johnson did not acknowledge

Alexander's help in his memoir, saying only that the story "remained unaffected by the change."

A thousand copies of the book were published by Harpers, bearing the full title, *The Philosophical Emperor: A Political Experiment; or, The Progress of a False Position*. It was dedicated to "The Whigs, Conservatives, Democrats, Loco Focos, Individually and Collectively of the United States." This time, since Johnson published it anonymously and did not wish to send copies to friends under his name, the book went through normal sales channels and the edition was sold out, but Johnson added, "As no pains were taken to bring the book into notice and I never avowed it, the book failed to attain any popularity, though I think it was an experiment in political discussion that merited attention. . . ." Acting, perhaps, on advice from his son, Johnson did, however, try to gain a wider audience for the *Philosophical Emperor* by sending a copy to Park Benjamin, a New York "literary man of much note in his day, and the editor of a widely circulated literary weekly called *The New World*." Johnson offered to give him all the proceeds on the sale of a new edition of 3,000 copies, but Benjamin replied that "the task would be futile." No book, he wrote, sells to the extent of 3,000 copies unless it is of "a popular character," for "people will not give themselves the trouble to think enough, fully to appreciate a political allegory, no matter how much pervaded by evidence of superior talent."

The *Philosophical Emperor* is a 110-page tale set in Johnson's favorite never-never land, Boresko—the scene of several later fables dealing with political and social problems of the period. Boresko was presided over by a Philosophical Emperor (Andrew Jackson), so-called for his fondness for "experimenting in the science of government." The Emperor had only one flaw: namely that he wanted "to originate no measure that was not popular, whatever might be its merits; and to repeal all measures that were unpopular, whatever might be their utility." In order to assure his popularity the Emperor often "emulated the quack doctor who, when asked why he had so many patients, replied that he was 'patronized by the fools who are numerous in every community, while regular physicians are patronized by the wise, who are few.' " The Emperor could not see why "the principle was not adequate to politics"; and this led him into a long series of "false positions." In a "false position," every step becomes compulsory with reference to the one that precedes; while in a true position, "every step is made voluntarily in contemplation of the one which is to follow."

Johnson, in his fable, laid much of the blame for Jackson's difficulties on the Emperor's "aristocratic, opinionated godmother," who was known as "Old Lady Felderal" (the Federalists), and who had decreed, throughout the Emperor's youth, that "everything he desired must be counteracted." She insisted (as in the case of the Federalists' reaction to General Jackson's unilateral decision to take New Orleans from the Spanish) that he be "invested in a strait jacket," and that his mouth be "gagged lest he employ unbecoming language." As Felderal tightened her grip on the Emperor, however, the people of Boresko began to cry out against her, suspecting that she had once been infatuated with "a young monarch of Glanden" (England), and that she planned to place a "Glanden saddle" (monarchy) on the Emperor's back. (A change frequently made against the Adamses.) Felderal retorted with the words of a hermit friend who lived in a cave:

> Boresko, Boresko, indulge not in pride
> For Jack's son shall girth you, and
>   his heir shall ride.

Finally, when the wrath of Boresko against her became too great, "Felderal spread the rumor that she was dead, and there was great rejoicing among the people." Among other things, the rumor caused "thousands of foreigners to flock into Boresko, and though they occasionally brought with them the mange, they also brought useful arts and sturdy arms enough to compensate for the evil" (the wave of immigration which took place during Jackson's presidency).

Johnson turned next to Jackson's archenemies, Nicholas Biddle and his Bank of the United States. Boresko's currency was in the form of sugar, but the Head Confectioner (Biddle) converted it into sugar plums (paper money) which were easier to handle, and more enticing. The Confectioner's first clash came when he attempted to defend against the "Imperial Plum Keeper" (Secretary of the Treasury Samuel D. Ingham), one of his shopkeepers who was suspected by the Emperor of dispensing sugar plums to the Emperor's enemies and withholding them from his friends. (Here Johnson was referring to Jeremiah Mason, the president of the Portsmouth, New Hampshire, branch of the U.S. Bank, who had been accused by Ingham of using his position for political purposes, and making loans to anti-Jackson men, including Daniel Webster, John C. Calhoun, and John Quincy Adams.) These charges by His Imperial Majesty's Plum Keeper infuriated the Head Confectioner, who promptly "mounted a very high horse, which is often employed in Boresko by short men on great occasions, and, riding directly to the Emperor, delivered a lecture on independence . . . declaring he would retain the shopkeeper, Emperor or no Emperor."

The Emperor was "a very roaring lion" when displeased, and his first impulse was to have the Confectioner and his shopkeeper shot— "but shooting, being attended by certain inconveniences, was eventually abandoned." The Emperor decided instead to try out his "popularity" theory by declaring the Confectionary unconstitutional—a very serious charge in Boresko, but one which the Emperor knew would appeal to the people. Here, however, the Emperor took his second step toward a "false position"—the first being his quarrel with the Confectioner over his shopkeeper. It also pushed the Confectioner into a "false position," and matters went from bad to worse, for, instead of "attending quietly to his sugar plums" and "leaving the matter to the good sense of Parliament and the people," the Confectioner decided to use his sugar plums "to wage war against the Emperor." To do this, "he supplied himself with an enormous breeches pocket which he kept full of the precious commodity to be distributed occasionally in addition to the regular streams which issued from the Confectionary." The Confectioner also used his sugar plums to bribe editors, and print long diatribes against the Emperor. "Happy were printers in those days . . . more than 7,000 plums were given by the Confectioner for the printing and distribution of one financial pamphlet, and 99,720 were employed in kindred operations." The ultimate consequences of the "false positions" entered into by the Emperor and the Confectioner were described by Johnson as follows:

The interference . . . in the appointment of shopkeeper to the government confectionary gave birth to a repulse on the part of the confectioner. This begat his majesty's doubts in relation to the constitutionality of said confectionary, which doubts begat the struggle of the confectioner, which struggles begat the veto, which begat the pressure, which begat the removal of deposits [Jackson's removal of specie from the U.S. Bank to the "pet banks"], which begat the panic [of 1837], which begat the entire prostration of business, which produced the expansion, which begat land speculations, which begat excessive deposits, which begat alarm for their safety, which begat . . . the prohibition of small sugar plums (bank notes of less than five dollar denominations), and the recommendation of prodigal expenditures, which later begat the distribution law, which begat the vaults and safes [Van Buren's Sub-Treasury plan], which begat the rejection of sugar plums in payment of duties, which begat the denial of any obligation to provide a currency for the nation, which begat the doctrine that people expected too much of their rulers, and that government must take care of itself and the people must take care of themselves.

Johnson's treatment of Van Buren displayed an unusual rancor. The new ruler, wrote Johnson, was "a humble man," but he could not "let his humility stand in his way, and exalted he must be." When the Philosophical Emperor chose him as his successor, "he submitted with a resignation that might become a Christian . . . and kindly promised that if he should be elected he would follow in the footsteps of his illustrious predecessor who never had any children of his own." He was suspected of insincerity, and on his countenance "he wore a never ending smirk." What bothered Boreskans most, however, was the fact that his most zealous supporters had been early friends of Old Lady Felderal, and that "his persistence in opposition to the will of the people was exceedingly like her belief that people are their own worst enemies." They also noted that his desire to obtain possession of government funds (the Sub-Treasury plan) was much like her desire to strengthen the power of the executive, as against the democratic notion of states' rights. Finally, the people rebelled, and a great battle was fought in which the ruler was slain "by two hundred and thirty-four bullets, or as they are called in Boresko, ballots." When his helmet was removed, the people were amazed to find that their dead ruler was none other than Old Lady Felderal herself—"proving that the defunct had been a magician, or rather, a witch." Her conqueror was an "old hero" (Harrison); and the day of his coronation was "welcomed as a day of deliverance." Unfortunately the old hero died a short time later and his successor (Tyler) began his successful reign during which the government, "relieved from its pecuniary embarrassments, discharged its debts . . . and accomplished its other national duties." The new emperor avoided false positions, and made no effort to curry popular favor; and "the past years of experiment and embarrassment seemed only like a troubled dream."

Johnson's next book, *Religion in Its Relation to the Present Life*, was published early in 1841 by Harpers, with Johnson, as usual, bearing the cost of publication. Though there is no record of Johnson's having actually delivered the text orally, his subtitle read "A Series of Lectures Delivered Before the Young Mens' Association of Utica, and Published at their Request." It reappeared in an 1862 edition under the title of *Morality and Manners*—a change he explained on the grounds that "the work was intended to be a complete system of ethics."

Johnson's own appraisal of the book in his later years displayed the familiar self-assurance mixed with defiance that characterized his view of all of his philosophical works. "The purport cannot be stated in a summary," he wrote, "the whole text being nothing more than a summary of general morality stated in the smallest compass." He added,

"Most authors write to communicate what they know, but I write to discover what I ought to know."

The title of Johnson's new work says exactly what he had in mind—far more so than *Morality and Manners*. "It is intended," he said in his preface, "to discriminate my subject from what is discussed in churches, and which is perhaps far too exclusively religion in its relation to a *future* life." In short, Johnson set out to create a practical manual of how to apply one's Christian precepts to the problems of daily life— a concept with a familiar ring to twentieth-century readers of religious "how-to" books, but which introduced some rather startling concepts into nineteenth-century protestant millennialism.

Johnson had already outlined his strictly utilitarian approach to religion and morality in his letter to John Adams about the practical advantages of being a Presbyterian, and in his lecture to Judge Bacon on "kindling appliances." The merits of religion and ethical behavior as passports to Heaven are ignored by Johnson; in fact, his only references to an afterlife in any of his writings are those conventionally pious allusions which turn up in the obituaries and letters of condolence he often wrote. Religion and morality are valuable because they produce better and more useful people here on earth—and they do so in accordance with natural laws which are most clearly set forth in the Bible in such statements as "The drunkard and the glutton shall come to poverty, and drowsiness shall clothe a man with rags."

At first glance, the thesis may seem embarrassingly simplistic and reminiscent of Poor Richard's approach to the universe; but Johnson does not let one off that easily.

"The science of morality," Johnson asserts, "is nothing but a knowledge of natural consequences which certain actions produce"— in other words, an empirical science based on factual information that any man can obtain through observation of nature, which obeys "determinate laws." Even when we understand this "science," however, it is not always easy to apply it in our human contacts since very often when we *think* we are behaving in a moral fashion, we are merly catering to our own self image, or what today might be called "role playing." Thus, we must first examine our own motivations before attempting to exploit the forces that motivate others. In a chapter called "The Art of Controlling Others," Johnson argues, "Men find it hard to deceive each other, for they are masquerading before others who have masqueraded themselves, and they know every turn of the game as well as you." Humility is considered a desirable moral quality, but "Why should you be exhalted for humility if you are humble for exaltation?" Disinterestedness is a virtue, but why respect for disinterestedness if you are disinterested to gain respect?" And finally, "If you do good to your enemy for the purpose of exciting his self reproach . . . you are no more deserving of his gratitude than if you feasted him on poisoned sweetmeats."

In a following chapter called "The Art of Self Control," Johnson returns to the theme of his letters to Watts Sherman and Judge Bacon. In learning to control oneself, which is a prerequisite for learning to control others, one must, he says, "refrain from every word, thought or action that would naturally proceed from the feeling you desire not to excite . . . even loud speaking is unfriendly to calmness of feeling, by reason of an exciting power which loud speaking seems to possess naturally."

For a brief moment, at least, it appeared that *Religion in Its Relation to the Present Life* might be destined for some popular success. Harpers wrote Johnson that they would like to publish it as one of the volumes of their Family Library, a highly popular series at the time. However, after Johnson had given his approval, the publishers submitted it to a prominent clergyman for appraisal, and this gentleman found certain sections objectionable on the grounds that they "inculcated hypocrisy, and that men should not act and speak benevolently till the feeling of benevolence was first possessed." Harpers asked Johnson to remove some of these passages, but Johnson "would not consent to expunge any part of it, and the book remained excluded from the 'Family Library.' " Another keen disappointment to Johnson was the new subtitle, "Lectures to the Young," which Harpers gave the 1862 edition. "This rather implied," he wrote, "that the book was designed for children. The book was designed by me for men," he expostulated in the autobiography.

Samuel Young, a New York State official of the Board of Regents, wrote Johnson that he was endorsing the work "for inclusion in the common schools," but there is no evidence that this produced any results. Governor Seward called it "an eminent success in the department of mental science," and Charles Frances Adams planned to read it "not without profit to myself." Beyond these few meager plaudits, however, the book went unnoticed.

CHAPTER 22

1841–1844

The Adams Connection

JOHNSON BEGAN THE YEAR 1841 well pleased with his domestic situation and "pecuniary condition." He was now worth, he said, some $180,000, with an annual income of about $12,000. When an "eminent politician" urged him to run for the State Comptroller's office, he declined, saying he was satisfied with his "private station." Most of his funds were tied up in bank stocks throughout the state, and he kept a wary eye on their progress. Opportunities for speculation often taxed the honesty of bank officials who held less rigid views of banking proprieties than he did, and when trouble was suspected Johnson lost no time in arriving on the scene. A surprise visit to the Bank of Rochester, for instance, turned up a dishonest cashier whom Johnson promptly removed, along with several of the bank's higher officers. John Jacob Astor's son, William, also had money invested in the same bank—about $30,000—but when Johnson called on him in New York he found Astor "amused" rather than concerned over the possible loss of "so trifling a sum."

Similar difficulties arose in the Watervliet Bank of Albany, and Johnson had another cashier replaced. He was less successful, however, with the Bank of Oswego, New York, where the other stockholders seemed to view the problem of occasional pilfering with equanimity. Johnson promptly disposed of his stock and "withdrew in disgust from the bank's affairs"—noting with satisfaction that, though it "lingered on for some time," it "eventually failed."

New York State's general economic condition, like that of much of the country, was unsettled, and its program of public improvements was lagging far behind what Johnson felt was necessary for the state's development. The Whigs and Democrats were squabbling over the rising costs of canal and railroad construction, and Johnson, going back to an old theme, prepared an essay entitled "State Debt and Public Improvement," which he sent to John Adams Dix, the editor of a monthly journal in Albany called *Northern Light* (Dix later became Lincoln's Secretary of the Treasury, and a major general in the Northern Army). Dix rejected the article, and his letter gave Johnson a chance to reflect once more, as he had earlier with John Quincy Adams, on the immature state of American letters. Dix suggested that he try his hand instead at a series of "popular" treatises on "astronomy, chemistry, natural philosophy, geography and other kindred subjects." Johnson commented:

> The letter gives us a clue to the literature most in request among us. It consists of bringing down existing treatises to a Common School standard, a species of abridged compilations of accredited writers. It constitutes a very cheap species of writing, and is wholly different from anything I ever attempted. I always wrote original thoughts, and avoided a republication of thoughts already known; and hence my writings have not been adapted to the wants of our readers. I was not a writer adapted to the *Northern Light*.

After his failure to please Dix, Johnson remembered Park Benjamin's *New World* magazine in New York City, and sent the piece on to Benjamin, whom Johnson recalled for his lectures in Utica—"chiefly noted for their humor, and often delivered in meter." Benjamin accepted the essay and assured Johnson that he would "at all times be happy to receive such articles."

Johnson, in 1865, had no recollection of what he had written in "State Debt and Public Improvement," and could find "no copy among my literary remains." The article, which appeared in the *New World* on January 22, 1842, however, is actually a rather tedious compilation of mathematical statistics figured down to cents and mills, but it may be of some interest to economic historians as another forerunner of certain ideas put forth in the 1930s. In it Johnson aimed to prove that the debts incurred by the building of railroads, canals, and highways, were of little consequence as compared with their eventual returns to posterity. "When we consider," he concluded, "the extent of our territory, the progressive compound increase of our population, we cannot avoid the conclusion that the use of our public works . . . must augment and keep pace with the above elements of increase."

On March 4, 1842, Eliza gave birth to a son, John Adams Johnson—"my third son by that name"—and the christening ceremony was conducted by Johnson's rector, Dr. Proal, during the summer. About this time, Proal was experiencing difficulty with his congregation, and called on Johnson for help. A number of the parishioners found Proal "uninteresting"; others simply "didn't like him," and a meeting of the parish was called for the purpose of removing him. Johnson intended to stay away at first, but at Proal's request, he appeared, and after a number of derogatory speeches had been made, he arose and addressed the meeting, applying a familiar argument to the problem. "To like Dr. Proal," he said "was the duty of his parishioners," and "not to like him was their fault, if not their crime." A man might dislike his wife, "but was he therefore to drive her from his house without any fault on her part?" Johnson added, "A man is bound to like his wife, and if he will try he will get to like her—such being our nature." His appeal, said Johnson, "disconcerted the meeting a great deal," and it broke up without taking any action. The next day Johnson penned a testimonial letter to Proal and circulated it among his fellow church members for their signature. Nearly all signed.

In August 1842 William Clarkson Johnson left his place as a law clerk and went on to the Harvard Law School. His buoyant letters from New England, filled with accounts of his visits with various Adamses around Quincy, must have taken his father's mind off his banking worries. After moving into his room in Cambridge, William went out to Quincy and called first on Mrs. Thomas Adams, the wife of Judge Thomas Adams, who greeted him "very heartily," and insisted on calling him "Cousin William—although I believe our relationship is rather that of aunt and nephew." He was also welcomed enthusiastically by his cousins, Elizabeth Adams, John, Jr., and Isaac Hull Adams. He noted: Mr Adams was very glad to see me and inquired much of you, Eliza, and all of the children. He and Mrs. A. knew the number of the children more readily than I did. . . . They seemed to think that my being at Cambridge might induce you to visit them."

William entered into his law studies with enthusiasm, but a later letter to his father indicates that the various Adamses around Quincy saw to it that he was well entertained during his spare time. He went to a "very temperate" temperance lecture by J. Q. Adams; heard Daniel Webster speak, and like his father, "was much disappointed." Mrs. J. Q. Adams invited him for a weekend, and on his departure told him to "come over as often as I would, and a room and table were always mine." Judge Thomas Adams and family aslo had him over for Sunday dinners. At one of the Adams get-togethers Mrs. J. Q. inquired how much it cost his father to send Sarah to school (Sarah had moved to a new private school run by a Madame Chegaray, and "was doing very nicely"). William guessed that it ran around $1,000 a year, and noted rather smugly in his letter to his father that Mrs. Adams had told him "this was more than she could afford to do for her daughter" (Louisa). William also filled his father in on other details. He had found a copy of Johnson's *Value and Capital* in a corner of J. Q.'s library marked "Private Interest." He had taken communion at the Quincy Episcopal church with Mrs. J. Q. who "except on communion days" went regularly to the Unitarian church. The former President thought William would do better as a lawyer in Philadelphia than in Boston, "as the Boston market was overstocked." Adams also informed him that he hoped "to visit Niagara next summer—so that we will have the pleasure of seeing him." Finally, William asked his father for $50, adding, "I am as economical as I can be."

Of the many entries in Johnson's autobiography concerning his and his children's relationship with the Adams family, the proudest, perhaps, began as follows:

> Early in the year 1843 I was honored by a visit from President John Quincy Adams. He was accompanied by the wife of his son Charles Francis Adams, and by her father, Peter Brooks of Boston, and by a son of Charles Francis. They arrived from the East in a railroad train that came in about twelve o'clock at night.

Part of the story of John Quincy Adams' visit to Utica has been told by L. H. Butterfield, editor-in-chief of the Adams Papers, in his essay "Alexander Bryan Johnson and the Adams Family," in *Language and Value* (pp. 183–206). We know that Adams had informed William of his plan to go to Niagara, but it was to be more than a mere vacation trip. An old friend of the ex-President's, General Peter Porter of Niagara Falls, invited Adams to come and see "the splendid exhibition of nature." Other western New Yorkers had also urged such a visit, including a rising attorney in Buffalo, Millard Fillmore. Adams had refused politely at first, writing in his diary: "I do not deceive myself by mistaking this earnest desire to hear me for anything more than mere curiosity. . . . I believe there is not a man in the world more unfit for self-exhibition at public meetings and banquet dinners." Meanwhile, however, events in the life of J. Q. Adams, now seventy-six, were pushing him toward at least a modest return to the public view. Since the 1830s he had been defying the gag rules imposed on Congress by southern and northern interests opposed to any discussions of slavery. He had been threatened with censure and expulsion. Among his most hated enemies was "His Accidency," John Tyler who, as Johnson would soon be doing, was pressing for the annexation of Texas. There was also Daniel Webster—and to make matters worse, both of them were coming to Boston for the dedication of the Bunker Hill monument. As Butterfield put it:

> To J. Q. Adams this seemed the last indignity. As a boy going on eight he had himself from the top of Penn's Hill in Braintree watched with his mother the battle that the monument commemorated. Now he would not travel the few miles to Boston to enter Webster's "gull-trap for popularity" by participating in a "pageant" designed "to bedaub with glory John Tyler, the slave-breeder, who is coming with all his Court in gaudy trappings of mock royalty . . . under color of doing homage to the principles of Bunker Hill martyrdom."

Adams wrote "I passed the day in the solitude of my study, and dined almost alone."

Though Adams rarely lifted a finger to attract popular support (a trait in him that Johnson deplored in his "Letter to the Democratic Electors of Oneida County"), shortly after a bitter battle over the "Gag Rule" in which his name had frequently been besmirched, he was tempted to test his popularity in some form or another, and began having second thoughts about a New York State tour. There were also family pressures. Abigail Brooks Adams, wife of Charles Francis Adams, at whose house in Braintree William had been so joyously received, was in ill health, and her family felt a trip to Saratoga Springs would be good for her. It was agreed that her ten-year-old son, John Adams, and her father, Peter Chardon Brooks, should accompany her, along with some members of the Adams family in Washington. However, as Butterfield says, there was the problem of who would take care of "the President." Still unnerved by the affair at Bunker Hill, Adams decided to join the family party at Saratoga Springs, "At the back of his mind," writes Butterfield, there was apparently "the thought that he might just possibly go on and visit Montreal, Quebec, and even Niagara Falls (which he had never seen) and some of his friends in New York State who had long and pressingly urged their hospitality upon him."

Butterfield gives a graphic picture of the rigors of Adams' New York State tour, including a reception in Canandaigua, where he was "whirled from factory to prison to young ladies' academy to lunatic asylum, and expected to say something appropriate and memorable at each." Adams' own dairy gives an equally terrifying picture of the arrival in Utica:

I was taken into a carriage and brought to Mr. Johnson's through a dense mass of population, I know not how or by whom. They brought me by the torchlight procession of the firemen. From the porch of Mr. Johnson's house I thanked them for their kindness, and I said I hoped and trusted we should all devote [Sunday] to the worship and service of Almighty God; and that [on Monday] I should have the happiness of meeting again my fellow citizens face to face. . . . Mr. Brooks was also lost for some time in the crowd; and Mrs. Charles, though in the charge of William C. Johnson, was so much alarmed that she actually screamed.

When Adams said that Sunday would be devoted to churchgoing, he meant exactly what he said, attending services at the Presbyterian, the Dutch Reformed and the Episcopal churches (in all of which, incidentally, Johnson had at one time or another held pews).

Johnson's own account of the visitation was more restrained, but added interesting details:

The next morning he went to Bagg's Tavern, as he had promised, and addressed a large number of persons who had collected for the occasion. I have been sorry that no arrangements were made to record his speech, but he said that he had come to Utica to visit the descendants of a deceased brother, and he was happy to find them so comfortably situated. . . . The next day we made up a party for Trenton Falls, which Mr. Adams had never seen. . . . I noticed at the Falls Mr. Adams kept picking up any stone that he thought singular, and placing it in his pocket, under the notion of preserving it as a memento of his excursion, and he returned to my house with his pockets pretty well loaded. . . . On our return home our grounds were illuminated, and we had a large party of our neighbors with a band of music and a supper. The guests danced till a late hour, and all passed off pleasantly. A deputation came up from Herkimer to arrange with President Adams to make some tarry in their village on his return. . . .

The next day Mr. Peter Brooks left us to return to Boston. He said he was tired of playing second fiddle to Mr. Adams. Mr. Brooks was about the same age as Mr. Adams and equally vigorous, and not unlike him in size and general appearance. He said that nearly all persons he met in our streets took off their hats to him, mistaking him for the President. He was one of the millionaires of Boston, but unassuming and very pleasant company. Besides Mrs. Charles Francis Adams, Mrs. Edward Everett was another of his daughters. Mr. Adams was fond of reading aloud, and occasionally indulged us in this way, reading even the small print of newspapers without the assistance of any glasses. He was visited during the day, by a deputation of colored men. The spokesman was a young barber of our city who delivered a short extempore address, recognizing Mr. Adams as the champion in Congress of the colored race. Mr. Adams answered him in a short speech, and the delegation departed well satisfied with their reception. Among them was a poor sickly colored man who frequently wrote poetry which our newspapers good-naturedly published. He wrote some on the present occasion. But he was also a painter, and expressed a desire to take a portrait in oil colors of Mr. Adams, and the President kindly consented. It was to be forwarded to Quincy when completed. The poor man faithfully performed his promise, and in due time, delivered to me a portrait which I forwarded to Quincy. It was not a bad painting nor a bad likeness considering who was the artist. After passing several days at my house, the President finally departed, leaving Mrs. Charles Adams with us to make a longer visit, and on the promise that my son, William, should accompany her home to Boston with my daughter Sarah. During his visit, several of our citizens proposed to take him to the old battleground at Oriskany. He expected to be required to make some remarks on the ground, and supposing his memory might need some refreshing on the events of the battle, I showed him Macauley's *History of the State of New York* and directed his attention to a description of the battle. He read it, but on returning from the excursion he said the visit had not resulted as he had expected, and no remarks were called for. He visited at the same time, some of the manufacturing establishments in our neighborhood, and among them the cotton mills at Yorkville. In presenting him specimens of their fabrics, they begged his acceptance of a piece of fine cotton cloth, but he observed that many years since, on entering into public life, he had adopted a rule to never accept any present, but if they would allow him to purchase the piece of cloth at their usual price, he would be glad to take it as a specimen of the degree in which the arts were cultivated. They of course assented, and he paid for the piece and brought it home with him to my house, where is was packed in his trunks.

The Adams diary provides still further details, saying that he stayed an additional day with the Johnsons "to give the opportunity for persons living in the neighborhood to come in and see the show." In addition to having his portrait painted, he was taken to Bishop and Gray's Daguerrotype Rooms to have some "likenesses taken of my head," of which he exclaimed that they were "all hideous." There was also an affair at a ladies' seminary where a reading from his mother's published letters by one of the trustees "was so affecting that I actually sobbed as he read, unable to suppress my emotion." At another meeting at the Bleecker House, following an introduction by Judge Ezekiel Bacon, he delivered a half-hour speech which he described as being "of mortifying inanity." Later he was whisked off to a local museum, where he was introduced to C. F. Stratton, "called General Tom Thumb, eleven years old, twenty-five inches high, dressed in military uniform, mimicking Napoleon."

The President's visit was nearly prolonged involuntarily yet another day. In Johnson's words: "In starting from my house to the cars, he came near being left behind, but on my running to the conductor, he delayed sufficiently long to enable the President to get on board, and the cars immediately started toward Albany."

After Adams' departure, Mrs. Charles Adams stayed on for a quiet week with the Johnsons, and wrote her husband (as quoted by Butterfield) that she had been "quite charmed" by the "unaffected kind manner" of her host, "who appears from what I have heard here to stand quite alone as a lovely domestic character." When it came time for her to leave for Boston, she took William and Sarah Johnson with her. William wrote his father an enthusiastic letter about a fishing trip with John Quincy Adams in which he out-fished the former president. He added that Adams was not at all fatigued by his trip to Utica, and was "on the whole much better than when he entered thereon."

When William finally returned home, he brought his father an inscribed copy of Mrs. John Adams' published letters edited by her son— the same letters which had brought tears to the eyes of J. Q. Adams at the Utica ladies seminary.

Mrs. J. Q. Adams more than shared her son's enthusiasm for the Johnsons, and William brought home a note from her saying she had hoped "his children could have stayed even longer"; and, as later developments indicate, her hope was probably shared by her granddaughter, fifteen-year-old Mary Louisa Adams, who some years later became Williams' second wife. "I am a poor broken woman," added Mrs. Adams, and her health would not permit her to travel to Utica, but Johnson and Eliza must allow her "to insist on a future visit by the Johnsons at Washington or at this place." The Johnsons made only one more visit to the Adamses, but son William, obviously a favorite, was to shared in a tour made by the indefatigable J. Q. Adams that fall which may even have outshone General Lafayette's triumphal procession through the Union in 1825—and which, incidentally, provided Johnson with what L. H. Butterfield describes as "one of the best accounts of this expedition" in existence.

The President has been invited to assist in the inauguration of an observatory in Cincinnati. William accordingly accepted his uncle's invitation." There is an ironic note to the story of the Adam's trip, for when, in his First Annual Message, Adams had spoken of astronomical observatories as "lighthouses of the skies," he had been the target of much ridicule in the press. Now, however, as a worn-out old man, he was roundly cheered as he made his exhausted way to this new "lighthouse in the sky."

Johnson excerpted his letters from William, the first mailed from Port Albina on Lake Erie on October 31, 1843, and the last sent from Washington on November 27 of the same year. The letters were accompanied by newspaper clippings giving further details, but William's own account was graphic enough to please his father.

We lay at anchor storm-bound since yesterday morning, having left Buffalo at eight o'clock. All day yesterday I lay on my back, seasick. We are in sight of Buffalo, but about twelve miles distant. At Buffalo we went to church with Mr. Millard Fillmore in the morning, and with Judge Rogers in the afternoon. In the evening we took tea with Mr. Fillmore and met the aristocracy, I suppose, of the city. Mr. Fillmore stated he was well acquainted with you, and desired I should present his regards to you. . . .

We reached Erie at about six in the evening. Guns were fired from the time we came in sight till we reached the wharf, when the whole town escorted the President to the Reed House, where they addressed him and he replied; and afterward he went through the ceremony of receiving the people individually. . . . We here found arrangements to convey us by land through Pennsylvania to Ashtabula in Ohio, and thence to Cincinnati. The roads, however, were in so bad a condition that we concluded to keep in the boat. We accordingly embarked (the boat having remained for our accommodation) at about nine o'clock, intending to stop at Ashtabula which we expected to reach at about one A.M. . . . We found, however, that a stoppage sufficient for the purpose might prevent us from reaching Cincinnati in season, unless we went by land over dreadful roads. . . . We went on, therefore, and arrived at Cleveland at about seven o'clock Wednesday morning. Our arrival was unexpected, as the people had sent on a committee who waited for us at Ashtabula, but after an exceedingly short time, our arrival at Cleveland became known; and by the time we reached the hotel, gentlemen were already in attendance to accelerate arrangements for our journey to Cincinnati. These consisted of a packet boat in which we were to proceed by the Ohio Canal, to Hebron on the National Road and thence by stage to Cincinnati. . . .

At the villages along the canal, the President was received with the greatest attention—I may say devotion. You can have no conception of the feeling that pervades the whole people. Along the stage route, every village had prepared for his arrival, the smaller settlements to form a line along the road to cheer him and obtain sight of him, and the larger settlements to receive him. At about midnight, a person left the boat and proceeded on horseback through a driving storm of snow and rain and through Ohio mud (of which you can form no adequate conception) to Akron, where we were to arrive at about seven in the morning. The inhabitants being thus notified, met us at the boat on our arrival at about a mile from the village, and escorted us to where we took breakfast. We were thence taken to the Court House, which was speedily filled with people. The President was then addressed, and to which he replied at some length, and then shook hands with all the men to the number of six or seven hundred, and kissed all the women of whom there was about two hundred. After this exploit, we returned to our boat and proceeded on our way. I forgot to mention that as soon as our cavalcade came in sight of the village all the bells of Akron were rung and cannons fired. I happened to meet here a friend of mine, and I inquired of him if he thought I could purchase a pack of cards in the village. He replied he did not know and would see. Shortly afterwards he brought me a pack, and told me to put them in my pocket and say nothing about them. What he meant, I am not sure that I know. On the boat, all the next day, Thursday, and the next, we amused ourselves playing cards. The President plays a strong game, and becomes so excited that it is a rich treat to observe him. At about midnight of Friday, another express met the boat bearing a letter from a former member of Congress inviting the President to spend an hour at Newark, where we should arrive at about six of Saturday morning. As soon as an answer was given to the messenger, he departed, the mud and storm still continuing. He had to travel fifteen miles. On our arrival we were received by a large concourse of people, and remained about two hours. We sent an express from this place to Hebron, some seven miles distant, to have a stage in readiness, that we might not be delayed a moment longer than necessary. We arrived accordingly at about eleven o'clock Saturday morning, and took leave of our boat on which we had passed three happy days, and of the young ladies, who had contributed much to our delight. The leave-taking was particularly affectionate. The President took the lead and bestowed a kiss on each young lady, and I need not say, I followed his example. . . . The people flock from all quarters to see the President, and they bring their children for him to look upon. He is constantly required to speak on political topics, and to give his opinion on past events, and prominent individuals, and I derive no little information from his answers, as I am constantly with him. I would not have missed this journey on any account.

On the return of the party to Washington, William wrote:

President Adams has been quite ill with his cold and great debility; though we think him improving now. We hope he will be well in time for the opening of Congress, for which he is very busily preparing. I wish with you that he could have been able to extend his visit to St. Louis, New Orleans, etc., but his health would not permit, and the attempt would have caused his health, like Gen. Harrison's who died from over-excitement and fatigue. You have no conception of what he had to undergo, making two or three speeches every day, shaking hands with from five hundred to a thousand persons. Mr. Grinnell and myself, during the latter part of our journey, were under the greatest anxiety lest he should not live to get home. At every village we passed through, the excitement deprived him of sleep, and when he ultimately reached home, and all excitement was withdrawn, he could scarcely walk or stand. . . . He seems under the impression that he will not live much longer, and says he has had quite glory enough. Hearing someone today express sorrow at the late death of an eminent man, he replied, "Why? He is as old as I am, he ought to die." At Cumberland in Maryland, we had great difficulty with the people. The President was so unwell that Mr. Grinnell and I thought it neither proper nor safe for him to be seen; and consequently no one was permitted to see him till we left. When he was seated in the railroad car, however, he shook hands out of the window with the people around, till the train started. . . .

William concluded by passing on some gossip:

President Tyler is reported to be sick, but he only had a chill and fever and nothing serious. He has begun to write his message and is rather nervous. Did you ever hear why his daughter-in-law, Mrs. John Tyler, Jr., is often sarcastically called the "acting" lady of the White House? It alludes to her having been from some eight years an actress. She is a daughter of the New York tragedian Cooper, which is deemed a great scandal by some over-good people; but Mrs. President Adams represents her as a very modest and interesting woman.

On August 9, 1844, it became Alexander S. Johnson's turn to pay a visit to his illustrious relatives in Quincy. Knowing his father's keen interest in the intimate details of Adams' family life, Alexander faithfully recorded his impressions in a series of letters begun in Boston and continued from New York City on his return there. Alexander was not as rapturous an Adams-watcher as his brother William, but he apparently asked many more questions about the Adams' past than William did. The first letter, with certain interpolations added later by his father, was written a few days after his arrival:

When we arrived at the President's house, we asked for the ladies, and presently Mrs. John [daughter-in-law to President John Quincy Adams] came down, to whom Mr. Thorn named me, and she sat down and continued in conversation with him. Presently Madame entered, and I was named to her also, but she took no notice of me and addressed herself to Mr. Thorn. She, soon, however, turned to me and inquired when I had left Washington. I replied that I was just come from Utica. She asked me if I was acquainted with the family of Mr. A. B. Johnson. I replied that the gentleman was my father; and she was very glad to see me. Miss Smith, a niece of Mrs. Adams, entered while this conversation in a low voice was going on, and she inquired of me after my sister, Sarah; when Mrs. John leaned forward to her, and whispered that I was not of that family. Happening to hear her, I told her I certainly was of that family, and we became acquainted. President Adams came in and greeted me cordially, and asked me to stay to dinner. I accepted, of course, and we dined together very pleasantly. After dinner he took me for a walk to his son's house [Mr. Charles Francis Adams], but Mr. and Mrs. Charles and the two Louisa's [one was the daughter of Charles Adams; the other, Mary Louisa, the daughter of Mrs. John, subsequently became the wife of William Johnson], being from home, we walked to the Quincy church and graveyard—the burial place of John Adams and his wife. At about seven in the evening I returned to Boston.

On Monday, I went again to Quincy to the house of Mr. Adams and delivered the presents and notes, and for which I am desired to convey many thanks to Sister Sarah and Eliza. . . . I occupied as my bedroom, the N. E. Chamber over Mr. Adam's library. It was half-filled with books that furnished me much gratification at night, the family keeping earlier hours than I do. I soon became well acquainted with all the family and spent my time delightfully. I kept my journal regularly, and have some fifteen pages of memoranda of things said and done. Mr. Charles and I went fishing to Cohasset, where we caught some twenty haddock in about an hour and a half. On Saturday, I went to Boston with Mr. Adams to visit the new ship, *J. Q. Adams*, a fine vessel of 650 tons for the China trade. Her figurehead is a full length statue of Mr. Adams, excellently done; and on her stern are his arms and motto—"Libertatem, Amicitiam, Fidem." He was addressed and replied very feelingly and handsomely. . . .

They all seemed sorry to have me leave, and pressed me to return at any and all times; and Mr. Adams thanked me much for my visit, and took leave of me with great kindness. He gave me a collection of such of his orations, etc., as he could lay his hands on, twenty-six in number, and promised to send me any other he should find. He also gave me an autograph to bind with them: "John Quincy Adams to his friend and kinsman, Alexander S. Johnson, Quincy, August 5, 1844." This at my request, of course. I had with him a good deal of conversation on many subjects, and of it I have memoranda which I propose communicating to you in a sort of a series of letters—how many I do not know.

Alexander's next letter came from New York, dated August 16. It read:

The library at Quincy belonging to the town is kept in a small room in the old house, immediately behind Mr. Adam's new house. The town has never taken any steps toward its preservation, or to render it available for use. Indeed, I suppose there are few persons in Quincy who are capable of using it, as for the most part, it consists of works in foreign and the dead languages. The disorder in which the books are kept is extreme, and the whole forms an apt comment on being a benefactor of the public. The Hancock lot [it was a donation given to the town by President John Adams] also, which the town received for encouraging education, is entirely unused, except as a pasture; and a railroad is being run through the center of it. When Mr. Adams took me to the church, to see the vault in which his father and mother are buried, we were told by the sexton that the key was lost. I do not know whether you have visited Quincy since 1826, nor whether you have ever seen a copy of the inscription on the marble tablet in the church. If you have not, I have a copy of it. I noticed in the graveyard, on one of the stones erected to mark the graves of the immediate progenitors of John Adams, he calls himself "The lawyer." It seemed to me so curious a mode of alluding to himself that I did not like to ask why it was adopted, but I fancied that I discovered the reason in an observation of Mr. Adams that in the early days of the colony lawyers were not tolerated, and even in his father's time they were looked upon with great dislike.

On November 21, 1844, he wrote again from New York:

Mr. [J.Q.] Adams arrived in this city the day before yesterday in the evening, and put up at the Mansion House. Yesterday morning I went to the Astor House and several other hotels to look for him, and on my return from an unsuccessful search, I found he had sent a gentleman to my office to tell me he was in town. I, of course, called on him immediately, and spent a couple of hours with him very pleasantly. He seems in better health and spirits than when I saw him in the summer, and he does not go to sleep when you are talking with him—a decided improvement I think. While we were sitting together, a Mr. Ellis of Massachusetts came in who said he had found a letter written two days after the Battle of Bunker Hill, by some man of note in those days, and which states that General Warren's death was owing to his being quite drunk on the day of the battle, and therefore not in a condition to retreat prudently, as did the other combatants when the Americans were compelled to retire. Mr. Adams said he recollected the day of the battle perfectly, that he was at Quincy with his mother, and they lived in considerable alarm lest they should be taken to Boston as prisoners by the British party; that hearing the cannonading, he went to the top of Pent's Hill in Quincy, and mounting on a stone fence could see Charlestown burning; that General Warren's death afflicted his mother exceedingly; that Warren was the family physician, and holding up his left fore-finger, he said it had been broken, and Dr. Warren had set it. His father and mother had always spoken in the highest terms of Dr. Warren, and never in any way alluded to his having a habit of drinking. I ventured to suggest to Mr. Ellis that even if it were true, it was scarcely worthwhile, at this day, to transform Dr. Warren's heroism into drunkeness, and that such a letter might better never see the light. In this he acquiesced, and I hope, therefore, that Dr. Warren's character will wholly escape the stain.

Mr. Adams asked me to write to him and promised to send me some documents this winter for which I shall be much obliged of course.

The long story of Johnson's ties with J. Q. Adams drew to a close in 1848 when the seemingly indestructible old man died in Washington on February 23—but not before one more of Johnson's children had descended on him. On December 27, 1847, Sarah Johnson left for Washington, at the former President's invitation, to attend a gala New Year's Eve party to be given in his honor. For some reason, Sarah was delayed in New York City, and, as Johnson wrote, "missed a great party," though "she received the kindest attention from her Uncle and Aunt." She remained in Washington at her uncle's house until the 23rd of February when, "after eating his breakfast in his usual health," Adams went off to the House of Representatives. A few hours later a messenger arrived stating that Adams had fallen from his seat, and was lying in some chamber in the Capitol. The messenger asked for something to cover him, and my daughter sent a large blanket shawl which she was wearing, and he was covered with it when he died." Adams' body was taken to Quincy for burial, and Sarah "left as soon as she could with propriety, and returned home."

There is one final note to the Johnson-Adams story—one which is of considerable importance to the genealogists of the Adams family. William C. Johnson first met his third cousin, Mary Louisa Adams, J. Q. Adams' granddaughter, during his visit to Quincy in 1843, but there is no evidence that he was deeply impressed. In 1847, he was married to a Miss Douw of Albany, who died in 1851. William then remembered his Cousin Louisa and married her in 1853. L. H. Butterfield, commenting on this union, wrote:

> Their descendants, who were and are numerous, were thus to be doubly descended from two Presidents of the United States. Few occurrences in his long and productive life, one may be sure, could have been more gratifying to William's father, the literary and philosophical banker of Utica.

CHAPTER 23

1844–1845

The State Constitution and the Slavery Question

O N OCTOBER 1, 1844, Johnson's fourth daughter, Mary Stebbins Johnson, was born. About a month later, he and Eliza took an excursion in his "one-horse buggy." While crossing a canal bridge, Johnson lost control of the reins. In attempting to stop the horse, he sprained two fingers in his right hand, and the horse plunged the buggy into a tree, fracturing a bone in Johnson's right arm. His son William, hearing the news, commandeered a passing wagon and rushed to his father's house, tipping over en route and injuring a leg. Johnson's injuries forced him to learn to write with his left hand, but anxious to let Rachel hear of his "lucky escape," he wrote her in his new calligraphy. The arrival of a letter from Utica in a strange handwriting frightened Rachel and her daughter, who thought some stranger was announcing his death, and elicited an alarmed note from Rachel, who wrote: "The recital cost us tears, particularly from my Catherine, who remarked on the intensity of her feelings, saying "How wonderful is the effect of blood!" Catherine added a postscript to Eliza: "I assure you, my dear cousin, that I feel extremely flattered and delighted at the kind and delicate proof of consideration you have shown me by naming one of your choice flower beds by my name."

Johnson's writing handicap was particularly unfortunate at this time, for he was about to embark on a series of essays dealing with national issues then stirring the country. He went doggedly on with his left hand, however, and the first fruit of his labor was a pamphlet entitled "The Annexation of Texas."

New York State, and particularly Johnson's own area, was by now strongly abolitionist, opposed to the extension of slavery into the new western territories. The issue came to a head with John C. Calhoun's bill to admit Texas as a territory, a move that would have opened it up to slaveholding, since most of the state was below the Missouri Compromise line. John Quincy Adams, writing in his diary on April 22, 1844, had said, "The treaty for the annexation of Texas to the union was this day sent to the Senate, and with it went the freedom of the human race." As the debate went on, Johnson felt the issues were being confused, and prepared his article, which was carried widely by the state press, and later republished in *Our American Union.* "It was animadverted upon severely by some politicians," he reported.

Johnson began by trying to reassure worried northerners who envisaged a host of problems rising out of annexation. He attacked Calhoun, however, for bad strategy in arguing that bringing in Texas as a slaveholding territory would give the U.S. a commercial advantage over Britain in the purchase of cheap cotton. "This," said Johnson, "had made the whole subject obnoxious to a large portion of mankind." As for the question of extending slavery, however, "both sides on the debate seemed to have forgotten that Texas, as an independent Republic, had had the power to import slaves directly if it wanted to, but that as a territory or state, it would be subject to the Federal law of 1808 making the direct importation of slaves punishable by death." (Johnson ignored the fact, however, that slaves could still be imported from the slave-breeding states.) The issue, Johnson argued, was not slavery, but whether Texas was worth having, whether an already large nation needed to grow larger, and whether there was any real danger, as many feared, that the annexation would produce war with Mexico or Britain.

Johnson began by describing the Texas potential:

> This immense country will become the home of millions of human beings, not drawn from other regions to depopulate them, but a new growth of immortal and intelligent beings. . . . Is the addition nothing, of such a territory to our home, such a multitude to our family circle, with whom we may interchange location without adopting a new allegiance, and interchange productions without the obstructions of conflicting nationality?

As for the fear that the addition of territory would "only encumber" an already huge nation, Johnson pointed out the fallacies in the analogy which opponents of annexation were making with other world "empires." These "empires," he said, "are composed of conquered nations, and every new acquisition divides the strength of the conqueror . . . but our Union is voluntary, and like an arch, constitutes a reciprocation of strength. . . ."

Johnson likewise dismissed the fear of conflict with Mexico and England as nonsense. Mexico, he said, had been defeated nine years earlier at San Jacinto by Texas alone, and had refrained from further attempts "from a want of power, or an abandonment of its exercise." Britain, too, had learned its lesson many times over, and would be "morally stopped, by her own practices, from any exceptions against the independent volitions of Texas."

In what may now seem an unfortunate peroration to his essay, Johnson reminded his readers how they had forced the "American aborigines to abandon to us such lands as they could not use themselves beneficially to the common rights of all." By this action, he said, "we were but fulfilling the command of Providence, to multiply and replenish the earth, and subdue it."

When, in February 1845, President Tyler, without waiting for the new President, James K. Polk, to take office, finally pushed through both houses an annexation bill, Johnson was jubilant, and produced a new essay entitled "Texas Annexed," hailing those "twenty million counsellors," the American people, who had defied the "spectres of sectional, partisan and abolition ravings." "Bless the people!" he wrote. "May their reign be perpetual!" He warned his readers against danger ahead, however, from legislators who would ask too high a price of the Texans themselves. "We have asked the Texans to surrender to us their forts, arsenals, navyyards, and ships of war . . . while the debts for these . . . are still to be paid by the constructors." He begged the next Congress to ease the terms of statehood and threatened it with the wrath of the people if it did not. Finally, he reiterated his faith in an expanding America, fashioned "by the dictates of nature." "The earth's occupancy is the right of man; and when men occupy, theirs is the right to pursue their own happiness under such form of government as they shall deem most conducive to that end, and in connection with any other government they shall wish, or in an independence of all connection."

Out in Galveston, Texas, Sam Houston, the first and only President of the Republic of Texas, and about to become one of the first two senators from the new state, received a letter from Johnson, enclosing a copy of "Texas Annexed." He responded gratefully, concluding: "The manner in which you have treated this subject of "Texas Annexation" is certainly executed with great ability. The value of Texas to the Union can only be appreciated a century hence."

Shortly after completing his article on the Texas question, Johnson turned to the New York State Constitution, which was scheduled for revision in 1845. This time he produced a series of seven articles which were also published in pamphlet form and finally included in *Our American Union*. The pamphlets were requested by several of the state legislators and publication was timed so that copies could be placed on the desk of every member of the legislature as the convention opened. Johnson later reported that "nearly every recommendation was adopted in the new Constitution," but added modestly, "I know not how far my pamphlet contributed to that end."

Johnson's concern with the issues at stake in the 1846 Constitutional Convention at Albany was far more comprehensive than it had been in 1826 when his sole interest had been the right of naturalized citizens to hold public office. Central New York State was no longer a comfortable oasis for Yankee Federalists, but a rapidly growing hodgepodge of newcomers from the coastal states and immigrants from abroad. Utica's population had doubled from 1826 to about 13,000 inhabitants. Along with the Presbyterian and Episcopalian churches, there were now two Catholic churches, one for the Irish and one for the Germans, two large Welsh congregations, a German Lutheran church, and shortly thereafter a "Beth Israel" synagogue.

With the influx of new groups came new tensions and new concepts of equality. In Geneva, New York, for example, journeyman shoemakers had the audacity, in 1835, to form a union, and a few months later New York City shoemakers followed their example. Both groups were struck down by the state courts as conspiring to fix prices, and dangerous riots were only narrowly averted. Whig newspapers blamed much of the agitation on "fannywrightism," and described the malcontents as a "dirty, loutish and foulmouthed set"; but the workers struck back by forming a Workingmen's Party, which, joining with the Locofocos, held a national convention in Utica and emerged as a coalition known as the Friends of Equal Rights.

By 1845 conservative factions had also mobilized, calling for severe retrenchment in state expenditures for public works, and for protection against legislative interference with private monopolies in transportation, banking, insurance, and so forth. In short, as the convention prepared to meet, the debate was building around the question of privilege versus equal rights. Johnson, whose reputation as a publicist was growing rapidly, stood firmly in the equal rights corner.

The egalitarianism which pervades Johnson's recommendations for a revised New York State Constitution comes something of a surprise from a man who, in his personal affairs, was so wedded to maintaining the status quo, so conscious of social position, and so prone to shy away from contact with the man on the street. One must remember, however, how deeply obsessed he was, as an English-born convert to Americanism, with the basic principles and the rhetoric of our democracy. The entire series of essays is pervaded with Jacksonian concern for the common man and a distrust of "a difference of privileges accorded arbitrarily to some men and denied to others."

Johnson opened with an attack on monopolies, singling out the Utica-Schenectady Railroad whose travelers were "helplessly subjected to virtually unrestrained rapacity." The existence of these monopolies, he charged, was "perpetuated by a constant process of logrolling and bribery." The same, he said, was true of state licensing in which the licenses were "reserved to reward favorites." Even the selection of delegates to the convention was based on a reward system. Delegates, he insisted, should be elected, not appointed. As for the State's right to create debt and impose taxes, in each instance the specific debt or tax proposal should be subject to a popular referendum. This proposal was known as "The Peoples' Resolution," and Johnson defended it stoutly.

In his essay "Aristocracy and Nativism," Johnson returned to his earlier crusade in behalf of the right of adopted citizens to hold office. He went further this time, however, arguing against the laws that made property holding a qualification for jury duty. "We have tried long enough," he wrote, "to benefit the poor by giving them soup in the winter, and penitentiaries at all seasons; let us give them the legal privileges of the rich, and haply they will cook their own soup and enjoy better incentives to worthy contact than fear of penitentiaries." Finally in his essay, "The Sovereignty of the People," Johnson presented a concrete formula for providing wider popular participation in the election of state assemblymen and senators. The one hundred and twenty-eight assemblymen should be chosen "not by counties as at present, but by small districts into one hundred and twenty-eight of which the State can be divided." The State's thirty-two senators should be elected in thirty-two districts, "instead of the eight as at present." Johnson noted triumphantly in his autobiography that his plan was "adopted in the new constitution." He also proudly transcribed a note from State Senator, George Geddes, a pioneer in state road building, congratulating him on his performance and adding, "Democracy should be taken in large doses to operate well upon the body politic—heretofore it has been taken in homeopathic doses."

In November 1847 Utica was hard hit by an epidemic of smallpox, and one of the Johnson's servant girls came down with the disease. His family had all been vaccinated, but the other help "left the house in terror," and "people whose occasion led them to pass the house, would cross the street to avoid the contagion." Johnson finally had the girl moved into an "empty brick building" and hired a couple to take care of her. "She was an Irish woman," Johnson said, "and I paid for her nurses and physician, and other expenses of fuel, feed, etc."

Another incident occurred at this time which Johnson found worth recording and which, in the manner of his telling it, sheds more light on his uncertainties about the Negro race which had so upset Beriah Green after Johnson's speech during the American Colonization Society debates. Johnson was appointed one of three judges in a Fourth of July oratorical contest sponsored by the Young Men's Association of Utica, and among the contestants was a "young mulatto by the name of A. A. Bradley." Johnson continued the story:

> He was studying law in Utica, but ultimately failed to obtain a license. I examined his production with a great desire to report favorably on it, but its composition proved to be inexplicable to me, and I concluded that the intellect of the colored race must be essentially different from that of the white race, for no doubt the production was entirely cogent to his intellect though not to mine. I have other reasons for believing that the intellect of different races may differ somewhat from that of other people. I think for instance that the intellect of the Jews differs somewhat from that of other people. While writing this present notice (1865), I have just read in a newspaper that the above A. A. Bradley was living in Savannah, and that he had been condemned to two years' imprisonment for uttering seditious language.

Of all of Johnson's notes on this period, however, the most intriguing perhaps concerns a literary effort of his which has never been discovered. It reads as follows:

> Park Benjamin was at this time . . . acting as a kind of godfather to unknown authors. I had a manuscript novel of a somewhat curious character, and I wrote him to ascertain whether I could obtain a publisher who would bring out the work on his own responsibility, I charging nothing for the copy.

Benjamin replied that he was no longer active himself in publishing, but added that if Johnson would pay him a fee of ten dollars, he would try to act as an agent. Johnson concluded the story:

I was not anxious enough to make the publication on the above terms, and the work has never been published, but remains by me. I have since occasionally revised the work, and I believe made a new copy thereof with emendations.

There are no clues at present writing as to the nature or the whereabouts of Johnson's "curious" novel.

Early in 1848 Johnson who, after the publication of his articles on Texas had become known as a middle-of-the-road mediator in the conflict between southern and northern interests, received a letter from Sidney Breese, U.S. Senator from Illinois. Breese was the son of Johnson's old friend Arthur Breese, the Utica lawyer who had preceded Johnson as president of the Ontario Branch Bank, and for whom he had named one of his sons. The letter invited Johnson's views on the reform of the old Fugitive Slave Law of 1793, which was still operative and which required enforcement by state authorities only. From the South's point of view the law had been ineffective, permitting the underground railroad to function with relative impunity in the North—particularly in upstate New York, where men like Gerrit Smith and Theodore Weld, along with such black leaders as Harriet Tubman and Frederick Douglass, were well organized to assist escaped slaves in their flight to Canada. Johnson promptly sat down to "draft a law" on the fugitive slave question, and sent it to the senator.

In the White House, Polk tried to steer clear of the question, and on becoming President in 1849 Zachary Taylor asked the Congress to "abstain from exciting topics of a sectional character." However, the discovery of gold in California in 1848, which drew thousands of immigrants, mostly from the northern free states, reopened the whole question of slavery. The "forty-niners" drew up a constitution which excluded slavery from California, and raised "exciting topics" again in Congress. Clay, Calhoun, and Webster engaged in some of their most impassioned oratory. Finally, on January 29, 1849, Clay presented his famous Compromise, calling for the admission of California as a free state, no slavery restrictions in New Mexico and Utah, a reduction in the size of slaveholding Texas, prohibition of the slave trade in the District of Columbia, and, finally, a stringent law to provide for the prompt recovery of runaway slaves. Webster vigorously defended the Clay Compromise; it was opposed with equal fervor by William Seward, the former New York governor, and now a senator from New York. The Compromise was adopted in August 1850, after Millard Fillmore, another of Johnson's acquaintances, had become President on the death of Taylor.

When the Fugitive Slave Law, in the form drafted by Senator Mason of Virginia, was passed in 1850, Johnson "recognized that it was in many essential particulars like my bill," and wrote quickly to Breese to "ascertain what he had done with the bill I sent him." Breese replied that Johnson's draft had been shown to Calhoun, "and I think he retained it," but he could not say whether Senator Mason had seen it or not. For himself, Breese added with considerable honesty, "I should have presented your bill to the Senate had not much excitement existed in my state on the subject, and I did not wish to increase it to my own detriment." He concluded, however, "I noticed the special similarity of Mason's bill with the one you sent me."

There is no clue as to the exact wording of Johnson's draft bill, but in speaking of it he said: "I thought that our citizens were so law-abiding that slaves could be reclaimed if the reclamation was made by our accustomed legal officers, and thus the peace of the Union now greatly endangered could be preserved."

Pennsylvania Congressman David Wilmot introduced his famous "Proviso" on the House floor in 1846 and again in 1848. It passed the House on both occasions, but was defeated in the Senate. Stated in its simplest terms, it provided that, with the end of the Mexican War and subsequent boundary settlements, "neither slavery nor involuntary servitude" should ever exist in any territory the country might acquire. Johnson saw the "Proviso," which was to become the chief plank in the platform of the Free Soil party, and later in that of the Republican party, as a clear case of federal interference, and a violation of states' and individual rights, and said so in an article written in August 1848, entitled "The Wilmot Proviso." In the earlier "Texas Annexed" he had risked the epithet of "doughface" which was being hurled at "northern men with southern principles," but this time he clearly invited it. A "doughface," he said, was merely a man who "will not be controlled in his votes by his geographical position." He repeated his claim that he "abhorred slavery," but denounced the "virtue which consists in voting self-denials on other people and attacking sins which our position disables us from committing." Reverting to his stand during the Colonization Society debates, he urged the North to remedy southern evils by their

good examples, rather than by coercion. . . . In such ways even slavery may in time disappear from our empire. . . . We are told that the North will never permit the acquisition of territory . . . which will tolerate slavery. Nay, all opposition to this fiat is silenced by an assurance of its universal favor among virtuous people—just as women are sometimes seduced in France, by being assured that chastity is unfashionable among the polite. But may we not hope something better?—that the North and South united will never permit the acquisition of territory whose inhabitants, flesh of our flesh, shall enjoy less power of self-government than we enjoy; that the North and South united will demand the neutrality of Congress on the disturbing subject of slavery, and that Congress shall neither establish it nor prohibit it?

During the same month, Johnson also published a more general essay entitled "The Slavery Question." Again he expressed his hatred for the institution of slavery, but uppermost in his mind was the preservation of his adopted Union:

> Nor let us delude ourselves by supposing we can compulsorily abolish slavery. Every effort we exert . . . calls into existence a counter-effort in others to retain it. We possess, therefore, no alternative but to retain the Union with slavery, or slavery without the Union. But what force cannot accomplish, forebearance may. Slaves were once lawful in New York and the writer has owned them in Utica. Had our State been pressed to the abolition of slavery by persons whose right of interference she denied, slavery might have existed among us now.

In the same article, Johnson unleashed one of his bitter attacks on Martin Van Buren who, in the 1848 campaign, was running on the Free Soil ticket against Governor Lewis Cass of Michigan, a Democrat (known as a "doughface"), and Zachary Taylor, the Whig nominee. Van Buren, said Johnson, was trying to claim a "monopoly" for his hatred of slavery. "All men hate it," exclaimed Johnson, "unless they are slaveholders, and many of the slaveholders hate it." Van Buren's campaign tactics included frequent anti-British pronouncements aimed at the Irish-American vote, but Johnson pointed out that by arguing for coercion of the South on the slavery issue, Van Buren was "making Irelands of our territories." The Irish Americans, he said, "must reject a candidate who will stultify himself by approving in Congress what he denounces in the British Parliament." In numerous letters to New York State newspapers, written under such pseudonyms as "Jefferson Junior," "Oneida," "Esculapius" and "The People," Johnson seized on a popular description of Van Buren as a "little Magician." Typical of these diatribes was one entitled "Unexampled Feat of Magic," describing a campaign speech by Van Buren in Utica:

The great Magician of Kinderhook performed in Utica on Thursday last one of the most extraordinary feats that was ever performed before any audience. Like Shakespeare's Prospero, he seemed determined by one great display of magic art to end his career, and then to bury his charms and conjurations forever. . . . All things being duly prepared, the great Magician suddenly appeared, and deliberately opening his mouth, swallowed himself up at a single mouthful—so that no trace of the late great Magician could be seen anywhere, although a strong smell of brimstone was very noticeable in the spot which he had occupied.

CHAPTER 24

1849–1852

The State of the Union

IN DECEMBER 1849, President Zachary Taylor announced to his Congress that California was ready for admission to statehood and that New Mexico would soon follow. In line with his efforts to avoid "exciting topics," he urged that the slavery question not be injected into the debate. Southern officials promptly objected to admission because the Californians had outlawed slavery, and Taylor informed them bluntly that he would use force if necessary if anyone resisted California's entrance as a nonslave state. Shortly before Taylor's bellicose announcement, Johnson opened a remarkable exchange of letters with Senator Richard K. Meade of Virginia—letters which he carefully preserved, but save for a few carefully chosen lines, omitted from his autobiography. Although they repeat much of what he had already said and written elsewhere, they indicate how far, and how dangerously, perhaps, he was willing to go in behalf of his convictions.

In his initial letter to Senator Meade, Johnson referred to a New York Senators charge, in a House of Representatives debate, that Meade was a "disunionist." Said Johnson, "A southern man is a unionist in the best sense of the word when he is contending against measures which would lead to disunion . . . nothing can be more patriotic than for the South to resist all congressional legislation on the subject of local slavery." Referring to the constitution, Johnson added, "We may well wonder how the principle of non-interference with domestic peculiarities came to be so well defined, and so well guarded against; and we shall have profited little if we now seek interpretations of the Constitution to authorize a congressional interference with local slavery." Johnson closed by saying, "I believe I express the views and feelings of a large mass of our fellow citizens in the North.

Meade replied promptly and with gratitude. "The opinion you express," he wrote, "about the views and feelings at the North is highly encouraging to one who really desires the perpetuation of our happy union. The North," he added, "has been deceived if it thinks we are afraid of our slaves—our slaves would be our friends in any conflict that would ensue."

Shortly after receiving Meade's reply, Johnson learned that Zachary Taylor had threatened to use force over the California question. He wrote again to Meade, saying, "Some persons seem to rely on military force of the general government as the bond which will hold the confederacy together, and I almost fear that . . . the President's recent message may intimate such a reliance by him." "Nothing," wrote Johnson, "could be more pernicious than such a reliance." Then he added: "the conduct of the North should be forebearing, for if we aggrieve the South by reason that we suppose they will submit to aggression, rather than lose the benefits of our Union, our aggression is doubly wrong; for to the sin of aggression we add the meanness of committing it under circumstances which we suppose will make resistance too costly to be attempted."

In 1850, with the controversy growing hotter, Johnson made a supreme effort to explain himself in a fifteen-page essay entitled "The Philosophy of the American Union; Or, the Principles of Its Cohesiveness." The essay, which is largely an elaboration of the Meade correspondence, featured a strong defense of "strict constructionism" in reference to the Constitution of the United States. The states, he said, went to the Constitutional Convention "as independent sovereigns," and they "severally retired from the Convention believing they retained all the sovereignty they had not specifically surrendered." However, to make the restriction on federal powers as "definite as language can make it, the First Congress added an amendment . . . that 'the powers not delegated to the United States by the Constitution, nor prohibited by it to the states, are reserved to the States respectively or to the people.' " John Adams, said Johnson, was a "loose constructionist" who worried for fear the liberties guaranteed to the states and to the people might leave the federal government "palsied" by the will of its constituents. But, said Johnson, "ours is a nation for only a limited number of purposes, and can continue as a nation only by adhering strictly to the limitations." As for being "palsied" by the will of its constituents, America, thanks to the initiative of its states and its people, had advanced "in all elements of progress to a degree which no other people ever witnessed, and to a degree which National government could not have obtained, had it been legally invested with the attributes of unrestricted sovereignty." Slavery might be a moral evil, but no strict constructionist could find any justification in the Constitution for federal intervention in bringing it to an end.

Johnson, in this essay, repeated all of his arguments for the annexation of Texas, the Fugitive Slave Law and those against the Wilmot Proviso. However, he also added some rather new dimensions to his philosophy. "Let not the truly Union men," he wrote,

> look with disapprobation at the disunion agitation which is pervading the South, for it is but the tempest which is to purify the political atmosphere; and a means which God has ordained for the purposes of longevity. Nations and society of every grade are kept peaceable and just only by the antagonisms which nature arouses between the aggrieved and the aggressor . . . Unrestricted submission in the intercourse of mankind with each other would be attended with universal ravage, rapine, and outrage. . . .

Echoing the thoughts in his letter to Meade, he urged the South to resist: "For the aggrieved to resist aggression is, therefore, the most patriotic of duties, and the fault of the South consists in not effectively having resisted in 1820, instead of compromising, by the circumscription of slavery, to obtain the admission of Missouri." Finally, in a passage that goes further than he had ever gone before—even in the letters to Meade—he affirmed the South's right to secede. "The right is not constitutional," he admitted,

> any more than our original Revolution was loyal, or than our War of 1812 was conformable to the definitive treaty made with Great Britain in 1783. . . . The right of secession is nevertheless among the "inalienable rights of life, liberty, and the pursuit of happiness" referred to in the Declaration of Independence, with which it says we are endowed by our Creator, and that "whenever any form of government becomes destructive of these ends, it is the right of the people to alter or abolish it, and to institute a new government."

In contrast to his Colonization Society speech, there is no reference to the "inalienable rights" of black men.

When in 1854 the Kansas-Nebraska Bill, sponsored by Stephen Douglas, became law, and left the question of slavery in new territories up to "the decision of the people residing therein," Johnson, of course, applauded it. This was good "strict constructionism," and Johnson felt that its legality was so "plain that it might be formed into an algebraic equation, and demonstrated mathematically." In one of the three essays he wrote on the Kansas-Nebraska question in 1854, he drew on his language philosophy, objecting to the purely verbal meaning of the word "Free-Soiler" "We speak he said as though a State consisted of a given portion of earth rather than of the people inhabiting a given locality, and this prevents us from seeing that Congress possesses . . . no greater control over the people of Nebraska or Kansas than over the people who reside in New York." Then, in a cutting reference to the Irish Americans in Utica who were holding frequent rallies in opposition to the Kansas-Nebraska Bill, he wrote:

> They abandoned Ireland because it is governed by a British Legislature; still they oppose the Bill because it permits the people of Nebraska to govern themselves. The Irish hate slavery, and doubtless a like hate of Irish religion and other Irish social peculiarities is equally honest with Englishmen, and if slavery is to be interdicted in Nebraska by reason that the Irish hate it, are they not justifying Englishmen in interdicting Irish peculiarities that Englishmen hate?

His last formal essay on the subject of slavery, "The Reserved Rights of the American People," was written in 1856, prior to the contest between the Democrat, James Buchanan, who was inoffensive to the South, and John Fremont, the Republican, who was demanding the admission of Kansas as a free state. Johnson ignored the third party (Know-Nothing) candidate, Millard Fillmore, and called vigorously for the election of Buchanan. His argument was simple, and, as events turned out, unproductive. "Each locality," he said, must "decide for itself the slavery question. . . . We may well hope that the disturbing topic, instead of being perpetuated and inveterated by the success of our opponents, will, by their defeat, be driven out of Congress forever." After this essay, Johnson's final pronouncements on slavery and the Union were in the form of letters and brief articles (sometimes signed with pseudonyms) to newspapers.

Johnson had long been dispensing advice to bankers through letters, speeches, and occasional articles, but in the winter of 1849 he decided that what was chiefly needed was a rule book for bankers, a body of theory and precedent such as existed for the law, a kind of bible for the would-be faithful. He went to work on what turned out to be a 44-page *Treatise on Banking* which he dispatched in April to the only American journal he thought could possibly be interested in the subject, J. Smith Homans' *American Bankers' Magazine* in Boston. The appearance of Johnson's essay in the June 1850 issue of the magazine was a happy event for both the author and the publisher. To Johnson it brought the first real taste of fame beyond the borders of New York State, attracting favorable notice abroad as well as in American financial journals. For Homans, it was a godsend, as he confessed to Johnson when he accepted the article, for the June issue of 750 copies was to have been the *American Bankers'* final appearance. Johnson's *Treatise* took up almost the entire issue, and its effect on Homans' fortunes can be gauged from the enthusiastic preface Homans added to his 1852 reprint of the essay in his *Bankers' Common-Place Book*. "The following *Treatise on Banking,*" he wrote,

> was extensively noticed in the daily press in many parts of our Union, and its information on the subject of banking was deemed so useful that several of the papers . . . recommended that a copy of the *Treatise* should be placed in every school district library. . . . The *Bankers' Magazine* of London quoted largely from the work, and with much commendation; and bankers everywhere who have seen it, unite in its praise. . . . As inquiries for this treatise are numerous (an order for a copy of the work has just been received from Paris), the editor has republished it, carefully revised by the author.

Homans concluded his preface by recommending the *Treatise* "to readers of every kind who desire a knowledge of what has heretofore been deemed the occult science of Banking."

For once, as Homans indicated, Johnson got one of his literary efforts into the right hands, sending off a copy of the *Treatise on Banking* to J. W. Gilbart of the London and Westminster Bank. Gilbart, the author of *A Practical Treatise on Banking* and *A History of Banking in America* was also the editor of the London *Bankers' Magazine,* and wrote Johnson:

> The pamphlet on banking which you have had the goodness to send me I have delayed to acknowledge in the hope of sending you at the same time, a notice of it in our *Bankers' Magazine,* but it will not appear before next month. I have the pleasure of seeing by your *Treatise* that your notions and mine perfectly accord as to the principles on which banks ought to be governed. I shall send you in January a copy in which your work will be noticed.

The review by Gilbart, whom Johnson identifies in his autobiography as "the father of joint-stock banking in England," was almost, in itself, a reprint of the *Treatise*—embellished by many kind words about the American author's "perspicuity"; and this praise from a famous Englishman set off a flurry of similar reviews, including one in the influential *Hunt's Merchants' Magazine,* in which the editor, Freeman Hunt, corroborated Johnson's (and John Quincy Adams') theories about the impact of British reviews in America by adding, "We are glad to see that English critics coincide with us in our high estimation of Mr. Johnson's *Treatise.*" As a footnote to the Gilbart review it should be added that, despite the disparities between the London and Westminster Bank and the Ontario Branch Bank of Utica, Johnson and Gilbart had more in common than they knew. Like Johnson, Gilbart had earlier been involved in a personal battle with a monolithic banking structure, the Bank of England, which resembled Biddle's "Monster" in many ways. When the Bank of England brought an injunction against Gilbart's own bank, ordering it to cease operations, Gilbart took the case to Parliament and won—after a fiery barrage of circulars and speeches. Even more intriguing is the fact that, at about the time Johnson was beginning his *Treatise on Language,* Gilbart was preparing a series of lectures called "The Philosophy of Language"—a copy of which he sent to Johnson in return for a copy of Johnson's later *Meaning of Words.*

Johnson's *Treatise* took what Sidney Wertimer, in his introduction to a modern reprint (New York, 1968), calls a "gloom and doom" approach to the responsibilities of a banker, warning that Providence is a guarantee of success when a banker "adheres with regularity to known forms of business and settled principles, but when he deviates from these, Providence is almost equally a guarantee of disaster both personal and official." The writing was larded with biblical references, coupled with sharp reminders of the facts of financial life. The use of money, said Johnson, "is too costly to permit anyone to retain it in inactivity . . . for 'dust thou art and into dust thou shall return' is not more applicable to the human body with reference to the earth than to bank currency with reference to bank loans."

Johnson was strictly practical in his statement of the banker's goal. "The object of banking," he said, "is to make pecuniary gains for the stockholders by legal operations." As Wertimer points out, there is no room in Johnson's philosophy "for acting altruistically," or "bringing benefit to the community." Johnson illustrated this point by referring to the suspension of specie payment in 1837 in order to spare debtors the losses "that would have resulted from paying their debts." Johnson clinched this argument with a typical analogy: "The owner of a steam engine regulates its business by the capacity of the engine, but should he regulate it by the necessities of his customers, he would probably burst his boiler."

In his final section entitled "The Man," Johnson was even more coldly realistic. If a man "wants to be more than a banker he should cease from being a banker." The banker is, of course, a human being, and is subject to unhappiness when he cannot help a friend, but "the moroseness which we abhor proceeds often from a sensitiveness that is annoyed at being unable to oblige; the amiability that is applauded springs from an imbecility that knows not how to refuse." As a family man, Johnson "knew not how to refuse," but as a banker, he hewed closely to the philosophy outlined in his *Treatise.* There is testimony to this effect in an amusing contemporary sketch of Johnson's career (one of the few outside of his obituary notices that exists) which appeared first in a short-lived newspaper called *The Utica Teetotaler* on October 12, 1850. The original, presumably by the *Teetotaler's* editor, Wesley Bailey, was entitled simply "A. B. Johnson," but it was reprinted in *Hunt's Merchants' Magazine* under the title of "Character of an American Banker: A. B. Johnson, Esq., the President of the Ontario Branch Bank." Hunt said he found it in the London *Bankers' Magazine* for December 1850—which raises the possibility that Johnson himself sent the not-entirely-flattering article to Gilbart shortly after it appeared in Bailey's newspaper. Hunt noted in his *Merchant's Magazine* reprint that "it is regarded by some of the many friends of Mr. Johnson as a rather 'hard likeness,' " but added his own feeling that the portrait was "faithfully sketched." The widely publicized article read as follows:

> A. B. Johnson is pretty well known in Utica, being one of the old inhabitants, and early identified with the fate and progress of the place. But some of our distant readers may not be so familiar with him, and to many of them he is an entire stranger. Mr. Johnson is, then, by profession a banker, and has been president of the Ontario Branch Bank of this city from the time that many of our young men were born, and as such the master spirit of his banking house. He must be some sixty years old, and is the father of near a dozen children. . . . Mr. Johnson is *rich;* all agree in this, and all agree that he has as honestly become rich as any banker anywhere. In banking, he is thought "to know no man after the flesh." He discounts notes not as a matter of *friendship,* but as a desirable "business transaction." It is reported of him that a neighbor once came to him, and desired him to discount his note, and urged his claims on the ground of long-standing neighborly intimacy; but Mr. J. replied, that he *"had never done such a thing in his life!"* Some may think this rather cruel; but then it is a question whether such a trait of character in a banker is not more praiseworthy than that inclination to favoritism which has involved and used up many banking institutions. . . .

Mr. Johnson is a model of industry and steady habits. Every day finds him at his post, and in performance of his banking duties. Indeed this is the ground of his great success in accumulating this world's "lucre," and the means by which he has acquired a vast amount of knowledge of the workings of money matters. Strict integrity is universally accorded to the President of "Old Ontario Branch"; but still some will have it that he is not as benevolent as he might be, and many persist in the belief that if they had half a million they would turn it to better uses. However this may be, probably Mr. Johnson will not consent to be relieved of the responsibility; and we who may be desirous of being charitable out of the fruits of his patient accumulation will probably never have the pleasure. . . . Of course it will be regarded as an oddity for one who has spent almost a life in a bank, . . . to find time or inclination for literary labors. Mr. Johnson is the author of several books, evincing much thought and study, in all of which chaste literature and utility are combined. His stories have the same merit. They have been written for a *practical* purpose, and not merely for amusement or literary fame. We have said Mr. Johnson is the father of a large family, thus copying to some extent the old patriarchs, with whom he is said to stand connected "according to the flesh." He loves his children as but few parents do. There is between him and them a sort of fraternity more resembling equality of position than is often seen between parent and child. He governs by reason rather than birchen authority. On this ground has originated his story-writing. When he would correct a fault in a child, or impart wholesome instruction, instead of calling him to him, and specifying the error or mistake to be corrected, he has sat down and written him a tale which should serve the double purpose of imparting correction and instruction, and at the same time prove a token of affection and a "keepsake" to be treasured up. All of the stories which have lately been reprinted in our columns, were written some time ago for this and similar purposes. They are tales in which it is sought to combine amusement and instruction, and for this purpose they are valuable contributions to the literature of the times. If any one of his offspring had been seriously afflicted with "heart-sickness"; if Alexander, or William, or Charles had ever experienced a serious derangement of the tender sentiment, we have no doubt that Mr. Johnson would have penned a story adapted to restore the tone of the affections and save the heart from breaking. We say this by way of apology for Mr. Johnson to that class of readers who admire no story but such as treat of hearts pierced by Cupid, and detail the art of getting married. Mr. Johnson writes because he has something to write about, and is always guided by the law of his life, *utility.*

The *Teetotaler's* reference to Johnson's "stories which have lately been reprinted in our columns" refers to four of his "Breviats" and "Apologues" which Bailey copied into his newspaper as soon as they appeared in the *Knickerbocker Magazine* during the year 1850, and which Johnson would republish later in his book *An Encyclopedia of Instruction* (1856). As to the rather coy reference to the "old patriarchs" with whom Johnson was said "to be connected 'according to the flesh,' " it is not known whether Johnson, by this time, would have regarded it as an indiscretion or not, but in all the biographical notes on Johnson by Utica historians, this is the only one that ever broached the subject of his Jewish ancestry.

Although Johnson never investigated further, the coincidence of Gilbart's having lectured on language philosophy made him enormously curious—as in the case of Roget's *Thesaurus* and his own "Collated Dictionary." Sometime in 1849 his son William visited the Smithsonian Institution in Washington and told his father he met a Professor Henry who claimed he had started to read Johnson's *Treatise on Language* "when he was a young man," but "the librarian handed as preferable an English work entitled *Prodromus* which Mr. Henry ultimately studied, but he thought it much like my work, and he wanted to know which book had been published first." Johnson immediately procured *Prodromus* and discovered it had been written by Sir Graves Champney Haughton under the full title: *Prodromus: An Inquiry into the First Principles of Reasoning, Including an Analysis of the Human Mind.* The book had been written somewhat before Johnson's *Treatise on Language,* and Johnson was relieved to find that it was "essentially different" from his own work, "it pursuing the old method of investigating the *verbal* meaning of words; while my book investigated only the *unverbal* meaning of words." Nonetheless, Johnson dispatched a copy of his *Treatise on Language* to Haughton, who replied cordially that, though he was ill with cholera at the time, he would "peruse the work with attention" as soon as he was strong enough. Haughton, a distinguished philologist, sent on a copy of *Prodromus,* along with the introduction to his *Bengalese and Sanscrit Dictionary.* This promising correspondence, which Johnson furthered with another letter to Haughton, was terminated, however, by a letter from the Englishman's niece telling of her uncle's death.

Johnson produced only one other essay between 1849 and 1852 in addition to the slavery articles and the *Treatise on Banking.* This was his piece titled "The Relative Merits of Life Insurance and Savings Banks," which has already been discussed in connection with John Greig's earlier attempt to get him to form an American life insurance company. The article appeared in *Hunt's Merchants' Magazine* for December 1851, and immediately came under violent attack from the life insurance companies, backed by a December 26 two-column editorial in the *New York Times* and a similar thrust in the editorial columns of the Boston *Commonwealth*. Hunt was, of course, delighted with the controversy, and encouraged replies from the insurance companies. Johnson said merely, "The article excited more attention than any other I ever wrote—life insurance companies, like the people of Ephesus, 'deeming their craft in danger.' "

Meanwhile, on the domestic front, three events had claimed Johnson's attention. On July 2, 1850, Eliza gave birth to Johnson's last child, a boy named John Greig Johnson, after his father's old friend and banking colleague in Canandaigua. Another happy event was the nomination in September 1851 by the Democrats at their Syracuse convention of his son Alexander for the post of judge of the State Court of Appeals. Alexander won the election and assumed his duties on January 1, 1852—the youngest man (at 35) ever to have held the post. Alexander had recently begun to prosper in his New York law practice, and, although Johnson was pleased with his son's political triumph, he felt Alexander had made "a losing exchange, pecuniarily speaking." A third family development, less pleasing to Johnson, was the marriage of his daughter Sarah to James Stoughton Lynch. Lynch was distantly related to Sarah (Johnson says "a second or third cousin"), and having been orphaned in his youth, had been brought up by Ann Masters. At Mrs. Masters' request, Johnson had taken the young man into his bank as a clerk some years earlier. Johnson wrote that the marriage "was not desirable to me," though the only reason he gave was that Lynch was "wholly destitute of property and that he felt his daughter could have made a more eligible choice." However, Johnson consented to the marriage in the belief that he could improve his new son-in-law's "pecuniary position." As it turned out, Lynch nearly succeeded in destroying Johnson's own "pecuniary position." After the couple's return from a New York wedding trip, Johnson presented his daughter with a "handsome brick dwelling house in Utica," along with money to furnish it; and, his old cashier at the bank, Thomas Rockwell, having "died opportunely for the new aspirant," Johnson replaced him with Lynch. Foreshadowing later events Johnson ended his story of Sarah's wedding with an understatement to the effect that he had "since had reason to believe that the bank never prospered" after Rockwell's death.

CHAPTER 25

1852

"The Most Distressing Event of My Life"

Eliza Johnson died tragically as a result of a fire in the Johnson home on March 28, 1852—a calamity which Johnson described as "the most distressing event of my life." She had stooped with her back to a stove to play with her youngest child, and her skirt, billowed by the draught, caught fire, burning her severely on her arms and back. She lived until May 25 that year, spending her last month in a wheel chair. As usual, Johnson, even in the throes of grief, speculated on the medical treatment she received. The physician, a specialist from New York City, had covered her burns each day with white lead paint, and her husband theorized, perhaps correctly, that the cause of her death was "painter's colic." She died two days before his sixty-sixth birthday, and fearing that his "intellect would give way under the shock, and to save my reason and perhaps my life," Johnson made hurried arrangements for a trip to Europe.

That Johnson was devoted to Eliza there is no doubt, but in writing later about her death there were no tender eulogies or reminiscences about her role in his life, such as he bestowed on Abigail. Instead what came back to him were painful memories of his own suffering—the war between his emotions, which at times appeared to be almost suicidal, and "my intellect which impelled me forward as my only safety." His family rallied around him swiftly; indeed, from the schedule of events that occurred in the Johnson household, it seems obvious that they had begun to arrange for his immediate future as soon as it became evident that Eliza would not survive. Three and a half days after her death he was aboard the steamship *Atlantic* with his son Charles en route to Europe for a four-month trip. There is no evidence that he had been planning any such trip earlier.

William and Alexander took charge of the immediate arrangements. William moved into his father's house to take care of the younger children and manage Johnson's affairs during the summer. Young Bryan and his brother John were sent to a boarding school in Poughkeepsie, New York, and Fanny was to stay at her boarding school on Staten Island. Alexander accompanied Charles and their father to New York and got Johnson aboard—though not without difficulty. Up to the moment of embarkation his father kept "alternating emotionally whether I should go or forfeit my passage money," and, as Alexander coaxed him into his stateroom, he took one look at it and announced violently that he was leaving the ship. Alexander replied, "On that side lies madness!"—and Johnson settled down—but there was still the return of the pilot to be reckoned with. The night of the scheduled departure there was a dense fog in the harbor, and the ship rode at anchor all night before discharging the pilot in the morning. Johnson, fortified by doses of "red lavender and hyoscyamus, anodynes to enable me to sleep," went to bed and awoke the next morning to find the ship under way and the pilot gone—"my destiny was not revokable." Meanwhile, Alexander had waited nervously at the Astor House until he received word that the pilot had come in without his father in tow. He dispatched a telegram to Utica announcing that Johnson "now might be deemed safely embarked," at which news, wrote Johnson, "my children at home felt greatly relieved."

Aboard the *Atlantic* Johnson found that he had been commended to the special care of the captain who, among other courtesies, arranged for a constant supply of "oranges, figs, calves' foot jelly, and milk" in Johnson's stateroom, where he took all of his meals alone. He managed to go on deck occasionally, and found that "by assuming a horizontal position" he could occasionally alleviate his bouts of seasickness. A lady passenger tried to entice him into an occasional sip of her brandy as a palliative, but he feared this would "make matters worse," and refused. Johnson's closest companion on the ship was a Mr. Laborteau of Cincinnati, who had also undertaken his trip to "divert his thoughts from the loss of a wife." Though he was much younger than Johnson, "the similarity of our condition made us sympathize with each other." He was disturbed to hear later, however, that Laborteau had remarried almost immediately, but that "the remedy had not produced the required effect," for the young man had left his new wife at home.

Charles Johnson, meanwhile, was suffering very little, and Johnson avoided him, "not wishing to oppress him with my cares." Charles and other young men "formed card parties and partook of other amusements," and much to his father's disgust indulged constantly in some "choice chewing tobacco he had brought with him and contrived to keep from the notice of the officers." When they got to Liverpool, Johnson persuaded him to give the remainder of his supply to a hotel waiter, suggesting that his American habit might not be appreciated by foreigners.

Nine days after its departure from New York, the *Atlantic* docked in Liverpool, the city from which fifteen-year-old Johnson and his mother, Leah, had embarked for New York in 1801. Johnson, with a day to spend before taking the London train, went off by himself looking for familiar sights, but found few. An ancient quarry he remembered had a railroad running through it, and everything else "was much enlarged and changed." Johnson was depressed by the beggars on the Liverpool streets, and was accosted by several prostitutes, to one of whom he said, "I would gladly change condition with you if it were possible—but the lady probably did not understand me, and passed on."

In London, the boardinghouse situation reminded Johnson of New York, "where before the establishment of the Astor House, I have been driven around for hours looking for a house with vacant rooms." He and Charles were turned away from three recommended establishments, and finally settled in at the Golden Cross on the Strand, where Johnson found his room "hardly as good as the rooms of the servants at home." This was to be the first of a long series of unfavorable comparisons Johnson would make between European and American life.

Johnson's brief account of his return to London after more than fifty-one years was a totally self-absorbed tale of little pilgrimages to the haunts of his youth, along with a few dutiful visits to Westminster Abbey. It is obvious, however, that uppermost in his mind was a reunion with Rachel and her brother Solomon—a reunion which he seems to have had qualms about—and from which Charles was excluded. The story of the eventual meeting was told guardedly, revealing nothing, save in one brief sentence, about the relationship that had grown up between Rachel and himself since the beginning of their correspondence following the death of his father, Bryan. Johnson recalled a few of the details of her troubled life which are already familiar through her letters, but which he described at this point with careful (and since we know the facts), almost cruel detachment. If there was any echo of the passionate exchanges between them on the subject of religion, Johnson gave no indication of it—though he did recount with painful honesty, and some self-castigation, some of the other tensions that marked their anticlimactic reunion.

When I left London in 1801, I left there a male and female cousin (brother and sister). . . . We had corresponded since, but had never seen each other. I knew their residence. She was a widow, and he a widower and they lived together. Before leaving New York, I had written them of my intended visit to London, and the day after my arrival, I took a cab and drove to their house. On getting out I knocked at the street door, and inquired if Mrs. Robinson (the name of my female cousin) was at home. She heard my inquiry, and rushing to the door, recognized me at once as her cousin, for she had been expecting me. When I left her, she was a beautiful young woman, a brunette with dark hair and eyes, of about twenty years of age, lately married and having one child. I now saw before me a woman more than seventy years old with a widow's cap on her head from which hair white with age profusely appeared—a form also rather corpulent, and dressed in dishabille, and calling me cousin! I was entirely shocked, and regretted that I had called, for till that moment, in all our epistolary correspondence, she appeared to my memory as she was in 1801 when we parted. In my gloomy state of feelings, and wrapt in my own despondency, I told her she was so altered, I was sorry I had called; and she remarked, "I suppose you think you are not changed at all."

True, I had not thought of my own change from a bright boy of about fourteen to an old sorrowing man of sixty-six. Her reply brought me to my senses, and I kissed her and walked into her parlour, where, sitting in an easy chair, I saw an old and quite infirm man. I asked, "Who is that?", and she replied, "It is my brother." When I had last seen him he was fond of dress, and was in the full bloom and spirit of approaching manhood. The change in him was even greater than in his sister, for she retained a vigorous intellect, while he, who was never her equal intellectually, was still less so now, under the influence of old age, ill health, and domestic afflictions by the loss of wife and property. She pressed me to remove to her house, but I felt not companionable, and declined the invitation. I believe she thought she had far more cause for my commiseration than I had for her's—she having been left a widow with three children, and but recently lost the last of them, a full grown young woman who had for some time been her chief companion and solace. . . . She found me so inexorably full of my own sorrows, that she tried to alleviate them, and when I was about departing from the house she said to her brother, "I have been acting the part of comforter, instead of being comforted." I found at her house the schoolbooks which belonged to me when a boy and which she had from affection to me preserved with great care. I recognized them and especially a cyphering book, from the circumstance that the word "addition," which was a caption on the first page had been spelled with one *D* instead of two, but which I had subsequently corrected at the schoolmaster's dictation.

Johnson and Charles remained in London for a week, during which time Johnson made many trips to Westminster Abbey, where he found the tombs of the "abbots and other distinguished ecclesiastics" much more interesting than those of "historically renowned warriors and statesmen." They then crossed the Channel from Folkstone to Boulogne, and Johnson was seasick all during the two-hour trip. In Paris they headed promptly for Meurice's Hotel, "a famous resort of American travelers . . . on one of the best streets of Paris, the Rue de Rivoli."

Johnson devoted pages of his autobiography to a dutiful, but wholly spiritless account of his continental tour. He journeyed from one landmark to another, but they elicited no special enthusiasm, and his comments seldom reached beyond the normal clichés of the American tourist abroad. There was the usual petulance over tipping, dining hours, and poor service in hotels (he went only to those which "cater to Americans"), and he made no effort to seek out those European intellectuals whose names and possible approbation might have meant so much to him in his younger days. Johnson regarded the trip as purely therapeutic, and, seemed to welcome each new hardship, including seasickness, as a counterirritant to his depression over his wife's death.

Johnson's reaction to the carefree gamblers and dancers at Baden-Baden was a reenactment of his melancholy visit, years earlier, to Ballston Spa. He was tempted by the roulette wheel, but resisted such dangerous experiments, "fearing where they might lead me." The mineral waters of Baden-Baden were avoided with equal caution. Prostitutes in the parks of Brussels and Naples behaved, he noted with approval, in "an orderly fashion"; and he ascribed their failure to molest him to his "forbearance from interfering with the inhabitants, moving about as a nice, quiet spectator." A guide in Pompeii explained the presence of a phallus on an ancient doorstep as denoting a "bad house," but Johnson held doggedly to the notion that it marked "the residence of a physician."

There were a few other typical Johnsonian reactions. Entering the Naples harbor, the Johnson party was held up for several hours while "the Russian Emperor's favorite counselor, Count Nesselrode" was ushered off the boat, and Johnson remarked that the "contrast between our treatment and that of the Count's was not very gratifying to our republican self-love." In Genoa he viewed some ancient statues "disfigured by rude plaster fig leaves," and on being told that the fig leaves had been placed there to please the Pope, Johnson commented, "I thought his Holiness unduly fastidious."

As for natural wonders, a trip on the Rhine "contrasted sadly with a trip up the Hudson," and the Mediterranean left him unmoved save for a moment of "exhilaration" when he spotted an American flag flying from the mast of a gunboat. In short, A. B. Johnson of Utica went methodically through the motions of an American traveler in Europe, but he told us nothing new—either about the sights he saw, or about himself.

Johnson returned alone to London, leaving his son behind in Paris, and put up at Morley's on Trafalgar Square—"still in no way comparable to the Astor House of New York." He then went immediately to take his final leave of Rachel and her brother.

> She made me take tea with her, and I also passed the evening with her and talked over old recollections. She related to me many incidents which she knew of my father and almost offended me by saying that my father "was always profuse but never generous." I always thought she was more nearly like me, intellectually, than any other person I ever knew. Her early education had been superior to mine, she being a fluent French scholar and a good musician, and she was my first teacher, having taught me the English alphabet. Like me, she made many attempts at original literary composition, and had published some articles of which she sent me copies; but I ultimately exceeded her in persevering study to a prescribed end, and in laborious attempts at composition. At one period of her life, she had accumulated a fortune by sending cargoes of flour to Spain and Portugal, during the occupation of those places by the army of Wellington. The last venture of the kind proved disastrous, by the freezing up of her vessels in the Thames, which prevented their arrival abroad till Wellington had pressed forward to France. This disaster she attributed to the laziness of an agent whom she directed one evening to visit the ships and direct the captains to move their vessels farther down the Thames, she fearing the coming frost; but the agent delayed till the next morning, and the apprehended mischief had been consummated. The whole of this information was new to me, but I finally left her house and never saw again either her or her brother, both dying after my return to America; the brother first, and his sister some year or more subsequently. They were the only blood relatives I knew of those who were alive when I left England in 1801.

Johnson and his son Charles left Liverpool for New York on the packet *Pacific* on September 8. Johnson again fought off the worst of his seasickness by "remaining horizontal," while Charles "amused himself with playing at cards, smoking, etc. in the cabin with other young men." They arrived home on September 18, and found Alexander and William waiting with a carriage at the dock to take them to Johnson's beloved Astor House:

> I returned home improved in my feelings, and on arriving in Utica, I found my family glad to see me; but my youngest child, John Greig,

had entirely forgotten me. He came to me with reluctance, and did not seem to understand when I claimed to be his father—for he had been taught to call my son William, father, who occupied my house in my absence. . . . On renewing my attendance at the Bank all seemed to be going on prosperously, and my own private affairs seemed accurate, and I again took both into my hands to serve as an amusing employment and to divert me from distressing reflections.

CHAPTER 26

1852–1857

"A Life of Literary Ease and Affluence"

JOHNSON WAS NOT ONE TO ENDURE FOR LONG the privations of a home without a wife. "I knew myself sufficiently," he wrote,

> to believe I had no prospect of happiness in life except by another marriage which would compel me to make an effort to regain a composure that otherwise, when left to my own reflections, would be unobtainable. I was excessively unhappy when the business of the day was ended and I withdrew to my desolate house—my habits disqualifying me from visiting or receiving visits.

It was his son William this time who served as his marriage broker, suggesting only a few days after his father's return from Europe that thirty-five-year-old Mary Livingston, of Livingston Manor, New York, might be willing to marry him if he felt "so inclined." Miss Livingston, a relative of William's recently deceased wife, had visited William's family often in Utica, and Johnson found her in every way "eligible." Before taking action, however, he took counsel with his family and with Ann Masters, Eliza's stepmother, who he felt was "entitled to be consulted." He proposed, and Mary Livingston "consented to the hazardous match . . . knowing my nine living children." (Johnson forgot two: there were eleven.) They were married on November 4, 1852, sixteen days after Johnson's return to Utica, at the house of Mary's brother, Brockholst, in Livingston Manor "whither I went for that purpose." The honeymoon was at the Astor House, and Johnson recorded that the marriage "was satisfactory in every respect":

> I know not which of us hazarded the most by this connection . . . but it yielded to my remaining years, which I had supposed were doomed

to bleak affliction, a domestic peace beyond anyone's most sanguine expectation. My children were also greatly relieved from the solace and attention that they felt bound to accord me, and gradually on our return to Utica, my house and family assumed a pristine cheerfulness.

While on the subject of marriage, Johnson also made note of several others which gave him satisfaction. During the preceding April, shortly before Eliza's death, his daughter Louisa Ann Smith Johnson was married at his house to George Bolton Alley, and four days after his own wedding, his son Alexander was married in St. Catherines, Ontario, to Catherine M. Crysler. Finally, in the following July, William brought home a new bride, the former Louisa Adams. Johnson again broke his rule against entertaining (since an Adams was involved), and had his "grounds and premises illuminated," hired an orchestra, and gave a large reception that "passed off happily."

Only one incident seems to have ruffled Johnson's feelings during the first months of his third marriage. For many years Johnson had been a senior warden in Trinity Church, keeping a close watch on its treasury, and standing firmly behind the rector, Dr. Proal, whenever the latter was in trouble with his congregation. About two years earlier, however, he had had some troubles of his own with Proal. Johnson "valued the Episcopal Church," he had said, "chiefly for its exemption from personal interference with its members," and was shocked one day to receive a letter from Proal chiding him for "setting a bad example" by "omitting to attend church in the afternoons as I had formerly done." Johnson promptly resigned as senior warden. The church, however, soon ran into difficulties over some land it owned in New York City, and Proal begged Johnson to rejoin the vestry and take charge of the matter. Johnson did so, but when he opposed the sale of the New York property, he was overruled by the rest of the vestry, and once more turned in his resignation. Proal asked him to remain, but, as Johnson put it:

I did not yield . . . and for the reason of a morbid interest which so identified me with all I undertook that it made me abidingly unhappy and disturbed my sleep when I was connected with what I deemed prejudicial and wrong. Most men when acting with others are wise enough to submit to an adverse majority, but I was never able to school myself into such a temper, for the reason, I suppose, that I was never compelled to occupy such a position.

Johnson's book *The Meaning of Words Analysed into Words and Unverbal Things, and Unverbal Things Classified into Intellections,*

Sensations and Emotions appeared in the fall of 1854 under the imprint of D. Appleton and Company. It cost him, he said, "$225.25 for the stereotype plates," with the publishers free to print as many copies as they wished. He made no stipulations about advertising the book, for, as in the case of his other books, he said, "I thought if they merited public attention they would obtain it, and I left them to float or sink of their own buoyancy." Of the contents he said flatly that they "represented my ultimate thoughts on language." However, the acknowledgments he received from persons to whom he sent the book were in the old familiar run. Gerrit Smith wrote that he would "be greatly pleased to read the book"; Charles Stebbins found it "a book more to be studied than read"; Charles Francis Adams promised himself "much instruction from the communication of your views"; and Henry Gibson was "greatly pleased" by what he had read "so far." From London, J. W. Gilbart, who should have had more to say but didn't, wrote, "It is gratifying to both of us to be able to show that our literary ambitions have not impeded the popularity of our banks." He sent a copy of his own lecture on the Philosophy of Language, which he had delivered many years ago, and added, "It is by no means so profound a work as yours." It remained for a Frenchman, however, to epitomize the world's indifference to the philosophical ruminations of a Utica banker. If Auguste Comte, the great positivist philosopher, had ever got around to reading *The Meaning of Words,* as Johnson had read Harriet Martineau's translation of Comte's *Cours de philosophie positive,* he might at least have reacted negatively to the American upstart who wrote these words: "That so recent a philosopher as August Comte—so acute, learned and discriminating—is still so bewildered by the homogeneity of words . . . is to me an encouraging proof that the present work is not unnecessary." Comte did not read the book Johnson sent him, and told Johnson firmly he had no intention of doing so.

> I pray you to accept my entire thanks for the small volume which I received yesterday, with your honored letter of the thirteenth of September. But although the question which you have broached may be one of the most fundamental we can agitate, I cannot promise you to read such an essay. For my part, I read nothing but the great poets, ancient and modern. The cerebral hygiene is exceedingly salutary to me, particularly in order to maintain the originality of my peculiar meditations. Nevertheless, without reading your book, I will confide its scrupulous examination to one of my best disciples. The question which occupies you has been directly treated in my positive philosophy, but I have fully demonstrated my positive theory of human

language in the fourth chapter of the great work, or a system of positive politics, of which I have just published the fourth and last volume, and according to the general plan of my labors I can never return to the subject.

Johnson dedicated his *Meaning of Words* to his son Alexander, and the dedication was highly praised in Utica newspapers—it being, presumably, one of the few portions of the book the reviewers could understand. It was a moving tribute to Alexander, and came about as close as this extraordinary father ever came to revealing the depth of his devotion to his eldest son—a devotion that was entirely reciprocated. It read:

I believe your recollections can extend back to no period when we were not companions of each other, and I often query which of us is more indebted to the other for intellectual and moral benefits thus received; but I usually adjudge myself to be the debtor. The topics of this book you have heard from me in every form which my intellect can conceive them, hence I inscribe the book to you, not to communicate its contents, but to record the social relationship which has always existed between us.

Of the merits of the book neither of us is in good position to judge—I from self-love, and you from prepossessions toward me. It has, however, exerted a kindly influence over my leisure during a long life that has been marked with sorrows of no ordinary magnitude. It has, indeed, been to me like the poor man's lamb in the parable of the prophet. "It has grown up with me and my children, eaten of my meat, drunk of my own cup, lain in my bosom, and been unto me as a daughter." Praying you may possess a son to whom you may be able to transmit a memorial of social intercourse like that recorded in this introduction.

I remain yours most faithfully,

The Author.

Johnson had come to feel that the *Treatise* was incomplete and "defective" in its insistence on verifying all verbal meanings by the evidence of the senses alone. These doubts were already evident even in the *Treatise* itself, where Johnson grappled with the problem of revelation. Man, he said, could never ascertain the meaning of revealed truth through his senses, or even through the power of reason. The only certain testimony was "within ourselves—the Holy Spirit acting on our feelings and producing the fervent acquiescence which we term faith."

The agnostic Fanny Wright had tried to steer him away from such metaphysical digressions, but he came back to them, pondering other meanings which could not be grasped through the functioning of the senses alone. How, for example, could one "contemplate anger unverbally," or arrive at an operative definition of words like *love, hate, hope, fear,* etc.? If his thesis about "unverbal things" to which words must refer was correct, then *they* must be seated somewhere beyond the power of the senses to identify; and thus, in *The Meaning of Words,* he located them in the extrasensory realms of "intellections" and "internal feelings."

In the *Treatise,* for example, Johnson dismissed as a caprice of language the notion that the sun had to have a "creator." Man could see that a ship had to have a "creator," for he could watch a ship being built, thus undergoing a "sensible experience," but having never seen, or felt, or heard the sun being created, the word "creator" in that context was an "empty salvo without signification." In *The Meaning of Words,* however, Johnson was forced to the conclusion that "men in all ages and in all places had conceived intellectually that the sun required a creator," and that such a "conception" must then "proceed from the organism of the intellect." The "unverbal thing" behind the word "creator," therefore, was an "intellection," and though it could not be seen, felt, or touched, the word had as much validity when applied to the sun as when applied to a ship.

To contemplate *anger* or *love* unverbally, as Johnson tried to do in *The Meaning of Words,* also required a widening of the scope of the *Treatise.* At this point Johnson called upon one of his favorite analogies, the deaf mute. A deaf mute cannot contemplate *love* or *anger* verbally. Words as "signs" are meaningless to him—as years later, the word *water* was meaningless to Helen Keller until her teacher connected the word *water* to specific sensations produced by water. However, Johnson decided, a deaf mute can experience the "emotion" of anger and love apart from their verbal designations, and thus *anger* and *love* exist and have an "unverbal meaning"—though so accustomed is man to "contemplate unverbal things through the medium of words, that to contemplate anger unverbally is at first an unintelligible requirement." The source of meaning in the words *love* and *anger,* then, was not a sense or an "intellection," but an "emotion" or "inner feeling."

Some Johnson students have argued that he was merely rationalizing here to provide an escape route for himself in the event his earlier nominalism should bring him into conflict with the orthodox. To deny the existence of the sun's "creator," for instance, would have been a serious heresy. A contemporary critic of Johnson's *Treatise,* theologian Horace Bushnell, did charge him with "ignoring language as a vehicle of the spirit,"* and John Quincy Adams had also chided him for neglecting metaphysics and biblical explanations of language. However, Johnson himself firmly denied these charges. "You may contend," he wrote in his preface to *The Meaning of Words,* "that my system is destructive not only of natural theology but of every other. If I thought this I would never have published these suggestions."

The Meaning of Words, though it repeats many of the propositions and analogies of the *Treatise,* is far livelier reading; for Johnson, among other things, had abandoned the notion that most of what he had to say would be fairly obvious to his readers. He also had given up to some extent the role of the ardent pedagogue, the zealous missionary leading his unwilling followers along the path of true understanding. Johnson is at his cleverest, perhaps, when he deals with the human animal's persistence in thinking that the meaning of a word always remains with a word no matter how we use or apply it. "Like the whistle of the winds," he began his first lecture, "the lowing of oxen, and the chirp of birds, words are mere sounds, apart from the signification they acquire conventionally or otherwise. . . ." Even his own book he said, would run into difficulty because it was made up of words, and

> every sentence of a book suggests to the reader something that he knows, while the writer may have intended something that the reader knows not. The difficulty presents an insurmountable obstacle against the direct communication by words of new intellectual conceptions. The most which verbal communications can accomplish . . . is by a species of fermentation or elicitation in the reader's intellect.

When two men agree, Johnson points out, that "George is good," they may be in agreement verbally, but the "unverbal" entity behind the word "good" in each case may be quite different.

Johnson also made an interesting foray into the field of "metacommunication"—as some modern semanticists call it—the "message behind the message" which a word conveys when used in some special context. "The words *rogue* and *rascal,*" he wrote, "we deem epithets of endearment when we know they proceed from feelings of affection. Indeed the feeling of love, when it is extreme, finds often in its struggles for utterance no words so expressive of its energy than those which literally are opprobrious."

In *The Meaning of Words,* Johnson is far more gentle with the giants of philosophy—men like Locke, Hume, Spinoza, Berkeley—than

---

* Horace Bushnell, *God in Christ* (Hartford, 1852), p. 44.

he was in the more obstreperous *Treatise*. No longer does he dismiss their propositions as "empty salvos." Rather, he feels that they might have overcome their defects had they only worked a little harder on understanding the nature of language. Locke, for example, said Johnson, was beginning to solve his problem when at the close of his *Essay on Human Understanding* he admitted, "Perhaps if ideas and words were distinctly weighed and duly considered, they would afford us another sort of logic and critic than what we have hitherto been acquainted with." Johnson exclaimed, "What a painful, but too late a dawning of light, must this have been!"

Johnson was now confident that his new trinity of the senses, intellections, and inner feelings remedied the deficiencies the *Treatise* had been guilty of years earlier in its reliance on the senses alone. He summed it all up in a concluding passage:

> Our unverbal knowledge consists of what our senses can perceive, what our internal feelings can manifest, and what our intellect (as interpreted above) can conceive; and if we keep each class distinct, so as not to confound them by means of their verbal transmutability into each other, we shall possess our knowledge devoid of all fallacy; and shall no longer deem perplexingly mysterious, that we cannot discover sensibly what we conceive intellectually, or commit any kindred solecism; and we shall pass through life exempt from all mystery except the one great common mystery that attaches equally and alike to all we know, or can know—an ennobling consummation abundantly remunerative of all the intellectual labor it may cost the man who shall attain it. The world also, when the consummation shall become general (and general it must become at some future day), will understand distinctly the kind of information it is seeking on any occasion, and by which of our three organisms to seek it; and will look back at our present indiscrimination of unverbal heterogeneities in things verbally homogeneous, as a man looks back at the speculations of his childhood.

Having created his two new categories of meaning, "intellections" and inner feelings, there remained for Johnson one final task in his explorations of the universe of language. He would have to take one more look at the phenomena of sight, sound, smell, and "feel." That he would do within a few years in a work called *The Physiology of the Senses*. Meanwhile, there were other matters to engage his attention.

The charter of the Ontario Branch Bank was due to expire on January 1, 1856, and after thirty-seven years as president, Johnson was strongly tempted to settle up the bank's affairs and retire. In 1845 Johnson had informed his son Alexander that he was considering such a course, and had asked Alexander to look around for a suitable house in New York City for himself and his family. (His son suggested an eighteen-room dwelling which could be bought for "upwards" of $30,000 or rented at from $1,500 to $2,000 per annum.) For the past several years he had been turning more and more authority over to his son-in-law James Lynch, coming into the bank only during actual banking hours, and using his office from time to time as a study away from the bustle of his family and servants. After talking things over with Henry Gibson of the parent bank in Canandaigua, however, Johnson decided to reorganize the Branch as a small independent institution to be known simply as the Ontario Bank. Johnson issued a circular to the stockholders describing his plan, and was delighted when many of the old shareholders in the Branch Bank applied for an even greater number of shares in the new bank. Johnson himself retained only $40,000 in stock (still a controlling amount), though he would have retained more "had not a regard for the wants of others restrained me." He also took the post of president, cutting his own salary from $2,000 per year to $1,500, and boosting Lynch's, whom he appointed cashier, to $2,500.

Nearing seventy, Johnson felt he still possessed "an undiminished vigor of body and intellect," but it seemed like a good time to transfer his bank to "younger hands." He could not say farewell, however, without a formal valedictory which he published in the *Bankers Magazine* of New York under the title, "A Eulogy on a Body Corporate." In it he announced the innovations he had brought about, paid tribute to his old colleagues, and proudly related the bank's long history. The article was widely quoted in the press, and was republished in *Our American Union*. The *Eulogy* caught some of the excitement of his pioneering days as a banker:

> We formerly depended on casual stage-coach passengers, often strangers, for transmission among their luggage of all our cash remittances to Albany and New York. When any accidents, and they were frequent, delayed unduly mail announcements that our packages had arrived safely, we have suffered paroxysms of anxiety which . . . time scarcely terminated before they were renewed by a repetition of the unavoidable hazard. From the sparseness, too, of population, our borrowers resided remote from the bank, often hundreds of miles, without our personal knowledge of their habits or pecuniary solvency.

Remembering, perhaps, that "hard likeness" of himself which appeared in the *Teetotaler* and the *London Bankers' Magazine*, Johnson also made an unusual, and somewhat wistful, confession. "I find nothing to regret," he wrote,

> though were the same duties to be reenacted, I should relax more than was my wont from the stern requirements of abstract justice with dealers whose notions of mercantile punctuality were, as farmers and followers of other commercial avocations, necessarily imperfect. . . . We could not, perhaps, always allow sufficiently for the short-comings of physical debility and pecuniary mischances.

Johnson felt, however, as he looked back over his career as a banker, that if he had been a hard man, he had also been an honest one, and he was proud of the rectitude with which he had conducted his affairs. He closed his "Eulogy" with the hope that those he had served would be able to say to him, in the words of the prophet Samuel, "Thou hast not defrauded us, neither hast thou taken aught from any man's hand." Johnson saw the "Eulogy" as the end of an old life and the beginning of a new. Looking back at this period, he wrote: "Having thus, as I supposed, fairly brought my banking cares to a successful termination, I calculated that the remainder of my life would be passed in literary ease and moderate affluence."

Johnson now set about tying up some literary loose ends. His first new work was something he felt he should have published prior to *The Meaning of Words*. He gave it the usual elongated title, *The Physiology of the Senses; or, How and What We See, Hear, Taste, Feel and Smell*. It appeared during the summer of 1856, published by Derby and Jackson in New York. Johnson's thought that his *Physiology* should have preceded *The Meaning of Words* is understandable, for in it he laid the foundation for the detailed analysis of sensory perception on which he constructed his theories of meaning.

As in the case of *The Meaning of Words*, Johnson had learned not to expect too much of his readers, and he began his book in an almost primerlike fashion using, he said, "the simplest truisms I could conceive, as, for instance, that hearing informs me of sound, seeing informs me of sight, etc., etc." This might seem absurd, he admitted, for these were all "acts which commence with our birth, and terminate only with our death." As is often the case, however, these "simple" elucidations of the obvious are deceptive, for they are followed by theorems and almost geometrically stated propositions which are by no means obvious.

The book is divided into two parts: "Of the Acquisition of Sensible Knowledge," and "Of the Extent of Sensible Knowledge"; and each part is broken up into a series of theorems. Typical theorems include: "Objects known in conjunction are not necessarily known separately." . . . "Pain is somewhat under the control of the intellect." . . . "How far a man can learn sights that he never saw." . . . "An infant sees nothing in flame to deter him from thrusting his hand therein." Each theorem is expounded with a flow of illustrations based on Johnson's own experience and observation, plus anecdotes from history and literature. In examining, for instance, the inadequacy of language for properly designating a "feel," a "sound," a "taste," Johnson takes us on a whirlwind tour of his own daily experiences and experiments. For example:

> By crossing the third and fourth fingers of the right hand, and placing the ends of the crossed fingers on a bullet, the person will feel two bullets when the bullet is gently rolled under the crossed fingers. . . . We occasionally infer something is crawling on our neck, but on examination, the inference is not corroborated by experience. . . . Dentists are often called upon to extract a painful tooth, which the sufferer is unable to identify with certainty. . . . If the battle of Waterloo had been narrated prophetically to Julius Caesar, all that differed from his sensible experience would have been sensibly unintelligible to him. . . . The Greek Fire is known words, but what the Greeks intended thereby is unknown to us. . . . If you and I have never seen the same white, we may, in the use of the word, seem to refer to the same sight, but our meaning will differ sensibly with any difference that may exist in our experience.

Johnson made a kind of parlor game out of this book, challenging his readers to produce their own experiences, and sometimes daring them to prove him wrong. What amateur philosopher, for instance, could resist the challenge of "no word can communicate to me:

1. Any sight I have not seen.
2. Any feel I have not felt.
3. Any taste I have not tasted.
4. Any smell I have not smelled.
5. Any sound I have not heard, unless the communicating word be the sound.
6. Any thought I have not thought, unless the communicating word be the thought.
7. Any emotional process that I have not experienced.
8. Any intellectual process that I have not experienced."

With all of its many complications, *The Physiology of the Senses* was, in a way, Johnson's hymn of praise to the mircale of the human organism. In his concluding paragraph he wrote:

> Philologists dignify their studies by saying that language is a greater work than all the arts and sciences it records, and we may safely add that our intellectual, emotional, and sensible organism, the matrices of language, are a greater work than language.

Interestingly enough, this was the one work of Johnson's to be noted by the most intellectually advanced of the English critical journals, the *Westminster Review,* which, under the heading of "Science," praised it rather highly in its October issue for 1856. The reviewer called it "an unpretending little book, the product (apparently) of an amateur in science, which is much more worthy of attention than such productions usually are." He suspected that the author was "evidently a thinking man as well as an observant one," and points out that many of Johnson's theories, "although familiar to those who have studied the subject more systematically," take on a novel aspect "from the guise under which they are presented." The book's great charm, said the reviewer, lay in the fact that it developed a "significance in the things of familiar experience which the millions pass unnoticed, but are always pleased to recognize when pointed out." Johnson was also complimented for his "agreeable raciness of style."

George Ripley, the literary editor of the New York *Tribune* gave the book a lengthy review in the August 1857 issue of *Harper's Monthly Magazine,* stating that it "should be regarded as a contribution to metaphysical, rather than physical science," adding that it also "made no small contribution to psychological science." *Physiology* received favorable notices in the literary columns of major American newspapers—not to mention the Utica Press, which was slowly awakening to the fact that its "distinguished fellow citizen" was becoming known beyond the narrow confines of the Mohawk Valley. Johnson singled out one compliment he received from a lady reader of *Harper's* in Virginia who begged him to correspond with her—a proposal he turned down on the grounds that he "was unfortunately past the age of such romantic gallantry."

It will be recalled that Gaylord Clark, the editor of *Knickerbocker,* had some years earlier urged Johnson to contribute to his popular monthly magazine, but that Johnson had turned him down, not wishing to "write for pecuniary gain." Johnson never explained what caused him suddenly to change his mind, but in 1849 and 1850 twelve

Johnson stories appeared in successive issues, plus two additional pieces in 1851 and 1852. These, together with ten other stories (or "apologues" as he called them) and sixty-six didactic pieces ("breviats"), which he had originally written as letters to his children when they were in school, formed the content of *An Encyclopedia of Instruction; or, Apologues and Breviats on Men and Manners,* published by Derby and Jackson (New York, 1857), and republished as *A Guide to Knowledge and Wealth.* He dedicated his 410-page book to the companion of his glass factory days in Geneva, New York, Henry Rowe Schoolcraft, now working in the Bureau of Indian Affairs in Washington. Schoolcraft, in 1851, had dedicated to Johnson his own *Thirty Years' Residence with the Indian Tribes on the American Frontier.* Shortly after the *Encyclopedia* was published, a fire broke out in the publisher's warehouse and many copies of the book were destroyed, with the result that, as he put it, "it was less diffused among the community than any other of my works."

As the editor of the *Teetotaler* in his sketch of Johnson had said, *The Encyclopedia of Instruction* was written "with one guiding principle in mind—utility." Johnson, with his scorn for pure fiction, and his distrust of poetry unless it could be translated into sensible prose, could not conceive of literature for its own sake, and fully embraced what Edgar Allan Poe, in his 1849 lecture "The Poetic Principle" derided as the "heresy of the didactic." The titles he gave to the fiction pieces are themselves indicative: "How to Live Where You Like—A Legend of Utica"; "How to Prosper; or, The Fatal Mistake"; "Feminine Perfections; or, The Unreasonable Bachelor." Reading these crude, moralistic tales today, one cannot help wondering how Johnson, far ahead of his time in many ways, could have produced these literary anachronisms, and how the *Knickerbocker,* which numbered Hawthorne, Whittier, Holmes, Bryant, and Longfellow among its regular contributors, could have accepted them. Despite the simplistic quality of the apologues—most of them are sermons sugarcoated in fiction—they do serve as companion pieces to some of his philosophical works. In "How to Be Happy," for instance, a kind of extension of *Gulliver's Travels,* he deals with the problem of how actions, and right thinking, affect behavior. A New England whaling ship lands in a country populated by Houyhnhnms, and the crew captures two intelligent colts that are brought back to America and hitched blindfolded to a grinding mill where they trudge endlessly in a circle. The colt named Grey imagines all kinds of pleasant things as he works, and enjoys the sounds and smells he encounters. The other horse, Black, however, deduces nothing but unpleasantness from the same sounds and smells that Grey loves.

When their blindfolds are eventually removed they discover to their surprise that they have been treading the same path—and Grey points the moral: "Happiness depends not on the road we travel, but on our own reflections thereon."

Another fable deals with a group of Indians at Oneida Castle, New York, and a set of girl triplets who have had a curse placed on them. Appetita is the only one who can eat; Limbina can only move her limbs; and Intellecta is limited to producing words. The triplets are, of course, Johnson's trinity in *The Meaning of Words*—the senses, the emotions, and the intellect, and not until the spell is removed and they become one child can they function normally and prosper. In another story, "How to Live Where You Like," a young lady named Lucinda leaves dreary little Utica and goes off, first to Albany, and then to New York where she leads a gay life, but acquires a spendthrift husband who wastes the fortune left to her by her father in Utica. The husband dies of dissipation, and Lucinda returns—sadder but wiser— to her old home, having discovered that "the only way to live where you like is to like where you live"— an act of volition which Johnson undoubtedly had to perform when he reluctantly left New York in 1814 to return to his father and mother in Utica.

The breviats are just what we would expect from the father who so carefully instructed his sons in the rewards of virtue, and reproved them only by indirection. In their aphoristic style, and their cataloguing of all the virtues, they are strongly reminiscent of Benjamin Franklin. There are also echoes from his letters to Watts Sherman and Ezekiel Bacon on the power of words and action to influence human behavior. Some of the breviats, in addition to being moralistic, contain some extremely practical and hardheaded advice—as in the case of the one entitled "Superstition." Johnson tells of a young lady who went to the races in her carriage and suffered severe injuries when her carriage overturned. He also describes the similar fate of a young man who took a carriage ride on Sunday. Both stories, he said, were used by parents to illustrate the punishments Providence reserves for people who attend races or pursue pleasure on the Sabbath. This is nonsense, says Johnson, for Providence doesn't work that way at all. "The sun shines on the wicked," he said, "as brilliantly as on the good, and the field of the infidel is watered by rain as beneficially as the field of a believer." It is totally wrong to tell children that going to the races or riding on Sunday will influence Providence, for "a ship loaded with missionaries is as liable to shipwreck as a vessel loaded with convicts, and lightning will strike a church as readily as a theater." Johnson concluded with the statement, "I respect too highly religion and morality to believe that they need the aid of falsehoods which are essentially irreligious and im-moral; and I respect too highly your understanding and feelings to believe that you cannot be both pious and moral without the coercion of a puerile superstition."

That Johnson realized his precepts were not always totally effec-tive in guiding the conduct of his children is evident in a breviat en-titled "The Inefficacy of Precepts." One of the boys, probably Charles at Geneva College, had received a letter from his father warning him to allow more time for his studies. The precept did not work with his son, and Johnson accordingly wrote the following:

> Parents imagine that they are accomplishing great objects when they place in the hands of youth books full of sage precepts. Such precepts aid our conduct about as much, and about as little, as a treatise on penmanship can aid our hand-writing, or a discourse on pigeon-wings can aid our dancing. To a man who can dance pigeon-wings the dis-course is significant; but to a man who cannot dance them, and for whom the discourse is designed, it is almost useless and unintel-ligible. . . . To the man who, by many disappointments and many victories, has learned how to commence his efforts early, the injunction that relates to early efforts is full of meaning; but to the inexperienced, the injunction teaches nothing.

Johnson followed this breviat, however, with another: "The Benefit of Precepts." Precepts are handy to have around when reflecting, after the act, on the perils of transgression. "They are therefore useful, though they lie by us like dry bones till our experience clothes them with life, flesh, muscles, and sinews."

It seems quite likely that the children must occasionally have rebelled against the steady stream of advice that came from their father's pen, but Alexander, at least, seems to have appreciated them, and it is difficult to question the sincerity of the letter he wrote his father June 26, 1846, on receiving a bound copy of most of the original letters on which the breviats were based:

> This morning I received from you another invaluable gift in the series of letters you sent me, containing as they do a record of almost every domestic event of interest to me or any of us for the term of sixteen years. More than this, looking them over I find them to contain a mass of moral and intellectual instruction which will ever keep present to my mind how deeply I am and shall ever be indebted to you for what-ever of excellence moral or intellectual I may ever attain.

The *Encyclopedia of Instruction* was not widely reviewed in the United States, but it did attract the attention of the *Athenaeum* in London in its issue for February 7, 1857. Johnson recalled that the reviewer had termed his book puerile, and remonstrated that the *Athenaeum* had "overlooked the fact that it was written for children." This is not quite the case. The reviewer had said:

> At first thoughts one might be excused for imagining that paternal epistles, crammed with apologues and breviats, could not have been very welcome to the younger people. But they are not badly executed, and had the writer been the driest of didactic sires, he may still have written pleasant things of home. . . . The paternal philosopher is, however, occasionally dreadfully trite, and his truisms are uttered like propoundings of discoveries, and his platitudes expressed with an amusing pomposity. Nevertheless, there are wholesome truths to be picked out of the chaff of "Apologues and Breviats."

Johnson's next work, *A Guide to the Right Understanding of Our American Union,* was also published in 1857 by Derby and Jackson. He described it as "a large number of articles I had written at different times for newspapers and pamphlets and magazines," and he said of it, "I know less of the fate of this volume than any other I have published." It was divided into three sections: "Of the General Government," "Of the State Government," and "Miscellanies"; and Johnson's opinion of the whole was that it should be of "perpetual interest and ought not to be lost." Many of the forty-eight essays written between 1830 and 1857 have already been discussed in connection with the events which occasioned them, but there was one additional piece, written for *Hunt's Merchant's Magazine* just prior to the book's publication, which is of special interest. It was called "The Almighty Dollar; or, Money as a Motive for Action," and it made it clear that Johnson had become every inch an American—and was proud of it. "The United States," he said, "is the paradise of millionaires" and "money pursuits engross the activity of nearly all its inhabitants. . . . The possession of a hundred thousand dollars confers a dignity equal to a baronetcy in England; five hundred thousand equals an earldom; a million makes a duke, and two millions, a prince of the blood royal." However, not being a "fawning people," we would not exchange our money for any of these titles. "We are like men debarred from champagne and ortolans who substitute coarser stimulants and grosser meats." Medals dispensed by royalty mean nothing to us, and if one were handed to one of our soldiers he would probably ask, "What metal the medal was composed of, and its value in dollars." This, says Johnson, is all to the good. In England, for example, medals, titles, and decorations "withdraw the elite of society from the ordinary utilitarian pursuits of life, while the money motive knows no distinction of employments but the lucrative and unlucrative." This country, in consequence, "excels all nations in utilitarian instrumentalities—in the swiftness and tonnage of its navy, in commercial enterprise, in the invention of machinery to save labor . . . and generally in restlessness of personal activity." This is also evident in our accommodations for ordinary people on our thoroughfares, "and in nothing is an American traveler more surprised than at the meagerness of board and lodging that he finds at the best hotels of London . . . the magnates of Europe not thus traveling in sufficient frequency to induce an adaptation of the means to aristocratic tastes." Johnson also maligns Canada, where the "toiling masses stagnate from conscious inferiority . . . and are active only to the degree necessitated by their animal wants." When a Canadian, however, comes to the States, he immediately "becomes vigorously active in a scramble for a common object." Another advantage to the pursuit of the almighty dollar is its tendency to promote peace rather than war, for many foreigners go to war for purely "honorary motives," whereas the American calculates the monetary risks involved.

Johnson admitted that there were some disadvantages to our system. Our art, for example, suffers. "Painters design only portraits to order, as tailors make coats; while our authors expend their efforts in compiling and imitating, rather than in originating." Our best national literary product is "coarse humor" (Johnson cites "Negro minstrelsy" as an example), because it "pays for the time bestowed thereon." The pursuit of money has also adversely affected the legal and medical professions, and lowered the public's esteem for good teachers. Johnson illustrates the adverse effects of the money scramble with the following interesting analogy:

The Jews of Europe exemplify some of the results that the money motive is eliciting here. Being debarred by law or prejudice from obtaining titular honors, they seek riches . . . and naturally subordinate thereto much that the honorary motive prefers. What a loss to the world has been their eighteen centuries of debasement, if, as is affirmed, they are more intellectually acute than any other race; an affirmation which they have, however, not verified here where they suffer no legal disabilities, and are continually vanquished at their own game of pecuniary accumulation; though probably, time enough has not elapsed to wean them from the petty traffic to which oppression originally crushed them, and to give their aspirations a higher aim.

Despite his reservations, Johnson concludes that the money motive is "more beneficial to mankind than the honorary, as witness our unparalled physical achievements, personal enjoyments, and national prosperity." When we have recognized our defects, he predicts, we will "control the evils of the money motive, and enjoy the good unalloyed."

At least one reader seemed to appreciate *Our American Union* and that was R. B. Taney, Chief Justice of the U.S. Supreme Court. Taney was particularly impressed with Johnson's essay "The Bank Panic and the Pressure," and complimented him on the "truth and clearness" with which he had described that "exciting period." Shortly after he had written his complimentary letter to Johnson, however, Taney suddenly became worried for fear the Utica author might use it as a testimonial for the book, and wrote another letter emphasizing that his remarks had been "written for yourself only," and that he would be "very unwilling to see the letter published." Johnson wrote him at once that his second letter had given him "as much pain as his first letter had given pleasure." He also returned Taney's letter "that he might be assured of its safety." Taney, in turn, sent the letter back to Johnson with profuse apologies for the wound he had inflicted, plus additional praise for *Our American Union:*

> I am still more strongly impressed with the force and perspicuity with which the principles and philosophy of our Union are stated . . . and also with the frank and independent spirit in which controverted questions are met and treated. You say you returned to me the letter to relieve me from anxiety. I cannot retain it on that ground. And feeling that it would not have been sent back from any other motive than the one you assign, I hereby re-inclose it.

Johnson commented, "Feelings so delicate as his to an entire stranger yield unequivocal evidence of an uncommonly estimable man."

Johnson, who often confessed unashamedly his hunger for literary fame and lamented his inability to attain it, added a proud note to his account of these fruitful years between 1854 and 1857 which saw the publication of four books and numerous essays in British and American magazines. In 1857 the first volume of Samuel Austin Allibone's *Dictionary of English Literature and British and American Authors* was published in Philadelphia, with Johnson, among scores of others, the subject of a 200-word biographical and bibliographical note. Allibone had written Johnson in 1856 to enquire what the "A" in his name stood for, and had ended his letter in a complimentary fashion: "Myself a merchant, I am always pleased to see men of business like yourself prove to the world that we are not altogether wrapped up in our ledgers and balance sheets, or cotton bags and bullion."

Johnson transcribed the letter in full into his memoir, commenting that it yielded an "insight into the immense labor of the author to obtain accuracy." What he does not mention, however, is that he also sent a letter to the editor of a Utica newspaper giving a glowing review of Allibone's work which he called "the greatest book of the age—available at a very low price." Johnson ended his review by saying: "As a family book it is next to an encyclopedia, and five dollars can in no way be expended more advantageously than in sending for the work." And a few days later, the newspaper carried further words of praise for the book. The work was commended for its "compactness and thoroughness," and, as "evidence of the fullness of its biographical notices of prominent living personages," the biographical sketch of Johnson was quoted in full.

CHAPTER 27

1857

The Ontario Bank Ruined

IN JULY 1857, a year and a half after the chartering of the new Ontario Bank, Johnson had every reason to be pleased with its progress. Each six months since the bank's opening, it had paid a four percent dividend to its stockholders, and his son-in-law James Lynch, along with the other officers of the bank, seemed to have things so well in hand that Johnson began to cut down on his daily office visits. Each Saturday Lynch presented him with a detailed account of funds, liabilities, and profits, all of which he checked against the ledger books, and found "uniformly correct." Johnson sent copies of the weekly statement to Gibson in Canandaigua, a stockholder in the new bank; and Gibson, by now far richer than Johnson, but still equally meticulous in money matters, wrote him on July 15: "The business and affairs and management of your bank are satisfactory to me in all respects."

On July 18, Johnson received a telegram from his son Alexander, now a judge in Albany. It read, "I shall be up at ten o'clock tonight." Johnson assumed "the visit was merely to be social, and as such, the communication excited no sensation but pleasure."

In the morning, after breakfast, we went on to our front piazza and took seats as usual on Sundays. He suddenly asked me how my bank account stood at Albany. I replied that the Albany City Bank owed us about $44,000. "No," said he, "your account is overdrawn more than $50,000!" "Then," said I, "they have paid some forged drafts." "No," he replied, "your cashier has been down to arrange and get forbearance on the overdraft." I was shocked. He must have gone down at night unbeknown to me and returned in the morning that his absence should escape my knowledge.

In this dramatic manner Johnson introduced in his autobiography the series of disclosures of malfeasance and deceit which ultimately revealed shortages of nearly a million dollars, and which led to the collapse of the Ontario Bank, with the loss to its stockholders of nearly all their investments, and to the destruction of Johnson's cherished image of himself as the irreproachable banker.

In addition to the story told in the autobiography, Johnson prepared at the time a much more elaborate record, complete with audits, and with the day-by-day account of his desperate efforts to stave off disaster. This verson he entitled, "Discovery by the President of the Falsification of the Books, Etc., and His Proceedings Consequent Thereto:—as Narrated by the President." He may have intended it for publication, but it was apparently never used. It was, however, handed on to Alexander, who carefully preserved it among his papers. Its early pages provide a lively narrative:

> I immediately went to the residence of the cashier, and was informed that he had left the town and would not be back till some time in the night, and arrange the facts, or something to that effect. I still hoped and even I discovered a hesitancy in telling me whither he had gone, nor was I told. I sent up one of my sons late at night to see if he had returned, but he had not. I now began to fear that he designed to abscond, and I induced my son William to watch at the depot when the first train was to go east about 1 A.M. and if he was about to depart with the train to prevent him in any way he could.
>
> July 20th, early Monday morning, I again went to the cashier's house and was told he was at home but had not yet come out of his bedchamber. I sent word to him that I wanted to see him and after some few minutes he came down the stairs and I told him I wanted him to walk with me, which he accordingly did. My intention was to take him to my house to meet my son from Albany, but he expressed a reluctance to go there. I then told him that I had discovered that the books were falsified . . . which he did not deny. I became excited and told him he had ruined himself and his family and that I could keep him no longer in the Bank than was necessary in the present emergency. I had still no conception that any other wrong existed than this instance, but as that evinced a difference of some $100,000 it was sufficiently alarming, as I saw that such a difference was nowhere represented on our statement. I asked him who in the Bank was knowing to the falsification beside himself. He replied they all knew it to the extent their knowledge was necessary in effecting the object. I then asked him what represented the missing $100,000 and he seemed unable or unwilling to explain except generally that he would explain as soon as he could arrange the facts, or something to that effect. I still

hoped and even supposed that the deficiency might be found without much eventual loss, and as he seemed unwilling to be seen walking with me to the Bank (our walking thus together being unusual) I told him to go to the bank and I would meet him there.

I soon followed after him to the Bank and immediately ordered the ledger to be brought to me. The bookkeeper said he was writing up an account for a dealer who was anxious to get it, but would send the book in a few minutes. I waited some five minutes and again called for the book and he again alleged that he was just through with his examination and would send it. I again waited for some minutes and becoming conscious that the bookkeeper was deceiving me, I peremptorily ordered the book to be brought to me forthwith and it was eventually brought. I immediately turned to the account of the cashier and on hastily footing it up, I found it overdrawn upwards of $17,000. I then examined in the same way the account of his brother in the name of France & Co. and found it overdrawn some $24,000, the Black River Railroad upwards of $26,000, and various other overdrafts to a large amount. I called him [Lynch] into my office and stated these overdrafts, which he made no attempt to deny except the overdraft of France & Co. which he said was larger than he expected. He said if I would be patient he could get them all made good in a few days. I accused him and the bookkeeper of deceiving me, they having constantly assured me that no overdrafts existed except some trifling sums that are accidental in every bank. The bookkeeper said that the cashier was the financial officer, and that it would not have done for him to have told me and made difficulty between me and the cashier, and that any such disclosures would have been improper for him. I found the bookkeeper's account overdrawn by some $700 which he soon brought me a note for endorsed by his father-in-law.

Over a hundred years later, Professor Sidney Wertimer, Jr., in his reprint of Johnson's *Treatise on Banking* (New York, 1968), included in his introduction a careful examination of the methods used by the perpetrators of this scheme which so thoroughly deceived one of the shrewdest banking experts in mid-nineteenth-century America, and made a mockery of those rigid commandments that had been laid down for bankers everywhere in "Eulogy on a Body Corporate." "In essence," wrote Professor Wertimer,

the ruin was accomplished by means of overdrafts in the balances which were ordinarily kept at correspondent banks. These were protested (often over entirely too long a period of time) by the presidents and officers of those correspondent banks. These letters of protest, however, were intercepted, and Johnson was never allowed, of course,

to see them. Copies of the "letter book," in which outgoing correspondence was copied, were falsified. Shortly, surreptitious postdated
drafts on New York were issued, "and surreptitious certificates of
deposit, and surreptitious certified checks; and, eventually the secret
obtainment of loans by hypothecating packages of the bank's bank
notes"—all of these stratagems were adopted. Bills receivable were
missing and discounts obtained on them were left unrecorded; the
total value of false securities issued, and bogus loans made, was
estimated by Johnson to be not less than a million dollars.

Johnson, writing in the "Discovery," explained further how the plotters
conducted their secret operations:

> Secrecy rendered further necessary that the securities should be
> fabricated outside of the bank—in shops and houses of the accomplices,
> in the bank at night and even after midnight, and especially on Sundays;
> till at length the business of the bank became divided into the legitimate
> business which was transacted during bank hours, and the illegitimate
> business that was conducted out of bank hours, and recorded in private
> books (if recorded at all) that remain still concealed and unknown.

A second device used to conceal the deception was the falsification
of the bank statements. These, however, according to Wertimer, "compared accurately with the books of the bank, so that the clerk who made
out the statements and kept the books from which the statements were
made could have been unconscious of the falsifications he was reporting.
Many checks that the bank paid the day preceding every weekly statement were not charged till the day after the statement was issued."
Johnson said that he called personally at the post office for his letters at
least three times a day. However, the plotters anticipated his calling
hours, and "means were employed to prevent suspicious letters" from
being placed in his letter box. They also, according to Johnson, employed other ingenious stratagems.

> Analogous to this species of espionage, an opening was made through
> a tin box that conducted heated air from the cellar of the bank into
> the directors' room, so that the deliberations of the directors could be
> heard by a listener. How long this expediency had been practiced is
> not known, and its existence was discovered accidentally after the
> suspension of the bank. Probably it was not invented till after the
> condition of the bank was discovered in July, and when the directors
> were consulting on the course to be taken with the implicated officers.

"In the last analysis," Professor Wertimer summed up, "the most effective means of concealment consisted in the board's lack of suspicion of the real character of the implicated officers of the bank, an 'unsuspicion,' as Johnson called it, 'promoted by nearly twenty years of supposed faithful services.' "

Not only did the colossal deception practiced against A. B. Johnson make a mockery of the *Treatise on Banking* and the "Eulogy," it became even more ironic in the light of another pronouncement of his entitled "Duties, Omissions, and Misdoings of Bank Directors," which had appeared in the April 1851 issue of *Hunt's Merchants' Magazine.* Johnson had written:

> The examinations of vaults and counting of money rarely reveal defalcations till the defaulter no longer endeavors to conceal his delinquencies. The counting is not pernicious, if the Board choose to amuse their vigilance therewith; but we have not attempted to designate modes in which frauds are detectable, the ingenuity of concealment being naturally as great as the ingenuity of detection.

The best insurance, Johnson had noted, was to keep a keen eye "on the general conduct, habits, and expenses of the manager." Johnson, in principle, was still the "manager" of the Ontario Bank, and on his own "conduct, habits and expenses," he certainly kept a keen eye. In reality, however, the bank was being managed by a clever cabal of ambitious men, including his son-in-law, to whom Johnson's rectitude and pious pronouncements on bankers and banking must have seemed tediously naive and moralistic. His keen eye had undoubtedly grown dimmer, and his old skepticism about human nature, so frequently expressed in his writings, had faded with the onset of benevolent venerability. One recalls, of course, his early reservations in connection with Sarah's marriage to Lynch, but those reservations were penned after the collapse of the Ontario Bank, and may well have been the product of hindsight.

In October 1858 The *Bankers' Magazine,* which had carried Johnson's proud "Eulogy," appeared with a long article on the collapse of the Bank entitled "Illegal Bank Drafts." It ended with these words: "This is the end of the Ontario Bank. Its powers as a bank have ceased. . . . No doubt is entertained that all the claims against the bank will be paid, though loss to the stockholders is variously estimated." The *Bankers' Magazine* also made it clear that New York State newspapers had given full coverage to the developing facts in the case, including the written opinions of the many courts involved in the prolonged litigation. "Had the discovery not been made at the time it was," the article added, "the whole capital would have been gone in less than two weeks."

"All the debts of the bank," wrote Johnson in his "Discovery" paper, "were ultimately paid by the receiver, including the bogus paper which the court of last resort held us, under the circumstances, liable to pay; and the stockholders lost all their investments except the 5% which the receiver ultimately returned to them." In his autobiographical account Johnson added a more personal note. Judge Daniel Appleton White of Salem, Massachusetts, who had also been a stockholder in the old Ontario Branch Bank, had invested $10,000 in the new Ontario Bank—"and, of course, it was all lost in the general ruin." The judge had recently retired to live on the income from his investments, and Johnson was deeply distressed over his plight. "His loss," wrote Johnson, "affected me more than that of any other of the stockholders, and I wrote to him that every time I thought of him, I felt a pang of distress, and to which he was kind enough to answer that my loss and disappointment affected him more than his own."

Johnson and the bank officers were involved in endless lawsuits regarding uncollected notes, but there is no evidence that Lynch or any of the others suffered at the hands of the law. Johnson, however, did make the following observations in his "Discovery" paper:

> By Section 29 of the Safety Fund Act of 1829, every officer or clerk who shall make or exhibit any false statement to any bank commissioner, was to be imprisoned in the state prison for not less than three years. If the law is obsolete, it should be reenacted, and made applicable to falsifying the statements prepared by officers of banks for the guidance of their respective directors—an offense against which no penalty exists—for, until the present case, it was an offense unimagined.

He added, "We had to contend against a body of men who, though guilty in different degrees, stood together, and were ready to defend each other to an extent that we dared not hazard." Wertimer explained the failure to take punitive action against the guilty parties, as follows:

> The false statements were not made or exhibited to any bank commissioner. The false statements were made to the bank's directors. Hence, Lynch escaped the clutches of the law. One can only speculate that the aggrieved stockholders did not take action against Johnson and his directors because, while they were thus proved negligent, they were unquestionably honest men of high reputation. They labored mightily to pay off the depositors and note holders and Johnson, in particular,

continued to be held in general respect throughout the countryside. Johnson, it should be remembered, was the bank's biggest stockholder ($40,000).

Looking back over Johnson's own frequent tales of the boisterous peccadillos and escapades of those early frontier bankers, politicians, and manipulators at a time when central New York State was undergoing its first frenzy of expansion, digging vast ditches, laying turnpikes and rails along the old Indian trails, and fastening grandiose names on the rude little trading posts that grew up beside them, the entire episode, including the "opening through a tin box" in the basement, may seem in retrospect close to low comedy. But to Johnson, the self-made new American, obsessed with his public image, pillar of Presbyterian and Anglican respectability, and spinner of moralistic tales in which rectitude eternally triumphed, it was a personal tragedy. The majority of his numerous obituary writers, after his death in 1867, passed charitably over the Ontario Bank disaster, but one of them, writing in the Utica *Daily Observer* for September 12, added this footnote to the story that everyone in Utica knew.

> His financial career was his pride; but educated in a school of mercantile and financial integrity and of antique virtue, he did not advance at an equal pace with the growing looseness and lack of principle which, in his later years, began to pervade the realms of finance and wealth; when trusts were more commonly betrayed than kept; when ledgers began to record lying figures instead of honest entries; and when all the arts of fraud, in which he was unversed, became the study and practice of the favored depositaries of private and public confidence.

There is no record of what happened to the funds that Lynch and his fellow conspirators got away with, but it was certain, as far as Johnson was concerned, that evil would reap its own reward. The "main actor" in the plot, Johnson indicated, made some temporary "pecuniary gain," but inevitably it turned into "pecuniary loss," and a fall from his "high social position with its attendant gratifications." Lynch was ostracized along with his family by Utica society for some years, but for Johnson, apparently, the ostracism was permanent and unforgiving. James and Sarah moved to Long Island with their children, where they lived in comparative penury, returning to Utica some years after Johnson's death. In 1863, six years after the "Discovery," we know that Sarah's sisters, at least, made an effort to effect a reconciliation between

Johnson and his once-favorite daughter, for on October 9 of that year
Louise Johnson Alley wrote to her younger sister, Mary, from Long
Island:

> I was very glad to know that you had told Father of Sarah's condition.
> I have wanted to for a long time. I have written many times to you for
> a year or more that she was very poor and is often in need. It is pitiful
> to see her, and know she is receiving charity from persons who feel the
> deepest sympathy for her but upon whom she has no claim. I think
> her family, one and all, should know how she is situated. I wrote to
> Alex last winter about her, but he never took the slightest notice of
> it, and I don't know whether he got the letter. She looks careworn and
> so low-spirited, and I fear often suffers for the want of money. . . .
> I am sure if Father was to see her he could not refuse to help her. It
> is hard she and her innocent children should suffer for the sins of her
> husband. I wonder if it will be so at the day of Judgment. I trust not.

CHAPTER 28

1857–1867

The Last Years

B Y THE TIME he completed in 1867 his painful narrative of the collapse of the Ontario Bank ten years earlier, Johnson had lost interest in continuing his autobiography. He was now 81. The only event after 1857 of any importance that he recorded is the publication of his last book, and the account is perfunctory:

> The last book I published was in 1861. I caused only one hundred impressions to be printed, and designed them for gratuitous distribution among my friends, though I have as yet distributed about half of them or less. I call the work, *Deep Sea Soundings and Explorations of the Bottom; or, The Ultimate Analysis of Human Knowledge.* It is a small volume and designed for a summary of the results I have aimed to accomplish in my several volumes on the same subject.

Johnson's philosophical swan song was the work of a tired, discouraged old man, and if it alone had survived, it might well appear to be the disjointed reflections of an eccentric amateur. Among other things he succumbed to a notion of embellishing the text with line drawings of trees with branches and offshoots bearing such labels as "Seeing," "Hearing," "Feeling," etc. The book, when viewed in relation to his other works, however, is not entirely without interest. It elaborates, for instance, upon some of his earlier thoughts on what we now refer to as "psychosomatic" therapy. He told, for example, of a woman who was cured "of what she thought was an incipient cancer by the application of cotton batting to her chest"; and of another woman who arose each morning with a headache, "and preserved it through the day by thinking of it in tactile thought"; while a friend of hers, also suffering from headache solicited other thoughts, "thus causing the pain to subside."

Johnson also examined his own sensory apparatus: "My memory," he wrote, "is more tenacious of sights than of any other part of my knowledge, and much that I think of absent persons and places is in visual thoughts"—an observation that is borne out by the early pages of his autobiography. Johnson may have become weary of philosophical inquiry, but he was not ready to give up hope, and he concluded his last work with these words: "I have devoted an unusually long life to speculations which the present terminate; and I claim that they constitute a better philosophy than can be found elsewhere, and more intelligible. This may not be saying much, and succeeding investigators will, I hope, accomplish more."

Johnson's literary and political activities in the years before the writing of *Deep Sea Soundings* in 1861 can be pieced together from the contents of his scrapbook, made up largely of press clippings he carefully preserved. The picture is often a lively, if somewhat confusing, one. Most of the clippings are undated, and only in a few cases are the newspapers identified, but the evidence shows clearly that neither the catastrophe at his bank nor the public's continued indifference to his philosophical writings had diminished his zest for disputation, and his concern with the world in which he lived. His chief concern was with the issues that were dividing the North and the South, and which would lead to the guns at Fort Sumter, and to the end, he thought, of his beloved American Union. To the majority of northerners as the great climax drew near, A. B. Johnson exposed himself first to the epithet of "doughface," and later to the more serious charge of "copperhead." To a minority, however, including many of the influential northern editors who published his increasingly bitter diatribes against those he thought were leading the nation into disunity and destruction, he was a model of consistency and good sense. His stand never wavered from that which he had first enunciated many years earlier in his speech against the American Colonization Society. Slavery was a moral wrong, but any interference with the rights of the sovereign states of the South was equally an injustice. His approach was a purely legalistic one and, as such, of course, was no match for the deadly passions that were steering the course of events.

During the battle for the presidency in 1856 between Fremont, Fillmore, and Buchanan, Johnson had published a number of sharp attacks on Fremont's supporters, the "Black Republicans," who, he felt, were bent on driving the South from the Union. The collapse of the Ontario Bank took his mind off national politics for a while, but as the election of 1860 drew near, he came back into the fray with a vengeance. Reflecting on the Dred Scott decision delivered in March 1857 by Chief

Justice Taney, Johnson replied to men like William H. Seward who were making it an issue in the campaign. He carefully explained that the decision, which denied a Negro's right to sue for freedom in Missouri, was merely a denial of the right of Congress to rule on the slavery question within a territory. The people of Missouri, he said, "still had the right to legislate on slavery as they can on any other question of property." John Brown's deadly raid on Harper's Ferry in October 1859, also an issue in the 1860 campaign, Johnson described as the work of "crazy conspirators—a class of men who possess great excitability of feeling, like crazy Millerites, crazy spiritualists, table-rappers and enthusiasts or any new doctrine who keep our lunatic asylums replenished with lunatics." When Horatio Seymour used the phrase "irrepressible conflict" in a Rochester speech, Johnson chastised him as a follower of Gerrit Smith, whom he suspected of having encouraged John Brown both in Kansas and at Harper's Ferry. During the election campaign, the Republicans were successful in passing a voters' registration bill which Johnson promptly denounced as a "Black Republican plot," in a series of newspaper articles signed "Oneida," "Long Pole," and "Anti-Humbug." The registration requirement, he said, would disfranchise the laborer and exclude Democrats from the polls, and was "a wanton and unnecessary burden, wicked also in its intention."

There is no record of any direct attacks by Johnson on Abraham Lincoln during the election campaign, but by 1864 Johnson was calling firmly for the repudiation of "Lincoln and his Republicans." Johnson's wrath even included Mary Todd Lincoln, whom Johnson excoriated in one of his letters to the press for having accepted the gift of "two black horses" from an upstate New York admirer, comparing her conduct unfavorably with that of John Quincy Adams who, during his visit to Utica, had turned down the gift of cloth from a local mill. Aside from these occasional petty outbursts, however, Johnson hewed mainly to his old states' rights position, punctuated by expressions of distaste for the "emotionalism" of the Black Republicans, which could lead to nothing but retaliation from the South. Much of this was undoubtedly due to his own personal temperament, his abhorrence of violence and his love of compromise—that same element in his nature which had appeared in his earlier stand against the "enthusiasm" of the Oneida Revivals, the fanaticism of the Utica abolitionists, and perhaps even in his own verbal excesses in his letter to the Presbyterian Session over the question of the Sunday mails. He would no more have been seen on the streets of Utica with Harriet Beecher Stowe than he would have, in the 1830s, with that other female firebrand, Fanny Wright. Above and beyond this rejection of any form of "ultraism," however, was his devotion to those rights "reserved" to states and individuals—plus, of course, his devotion to the party of Andrew Jackson, which he had deserted only temporarily out of distaste for the policies of Martin Van Buren. In place of the Whigs had come the "Know-Nothings" and the Republicans, with the latter capitalizing in New York State on the growing sentiment against the extension of slavery into the new territories, thus violating once more, he felt, the principle of self-determination. The Republicans had gained control of the state legislature and the governorship, while the Democrats were degenerating into squabbling factions, with a growing split between the party in New York City and upstate. The city Democrats were strongly under the influence of a large Irish element that feared the competition of freed slaves, and bridled at the high moral tone toward slavery taken by the upstaters. Horace Greeley of New York editorialized in the *Tribune* about letting the South "go in peace," while upstate editors were endorsing the fiery abolitionist pronouncements of William Lloyd Garrison.

Only one thing kept the Democrats together in 1861, and that was the lesson of the 1860 party convention in Charleston when some of the Democrats had bolted and nominated Breckinridge. Democratic disunity had resulted in the election of Lincoln, and the future looked bleak to both the city and the upstate factions. Accordingly, the Democratic State Convention at Albany in 1861 was called to "avert the threatened destruction of our National Union" and, by the same token, of the Democratic party. It was made up of what Greeley called "the most imposing assemblage of delegates ever assembled within the State"—and among the speakers was Alexander Bryan Johnson.

Johnson began by saying, "I am an old man, as is but too apparent, and still, Sir, I am quite young in such an assemblage as this. This is the fourth time I have ever met in such a convention." He recalled his presence at the Baltimore Convention that nominated Van Buren, and was greeted with applause as he added, "who at that time was a Northern man with Southern principles—meaning, as we supposed, that he was a man who was willing to give the South equal privileges with the North in the Union."

Throughout the first part of his speech, Johnson upheld the doctrine of states' rights with a fervor that would have won the admiration of John C. Calhoun. Then he turned to the "real enemy," the Republicans:

> To a superficial observer, our difficulties consist of revolutionary movements in the Southern States, but these movements are only symptoms of a disorder . . . and before we can treat the disorder understand-

ingly with a view to its remedy, we must understand its cause, and we shall find it in the avowed principles on which the presidential election [1860] was conducted to its final triumph—principles inculcating sectional hate in place of federal kindness, in direct contravention of the dying injunctions of the father of his country, and of the most eminent of his successors in the Presidency, General Jackson.

After a lengthy discussion of the question of constitutionality, and the differences in physical productivity, temperament, and attitude among the "sovereign states," Johnson in his peroration, echoed the sentiments of Horace Greeley:

> If Congress cannot, or will not, win back our Southern brethren, let us, at least, part as friends; and then possibly, if experience shall, as we suppose it will, show the departed states that, in leaving the Union, they have only deserted a happy home, they may be willing to sue us to re-admit them; or, if they shall find a permanent separation more desirable than Union, we may still exist together as useful and profitable neighbors, assisting each other when either is threatened by injustice from the nations of Europe; and the two sections, instead of wasting their time and energies in quarreling with each other about slavery, will at least have more time to severally employ all their energies in seeking their own prosperity in their own way.

In August 1861 his daughter Louise Alley wrote to him asking, "What are your feelings in regard to the war? I am continually asked the question, but not knowing, I can never answer." Johnson referred her sternly to the pamphlet he had printed containing his Albany Convention speech. Louise's reply was humble: "I fear you will think I did not read your pamphlet, but I did. I merely asked the question not knowing whether your ideas had changed since the actual fighting had begun." Her question was not an unreasonable one, for, as the war grew in intensity, most of the delegates who had vigorously applauded Johnson at the convention joined the crusade to "conquer a peace." Johnson was a notable exception, and not deviating for a moment from his principles, he began to turn his pen against the Democrats as well as the Republicans. He noted with sorrow, for instance, in a letter to an Albany newspaper, that "the Democratic leaders had been out for war," adding, "I maintain that the Democratic party is more responsible for war than the abolitionists. The South would never have hazarded rebellion if they had expected an undivided North."

Louise Alley wrote again, on September 7, 1863, full of trepidation:

The drafting has made trouble all over. At New Rochelle we hear several houses were threatened to be burned in our neighborhood. Mr. Davenport came very near being killed, for he was one of the enrolling officials. We hear New York is in an irritated state from the soldiers who congregated there. The parks are all filled and persons tell us the air is dreadful, and that it is dangerous to be there. Mrs. Alley is alarmed, and has to stay there much against her will, for there are so many in the square in front of her house, and she hopes they are full of fleas from the horses. She wants to go home, but is afraid to.

On December 3, 1863, five months after Gettysburg and Vicksburg, the Boston *Courier* published on its editorial page excerpts from a pamphlet entitled "Where We Stood and Where We Stand." The editor noted that, "without obtaining any clue to its authorship, we have found it one of the most succinct . . . expositions of our national troubles we have yet seen." The article was by Johnson, and it restated all the old arguments. This time Johnson laid some of the blame for the conflict on a "controlling New York Senator" (probably William H. Seward) who, when California was brought into the Union as a free state, giving the northern views a majority in the Senate, announced, "The battle has been fought and won." Thus, Johnson explained,

from his eloquence, and from lay and clerical partisan assistance, the Federal government had become hateful to the South. In short, the North was tired of the Confederacy and desired a national government as ardently as the Jews desired a king, . . . and these tenets, which the South abhorred as heresy, the North insisted were only a return of the Government to the intention of the founders.

The *Courier*'s editor (obviously also a "copperhead") commented: "The several propositions embraced here are each of them incontrovertably true."

Johnson, however, never abandoned his legalistic approach, and later, after the South had been defeated, made a sudden shift to a hard line toward the South, which was perhaps logical according to his premises. The South had had a right to secede, and had done just that in 1861, thus ending the Union, or "Confederacy" (as he preferred to call it), of the founding fathers. Since there was now no longer any Union, no President had the right to reconstitute one by readmitting the seceded states.

While Johnson was inveighing against the war, two of his sons, Charles and John, were serving in the Union Army. There were brief communications asking for money (which Johnson supplied) to buy their swords and uniforms, and describing some of their activities. The letters were circulated among Johnson and the other children. One from Charles at Manassas Junction expressed the hope that he would see his brother Alexander soon—"if fighting Joe doesn't get me killed first." Both boys came through their battles successfully, though Charles was wounded slightly and was brevetted major general.

The Civil War, to which many young men of Utica went off singing "Belle of the Mohawk Vale," left the growing city with its toll of dead and wounded and the usual number of plaques and monuments to the "boys in blue." The Utica "Citizens Corps," organized mainly for social purposes in 1837, held a meeting two days after the war started, and informed the government that it would be ready to march "fully equipped on two days notice."* After a brief training period in Albany, and now known as "The First Oneida," it saw fighting at Malvern Hill, Fredericksburg, and Chancellorville. The "Second Oneida" was mustered in on May 21, 1861, and served at Cedar Mountain, Antietam, and Fredericksburg. Between them the two Utica corps contributed six major generals to the Union Army, including Charles A. Johnson.

Johnson was also busy watching over the affairs of his beloved city. For many years now, the word "venerable" had become a favorite adjective in editorial introductions to communications from A. B. Johnson.

The *New York Times,* in reprinting one of his articles on finance, went so far as to call him "the most venerable banker in America." Venerability, however, had its responsibilities as well as its rewards, and Johnson was called upon to write some twenty obituaries as old friends and acquaintances passed from the local scene. Among his subjects were his colleague Henry Gibson; Watts Sherman, whom he had twice steered into lucrative matrimony; John Greig, after whom he had named a son; his rector, Dr. Proal; and Thomas Rockwell, his stalwart cashier at the Ontario Branch Bank. Johnson also paid tribute among others to Samuel Stocking who, in 1804, had founded the Utica Fire Department (in which Johnson, wearing a white helmet, had served briefly); and to Benjamin Franklin Cooper, an "honest farmer," who despite his scorn for "pecuniary gain" had been a man of "outstanding probity."

As the local literary savant, Johnson reviewed such books as Henry T. Tuckerman's *Essays Critical and Biographical* for the Utica press; he attended oratorical contests staged for the benefit of the Utica Lunatic Asylum and praised or criticized the speakers; and he contributed brief

* T. Wood Clarke, *Utica for a Century and a Half* (Utica, 1952), p. 53.

notes on the etymology of such words as "teetotal" and "botheration" to local literary columns. The author of *An Encyclopedia of Instruction* also felt obliged from time to time, as he had in the past, to instruct parents on the upbringing of their young. Parents of college students were warned that "the deteriorating commences with tobacco and then with drink, and many a student graduates a sot more often than a scholar." The remedy, he said, was to have colleges emulate the preparatory schools where the students "study gregariously rather than in the privacy of their rooms without adequate supervision." As for young bank clerks and other youthful employees, Johnson warned against early closing hours, advocating that the young be kept at work until their "ordinary bedtime," thus discouraging immorality and increasing productivity. He was still opposed to corporal punishment, however, and inveighed against it in several letters to the press.

One of the rewards of "venerability," of course, was the privilege of reminiscing about Utica's past, and, as he began to go through the notes for his autobiography, he often shared them with the readers of Utica newspapers. "Thirty-four years ago," he recalled on one occasion, "the people of Utica became much interested in the revolt of the Poles against Russia," and he documented that early event with copies of his letters to and from General Lafayette. An 1861 Fourth of July celebration brought forth the memory of his own oration in 1824 which he described in an article entitled "What Was Thought of the Black Man Forty Years Ago." Writing in the third person, he recalled: "The orator expressed his wish that our constitutions shed their blessings in an indiscriminate profusion not on a sect, nor a color, nor a nationality, but on all men who dwell within their boundaries." His most ambitious attempt to revive the past, however, was a series of six long articles published in the *Bankers' Magazine* in 1861. They were printed under the general title of "Recollections of an Old Banker," bearing such subtitles as "A Disobliged Dealer," "An Accommodation Endorsement," etc., and each was described as "A Romance of Real Life." The stories were told in a colloquial vein, and dealt with his own banking experiences, with the inevitable moral cropping up at the end.

Local politics came in for its full share of attention from Johnson. Now in a neutral position as far as other Utica banks were concerned, he lashed out under such pseudonyms as "Anti-Breeches-Pocket" and "Anti-Gouger" at local authorities who had made certain lucrative arrangements between the State Lunatic Asylum and his old rival, the Oneida Bank. The Utica City Council also came under attack for its tax policies, and Johnson proposed many amendments to the city charter. Johnson still reserved his heaviest ammunition for his political opponents, but with the close of the war and advancing age and infirmity he was finally willing to lay down his arms.

The date, February 7, 1867, appears on the final page of Johnson's manuscript biography. A letter to his son William bears the same date. It reads:

My dear Son,

The brevity of my letters referred to in yours of the fourth is owing to ill health. I am evidently in the last stage of existence and failing very fast with heart disease. I can no longer walk from my office to my house, but have to ride, and though I make out with increasing difficulty to walk to my office, the distance being a descent which is easier to me than an ascent, going upstairs even to my office causes me to struggle for breath in a very painful manner. I am not, however, afraid of death, and await patiently as I can the inevitable result. With much love to you all.

Yours very truly.
A. B. Johnson

When the autobiography was completed, it was transcribed by a number of copyists and bound as a "fair copy." The rough draft in his own handwriting, Johnson likewise had bound. He presented it to his wife, Mary Livingston Johnson, with a one-page dedication dated May 22, 1867. "As it is disfigured by erasions and interlineations," he wrote,

it is not worthy of your acceptance; but these defects make it assimilate with my own personal defects which you have borne with in the most exemplary manner for many years; and hence I have the presumption to hope you will accept these memoirs with all their defects, as a remembrance of me when Providence shall order our final separation. I believe they will cause you no reason to blush for your husband, as you may chance to revert to these pages for a recollection of his conduct during his long life; though they may fail to occasion you any gratulations for great achievements which his seclusion and public favor never called on him to perform. However, such as these memoirs are, he dedicates this copy to you, to be preserved or destroyed, or to be used at any time in any way you may think proper; and especially as a tangible recognition of my love and respect for you as the solace of many of my last years, that without you would have been desolate and unendurable.

Less than four months after writing this dedication, on September 10, 1867, Alexander Bryan Johnson died quietly and contentedly, surrounded by his family, in the house on Genesee Street where he had once entertained Lafayette and John Quincy Adams. Earlier, in the final essay of his *Encyclopedia of Instruction* (an essay which had originally been sent as a breviat to his son Alexander) he had written:

> We exaggerate the pain of dying, and thus illusorily aggravate our sorrow for the dead. As life wanes by decay or disease, sensibility diminishes with it; so that necessarily the moment of dying is a moment of the least possible sensibility. I believe that death is an animal pleasure. The man who is sleepy finds a pleasure in falling asleep; the man who is faint, finds a pleasure in fainting; the man who is too feeble to stand, finds a pleasure in recumbency. Every pain and every agony that accompanies disease, fits dissolving nature for death. Death thus becomes an animal want to the dying; as sleep becomes an animal want to the sleepy; and death when it arrives, is a gratification of the want, just suited to our condition, and hence, is pleasurable.

The funeral cortege that moved up Genesee Street to the cemetery was the longest in the memory of his fellow Uticans. His obituaries, one of them written by his former antagonist in the Van Buren campaign, Judge Watson Williams, were longer than any he had ever composed himself. Williams praised his philosophical works (though he confessed he had not wholly understood them); he lauded his "scrupulous and undeviating honesty," and he regretted "his invincible repugnance to the general social intercourse which prevented him from working harmoniously with other men." Concluding his tribute, Williams wrote,

> He knew himself and frankly confessed more defects than he claimed virtues; and yet a fair judge will allow that few men have passed so long a life, actively employed from the beginning to end, with so few positive stains, and so many unassuming merits.

The tall marker that stands over the Johnson family plot in what is now Forest Hills cemetery in Utica bears the following inscription, probably written by his son Alexander:

ALEXANDER BRYAN JOHNSON
BORN MAY 29, 1787
DIED SEPTEMBER 9, 1867
BORN IN ENGLAND, FROM 1801 HE LIVED
IN UTICA, THRICE MARRIED, SEVEN

SONS, AND FOUR DAUGHTERS
AND HIS WIDOW SURVIVED HIM.
THE AUTHOR OF MANY BOOKS:
A LAWYER BY EDUCATION
A BANKER DURING ACTIVE LIFE:
A STUDENT OF PHILOSOPHY ALWAYS:
THIS FOR THE WORLD
THEY WHO LOVED HIM KNOW THE REST.

There is, however, a more fitting epitaph for A. B. Johnson—one he wrote himself as a kind of appendix to his brief account of the publication of *Deep Sea Soundings*. It was an attempt to provide a retrospect of all of his philosophical writings, and a summary of his intellectual efforts. It is tinged with despair at times (". . . though my life may be deemed a miscarriage . . ."), and at others, with proud defiance ("I am the only writer that has ever thus analysed all words into things that are not words"). Many of the old analogies used in the *Treatise* are placed on exhibit once again—"the ray of light passing through a crystal . . . the spark falling on gunpowder"—and the old questions are restated. In this world "which is a congeries of wonders" are these phenomena merely "a sensible sequence of sensible events," or are "the events connected by nature so that the events must succeed each other"? Johnson's long retrospective begins on a melancholy note:

And now in taking a review of my various writings that have engrossed a large portion of my active and long life, I feel that I have labored in vain so far as my teachings have been accepted by the world or influenced the thoughts of reflective men. Teachings which, like mine, require an eradication of existing notions, labor under disadvantages that may be well deemed insurmountable, while teachings which harmonize with prevailing opinions are readily accepted. My studies have been intellectually beneficial to myself and to that extent they solace me for the time I have devoted to them. In artistic construction I believe they are unsurpassed for brevity of expression and perspicuity of meaning. I shall leave much unprinted manuscript, but whether any of it deserves publicity I cannot conjecture, and judging from the past, the dead may be well left to bury its dead. . . .

Finally, however, in the last paragraph the exhausted philosopher abandons his questions and his answers, and ignoring those contemporaries of his to whom his truths, he thought, should have been "self evident" but never were, he speaks across a century to thinkers not yet born. There is some arrogance, perhaps, in this sweeping valedictory, but it was an arrogance based, at least, on certainty. No longer does he merely "hope" that future philosophers will comprehend—he "trusts" they will; and in some few quarters where men and women are attempting to cut through the verbal static that afflicts our clamorous world, A. B. Johnson, the philosophical banker of Utica, is beginning, at least, to find an understanding audience. "All speculative philosophies precedent of mine," he wrote,

> are like tunes which skillful musicians play on a pianoforte. Each philosopher plays with words such a tune as he deems best; but my philosophy plays no tune, but refers every tuneful note to the internal machinery of the piano from which the tuneful note proceeds. I am the first philosopher that has gone deeper than language, and has sought to discover the meaning of words in man's internal organism, a meaning that is not words. The verbal systems of speculative philosophy are as interminable as the different tunes that can be formed out of the notes of a piano, and realizing how barren such philosophies have ever been for the settlement of the questions for which such philosophies are employed, I have essayed the new system as an ultimate and fixed limit of all speculative knowledge, and which will in time, I fondly trust, cause an abandonment of the old and endless speculations of the verbal philosopher.

Index